D1084427

State Criminality

Issues in Crime & Justice

Series Editor
Gregg Barak, Eastern Michigan University

As we embark upon the twentieth-first century, the meanings of crime continue to evolve and our approaches to justice are in flux. The contributions to this series focus their attention on crime and justice as well as on crime control and prevention in the context of a dynamically changing legal order. Across the series, there are books that consider the full range of crime and criminality and that engage a diverse set of topics related to the formal and informal workings of the administration of criminal justice. In an age of globalization, crime and criminality are no longer confined, if they ever were, to the boundaries of single nation-states. As a consequence, while many books in the series will address crime and justice in the United States, the scope of these books will accommodate a global perspective and they will consider such eminently global issues such as slavery, terrorism, or punishment. Books in the series are written to be used as supplements in standard undergraduate and graduate courses in criminology and criminal justice and related courses in sociology. Some of the standard courses in these areas include: introduction to criminal justice, introduction to law enforcement, introduction to corrections, juvenile justice, crime and delinquency, criminal law, white collar, corporate, and organized crime.

TITLES IN SERIES:

Effigy, By Allison Cotton

Perverts and Predators: The Making of Sexual Offending Laws, By Laura J. Zilney and Lisa Anne Zilney

The Prisoners' World, By William Tregea and Marjorie Larmour

Racial Profiling, By Karen S. Glover

State Criminality

The Crime of All Crimes

DAWN L. ROTHE

LEXINGTON BOOKS
A division of
ROWMAN & LITTLEFIELD PUBLISHERS, INC.
Lanham • Boulder • New York • Toronto • Plymouth, UK

5/19/10
WW
#80 —

Published by Lexington Books
A division of Rowman & Littlefield Publishers, Inc.
A wholly owned subsidary of The Rowman & Littlefield Publishing Group, Inc.
4501 Forbes Boulevard, Suite 200, Lanham, Maryland 20706
http://www.lexingtonbooks.com

Estover Road, Plymouth PL6 7PY, United Kingdom

Copyright © 2009 by Lexington Books

All rights reserved. No part of this book may be reproduced in any form or by any
electronic or mechanical means, including information storage and retrieval systems,
without written permission from the publisher, except by a reviewer who may quote
passages in a review.

British Library Cataloguing in Publication Information Available

Library of Congress Cataloging-in-Publication Data

Rothe, Dawn, 1961-
    State criminality : the crime of all crimes / Dawn L. Rothe.
        p. cm. -- (Issues in crime & justice)
    Includes bibliographical references and index.
    ISBN 978-0-7391-2671-4 (cloth : alk. paper) -- ISBN 978-0-7391-2672-1 (pbk. :
alk. paper) -- ISBN 978-0-7391-3250-0 (electronic)
    1. Criminology. 2. International offenses. I. Title.
    HV6030.R68 2009
    364.1'3--dc22   2009016010

⊖™ The paper used in this publication meets the minimum requirements of American
National Standard for Information Sciences—Permanence of Paper for Printed Library
Materials, ANSI/NISO Z39.48-1992.

Printed in the United States of America

In memory of Tasha

Contents

Foreword

Over two thousand years ago the Chinese philosopher Mozi (Mo-tzu, c. 470–c. 391 BCE) observed that the rulers of the earth "recognize a small crime as such, but do not recognize the wickedness of the greatest crime of all—the waging of war on another state" (quoted in Kurlansky 2006). It appears that nothing much has changed. As I write the foreword to this important book about state criminality, the presidency of George W. Bush is coming to an end. The Bush administration has been one of the most lawless in U.S. history. Senior officials in this administration have perpetrated a veritable state crime wave. By invading Iraq in 2003 in violation of the United Nations Charter they have engaged in an illegal war of aggression, the "supreme international crime" according to the Nuremberg Tribunal. They committed a variety of war crimes, violations of International Humanitarian Law, during the brutal occupation of Iraq that followed, which has resulted in the deaths of hundreds of thousands of Iraqis. They have tortured detainees in U.S. custody at bases in Afghanistan, Abu Ghraib prison in Iraq, and Guantanamo, Cuba, in violation of the 1949 Geneva Conventions and the 1984 UN Convention Against Torture. And these offenses are only the top of a long list of state crimes this administration has engaged in.

Given these great crimes, important questions arise. Will the officials responsible for the crimes be held accountable? Will the new Obama administration appoint a special prosecutor to investigate the alleged illegal actions of Bush officials and perhaps bring indictments? Will there be justice for the victims? Are senior administration officials in the U.S., including the President and Vice President, above the law?

I am not optimistic that there will ever be any accountability for the crimes the Bush officials have committed. It appears that many political leaders and citizens still "do not recognize the wickedness of the greatest crime of all." President Obama has been advised by some politicians and by the mainstream media that war crimes prosecutions would be a "politically fraught" step, and he seems reluctant to go down that road (Johnston and Savage 2009). It appears that many Americans would prefer to look the other way and not think about the whole issue of criminal activity on the part of U.S. leaders.

As Dawn Rothe so rightly points out in this volume, state criminality is not generally a topic of everyday life. From the time of Mozi down to the current post-9/11 era, most people do not see the socially harmful and illegal actions of state officials to be a problem, let alone a crime. Despite the brutal and murderous impact of state crimes around the world, few government officials, and fewer still average citizens, think much about these offenses or do anything to prevent or control these grievous harms. Above and beyond the various reasons that Professor Rothe adduces for this state of affairs, there are two other critical factors that should be noted. One is the phenomenon of the *normalization of deviance* within state organizations and national political cultures (Vaughan 1996, 2007; Kramer 2008); the other is the fact that orthodox criminology generally tends to operate in the service of power (Michalowski and Kramer 2006; Michalowski 2009).

As Mozi astutely pointed out so long ago, political rulers (state officials) generally do not see themselves as criminal. In fact, in the modern era, despite the existence of widely accepted moral and legal standards by the international political community, they often come to define their violation of these standards as normal and acceptable. Diane Vaughan defines this phenomenon as the "normalization of deviance." According to Vaughan (2007: 12):

> When deviance is normalized, the action is not seen as wrong by actors in that setting—thus making it important to study decision-making as situated action. It is not concealed from other members of the organization; it is, in fact, culturally approved and therefore rewarded. Deviant actions are viewed as normal because they fit with and conform to cultural mandates of the group to which the actor belongs.

For example, my research on the bombing of civilians during World War II demonstrates that during the course of the war the socially constructed morality of nationalistic and imperialistic war goals, the "technological fanaticism" of the bureaucracies charged with military planning, the legitimation of state violence through the failures of international law, and a variety of social psychological and emotional factors all contributed to the overall erosion of social and moral constraints on the state crime of terror bombing civilians (Kramer 2008). The social and cultural forces that developed during World War II resulted in a "normalization of deviance" that continues to provide normative support and institutional benefits for the military targeting of civilians from the air within various state organizational structures and the general culture down to the present.

Not only do state officials tend to view their harmful and illegal actions as normal and acceptable, criminologists have generally failed to subject these moral and legal violations to the same level of critical scrutiny they give to other forms of criminal behavior. In two separate studies, both Michalowski and Kramer (2006) and Toombs and Whyte (2003) found that research articles focusing on the crimes of the powerful (corporations and states) typically constituted less than three percent of all articles in the major U.S. and British journals of criminology and criminal justice. Within the discipline of criminology, formal legalism, methodological individualism, an emphasis on ameliorating private crimes, the cultural dynamics of mass communication, and the pro-systemic character of the criminological profession all combine to limit the attention of criminologists to state crimes (Michalowski and Kramer 2006; Michalowski 2009).

Given the normalization of state crimes by state officials and the failure of traditional criminology to confront the crimes of the powerful, *State Criminality: The Crime of All Crimes* offers an important corrective. Attempting to generate greater awareness of these crimes, Professor Rothe shows that a number of scholars from various disciplines have begun in recent years the significant task of analyzing state criminality in all of its forms. This book brings that important work together and presents it in a coherent framework that will be helpful to students and future researchers as well as fellow citizens. Thanks to efforts of Professor Rothe, those with an interest in the topic of state criminality will be able to assess what has been accomplished thus far both empirically and theoretically in this area, and what remains to be done. And we may hope that, thanks to the work of Dawn Rothe and other criminologists who are now focusing their attention on the neglected issue of state crime, greater awareness will be raised, the normalization of such crimes will be shattered, and future Presidents will not escape accountability for the commission of "the crime of all crimes."

Ronald C. Kramer
Kalamazoo, Michigan
January 2009

References

Johnston, D. and C. Savage. 2009. "Obama Signals His Reluctance to Look into Bush Policies." *The New York Times* (January 12): 1.

Kramer, R. 2008. "From Guernica to Hiroshima to Baghdad: The Normalization of the State Crime of Terror Bombing Civilians." Paper presented at the Annual Meeting of The American Society of Criminology (November 13). St Louis, Missouri.

Kurlansky, M. 2006. *Non-Violence: The History of a Dangerous Idea*. New York: Modern Library.

Michalowski, R. 2009. "Power, Crime and Criminology in the New Imperial Age." Forthcoming in *Law and Social Change*.

Michalowski, R. and R. Kramer. 2006. *State-Corporate Crime: Wrongdoing at the Intersection of Business and Government*. New Brunswick, NJ: Rutgers University Press.

Tombs, S. and D. Whyte. 2003. "Scrutinizing the Powerful." Pp. 3–48 in *Unmasking the Crimes of the Powerful: Scrutinizing States and Corporations*, edited by S. Tombs and D. Whyte. New York: Peter Lang.

Vaughn, D. 1996. *The Challenger Launch Decision: Risky Technology, Culture, and Deviance at NASA*. Chicago: University of Chicago Press.
Vaughan, D. 2007. "Beyond Macro- and Micro-Levels of Analysis, Organizations, and the Cultural Fix." Pp. 3–24 in *International Handbook of White-Collar and Corporate Crime*, edited by H. Pontell and G. Geis. New York: Springer.

Acknowledgments

I want to acknowledge and thank my family, Christopher, Nathan, and Hahnna, for their love, pride, and support. Of course, I cannot forget to mention the importance of my two newest additions to my life, Danny and Breahnna, who let me know I have done some things right in life. I also wish to thank my wonderfully supportive colleagues who have encouraged me, advised me, and just been there for me along the way. I am grateful for all of your work, support, and having the chance to have you as colleagues and friends. I want to specifically thank Ron Kramer for being the best mentor a person could ask for and for all of his support and friendship. Additionally, I thank him for his insightful comments, suggestions, and review of this manuscript. Last but not least, I want to thank Hope Smith who has truly given me hope. Thanks for your help in editing and formatting—I still have hair because of you.

State Criminality:
The Crime of All Crimes

There I see a miserable people groaning under an iron yoke, the whole human race crushed by a handful of oppressors, and an enraged mob overwhelmed by pain and hunger whose blood and tears the rich drink in peace. And everywhere the strong are armed against the weak with the formidable power of the law.

Jean-Jacques Rousseau, *The State of War*

Introduction

State crimes are historically and contemporarily ever-present with atrocious results leading to more injury and death than all traditional street crimes put together. Consider that genocide and/or crimes against humanity during the 20th century in Albania, Bosnia-Herzegovina, Cambodia, Chile, Darfur, Germany, Rwanda, Turkey, Uganda, Ukraine, and other regions claimed the lives of tens of millions and rendered many more homeless, imprisoned, and psychologically and physically damaged. The post-World War II era has been marked as one of the most violent periods in human history (Erikson and Wallensteen 2004). The majority were intrastate conflicts involving systematic and widespread massive human rights violations. It is estimated that between 1945–1996, 220 conflicts resulted in 87 million deaths (Balint 1996).

An important question to ask ourselves is why relatively few criminologists study these types of crimes. Perhaps as important, why are most students and/or the general population unaware of the magnitude of crimes of the state that have occurred in the past or are ongoing as of 2008 (i.e., the Darfur genocide or crimes against humanity in Uganda)? Moreover, why is there an absence of curiosity of the worst of the worst criminal acts: government criminality and other violators of international law? My goal for this text is to impact, in some small way, relatively speaking, this lack of curiosity and awareness. Thus, my aim is not to just provide readers with the core knowledge of state crime, but to instill a curiosity that goes beyond the last pages of this book. Indeed a lofty goal; nonetheless, it is with this goal that I continue.

Chapter 1 begins with an introduction to some of the basic terminology about and theoretical understandings of a "state." I then introduce the field of state crime, its history, developments, and core issues that have often belea-guered the field. Variant strands or hybrid forms of state crime including state-corporate crime, crimes of globalization, environmental, and political crimes are then introduced. Chapter 2 provides description of the various types of crimes that are committed by governments, acting alone, or in collusion with militias, paramilitaries, and/or transnational corporations. This includes the relevant laws prohibiting such acts as genocide, genocidal rape, crimes against humanity, crimes of aggression, state-sponsored terrorism and assassinations, political corruption, torture, slavery, forced displacement, and the militarized use of children. Chapter 3 describes the various hybrid forms of state crime as well as the crimes covered in chapter 2.

Chapter 4 focuses on depictions of state crime and how the marginalization of the topic lends to the lack of curiosity or outrage (e.g., mass media including newscasts, print, and films and the university setting and criminological textbooks), the various types and costs of these acts (direct and indirect), and, lastly, some fundamental methodological issues associated with the study of state crime. In chapter 5, I provide a review of relevant criminological theories that can contribute to our understanding of how and why these types of criminal acts occur. From this, I introduce an integrated theory for international criminal law violations.

Chapters 6 and 7 introduce a typology of governmental structures that are most conducive to specific forms of state criminality. Specifically, chapter 6 introduces governmental structures including democratic, parliamentary, and federal republics, their commonalities for types of crime, as well as enactment procedures. Chapter 7 then explores governmental structures such as authoritarian, dictatorships, communism, military juntas, republic (one-party rules), and theocracies. As with chapter 6, other core structural conditions are examined along with enactment procedures.

Chapter 8 introduces the extant international institutions of control: specifically, the institutions of international law, United Nations, International Court of Justice, International Criminal Tribunals for Yugoslavia and Rwanda, and the International Criminal Courts structures, functions, strengths and weaknesses are presented. The chapter concludes with a summary of their potential and the critique of such institutions that are said to be based on retribution versus social justice and reconciliation.

Chapter 9 then examines domestic controls, including those that were created to act simultaneously with the international systems of control: gacaca, hybrid tribunal for Sierra Leone, truth and reconciliations commissions, amnesty projects, and countries' own domestic laws and criminal justice systems. Through the discussion of the various types of controls, each is not only presented but also critiqued. Chapter 10 concludes the overview for potential or real barriers to state crime by exploring the fundamental mechanisms associated with constraints. Key international constraints are presented along with several examples, including international citizen's tribunals, the media, political pressure from states, and public movements. The chapter closes with some key distinctions between the international and domestic forms of restraint and the need to be mindful of issues that may rise if we over-generalize expectation of these institutions' efficacy for all cases of state crime.

The book closes with chapter 11, which presents a brief overview and summary of state crime. This is followed by a discussion of future directions and policies that include the idea of a "true" international community, cosmopolitism, and universalism in the face of the realpolitik of international relations, human nature, and power.

Chapter 1

An Introduction to State Criminology

State crimes result in more injury and death than traditional street crimes such as robbery, theft, and assault. Yet, despite the gravity, costs, and extensiveness of crimes committed by states and political leaders, these harms have been understudied relative to conventional street crimes in the field of criminology and criminal justice. Nonetheless, in the last decade, considerable theoretical, conceptual, and empirical progress has been made by criminologists to better specify the nature, extent, distribution, causal variables, and potential social controls of state violence. This chapter will review the history and extant literature on crimes of the state along with providing some basic terms and definitions of states.

Introduction to the History and Terminology of State Crime

Only recently have criminologists studied state crime. Yet, state crime has been approached in a number of ways by a number of disciplines (i.e., criminology, history, political science, sociology). For example, at the end of the nineteenth century, a French judge, Louis Proall (1898), in his book *Political Crime,* focused on the crimes of statesmen and politicians. Becker and Murray (1971) analyzed how state governments break the law, as did Lieberman in 1972. Sociologists, such as Giddens (1987a) and Tilly (1985), explored the use of organized violence used by states. Keelman and Hamilton (1989) analyzed crimes committed by individuals acting in obedience to government authorities.

The intellectual history behind White-Collar Crime (WCC) research on state crime can be traced back to Edwin Sutherland (1939), who called attention to a then-neglected form of crime, namely the crimes of respectable people in the context of a legitimate occupation, and of corporations. Although the significance of such crime—white-collar crime—was conceded by some criminologists in response to Sutherland, only a few began to focus on white collar crime until several decades after his 1939 speech and the publication of his landmark book, *White Collar Crime* (1949).

Since the 1970s, however, a fairly rich literature and substantial interest in white-collar crime developed within criminology (e.g., Friedrichs 2004). Yet, Sutherland himself was not at all interested in crimes of states. For him, "war crime" referred to black market activity of businessmen, and he disregarded the massive crimes of the Nazis that were taking place during the time that he was working on his *White Collar Crime* book (Rothe and Friedrichs 2006). But his extension of the concept of crime beyond its conventional parameters did provide an important foundation built upon by several later scholars (Clinard 1946; Geis 1967; Kramer 1982; Michalowski and Kramer 1987; Schwendinger and Schwendinger 1970; Turk 1982; Vaughn 1982). Nonetheless, for most of the twentieth century, criminologists largely disregarded the topic of crimes of the state (Rothe and Friedrichs 2006). For example, in 1988, Martin, Romano, and Haran stated that criminologists neglected the study of large scale economically motivated international criminal networks. At about the same time, Manual Lopez-Rey complained "about the neglect of criminology of nonconventional crime," including state-sponsored terrorism (Martin et al. 1988, cited in Barak 1991: 7).

State crime was also conceptualized as political crime. Austin Turk, however, viewed this as crimes against the state, not by the state. Instead, Turk (1982: 35) stated, "No matter how heinous such crimes may be, calling them political crimes confuses political criminality with political policing or with conventional politics, and therefore obscures the structured relationship between political authorities and subjects." Hagan (1997), on the other hand, argued that political crimes were crimes committed by the state. Ross (2000, 2003) combined the earlier work of Turk and Hagan and defined political crime as both crimes against the state and crimes by the state. Other criminologists began exploring state crime from a political economy model. For example, Michalowski (1985) utilized a political economy model to explore crimes of capital committed by organizations.

While the concept of state crime had been addressed by a few criminology scholars, one can argue that Chambliss' 1989 American Society of Criminology Presidential address (Chambliss, 1990) provided the more direct and immediate inspiration for more systematic attention to crimes of the state on the part of a number of criminologists (Barak 1990; Friedrichs 1992; Kramer 1992, 1995; Ross 1995; Tunnell 1993). These early works (though often plagued by definitional issues) examined the crimes of the state as well as potential controls of such crime. The two issues that generated much debate in these early works were (1) whether the individual or the state (organization) was culpable for acts deemed a state crime, and (2) what standards should be used to define state criminality.

Definitional Issues I: Individual Versus State Entity

Dating back to Sutherland, the notion of an organization being criminally liable had consistently been met with resistance by criminologists until the late 1970s through the mid 1980s. It was then some criminologists began to incorporate ideas from organizational sociologists' research (Ermann and Lundman 1982; Gross 1978; Schrager and Short 1978; Vaughn 1982, 1983). In the 1970s, the organizational sociologists' emphasis argued that social scientists needed to move beyond focusing on the individuals who make up an organization and to recognize that the aggregate whole "functions as an entity" (Hall 1987, quoted in Kauzlarich and Kramer 1998: 7). Moreover, they are capable of actions that affect a community (Perrucci and Potter 1989). As such, it was argued that organizations, as social actors, "can and should be the primary focus of analysis in state and corporate crime" (Kauzlarich and Kramer 1998: 9). Others strongly objected to the notion of a state, as a social actor, in an analysis of state or corporate crime (Cressey 1989). Nonetheless, research on state and corporate crime that defined the state as a social actor continued. However, within the international legal arena, the notion of a state actor was already well underway.

The concept of a state as an entity possessing individual rights and subject to criminal liability emerged back in the mid 1900s. As Henkin (1995: 111) points out: "At Nuremberg, sitting in judgment on the recent past, the Allied victors declared waging aggressive war to be a state crime (under both treaty and customary law) as well as an individual crime by those who represented and acted for the aggressor state."

In 1976, the International Law Commission again discussed the notion of state criminal responsibility (Jorgensen 2000: 28). Moreover, several legal scholars have observed, there is a connection between individual criminal responsibility and state criminal responsibility under international law (Kramer, Michalowski, and Rothe 2005). Cassesse (2002: 19) suggests that most of the offenses proscribed under international law "for the perpetration of which it endeavours to punish the individuals that allegedly committed them" are considered by international law "as particularly serious violations by States"; consequently, when a crime is committed by an individual "not acting in a private capacity, a dual responsibility may follow: criminal liability of the individual, falling under international criminal law, and State responsibility, regulated by international rules on this matter."

Furthermore, during the process of negotiations of the Rome Statute of the International Criminal Court in 1998, the French delegate introduced a proposal for the inclusion of organizations including states. Of the two drafts proposed, one Draft Statute contained an article that would subject legal entities to the Court's jurisdiction if the crimes were committed on behalf of such legal persons or their agencies or representatives. In the end, this was dismissed as contradictory to the principle of a complimentary system (Sadat and Carden 2000). Jorgensen (2000) also has called for the use of state criminal responsibility. I agree with her claim that there is a link between state and individual criminal responsibility. As social actors, an organization is nonetheless composed of agentic individuals.

Moreover, a state will not necessarily be deterred from criminal action if it can merely sacrifice individual agents to the court as it can sacrifice individual soldiers and units on a battlefield. With the precedent set at the Nuremberg Trials, acting Heads of States would be held liable. Furthermore, Kauzlarich and Kramer's (1998) work emphasizes that the center of state criminality is the state, not the individual. Structural and organizational conditions combine with individual predilections and positions to generate these offenses; punishment of individuals will not be able to deter the polities themselves from offending (Rothe and Mullins 2006a). One can sanction numerous bureaucrats, soldiers, and spies without eliminating a state's ability or motivation to engage in criminal behaviors. The most powerful motivational elements arise within the state itself, not within the state's agents. Moreover, states as criminal actors would further ensure victim(s) compensation and a sense of justice for those victimized. It also would allow for sanctions to be set against the state versus utilizing the underpowered International Court of Justice or trying to get the United Nations Security Council to grant such a sanction with existing veto votes.

Obviously, one cannot incarcerate a state. However, the ability to levy trade and other sanctions upon criminal states may act as further controls. Restriction of trade, imposition of tariffs, denial of loans from foreign powers or the International Monetary Fund, or insistence upon collection of outstanding debts are all tools which the International Criminal Court (ICC) could use to exert social control. This requires that there exist political and economic bodies capable of and willing to engage in such sanctioning behaviors. While sanctions are often criticized as ineffective, these claims are often made disingenuously as part of broader political rhetoric or the specificities of a case are inappropriately generalized (Rothe and Mullins 2006a).

If we accept that a state is indeed an actor that may be held liable for its actions, we must then discuss what standards we should use to judge a states' action as criminal. This was the other issue of the contentious debate engulfing earlier works of state crime research.

Definitional Issues II: Standards to Be Used

Within criminology, the idea of a state being criminally liable was met with significant resistance. There were those that denied state criminality was possible. The common argument against state criminality was that "governments and their agencies do not commit crimes, but only because the criminal law does not take cognizance of them as criminal actors." Instead, states can only commit "noncriminal deviance" (Cohen 1990: 104). On the other hand, scholars who supported the idea of state criminality were divided upon the standards to be used between a legalistic frame and a broader frame including social harms to human rights.

Several criminologists argued that the standard for defining a crime by the state needed to be expanded to include social definitions. The earliest proponents of this view were the Schwendingers (1970), who proposed crime could be socially defined based on the notion of human rights. While some criminologists followed the idea of human rights (Galliher 1989), broader definitions were also put forth. For example, Michalowski (1985) suggested that socially analogous harm could be used to define state or corporate crimes (see also Barak 1990). Nonetheless, from its inception, the growth and development of state crime studies have been faced with a key conceptual problem: how can the state be a criminal actor when legally it is the state itself that defines criminal behavior? Barak (1991: 8) points out that "the study of state criminality is problematic because the concept itself is controversial, in part because of a debate over whether one should define crime in terms other than law codes of individual nations. Some argue that if a state obeys its own laws, it should be judged by no higher criterion."

Sharkansky (1995) presented such a critique, arguing that while states may commit many undesirable behaviors, one cannot call them criminal unless they expressly violate their own laws. Labeling a state criminal on other grounds violates key precepts of national sovereignty and a nation's right to regulate itself. However, this critique sees even well recognized instances of state criminality, like the Holocaust, as "nasty" behaviors but not criminal.

In Chambliss' 1989 presidential speech, he suggested that state crimes are those "acts defined by law as criminal and committed by state officials in pursuit of their jobs as representatives of the state" (1990: 184). Kramer and Michalowski (1990) quickly followed with the definition of state-facilitated crime, those activities of the state which fail to constrain criminal and dangerous behaviors. Chambliss (1995: 9) subsequently again called for resolving the key question at the foundation of the discipline, the definition of crime, so that the discipline could remain viable and vital. He stated: "State organized crimes, environmental crimes, crimes against humanity, human rights crimes, and the violations of international treaties increasingly must take center state in criminology. . . . Criminologists must define crime as behavior that violates international agreements and principles established in the courts and treaties of international bodies" (Chambliss 1995: 9).

Green and Ward (2000) have critiqued definitions of state crime that are based on a highly legalistic use of international law. They define state crime as the area of overlap between two phenomena: (1) violations of human rights, and (2) state organizational deviance. They suggest that state organizational deviance is a violation of human rights—the elements of freedom and well-being that human beings need to exert and develop their capacities—conducted by persons working for state agencies, in pursuit of organizational goals, and that if their actions were to become known, some social audience would expose the individuals or agencies concerned to a sufficiently serious risk of formal or informal censure and sanctions, thus affecting their conduct (Green and Ward 2000: 110).

They have opted for a deviance-based definition that draws upon the work of Howard Becker (1963) and other labeling theorists. Green and Ward assert that state crimes are offenses only when the action is labeled as such by a social audience. Other definitions, they claim, lack legitimacy. Moreover, their latest work (2004) examined state crime in relation to corruption, state-corporate crime, natural disaster, police crime, organized crime, state terror and terrorism, torture, war crimes, and genocide all under the rubric of International Human Rights Law (IHL) and the labeling of such by some social audience. This approach is far too vague concerning what constitutes a social audience and which audiences may legitimately label behavior a crime. Others, such as Kramer and Michalowski (2005), have responded to the call of Green and Ward for using international human rights by claiming that human rights and/or more vague frames can indeed be incorporated within the body of an international legalistic frame.

In general, the critique of using legal codes as the base definition of crime is well discussed in the state crime literature. Alternative formulations have been advanced, ranging from international legal codes to basic human rights precepts to the perceptions of the state's citizens (Barak 1991; Chambliss and Zatz 1993; Friedrichs 1996b; Green and Ward 2000; Kauzlarich and Kramer 1998; Ross 1995; Ross et al. 1999; Tunnell 1993). The controversy over the appropriate definition of crimes of the state is sure to continue, as standards used for defining state crime remain problematic and have not been fully resolved (see Rothe and Friedrichs 2006). However, I contend that in general, most critical criminologists studying state crime agree that using international law (customary, treaties, charters, and the newly emerged criminal law) constitute a basic foundation for defining state crime as this framework includes standards such as human rights, social and economic harms, as well as providing a legalistic foundation (Rothe and Friedrichs 2006). Furthermore, international criminal law covers individuals as well as states, thus resolving any ongoing reservations of the state as actors versus individuals. As Jorgensen (2000: 139) suggests, "all acts which constitute international crimes may in principle entail individual or state responsibility, or both, depending on the nature and circumstances of the breach, and that the two notions can complement each other." In sum, the emergent principle of criminal law is that states themselves can commit crimes, and they can and should be held criminally responsible for them (Kramer, Michalowski, and Rothe 2005). Consequentially, I define state criminality as: "Any action that violates international public law, and/or a state's own domestic law when these actions are committed by individual actors acting on behalf of, or in the name of the state, even when such acts are motivated by their personal economical, political, and ideological interests" (see also Rothe and Mullins 2006a).

Theories and Definitions of States

The growing interrelationships between the state, international organizations, transnational corporations, the mass media, and globalization generates a situation where the interplay and reinforcement of these processes in multiple institutions create profound implications for defining states. Moreover, as the state has been reified to the point of it being a seemingly natural institution, social scientists in general, and criminologists more specifically, often analyze the state without ever providing a clear definition of the concept. Likewise, academics that do attempt to create a theory of state, describing its functions and/or roles, simultaneously often fail to provide a working definition of the apparatus they are discussing. Since I have now spent some time discussing what state crime is and how a criminology of state crime has evolved over the last decade, it seems like a natural time to pause and consider what exactly a state is and what role it plays.

State Theories

Attempts to develop a theory of the state have occurred for centuries. Philosophers such as Aristotle, Hobbes, Locke, and Rousseau all attempted to explore the political components of society and civil governance. Classical theorists, such as Marx (1906), Weber (1947), and Durkheim (1933) also developed theories of the state and its function. By mid twentieth century, contemporary theorists continued to explore theories of states. These works come from several scholars including Miliband (1970), Poulantzas (1969, 1976), Habermas (1975), O'Conner (1973), and Gramsci (1971). The modernity and dependency schools also explored state theory in terms of globalization (see Santos 1971; Smelser 1964; So 1990; and Wallerstein 1986).

Nonetheless, during the 1980s, state theory waned considerably, so much so that the last decade was "notable for the impoverishment of state theory" (Barrow 2005: 1). There were negligible theoretical advances and many radical scholars, including critical criminologists, drifted away from state models. This was in part due to the complexities of the topic itself and a stalemate between "proponents of various theories."

In addition, there was a broad abandonment of grand theory and grand scale meta-narratives. The move from a Neomarxist model to post-structuralist and post-modern theory shifted analysis from the macro to the micro forms of power and to "technologies of power" (Foucault 1972; Henri-Levi 1977; Mitchell 1991). As such, there could be no "grand theory of the state-political . . . or of the economy" (Poulantzas 1978: 19). Instead, merely "general propositions can be made" concerning the state unless specific to one country. The recognition that a meta-theory of the state was unrealistic resulted in a shift in focus of the state in general to the capitalistic state in particular. "What is perfectly legitimate is a theory of a capitalist state . . . made possible by the separation of the space of the state and that of the economy" (20). This change also led to a neglect of state definitions once present in Classical models.

There was also an emerging trend towards theories of globalization and states. The new interest in globalization sparked a renewal of political economy models. These began to take on an a priori assumption that state interests based on the political economy were "considered eternal and self-evident" (Creveld 1999: 415). Capital accumulation is seen as directly dictating the rhythm of state activity and is articulated to and inserted into state global policy (Poulantzas 1978; Wallerstein 1977, 1979, 1986). Moreover, the concept of one grand economy, the global economy, took center stage and was reified. Simply stated, the development of a capitalistic world economy was seen as "self-perpetuating."

At the same time, recognition of the state as a more complex political apparatus surfaced wherein the state was recognized as a peculiar political entity composed of an assemblage of impersonal and anonymous functions distinct from economic power (Poulantzas 1978: 54). The state "is a specific and highly complex phenomenon, and it can by no means be reduced to, or treated as a simple variant of, the capitalist state" (Poulantzas 1978: 24). This included recognition of the relative separation of the political from the economic. Nonetheless, the political, as conceived, still failed to take into account agency or the forces of individuals' ideological, religious, and moral interests framed as state interests. As Seabrooke (2002) noted, the state was effectively a faceless rational actor.

The globalization literature tended to analyze the state as potentially irrelevant in international relations (Whyte 2003). State theories waned due to assumptions that the state, as a meaningful unit of analysis, in the global economy, was ending (Ohmae 1995). Griffen (1995) concurred with the deterministic view of globalization as inevitable as well as the growing diminution of the state. Simply stated, the notion of sovereignty erosion was becoming popular leading to a further decline in state theories that focus more broadly on state functions domestically and internationally (Krasner 1995). Models accepting this premise focused on the undermining of state sovereignty by the globalization of markets beyond the institutional boundaries of states. Not only were states seen as declining in relevance, but the actors within the political process were completely omitted. Furthermore, these assertions rested upon a highly idealized and reified account of globalization (Whyte 2003). State policies were viewed as inevitably market-driven and focused on the dynamics of a global and capitalistic economy, most notably, U.S.-centered. For example, Aglietta (1990) focused on imperialism as the emerging theme of globalization. This inevitably led to a state analysis that was "incomplete" as it was "restricted to the structure and dynamics of wage relations in the U.S." (Aglietta 2000; Barrow 2005). On the other hand, other scholars (Domhoff 1998) noted that theories of imperialism could not be constructed on the basis of economics alone.

In general, political scientists examined state relations and foreign policy using two approaches: (1) the structure of the international system (based on economics and rational choice models), and (2) decision-making analyses that attempt to explain political processes from within states (Spiegel and Wheeling 2005). Both of these orientations failed to adequately address the dialectic process between states and the international arena. Concerning this point, Seeley (1986: 133) stated, "Never be content with looking at states purely from within; always remember that they have another aspect which is wholly different, their relation to foreign states." These interstate relations need not be limited to or solely based on political-economic relationships, but could incorporate tradition, religion, or ideological interests.

The focus for other scholars shifted to an elite-centered model where states were seen as captured by a "mere fraction of capital that is pursuing a myopic definition of national interest rather than the larger neoimperial interests of globalizing capital" (Barrow 2005: 20). This attention coincided with a renewed interest in class conflict now seen as intrastate, contradicting interstate class interests. Simply stated, the state took on the personification or representation of class interests within a global conflict. As stated by Wallerstein (1977: xi), "we shift from seeing classes (and status groups) as groups within a world-economy."

Interest also began to shift towards state models that could explain the significance of interstate relations more broadly. This shift inevitably led back to the ongoing debate over the significance of state theory within a global order. For example, Cox (1996: 31) challenged the idea that the state was in retreat and proposed an internationalization wherein the state was being transformed "into an agency for adjusting national economic practices and policies to a perceived global economy." Others claimed the state was growing stronger in its role within the international arena because state-specific resources remain core to economic activity. For example, transnational organizations "utilize the most advanced states for foreign investment and remain tied to specific dominant states" suggesting state economies may supersede a "global economy" (Hirst and Thompson 1996).

In general, models of the state either focus on domestic affairs or on international relations and/or globalization. There are few accounts of state theory that are capable of addressing both without reducing one or the other to a point of irrelevance. Moreover, the few theories that do address both usually focus on the Western capitalist state to do so (Barrow 2005; Cox 1996; Whyte 2003). With the reemergence of interest in political economy models, variables at the level of agency are often ignored. There are exceptions. For example, in exploring international relations and prohibitions on state behavior, Passas (2004: 1) states:

> [I]t is also true—despite the inattentions of most international relations scholars—that moral and emotional factors related to neither political nor economic advantage but instead involving religious beliefs, humanitarian sentiments, faith in universalism, compassion, conscience, paternalism, fear, prejudice, and the compulsion to proselytize can and do play important roles in the creation and the evolution of international relations.

Intrasocietal interactions as well as interstate relations entail highly complex processes in which not only "economic and security interests but also moral interests play a prominent role, in which the actions of states must be understood as the culmination of both external pressures and domestic political struggles" (Nadelman 2004: 2). This is not an argument suggesting states have moral views; rather, "the capacity of particular moral arguments to influence government policies, particularly foreign policies, stems from the political influence of domestic moral entrepreneurs as well as that of powerful individual advocates within the government." Others, such as Charles Beitz (1979) and James Mayall (1982), also focused their research on morality in international politics, centered on individuals with agency, as opposed to a focus on the state.

In essence, these premises bring back the agentic forces that compose the state political apparatus and allow for an understanding of state actors beyond capital accumulation and domestic legitimation. It allows for the interactional level within the structural and international levels to be explored. This view, coupled with international critical legal theory (Carty 1991) that recognizes the diversity of states and state functions within international relations moves beyond the limitations of state theories that are focused on the economic relations wherein capitalism lies at the heart of the analysis.

From this brief review of state theories, a general lack of operationalizing of states is evident. As previously stated, there are relatively few contemporary state theories that provide a working definition of the state within their research. Exceptions to this include Giddens (1987a), who suggested the state can be defined as an apparatus of government of a definite type within a society. Neuman (2005: 17) recently defined the state as "all the government, or the public sector, plus much of what immediately surrounds it, connects it to society, and holds it together." Yet, in general, most political sociologists and critical criminologists, while putting the state at the center of their field, fail to provide a definition of the state at the core of their analysis. In part, this omission is simply because "defining the state is a notoriously difficult task" (Faulks 2000: 20).

As for the role or theory of state action, I concur with Faulks; it is too complex for one theoretical concept to cover the variations of state apparatuses. As such, let us turn know to how states are defined by political entities.

Political Definitions

The preceding brief overview demonstrates the multiple ways the state has been analyzed. Yet, defining a state is also done within the political arena, both internationally and domestically. For example, The Foreign Relations Law of the U.S. (S 201), restated in S101 1987, and the 1933 Montevideo Convention on Rights and Duties of State used a more simplistic model for defining a state wherein the state has (1) a defined territory and population, (2) said territory and population are under the control of its own governmental apparatus, and (3) the entity engages in or has the capacity to engage in formal relations with other states. Another working definition used by the United States' State Department when dealing with international legalistic matters and its foreign policy relating to other states includes these characteristics: the entity (1) has effective control over a clearly defined territory and population, (2) possesses an organized governmental administration, (3) has the capacity to act effectively to conduct foreign relations and fulfill international obligations, and (4) has been recognized as a legitimate entity by the "international community."

The defining of a state can often be done ad hoc and for self-serving interests of the state such as that offered on November 16, 2001, by President Bush. He defined the state as "any State, district, territory, or possession of the United States" (Federal Registrar, Vol. 66, p. 57835). While this definition is much more expansive than those offered by sociologists, the 18 USC goes further and defines the state as "all areas under the jurisdiction of the United States including . . . all places and waters, continental or insular, subject to the jurisdiction of the United States" (18 USC Section 5 and 49 USC 46501 [2]).

International Governmental Organizations also define states. For example, Article 4(1) of the UN Charter explicitly mentions the ability and willingness "in the judgment of the Organization" to carry out international obligations as a criterion for admission of new members to the United Nations, thus, as recognition of statehood. This stipulates what constitutes statehood in accordance with international law, i.e., the essentiality inherent to the state as a subject of international law. All other requirements for statehood, according to international law, in particular the existence of effective power of control over a territory and its inhabitants, are derived from this one criterion: the necessary ability and readiness to act in accordance with international law. Moreover, admission of new states as members of the United Nations takes place by an act of collective recognition by existing states.

Thus, statehood becomes defined by more abstract concepts such as recognition, self-determination (UN Charter 1: 2), and willingness to fulfill international obligations and relations. Simply stated, statehood becomes defined internationally using the constitutive approach—recognition by other states, and/or by the declarative approach—states have a legal personality de facto regardless of international recognition or UN membership.

While international and state definitions are based on political interests, legalistic criterion, and/or legal obligations, they demonstrate the ambiguities of defining a state. Consequently, it seems, as social scientists we must be aware of the socially constructed nature of and implicit assumptions of the term *state*. As such, it is essential that we operationalize such an ambiguous term, perhaps even more so when we claim criminal liability on the part of a state. Therefore, we suggest that the state be defined as: "[T]he institutions, organizations, and/or agencies composed of actors representing and entrusted with the functions of the political apparatus governing the corresponding population via the legitimate and symbolic use of power, contained within a historically and culturally defined milieu and bound territory."

This definition allows us to conceptualize the state as composed of individuals and also as an entity that has been reified as the institution of political power within the existing territory and culture. Moreover, by recognizing the agentic forces that compose the administrative machinery, we are not limited to political-economic or capitalistic models of the state, but can consider the political, ideological, and religious views of the actors that often frame the socially constructed "state interests." After all, ideology always has roots "which go beyond the state apparatus and which always consist in relations of power" (Poulantzas 1978: 37).

A Typology of Governmental Crimes

This section provides a general conceptual and definitional overview of different forms of governmental crimes.[1] The forms of state crime that I introduce here are "not easily classified as corporate, occupation, or governmental crime. They are hybrids that combine attributes of two or more of the established forms of white-collar crime" (Friedrichs 2007: 145). As they incorporate attributes of other forms of crimes along with state crime, the following section will briefly introduce state-corporate crime, crimes of globalization, political crime, and environmental crime.

State-Corporate Crime

Scholars of state crime have explored how crimes occur when states and corporations are intermingled: a crime can be attributed to the actions (or lack thereof) of both a state and a corporation(s). Building upon the growing interests in political and state crimes, several presentations and/or articles brought the concept of state/corporate crime to the attention of criminologists. Kramer and Michalowski (1990: 4) provided the most widely cited definition of state-corporate crime: "State-corporate crimes are illegal or socially injurious actions that occur when *one* or more institutions or political governance pursue a goal in direct cooperation with one or more institutions of economic production and distribution."

State-corporate crime increasingly came to be seen as taking two forms, although these types often interacted with each other. Accordingly, a distinction emerged between state-facilitated and state-initiated crimes (Kramer 1992; Kauzlarich and Kramer 1993). These earlier works proposed and explored a "framework for examining how corporations and governments intersect to produce social harm" (Kramer, Michalowski, and Kauzlarich 2000: 263). Such intersections can work in a myriad of fashions. States can create laws that facilitate corporate wrongdoing and crimes (e.g., the infamous Savings and Loan debacle within the United States); regulatory and advisement agencies can simply fail to do their appointed tasks (e.g., OSHA's failure to provide remedy to safety violations at an Imperial Chicken plant in Hamlet, North Carolina [Aulette and Michalowski 1993]; the FAA's failures to ground ValuJet [Matthews and Kauzlarich 2000], and NHTSA's failure to investigate tire failures and roll over incidents on Ford Explorers [Mullins 2006]). States and state actors can also directly collude and conspire with private corporations to violate laws as in the case of Halliburton's war profiteering since the war on terror or Blackwater's killing of innocent civilians (Rothe 2006).

The Crash of ValuJet Flight 592:
A Case Study in State-Corporate Crime

by Rick A. Matthews and David Kauzlarich (2000)

"The Crash of ValuJet 592: A Case Study in State-Corporate Crime" is a seminal piece within the body of corporate crime research. It not only serves as one of the leading well-cited cases of corporate crime by scholars of white-collar crime, but was one of the earliest case studies of state-corporate crime. The recognition of the relationships between a state regime and corporate actors, while not Matthews and Kauzlarich's original conception, is skillfully applied to the ValuJet case. Simply, on May 11, 1996, ValuJet flight 592 crashed in the Florida Everglades, killing all 105 passengers and five crew members. Matthews and Kauzlarich then show how the immediate cause of the crash was a fire that erupted after oxygen generators exploded in the cargo compartment. As such, ValuJet and SabreTech (an airline maintenance company) failed to comply with regulations for the presentation, storage, and transportation of hazardous materials. The authors then suggest that the Federal Aviation Administration (FAA) was negligent in its oversight: not adequately monitoring ValuJet or instituting safeguards and guidelines that would have protected the passengers and crews.

Matthews and Kauzlarich spend some time reviewing the concept of state-corporate crime within the criminological literature, which also provides readers with a basic foundation of the field's history up to the time of the publication. Further, the authors provide the necessary, yet succinct, background factors leading up to the crash. From this, as is generally followed in these types of case studies, Matthews and Kauzlarich apply a theoretical analysis. In this case they have chosen the integrated model previously developed by Kramer and Michalowski (1990) and later added to by Kauzlarich and Kramer (1998). While this article provides an analysis of the crimes committed by the ValuJet Corporation, it also addresses a key factor in many examples of state-corporate crime: crimes of omission. Simply, the authors argue that state-corporate crime, in the case at hand, was the result of the corporation's actions, outsourcing, but more importantly, the omission of state regulatory agencies to do their role in oversight.

With the increasingly international nature of corporate operations, capital accumulation and dispersement, these types of crimes take on an increasingly international flavor and situation (Friedrichs and Friedrichs, 2002; Rothe, Muzzatti, and Mullins 2006). Moreover, as states continue to privatize war efforts and to utilize mercenaries and corporate warriors, the notion of state/corporate crime highlights the role that transnational organizations can play in crimes by the state (Singer 2003).

State-Corporate Crime: The Democratic Republic of Congo

The Democratic Republic of Congo (DRC) has devolved into uncontrolled genocidal warfare between ethnically-based factions within an unresolved civil war, due to international involvement on behalf of its neighbors (e.g., Uganda and Rwanda), transnational corporations (e.g., AngloGold Ashanti), and those corporations' Western trading partners (Metalor Technologies and the nation of Switzerland). Central within the conflict is the control of rich mineral fields of the country. When Uganda and Rwanda decamped from Congo in 2003 and 2002, respectively, they left behind factional militias that continued the conflicts. Uganda supported the Front des Nationalistes et Integrationnistes (FNI), a Lendu-based ethnic armed force; Rwanda supported the Union des Patriotes Congolais (UPC), a Hema group. These ethnic groups have a history of conflict over land rights; with Ugandan occupation of the region, the tensions flared and Rwanda and Uganda poured arms into the struggle, using the ethnic warfare as a proxy for their own conflicted control of the region. The Lendu and Hema have continued to struggle over control of the rich gold fields, especially those in the Mongbwalu and Durba areas (both of which share a border with Uganda). Fighting has been intense, with war crimes and massive human rights violations committed frequently by all parties (Amnesty International 2003; Human Rights Watch 2003b, 2005a; UN Security Council Report 2003).

The major reason this region has been so heavily contested is the mineral deposits, which represent a major source for profit in an overall, destabilized African economic system. During the Second Congolese War (begun in 1998), Uganda occupied gold-rich lands in the north, establishing control over the Gorumbwa, Dubra, and Agbarabo mines. According to Human Right Watch (2005a), almost a ton of gold was extracted during a four-year period (1998–2002) worth approximately 9 million USD. Without the resources to engage in industrial mining practices, they forced miners to engage in artisan labor practices, which are very dangerous and reckless. Ugandan soldiers frequently beat and extorted the local miners by required monetary payment to enter the mines and by taking a percentage of the ore that they mined.

Due to the highly valued mineral wealth found especially in the northeastern portion of the nation, both transnational corporations and Switzerland were either directly involved or duly complicit with the violence in northern Congo (Human Rights Watch 2005a; UN SC 2003). Gold, silver, diamonds, coltan, and other precious minerals constitute the major exploitable natural resources of the area. With the political and economic chaos instigated by the civil war of 1998 and the continued unrest since, these mineral resources are effectively controlled by militia groups. While the sitting government can, and has, issued contracts and deeds for mineral extraction, such official permissions are meaningless in the hinterlands. To actually take advantage of these economic agreements, companies must also negotiate with the on-the-ground powers or establish relationships with neighboring nations to purchase raw materials illegally taken over the border and then shipped into major global markets (Human Rights Watch 2005a; UN SC 2003).

Involvement in this sort of trade can violate human rights laws when the nature of mining operations fails to follow existing international guidelines. This is precisely the situation which has widely existed in the northeastern region of DRC. The UN Panel of experts (UN SC 2003) named over 100 corporations with problematic or suspect dealings within the DRC during the chaos of the past 8 years (see the UN SC 2003 report for a full accounting of those involved). While the majority of these were African-based companies (most based in neighboring nations), major transnationals, like DeBeers, were also named. Belgium, Canada, Germany, Israel, the Netherlands, Switzerland, the United Kingdom, and the United States all have multiple companies on the list. For example, Metalor Technologies, a leading Swiss refinery, is responsible for purchasing Congolese gold from Ugandan sources (Human Rights Watch 2005a). While claiming to follow all Swiss and international laws, Metalor's due diligence is problematic; they knew the gold was coming from Uganda. It is also well known that there is essentially no indigenous Ugandan gold production and Uganda does not import gold from other states. This leaves one likely source of the metal: northeastern Congo. Metalor's purchases were facilitated by the Swiss freeport system. Freeports provide a place for the importation of goods that are legally outside the realm of governmental control. No duties or tariffs are applied to goods brought in through these zones, and thus no governmental record-keeping or oversight occurs. A company like Metalor can buy gold within the freeport zone with no official taxation or, more importantly, with no tracing of its origins. As with the other transnational organizations listed, Metalor actively and knowingly participated with the militias to illegally purchase gold. When such militia groups are involved in war crimes, forced labor, and other crimes against humanity, and transnational corporations are actively supporting them or providing outlets and business, transnational corporations become both complicit and responsible itself for these crimes. (For a more detailed discussion see Mullins and Rothe [2008].)

The notion of a state as an actor did indeed raise scrutiny within academe, while the idea of corporations as criminally liable has been generally accepted. However, within the courts domestically and internationally, liability of corporations has often been viewed as a civil case at best (Singer 2003). Nonetheless, international legal precedence has also been set for criminal liability of corporations and transnational organizations.

Transnational Organizations

The idea of criminal liability of organizations is not new. Within the scope of criminological research, such claims have been made for several decades. Moreover, during the Rome Statute Preparatory Committee meetings (1996–1998) the concept of organizations and states were added into one of the existing Drafts (see chapter 3). Recently, agreements have been framed by the United Nations that compel transnational corporations to obey human rights laws. For example, the 2003 Norms on the Responsibilities of Transnational Corporations and Other Business Enterprises with regard to human rights agreement expressly bring the behavior of corporations operating in multiple nations under the rubric of human rights laws. Drawing heavily upon the UN Charter, especially Articles 1, 2, 55, and 56, this agreement acknowledges that globally active for profit corporations are major players in the international arena.

Traditionally, it has been the internationally held expectation that states are the key players responsible for the maintenance and enforcement of human rights standards. Yet, due to the increasing power and influence of these corporate entities, it is their obligation as the core of a key social institution—e.g., the international society's economy, to abide by existing human rights law. If they are either active or complicit in such actions, then they are prosecutable by the ICC. Corporate actors, state agents, and even private citizens unconnected to a transnational or national entity are currently under the court's jurisdiction as long as the action in question occurs within a signatory state that has ratified the Rome Statute or they are nationals of signatory states. This means that representatives of transnationals who operate within signatory states must abide by international human rights law or face prosecution (Rothe and Mullins 2006a).

Furthermore, the recent Agreement by the United Nations Economic and Social Council (2003), to which the U.S. is a signatory, specifically addresses the criminal liability of transnational organizations and that these organizations (actors within the organization) fall under the purview of international law and the ICC. Article 18 also of this Agreement sets up criminal liability to which even the ICC could potentially have jurisdiction. It states: in connection with determining damages, in regard to criminal sanctions, and in all other respects, these Norms shall be applied by national courts and/or international tribunals, pursuant to national and international law (E/CN.4/Sub.2/2003/12/Rev.2). Previously, individual and organizational criminal liability was avoided through "transnational loopholes" (Michalowski and Kramer 1987). Thus, the notion of transnational criminal liability is relevant to the ongoing subfield of state-corporate crime as well as the case at hand (Rothe and Mullins 2006a).

State-Corporate Crime: War Profiteering and the Ali Babba

The intersection of state and corporate interests during times of war is a fundamental part of the war-making process. Every capitalist country must rely on private-sector production to produce the weapons of war. In the United States, for example, major auto manufacturers such as Chrysler, Ford, and Chevrolet retooled to produce tanks, guns, and missiles instead of cars during World War II, while many other companies refocused some or all of their production to serve the war effort. With the introduction of a permanent wartime economy after the end of World War II, amid concerns that the United States was coming to be dominated by a military-industrial complex (Melman 1974), major providers of weapons and logistical support such as General Electric, Boeing, Bechtel Group, and Lockheed Martin became regular recipients of government contracts. They were also repeatedly at the center of controversies concerning cost overruns and questionable charges (Grieder 1998).

The close alignment of corporate and government interests in the production and procurement of the weapons of war is a vivid example of the "revolving door" effect as described by C. Wright Mills (1954) in the Power Elite. As executives from major military contractors fill elected or appointed government positions, the interests of the state become increasingly entangled with prior corporate loyalties. In recent years, the integration of state interests with those of the private corporation has intensified. This integration began with efforts to adapt to a downsized military through increased reliance on "just on time" privatized logistic contracts. The move to an active war footing following the attacks of 9/11, including the wars in Afghanistan and Iraq and the permanent "war on terror," further cemented the private-public strategy for war-making in the United States (Rothe 2006).

The controversy surrounding links between Vice-President Dick Cheney and Halliburton, the company he formerly headed, provides a demonstration of the potential for state-corporate crime embedded in this new policy of war by subcontract. There have been claims that the association between Cheney and Halliburton resulted in no-bid, cost-plus contractual work without competitive pricing or oversight. According to some, the affiliation between Cheney and Halliburton has established war profiteering as an acceptable and systematic practice within the Bush Administration by rewarding "corporations for who they know rather than what they know, and a system in which cronyism is more important than competence" (Hartung 2003: 26).

Although the relationship between Cheney and Halliburton appeared to be a major factor in awarding contracts to Halliburton (Chatterjee 2004), Cheney denied any involvement in the contracts contracting process. On "Meet the Press" he said, "As Vice President, I have absolutely no influence of, involvement of, knowledge of in any way, shape, or form of contracts led by the Army Corps of Engineers or anybody else in the Federal

Government" (NBC "Meet the Press" with Russert 2003).

Private memos, however, proved otherwise. An internal Pentagon e-mail (March 5, 2003) sent by an Army Corps of Engineer official, claimed that Douglas Feith, Defense Department's undersecretary for policy, approved arrangements for a multi-billion dollar contract for Halliburton "contingent on informing the WH tomorrow. We anticipate no issues since action has been coordinated w VP office" ("From the Editors," *New York Times* 2004: 1). Within three days Halliburton received one of the first State Department contracts for Iraq worth as much as $7 billion (Gongloff 2003). Not only did Halliburton receive billions of dollars from the State through competitive and non-competitive contracts, most of them were cost-plus contracts. Cost-plus contracts are essentially blank checks that ensure whatever Halliburton bills for services is reimbursed for those costs as well as an additional percentage (between 2 and 7 percent) for the company's profits (fees). These types of open-ended contracts are incentives to maximize expenditures to increase the total value of the contract and profits. Moreover, the larger the contract, the more valuable becomes Halliburton's stock.

For example, October 2002, Halliburton's stock was $12.62 a share; however, when the KBR Iraq restructure contract was awarded, Halliburton's stock rose to $23.90 a share (see Halliburton stock portfolios 2001–2004). According to Henry Bunting's testimony to the Democratic Policy Committee, the Halliburton motto in Iraq is "don't worry about it, it's cost plus" (Bunting 2004). In essence, no one questioned pricing. "The comment by both Halliburton buyers and management was 'it's cost plus, don't waste time finding another supplier'" (Chatterjee 2004: 32).

To date, Halliburton has over 24,000 workers in Iraq and Kuwait alone, 11,000 more than the number of British soldiers deployed there (Chatterjee 2004; "Halliburton" 2004; "Iraq Reconstruction" 2004). By 2005, KBR had earned contracts worth over $2.2 billion from work in Iraq (of this, 42 percent was spent on combating oil fires and restoring pipelines, and 48 percent for housing and transportation for troops). Overall, it has been estimated that Halliburton has received more than $8 billion in contracts since Cheney became V.P.

The close relationship between the Administration and Halliburton constitutes a form of state-initiated war profiteering. While Halliburton may be guilty of inflating total contract values through overcharges and/or charges for services not provided, the opportunities for profiteering were the products of the cozy relationship between the company and a sitting administration whose vice-president was Halliburton's former CEO. Thus, the economic gain was both personal and political (Rothe 2006).

State-International Organizational Crime

The concept of "crimes of globalization" (Friedrichs 2004; Friedrichs and Friedrichs 2002) is the newest addition to the list of forms of crime with a cognate relationship to crimes of the state. Informed by Falk's (1993) observation that globalization is driven by the interests of capital over people, "crimes of globalization" refers to mass harms of people, especially within developing countries, that arise as latent consequences of the development and expansion of global capital. According to Friedrichs and Friedrichs (2002: 18), crimes of globalization have characteristics of "state crime, political crime, white-collar crime, state-corporate crime, and finance crime" but do not fit neatly into any of these categories. Specifically, these crimes "involve cooperative endeavors between international financial institutions, transnational corporations, and state or political entities that engage in demonstrably harmful activities in violation of international law or international human rights convention."[2]

Friedrichs' approach highlights the role of international financial institutions, transnational corporations, and states in the context of criminogenic tendencies within globalization. Friedrichs and Friedrichs (2002) examined the role of policies put forth by the World Bank, the International Monetary Fund, and the World Trade Organization in developing states that result in socially harmful practices and human rights violations. The policies and practices of these international finance institutions can have dramatic societal effects, as reflected in the "structural adjustments" imposed on countries such as Argentina, Senegal, and Rwanda that destroyed the way of life of large numbers of indigenous peoples (Rothe and Friedrichs 2006).

International finance institutions may not intend to do harm. Indeed, they claim that their central mission is to alleviate economic and other forms of suffering. But the privileging of transnational corporate interests and the interests of powerful states, coupled with the arrogance with which these institutions implement a "top down" form of global economics, results in immensely harmful consequences that conflict with the ideology and promotion of human rights. Moreover, since international financial institutions work closely and cooperatively with high-level government officials in both developed and developing countries, the crimes of globalization they facilitate are inevitably intertwined with crimes of the state (Rothe and Friedrichs 2006; Rothe, Muzzatti, and Mullins 2006; Rothe, Mullins, and Sandstrom 2008).

Political Crimes

White collar crime scholarship in general has differentiated between occupational crimes—illegal acts committed during the course of one's daily job activities for the purposes of the attainment of personal goals, and organizational crimes—those illegal acts committed during the course one of one's daily job activities for the purposes of corporate goal attainment (see Friedrichs 2004).

Crimes of Globalization: *Rwanda*

After its independence in 1962, Rwanda's relations with its former colonial powers and international financial donors became exceedingly complex. The catastrophic impact of structural adjustment policies dictated by the IMF and World Bank, along with the fall in coffee prices on the global market (a fall linked to the policies of the institutions and the International Coffee Organization), played a key role in establishing the socioeconomic context within which the Rwandan crisis emerged. As often occurs in heavily indebted countries undergoing additional economic stressors or near collapse, the Habyarimana regime requested help from the international arena. It accepted the IMF-WB's proffered structural adjustment program. The "With Strategy Change" plan was adopted and almost immediately a 50 percent devaluation of the Rwandan franc was carried out in November of 1990. The devaluation was posited as the key to boost coffee exports by increasing the purchasing power of international trading partners.

The plunge of the Rwandan franc triggered severe inflation within the Rwandan economy. Outstanding external debt increased by an additional 34 percent between 1989 and 1992. Import prices soared, yet the price at which coffee was bought from local producers was frozen by the IMF's structural adjustment program (SAP) requirements. In June 1992, the IMF ordered a second currency devaluation; prices for fuel and consumer essentials rose again. With trade liberalization and the deregulation of grain markets as recommended by the SAP, cheap food imports and food aid from the other countries were destabilizing the few local markets that had managed to sustain themselves. The entire agricultural system was pushed into crisis as a result of the austerity measures and sinking civil service salaries. These policies inevitably exacerbated the overarching climate of insecurity (Toussaint 2004).

Like the poorest sectors of the urban population, these destitute farmers became a permanent reservoir of recruits for the Interahamwe militia and the army. The fall of the market in the late 1980s also corresponded with the political disintegration of the Habyarimana regime. In turn, massive social discontent from the devastating economic conditions was channeled by the regime's hardliners into implementing their plan for genocide. (For a more detailed account of the Rwanda genocide and Rwanda's history, see also Mullins and Rothe [2008] and Prunier [1995]).

By 1990, Rwanda was in a pervasive crisis. The Rwandan crisis of the early 1990s became a spectacle of donor roundtables in Paris, broken cease-fire agreements, and failed peace talks. Initiatives were closely monitored and coordinated by the economic donors in a tangled web of conditions (Toussaint 2004). When the fighting between the RPF and the regime started, millions of dollars of balance-of-payments aid from multilateral and bilateral sources came pouring into the coffers of the Rwandan Central Bank. Earmarked for commodity imports, a sizeable amount of these loans were diverted toward the acquisition of military hardware. After October 1990, the Rwandan Armed Forces expanded from 5,000 to 40,000 men, requiring a sizeable influx of outside money to pay the new recruits. The new recruits were drawn from the urban unemployed who had dramatically increased since the collapse of the coffee market in 1989. Thousands of youths were also drafted into the civilian militia.

The stage was set for the upcoming genocide. International financial institutions became wary of such large military expenditures and demanded that the regime decrease military spending. At the same time, however, they allowed the regime to account for the sums loaned by the WB and the IMF by presenting old invoices based on a flawed accounting system for all imported goods (Toussaint 1999). By using invoices versus receipt-based accounting for imported goods, the dates and amounts were easily altered. This strategy allowed the regime to finance massive arms purchases that would later be used in the 1994 genocide. For example, trucks imported for the army were put on the Transport Ministry's account, and fuel used for militia and army vehicles was recorded on the Health Ministry's account (Toussaint 2004).

When the IMF and WB suspended lending at the beginning of 1993, they failed to freeze the large sums of money held in accounts in foreign banks, which the Habyarimana regime used to buy more arms. The WB and IMF had knowledge of intelligence and NGO reports from within the county that indicated that ethnic hostility between the Hutus and Tutsis had increased and genocidal rhetoric had become more amplified. While the WB eventually did respond by suspending lending in early 1993, military usages of international funds began in 1989, specifically in the financing of troop increases. The WB's delay in responding to the Rwandan government's misuse of funds allowed for the development of a military hardware and personnel infrastructure that facilitated the 1994 genocide. Actions such as these indicate how, through acts of omission, the institutions failed in their duty to monitor loan money.

Further, the full democratization of Rwanda envisaged by the IMF, WB, and the 1993 Arusha accords was impossible due to the widespread impoverishment of the population. Instead, the objectives of democratization and interethnic solidarity were subsumed to the demands of *realpolitik*, which meant meeting the conditions of "good governance" by international finance lenders and Habyarimana. The installation of a multiparty coalition government under the trusteeship of Rwanda's external creditors fueled the various political factions within the regime, leading to the assassination of Habyarimana—the oft cited trigger of the genocide.

Clearly the international financial institutions did not intend to produce the Rwandan civil war and the 1994 genocide. However, the austerity measures combined with the impact of the IMF-sponsored devaluations contributed to impoverishing the Rwandan people at a time of acute political and social crisis. The deliberate manipulation of market forces destroyed economic activity and people's livelihood, fueled unemployment, and created a situation of generalized famine and social despair that enhanced the growing, though constructed through colonial and religious leaders, ethnic divisions (Toussaint 2004). Additionally, the requirements mandated by the policies for aid enhanced the political upheavals and uncertainties, which led to the additional rift in the regime and Habyarimana's assassination. The anomic conditions were developed and intensified by the IFIs, ensuring what may have been preventable: the 1994 genocide (Rothe, Mullins, and Sandstrom 2008).

Similarly, state crime research distinguishes between political crimes—those illegal activities committed by state actors for the fulfillment of personal goals or those of non-polity organizations working within, and other state crimes (see Friedrichs 2004; Ross 2003). Political crimes, such as corruption and election fraud, are typically done by state actors who use their access to state resources for the accomplishment of the criminal act. Yet, motivational drives and criminal outcomes are focused on personal enrichment and/or direct benefit to non-state groups, such as political parties. As with occupational crime, I see the key trait of political crimes being individuals taking advantage of their occupational positions of trust (Sutherland 1939) to enhance their own social status and positions. Archetypical cases of this type of political crime include Boss Tweed's corruption of Tammany Hall, the Teapot Dome Scandal of the Harding Administration, and the Watergate break-ins ordered by the Nixon White House. Such scandals and abuses of power are nearly omnipresent in modern states (see Ross's 2003 volume for a comprehensive list of criminal corruption in modern democratic states). While others do classify this type of behavior as a form of state crime, I view these as occupational crimes—for self gain, not in pursuit of organizational goals as such; they are out of the purview of what I consider to be forms of state crime. For this reason, these types of criminal activity are not addressed in this book.

While there are several regional documents regarding corruption, in December 2005, The United Nations Convention against Corruption (UNCAC) was one of the most important developments towards a global fight against corruption. Nonetheless, unlike the other types of crimes listed in this chapter, the Convention is designed, not as a criminal law, but as a set of guidelines and principles. For example, Article 1 states:

The purposes of this Convention are: (a) To promote and strengthen measures to prevent and combat corruption more efficiently and effectively; (b) To promote, facilitate and support international cooperation and technical assistance in the prevention of and fight against corruption, including in asset recovery; (c) To promote integrity, accountability and proper management of public affairs and property.

Political corruption includes the rigging of electoral processes and lack of transparency, and is usually followed by political repression (i.e., censorship, expulsion from country, death, and/or imprisonment). Economic corruption includes the misuse of state funds, the receiving of kickbacks, and the use of black market monies, and is often followed by reversal of laws and/or political repression (i.e., reversal of domestic whistle-blower protections, lack of financial transparency, and/or limitations on freedom of information acts). These offenses are widespread and regretfully are common to multiple forms of government, whether they are democratic or authoritarian regimes. As such, these acts are not limited to countries that have been labeled as examples of "bad governance," but instead, state corruption transcends into all forms of governance (including the United States).

Political and Economic Corruption: Zimbabwe

According to INTERPOL (2007: 1), "Corruption undermines political, social and economic stability. It threatens security and damages trust and public confidence in systems which affect people's daily lives. Although corruption frequently occurs at local or national level, its consequences are global; its hidden costs immense." Perhaps one of the worst offenders of political and economic corruption is Zimbabwe, where corruption in government and private sectors is endemic. For example, in August 1998, President Mugabe sent one-third of the Zimbabwean army into neighboring Congo, where government agents become rich from diamonds. In July 2000, the government launched its resettlement program of land reform, resettling 162,000 families that built houses on the land. The resettlement program, however, benefited only government ministers and officials rather than the landless poor and led to food shortages and nationwide famine. In 2004, the ex-Finance Minister, Christopher Kuruneri, was charged with illegally exporting foreign currency for the purpose of building a luxury home in South Africa. Both petty and grand-scale corruption has been steadily increasing over the last five years, according to Transparency International of Zimbabwe (TIZ) and the African Parliamentarians Network Against Corruption (APNAC). It has now become so endemic that corruption is a way of life even for the citizens. They now pay bribes to attain official documents. Public officials say they need the bribes to supplement salaries in a country where the average person lives on less than one U.S. dollar per day. Transparency International of Zimbabwe states that "although the country has ratified various international protocols and entered into regional partnerships to fight corruption, it continues to move up the corruption barometer due to massive illegal deals, which have become the normal way of doing business." Since 1987, Zimbabwe saw an exponential rise in large-scale cases of corruption (Shana 2006). Politicians still active in politics and or government have been recycled back into positions of authority, even if they were previously convicted and sentenced for corruption. "Involvement in corruption appears to have enhanced their political careers, not damaged them" (Shana 2006: 2).

Examples of corruption scandals (Shana 2006):

1986 – National Railways Housing Scandal
1987 – Zisco Steel Blast Furnace Scandal
1987 – Air Zimbabwe Fokker Plane Scandal
1988 – Willowgate Scandal
1989 – ZRP Santana Scandal
1994 – War Victims Compensation Scandal
1995 – GMB Grain Scandal
1996 – VIP Housing Scandal
1998 – Boka Banking Scandal
1998 – ZESA YTL Soltran Scandal
1998 – Telecel Scandal
1998 – Harare City Council Refuse Scandal
1999 – Housing Loan Scandal
1999 – Noczim Scandal
1999 – DRC Timber and Diamond Scandals
1999 – GMB Scandal
1999 – Ministry of water and Rural Development Scandal
2000 – VIP Land Grab Scandal
2001 – Harare Airport Scandal

There are other types of political crimes as well—those crimes whose primary direction and motive is a political statement—including forms of terrorism. These are actions that violate established legal code whose primary motivation and the direction is an attempt to influence a political process or entity. Thus, one can commit a political crime without access to mechanisms of the state if the intent is to accomplish political change. These crimes can include nonviolent but illegal protests, treason, and forms of assassinations and/or terrorisms; however, as non-state agents, they would not be considered a state crime, nor the focus of this work. Nonetheless, the later two crimes are perhaps the most horrific when committed or sponsored by a state against another country for purposes of altering a political process. This type of political crime is considered to be a form of state crime as it is committed, not just in the name of a state, but for the purpose of attaining a state's interests.

Environmental Crimes

Environmental crimes can also be classified as either a state/corporate crime or a crime of globalization. The criminality can involve governments, corporations, and, in some rarer cases, individuals acting on their own behalf (the latter would not be an example of environmental crimes or state crimes discussed here). The involvement of states can be classified as crimes that are state-initiated or facilitated through acts of omission. After all, in many cases, crime networks are aided by government agencies due to their lack of efficacy. Broadly speaking, there are seven main areas of environmental crime: illegal wildlife trade; fishing; logging; trade in ozone-depleting substances; biopiracy, which includes the illegal transport of controlled biological or genetically modified materials; illegal waste disposal; and illegal transportation and dumping of hazardous wastes. Two definitions of environmental crime are suggested by Mary Clifford (1998). The first is a broader definition that encompasses social harm as a standard: an act committed with the intent to harm or with a potential to cause harm to ecological and/or biological systems and for the purpose of securing business or personal advantage (see also Green and Ward 2004). The other definition is based on a legalistic standard: any act that violates an environmental protection statute. A more recent reclassification of environmental crimes included the use of "green crimes" (Lynch and Stretsky 2003).

Numerous treaties exist in response to controlling this illegal global commerce: the *Convention on International Trade in Endangered Species* (includes the range of protected animals, plants, and products); the *Convention on Conservation of Antarctic Marine Living Resources*; the *Stockholm and Rotterdam Convention* (covering certain pesticides or toxic chemicals); the *Montreal Protocol* (covering chemicals such as ozone depleting substances); and the *Basel Convention* (addressing hazardous waste materials), for example. In all, there are approximately 240 environmentally-related international treaties, conventions, and protocols (UN Millennium Project 2007).

Recent examples of environmental crimes include France's (2005) decision to send the asbestos-riddled aircraft carrier Clemenceau to India for breaking, regardless that it violated European Union law on the export of dangerous waste. Additionally, according to Euro Correspondent (2007: 1), English authorities deal with "around 44,000 incidents of commercial waste flytipping per month, including chemicals and fuel, asbestos, clinical waste, and animal carcasses." A London waste company, Community Waste Ltd. of Earls Court in London, was fined £30,000 after attempting to illegally export maggot-infested household waste to India. Petro Canada was found guilty of unlawfully discharging oil from one of its oil-production platforms (May 2006). Such cases are typical forms of environmental crimes. As I noted, these types of crimes can also be considered crimes of globalization. Take, for example, the case of the dam at Pak Mun in Thailand that was constructed under the structural adjustment policies of the World Bank (Friedrichs and Friedrichs 2002). Like other dam projects overseen and funded by the WB, the Pak Mun dam project resulted in hundreds of citizens being displaced, environmental harm to the ecological system, and a loss of livelihood for rural fishermen.

Environmental Crimes, Nuclear Weapons, and Waste

The threat to use or the use of nuclear weapons by states has been deemed illegal (Kauzlarich and Kramer 1998). Specifically, in 1996, the International Court of Justice ruled that the threat or use of nuclear weapons was illegal in response to a request by the UNGA for an advisory opinion. In a classical study of state crime, Kauzlarich and Kramer (1998) trace the legal standards to classify the U.S. production of, threat to use and/or use of nuclear weapons as a state crime. In their research, they note that "the nuclear weapons facilities at Oak Ridge TN polluted the environment with about 300,000 pounds of mercury along with other toxic and radioactive materials. . . . Mercury-contaminated soil was used as fill at a local church and for a public school playground" (3). Kauzlarich and Kramer also note that in 1986, at a Savannah GA nuclear facility, over 200,000 gallons of waste each day was generated. The waste disposal practices at this time were based on the assumption that the soil would just absorb it, eliminating the dangers and hazards. Yet, the Savannah River Plant has been identified as one of the most environmentally damaged of the nuclear weapons facilities. While this type of contamination from nuclear production was indeed horrific, it was nothing in comparison to the damage caused by the U.S. nuclear bombing of Hiroshima and Nagasaki. As such, I argue here that the use and production of nuclear weapons should not only be considered a state crime, but also be considered an environmental crime committed by states and state-corporate actors. As noted by Makhijani, Hu, and Yih (1995, quoted in Kauzlarich and Kramer 1998: 95), "The production of nuclear weapons, unfortunately, has led to massive pollution of the environment."

Chapter Summary

The goal of this chapter was to familiarize readers with the basic history and forms of state criminality. Unlike a criminology of traditional street crime, state crime is far more complex and as such requires a much more in-depth explanation of the actors involved and various forms it can take, including common patterns of collusion with different "criminal partners." Consequentially, this chapter has thoroughly explored the "birth" of a criminology of state crime, including the problematic nature of operationalizing states. With a working definition, standards used to define a state's behavior as criminal, I then presented different forms of state crime that can transpire: state-corporate crime, crimes of globalization, political crime, and environmental crime.

Notes

1. The term *governmental crime* is being interchanged here for *state crime*, as a territory does not commit a crime, yet we commonly call the government and its agencies the *state*.

2. For a more complete discussion of the typology, see Friedrichs (2004).

Chapter 2

Laws Prohibiting the Most Deleterious Acts of State Criminality

Regrettably, state criminality generally involves the worst harm known to humans. The same is true for other violators of international criminal law. After all, international laws banning these types of behaviors do so only when they are systematic and widespread efforts. As such, whether they are states, paramilitaries, or militias acting with a government, the crimes covered in this chapter can indeed be classified as the worst of worst. To better understand the meanings, requirements, or legal standards to which we can classify these behaviors as crimes, I provide you with a brief overview of international followed by the main crimes, including the relevant laws, treaties, charters, and/or principles.

Overview of the Development of International Law

Although International Law has existed for centuries, only in the past few decades has it evolved to become an established legal framework for the control of individual and organizational actions. As the twenty-first century begins, numerous bodies of international law are in effect: from the laws of war, to the laws of the air and seas, and human rights law. However, all of these do not hold the same justicability status; they are enforceable in various modalities. There is no single collected body or jurisdiction that constitutes international law. It is a culmination of bilateral and multilateral treaties, conventions, resolutions, customs, and precedents. States have varying levels of adoption and commitment to these bodies of law; the ability to adjudicate violations of the law is similarly dispersed and varied.

Generally, scholars recognize international law arises from four different sources. The most generally recognized by legal and non-legal scholars alike are international conventions, or treaties, that specifically create rules acknowledged by states. Whether these are bilateral or multilateral agreements or domestically ratified conventions of the United Nations, they bear the most resemblance to traditional state legal codes. Although such agreements are neither as legally solid nor as adjudicatable (be it from vagueness, lack of will, or the common practice of signing/ratifications with reservations) as traditional state law, they do hold international force. The second source of international law is international customs, the acknowledgment of historical past practice and belief by states. This was the original source of the laws of war, which have since been codified into probably the most solid example of extant treaty law. Further, they are considered general legal principles recognized by all countries. Customary laws are based on common and constant practices of states out of a sense of *opinio juris*—an ideal of natural law based upon legal obligation and principles. Simply stated, the fundamental principles behind customary laws are founded on willing state participation and a historical recognition of consistent state practices. Customary laws often find their way into multilateral treaties and as such are not only universal in nature but justicable as well. The third source of international law is judicial decisions; however, precedent decisions do not hold the same level of influence in international law that they do in common law legal systems. Yet, they are significant in guiding the behavior of courts and legal processes. The fourth source includes some of the writings of influential legal scholars whose ideas have been brought into adjudication processes over the decades.

Genocide and Genocidal Rape

The concept of genocide dates back to Ralphael Lemkin's (1933) Madrid proposal for the creation of a multilateral convention, making the extermination of human groups an international crime and later defined by him in 1943.[1] Lemkin suggested a treaty should be created to make attacks on religious, ethnic, or national groups an international crime. He called this *genocide*: from the Greek word *genos*, meaning race or tribe, and *cide*, the Latin term for killing. Four years passed after Lemkin first defined genocide before it was recognized as an international crime by treaty. However, the legal foundation was first put in place during the 1945 Nuremberg Trials and subsequent Nuremberg Charter. Genocide was used in the indictment against the Nazi war criminals that stated that those accused "conducted deliberate and systematic genocide . . . the extermination of racial and national groups, against the civilian populations of certain occupied territories in order to destroy particular races and classes of people and national, racial or religious groups" (Orentlicher 2006: 2). Nuremberg prosecutors also invoked the term in their closing arguments. While the Nuremberg Charter did not use the term *genocide* per se, its definition of crimes against humanity was very close to the idea of genocide Lemkin proposed. The difference was the requirement of specific intent in the case of genocide, which is lacking in the definition of crimes against humanity.

In 1946, the United Nations General Assembly adopted a resolution establishing genocide as an international crime. In its preamble, the Resolution defined genocide as "a denial of the right of existence of entire human groups, as homicide is the denial of the right to live of individual human beings" (Resolution 95 [1]). In 1948, *The Convention on the Prevention and Punishment of the Crime of Genocide* was adopted by the United Nations. Article 1 states that "the Contracting Parties confirm that genocide, whether committed in time of peace or in time of war, is a crime under international law which they undertake to prevent and to punish" (General Assembly Resolution 260 A [III]). Thus, genocide may be committed by an individual, group, or government, against one's own people or another, in peacetime or in wartime. This last point distinguishes genocide from "crimes against humanity," whose legal definition specifies wartime.

As with any Western criminal law, the establishment of an action as genocide not only involves *actus reas*, or the act itself, but also *mens rea*—intent. Establishing that a series of actions not only had the effect of near eradication of a category of persons is not enough to constitute genocide. Prosecutors must also establish that the intent of the actions was the entire or the partial annihilation of an entire or partial given group. This creates a legal space for denial, equivocation, and obfuscation, where the accused party denies genocide not by denying a series of systematic actions, but rather, denies intent. As intent is extremely difficult to prove, this definition included a restrictive component that has allowed state and political leaders to deny and/or raise doubt about whether genocide has occurred. However, the 1948 Genocide Convention, Article 3, also forbids the acts of conspiracy to commit genocide, direct and public incitement to commit genocide, and complicity in genocide.

Nonetheless, since the Conventions development there has been a dearth of precedents that enforce it. Specifically, it was not until the 1990s that the international arena recognized and prosecuted acts defined as genocide: the establishment of the 1993 International Criminal Tribunal for Yugoslavia (ICTY) and 1994 International Criminal Tribunal for Rwanda (ICTR). Then in 1998, with the development of the Rome Statute for the International Criminal Court (ICC), the crime of genocide was again reaffirmed as an international crime; the requirements of both a physical element (comprising certain enumerated acts) and a mental element (intent) are central to Rome's definition. Case law developed especially through the ICTY has emphasized that this later element be present for a genocide label to be applied. Specifically, Article 5 of the ICC lists genocide (and crimes against humanity) as a crime of "most serious crimes of concern to the international community as a whole." Genocide is then defined in Article 6. Both the physical and mental requirements of the 1948 Convention were carried over and included in the Rome Statute (Rothe and Mullins 2006).

International criminal laws are also hierarchically organized. Specifically, genocide is considered a graver offense than crimes against humanity. The ICTY Trial Chamber developed such a distinction when it produced the following rank order among crimes against humanity: (1) genocide, (2) crimes against humanity of a persecution type, and (3) crimes against humanity of a murder type. This is significant when considering not just the gravity of actions but also the subsequent punishment and charges of those who partook in such atrocities. While, to date, an international equivalent to sentencing guidelines has not yet emerged, the ICTR and ICTY judges focused on the gravity of the offense, the level of involvement of the accused in the crimes, and other aggravating and mitigating factors to determine sentences. The determination of the relative gravity has concrete implications for the application of punishment (Frulli 2001). As such, it would stand to reason that charges of genocide would merit a harsher sentence than one based on crimes against humanity (Rothe and Mullins 2006; Mullins and Rothe 2008).

Even with the existing definitions, defining acts as genocide have been heavily debated based on two components: a legal definition that satisfies the requirement of intent; and one based on the political interests of given states, be they economic, political, or military. Together both of these have led to a bleak perspective on the international society's seriousness of ending genocides. The verbal manipulation of the term has led to a plethora of instances wherein interest groups claimed genocide under circumstances far from intentional mass killings of a protected group (e.g., oppression, famines, and widespread malnutrition). Additionally, political leaders have manipulated the use of the term to ignore acts as genocide when it is not in their state's political, economic, or military interests (e.g., Yugoslavia, Rwanda, and Darfur).

As is typical within any legal system, the laws governing genocide have been modified and extended through the processes of case law precedent. For genocide jurisprudence, both the International Criminal Tribunal for Yugoslavia and the International Criminal Tribunal for Rwanda have made major decisions that have refined and reinforced extant laws concerning the willful slaughter of an entire category of peoples. In the Akayesu Trial held before the ICTR in 1998, paragraph 497 of the ruling states that "genocide does not imply the actual extermination of [a] group in its entirety, but is understood as such once any one of the acts mentioned in Article 2(2)(a) through 2(2)(e) is committed with the specific intent to destroy 'in whole or in part' a national, ethnical, racial or religious group" (see also Rutaganda, December 6, 1999, ¶ 48–49).

Such a reconfiguration places the prosecutorial emphasis on intent, which has two simultaneous effects. First, it can make prosecution more difficult in that establishing the existence of a mental state—notoriously difficult to factually establish—becomes primary. Second, it allows for the prosecution of "interrupted" genocides, allowing justice after an international intervention before widespread death, though such international interventions often occur well after genocide is well underway.

Recent case law developed by the ICTY and ICTR have further refined the legal category of genocide within international law. The primary precedents include, most significantly, the recognition of rape as a form of genocide, protections applying to specific groups within the domestic populations, and the requirement for intent of a group in whole or in part. For example, in the Akayesu case, the ICTR found Jean-Paul Akayesu guilty of rape as a form of genocide (September 2, 1998). This was a landmark decision in that it was the first time that rape was legally found to be both a form of genocide and a crime against humanity. The tribunal's decision was based on evidence that he, as a community leader, had witnessed and encouraged the rape of women in the course of a genocidal campaign against the Tutsis. In this decision, the ICTR described a situation in which a rapist might deliberately impregnate his victim with the intent to force her to give birth to a child who would, because of patrilineal social conventions, not belong to its mother's group. The tribunal noted that such an act might be a constitutive element of genocide. The Rwanda tribunal statute enumerates "outrages upon personal dignity, in particular humiliating and degrading treatment, rape, enforced prostitution and any form of indecent assault" as war crimes, following the formulation of Common Article 3 of the Geneva Conventions and Article 4(2)(e) of Protocol II. The Akayesu Trial Chamber (September 2, 1998, ¶ 731) also stated that "these rapes resulted in physical and psychological destruction of Tutsi women, their families and their communities. Sexual violence was an integral part of the process of destruction, specifically targeting Tutsi women and specifically contributing to their destruction and to the destruction of the Tutsi group as a whole" (see also Kayishema and Ruzindana, Trial Chamber, May 21, 1999, ¶ 95). The Chambers held that acts of sexual violence can form an integral part of the process of destruction of a group. As a result of these landmark findings, the law on sexual violence as an international humanitarian crime has developed at a startling pace. By virtue of a combination of statutory law and case law, massive and systematic rape is now considered a type of genocide, a war crime, and a crime against humanity.

Crimes against Humanity

The term *crimes against humanity* has its origin in the laws of piracy. While crimes against humanity have been attributed to the 1907 Hague Convention preamble, this refers to the Martins Clause and the laws of humanity . . . and the dictates of public conscience. At this time, the concept was based on existing state practices derived from the values and principles deemed to constitute the "laws of humanity" (Bassiouni 2006). After World War I, in connection with the 1919 Treaty of Versailles, a commission to investigate war crimes was created. They relied on the 1907 Hague Convention as the applicable law. In addition to war crimes committed by the Germans, the commission also found that Turkish officials committed "crimes against the laws of humanity" for killing Armenian nationals and residents during the period of the war (Bassiouni 2006: 2).

In 1945, the United States and Allies (Great Britain, France, and the Soviet Union) developed the Agreement for the Prosecution and Punishment of the Major War Criminals of the European Axis and Charter of the International Military Tribunal (IMT), which contained crimes against humanity in Article 6(c) (Bassiouni 2008). The Nuremberg Charter was the first document wherein crimes against humanity were established in positive international law. The concept originated in order to prosecute Nazis and Japanese individuals responsible for the atrocities of WWII that were outside of the existing 1907 Hague Conventions. Acts like the Nazi Holocaust cried out for international legal action, but there was no international law to draw upon. As many of these actions were not committed by uniformed armed forces on the field of battle, existing war crimes laws did not hold jurisdiction.

Crimes against humanity have been included in the statutes of the ICTY and ICTR. Additionally, the ICC has included it within the Rome Statute. Specifically, Article 7 states that "crime against humanity" means any of the following acts when committed as part of a widespread or systematic attack directed against any civilian population, with knowledge of the attack:

> Murder; Extermination; Enslavement; Deportation or forcible transfer of population; Imprisonment or other severe deprivation of physical liberty in violation of fundamental rules of international law; Torture; Rape, sexual slavery, enforced prostitution, forced pregnancy, enforced sterilization, or any other form of sexual violence of comparable gravity; Persecution against any identifiable group or collectivity on political, racial, national, ethnic, cultural, religious, gender; Enforced disappearance of persons; The crime of apartheid; and Other inhumane acts of a similar character intentionally causing great suffering, or serious injury to body or to mental or physical health.

The term *crimes against humanity* is far more expansive than genocide. In many ways it has come to "mean anything atrocious committed on a large scale" (Bassiouni 2006: 1). To some extent, crimes against humanity overlap with genocide and war crimes. But crimes "against humanity are distinguishable from genocide in that they do not require an 'intent' to 'destroy in whole or in part,'" as cited in the 1948 Genocide Convention, but target only a given group and carry out a policy of "widespread or systematic" violations (Bassiouni 2006: 2). This body of law governs the behaviors not only of one state on another's citizens, but also a state's treatment of its own peoples.

Torture

Universal condemnation of torture is not merely the abstract ideology of political theorists, philosophers, or international legal scholars. The principle can be found in most of the basic documents of international law including The Fourth Hague Convention, Annex Article 4 of 1907, the 1948 Declaration of Human Rights, the 1975 Declaration Against Torture, two UN covenants against human rights violations in 1976 (making torture a crime against humanity), and the UN Convention Against Torture and Other Cruel Inhumane or Degrading Treatment or Punishment (1987).

The *Universal Declaration of Human Rights* (1948) was drafted by the United Nations Commission on Human Rights in 1947–1948 and adopted by the United Nations General Assembly on December 10, 1948. Article 5 prohibits torture and cruel, inhumane, or degrading treatment: No one shall be subjected to torture or to cruel, inhuman or degrading treatment or punishment.

The 1975 Declarations Against Torture Article 1 defines and prohibits torture as follows:

> For the purpose of this Declaration, torture means any act by which severe pain or suffering, whether physical or mental, is intentionally inflicted by or at the instigation of a public official on a person for such purposes as obtaining from him or a third person information or confession, punishing him for an act he has committed or is suspected of having committed, or intimidating him or other persons. It does not include pain or suffering arising only from, inherent in or incidental to, lawful sanctions to the extent consistent with the Standard Minimum Rules for the Treatment of Prisoners. (*General Assembly Resolution 3452 (XXX) of 9 December 1975*)

The Convention Against Torture and Other Cruel and Inhumane Treatment or Punishment of 1987 defines and prohibits torture as:

> Any act by which severe pain or suffering, whether physical or mental, is intentionally inflicted on a person for such purposes as obtaining from him or a third person information or a confession, punishing him for an act he or a third person has committed or is suspected of having committed, or intimidating or coercing him or a third person, or for any reason based on discrimination of any kind, when such pain or suffering is inflicted by or at the instigation of or with the consent or acquiescence of a public official or other person acting in an official capacity. It does not include pain or suffering arising only from, inherent in or incidental to lawful sanctions. (*Part One, Article 1, Paragraph 1*)

The United Nations Committee further delineated specific practices for inclusion under torture and/or cruel and inhumane treatment including, but not limited to, daily beatings, detaining individuals in small uncomfortable spaces for two weeks, forcing individuals to sleep on the floor while handcuffed following interrogation, sleep deprivation, depriving food and water, being hooded, loud music for prolonged periods, using cold air to chill, and the threat of torture. The UN Committee has also recommended that the use of blindfolds during questioning be prohibited by states (Committee Against Torture, United Nations Documents).

Torture is also defined within the context of the International Criminal Court (ICC) under both war crimes and crimes against humanity. Article 7 defines crimes against humanity as acts that are widespread or a systematic attack against a civilian population. This includes acts of torture, intentional causing of great suffering to body or mental health, murder, and attacks directed against a civilian population. It is also listed in Article 8 with other war crimes that include torture or inhumane treatment, biological experiments, extensive destruction and appropriation of property, and willfully denying a prisoner of war or other protected person the right to a fair and regular trial.

Legal precedence has also been set reinforcing the notion of torture as universally condemnable, or customary law, and prosecutable offense, domestically and internationally. For example, dating back to 1900, in Paquette Habana 175 US 677, the U.S. Supreme Court ruled, "like all the laws of nations, it rests upon the common consent of civilized communities. It is of force, not because it was prescribed by any superior power but because it has been generally accepted as a rule of conduct" (Harbury 2005: 127). More recently (1980) the U.S. Appeals 2 Circuit Court in *Filartiga v. Pena-Irala* stated:

> Turning to the act of torture, we have little difficulty discerning its universal renunciation in the modern practice and usage of nations. . . . In light of the universal condemnation of torture in numerous international agreements, and the renunciation of torture as an instrument of official policy by virtually all the nations of the world, we find that an act of torture committed by a state official against one held in detention violates established norms of international law of human rights, and hence the law of the nations. (Harbury 2005: 114, 127–28).

Again in 1992, in *Siderman v. Republic of Argentina*, the Court of Appeals, Ninth Circuit, stated, "The right to be free from official torture is fundamental and universal, a right deserving of the highest statutes under international law, a norm of jus cogens." This reinforces not only binding codified laws, domestic and international (even with reservations), but also precedence as customary law.

While torture is universally prohibited and reinforced via criminal law and customary law (jus cogens), it cannot be denied that torture continues to be used by supporters of the universal judgment against it (state signators) as well as those opposing or non-signators. For example, states that ratify treaties outlawing torture do not necessarily have a better record for adhering to their obligations than those that do not (Hathaway 2004). Likewise, states that have a worse record of using torture are slightly more likely to ratify the Convention than those who have been found to use torture less. Specifically, out of 160 states, Hathaway reports that 41 percent of countries that seldom practice torture are ratifiers of the Convention Against Torture. This is compared to 47 percent of countries that have ratified the Convention that use torture as a military or political means more often. Simply stated, there is a larger percentage of signators and ratifiers that use torture more commonly than those that rarely use it. Comparing democratic with nondemocratic states, Hathaway (2004) states that 24 percent of nondemocratic states with better torture ratings have signed the convention compared to 40 percent of nondemocratic with worse torture ratings. Moreover, among democratic states, 57 percent of those with better torture ratings ratified the Convention compared to 62 percent with worse torture ratings. Hathaway further found that torture is not limited to the myth of dictatorship; 43 percent of dictatorships signed and ratified the Convention. However, democratic states that have signed and ratified (which is necessary for a state to be legally bound by its signator) the Convention, and where torture is the most prevalent, constitute 60 percent of all the states legally bound domestically and legally by their ratification (Hathaway 2004). Thus, it appears that a state's public support of the Conventions and Treaties as well as its legal obligations do not dissuade it from the practice of torture.

Torture has a long history of use that varies in its extremism (e.g., death and dismemberment to stress and duress positions). Some of the "lesser" means of torture, such as sensory deprivation and stress positions are common methods used by modern intelligence services.. Other extreme forms of torture are commonplace in states (overtly and covertly practiced) such as Afghanistan, Israel, Jordan, Egypt, Saudi Arabia, China, North Korea, and Russia. Moreover, the U.S. has covertly used torture tactics over the past 50 years. One need only remember the CIA's "Kubark Counterintelligence Interrogation Manual" (1963–1975), the Phoenix Program (1968–1971), the "U.S. Psychological Operations Manual" (1962), the "Human Resource Exploitation Training Manual" (1983), and the "Handling of Sources Manual" (U.S. School of the Armies guide) to recall the systematic training and use of such practices covertly in Vietnam, Latin America, and the Philippines.

The ideology for and/or the end of practicing torture is far from being recognized as it persists today just as it did during times of the Gulag and the Holocaust predating criminal liability. What is more, states not only ignore their legal obligations by pursuing this tactic but many attempt to create legal loopholes justifying the systematic use and practice of torture. This is well illustrated by the U.S. attempt to create a legal loophole excluding its obligations to IHL with the classification of detainees as enemy combatants versus prisoners of war (which alleges to guarantee treatment of detainees in a conflict) post 9/11.

State-Sponsored Assassinations

Domestic and international law prohibits all forms of extrajudicial executions, including state-sponsored assassination. State-sponsored assassinations are premeditated and intentional killing(s) of a public or political figure for a political purpose. The act involves the murder of a specific public figure or leader for a political purpose. Most all domestic laws have some legal prohibition against state assassinations, including the United States. Under international law, the prohibition of the assassinations of state political leaders is drawn from humanitarian laws, the UN Charter, and human rights documents. These are guided by the basic assumption of the right to life, guaranteed in several international documents. For example, the Universal Declaration of Human Rights, Article 3 states that "Everyone has the right to life, liberty and security of person." The International Covenant on Civil and Political Rights (6:1) states that "every human being has the inherent right to life. This right shall be protected by law. No one shall be arbitrarily deprived of his life."[2] The UN Human Rights Committee also stated that the protection against arbitrary deprivation of life, which is explicitly required by the third sentence of Article 6 (1), is of paramount importance. The Committee considers that state parties should take measures not only to prevent and punish deprivation of life by criminal acts, but also to prevent arbitrary killing by their own security forces. The deprivation of life by the authorities of the state is a matter of the utmost gravity. Therefore, the law must strictly control and limit the circumstances in which a person may be deprived of his life by such authorities (The Right to Life [Art. 6]: 30.7.82, Human Rights Committee, General Comment 6, Art. 3).

State-Sponsored Terrorism

The use of the term *terrorism* is indeed politically charged. The familiar saying, one man's terrorist is another man's freedom fighter, points to the malleable definition and categorizing of the term. Most often, terrorism is equated with "non-state actors," or groups that are not responsible to a sovereign government. Nonetheless, the idea of state-sponsored terrorism is a very real phenomenon and a part of state criminality. It is generally agreed upon by scholars that state-sponsored terrorism is generally committed for political purposes, targets the citizenry, and exploits fear and terror by authorities normally considered legitimate agents of the state. After all, states often resort to violence to influence, control, or repress a population. This can take the form of security forces using terror to aid in repressing dissent (i.e., Chile), and intelligence or military organizations that commit acts of terror designed to further a state's policy or diplomatic efforts (i.e., Israel). These forms of state terrorism often make use of the state's official agencies, including the police, military, other governmental agencies, and/or the judicial system to terrorize (i.e., Stalin's purges and the Gulag). States can also facilitate acts of terrorism—state-supported terrorism. This can include governments providing supplies, training, and other forms of support to non-state terrorist organizations. An example of this type of terrorism would include the United States' support of the Contras, who were systematically oppressing the population, targeting soft targets (civilians and civilian infrastructures), in an effort to overthrow or de-legitimize the Sandinista government.

Enforced Disappearances of Persons

The disappearance of individuals refers to the arrest, detention, or abduction of persons by, or with the authorization, support or acquiescence of, a state or a political organization, followed by a refusal to acknowledge that deprivation of freedom or to give information on the fate or whereabouts of those persons, with the intention of removing them from the protection of the law for a prolonged period of time. Such practices are often used by autocratic regimes, including militarized governments. For example, after Augusto Pinochet successfully led the 1973 military coup and the overthrow of President Salvador Allende, it has been documented that he ordered the disappearance and/or deaths of an estimated 3,000 people the regime viewed as political dissidents and/or opposition to state policies. The goal, as with most cases of forced disappearance, was to eliminate opposition while simultaneously generating fear in its citizenry to enhance compliance and obedience as well as to ensure a level of secrecy, ensuring immunity.

Enslavement

Slavery or enslavement is prohibited under international humanitarian laws. It is also banned by the International Criminal Court. Enslavement refers to the exercise of any or all of the powers attaching to the right of ownership over a person and includes the exercise of such power in the course of trafficking in persons, in particular, women and children (Rome Statute 1998: Article 7, 1c). Typically, the use of enslavement occurs with the use of child soldiers; female enslavement during civil or interstate wars for the purposes of sex and servitude; and/or the trafficking of children and females for purposes of sexual enslavement, domestic workforce slavery, and/or by militias or regimes for economic purposes such as forced labor (i.e., working in mines or collecting rubber). Countries that have been complicit in enslavement include, but are not limited to, the United States, Saudi Arabia, Indonesia, Guatemala, Guinea, Singapore, Sri Lanka, and the United Arab Emirates. Human Rights Watch has found consistent patterns in the trafficking of women. In all cases, coercive tactics, including deception, fraud, intimidation, isolation, threat and use of physical force, or debt bondage, are used to control women. Without such corruption and complicity on the part of state officials, trafficking could not thrive (Human Rights Watch 2007). Often local police officers facilitate the trafficking of females by creating false documents, visiting brothels to partake of free sexual services, and sometimes engaging in trafficking directly (i.e., Bosnia).

Child Soldiers

There are four kinds of international law prohibiting the use of child soldiers: international human rights law, international humanitarian law, international criminal law, and international labor law (Human Rights Watch 2007). This includes the 1977 Additional Protocols I (Article 77:2) and II (Article 4:3c) to the four Geneva Conventions, the Convention on the Rights of the Child (1989), The Optional Protocol to the Convention on the Rights of the Child on the Involvement of Children in Armed Conflict, and the Child Labour Convention 182.

For example, Additional Protocol II, which is applicable during non-international armed conflicts) states that "children who have not attained the age of 15 years shall neither be recruited in the armed forces or groups nor allowed to take part in hostilities." The Optional Protocol to the Convention on the Rights of the Child on the Involvement of Children in Armed Conflict (2000) states that State Parties shall ensure that persons who have not attained the age of eighteen years are not compulsorily recruited into their armed forces (Article 2). Additionally, Article 4 states that "armed groups that are distinct from the armed forces of a state should not, under any circumstances, recruit or use in hostilities persons under the age of eighteen," thus covering the use of child soldiers by militias and/or paramilitaries. Under the Rome Statute of the International Criminal Court (Article 8), it is a war crime to use conscription or enlistment of children under fifteen years in either national armed forces or armed groups, including using them in active hostilities.

The International Labor Organization (ILO) adopted the Worst Forms of Child Labour Convention 182 (1999), which commits each state that ratifies it to "take immediate and effective measures to secure the prohibition and elimination of the worst forms of child labour as a matter of urgency." This includes all forms of slavery or practices similar to slavery, such as the sale and trafficking of children, debt bondage and serfdom and forced or compulsory labor, including forced or compulsory recruitment of children for use in armed conflict. Nonetheless, an estimated 200,000 to 300,000 children are serving as soldiers for both rebel groups and government forces in current armed conflicts as of this writing.

International Humanitarian Law: War Crimes

As a result of immense suffering, devastation, and death, laws of war were created to regulate acceptable behaviors during times of international armed conflicts. The first attempt to regulate acts during war occurred at the Diplomatic Conference of Geneva in 1864, which resulted in the first treaty to establish international humanitarian law also known as the rules of war: The Geneva Convention for the Amelioration of the Condition of the Wounded in Armies in the Field. Additional conferences were held that extended the laws of war to other categories including principles for war at sea (Hague Convention of 1899) and for treatment of prisoners including their status (Geneva Conventions of 1907), the Hague Rules of Ariel Warfare of 1923, the Geneva Convention of 1929 (Articles 2, 3, 4, 46, and 51), and the International Military Tribunals of German War Criminals (The Nuremberg Principles 1945) (see Yearbook of the International Law Commission, 1950, Vol. II, pp. 374–78; English Text published in Report of the International Law Commission Covering its Second Session, 5 June–29 July 1950, Document A/1316, pp. 11–14).

After the Nuremberg Trials were conducted, the United Nations took the first step to combine the previously established rules of war into four separate conventions and added provisions for the protection of civilians during armed combat (The Geneva Conventions of 1949 I, II, III, IV). These include Convention I (relative to the Amelioration of the Condition of the Wounded and Sick in Armed Forces in the Field), which provides for the care of the wounded and sick combatants to eliminate torture, murder, and biological experiments; the II Convention (relative to the Amelioration of the Condition of Wounded, Sick and Shipwrecked Members of Armed Forces at Sea), which covers the wounded, captured or sick combatants at sea; the III Convention (relative to the Treatment of Prisoners of War), which covers prisoners of war to be treated humanely, adequate housing provided, food, clothing, medical care, the prohibition of torture, medical experiments, acts of violence, insults and public curiosity against those captured; and the IV Convention (relative to the Protection of Civilian Persons in Time of War), which covers civilians by stating that all parties to the conflict must distinguish between civilians and combatants and direct their operations only against military targets. Civilians must be permitted to live as normally as possible and to be protected against murder, pillage, torture, reprisals, indiscriminate harm, indiscriminate destruction of property, and being taken hostage. "Their honor, family rights, and religious convictions must be respected. Occupying forces shall ensure safe passage of food and adequate medical supplies and establish safety zones for the wounded, sick, elderly, children, expectant mothers, and mothers of young children" (Geneva Conventions, August 1949).

Two additional Protocols to the Geneva Conventions were added to the body of law by which war crimes are classified. These include Protocol I and II (additional to the Geneva Conventions of 1949), which relate to the Protection of Victims of Non-International Armed Conflicts (June 8, 1977). Protocol I provides further details of civilian protections in international conflicts, and Protocol II extends protection to victims of internal conflicts in which an armed opposition controls enough territory to enable them to carry out sustained military operations.

Further precedence for the body of international humanitarian law was set by the recent development of the Rome Statute of the International Criminal Court (ICC) 1998. The International Criminal Court utilizes customary law, human rights law, and the Geneva Conventions as a basis for what constitutes war crimes. Consequently, there is not a single unified Convention or text for the laws of war, as they have been assembled throughout history in attempts to minimize the atrocities of armed conflicts, and they continue to expand and change in specificity.

In summary, the rules of war constitute a significant body of law aimed at constraining the means of violence and harms during an armed international or internal conflict. The essential body of law that defines war crimes has been expanded throughout history at specific historical contingencies (such as World War I, World War II, with the creation of the United Nations, precedent international military tribunals, and the Rome Statute of the International Criminal Court). The rules of war also include two other components for regulating armed conflict behaviors, which are crimes against peace and crimes against humanity. While these crimes are considered crimes of internal or international armed conflict (in a broader sense, crimes of war), they cover a more expansive component of principles than war crimes.

Relevant International Statutes, Treaties, Charters

Convention (IV) respecting the Laws and Customs of War on Land and its annex: Regulations concerning the Laws and Customs of War on Land. The Hague, 18 October 1907.

Convention relative to the Treatment of Prisoners of War. Geneva, 27 July 1929.

Principles of International Law Recognized in the Charter of the Nüremberg Tribunal and in the Judgment of the Tribunal, 1950.

Convention (I) for the Amelioration of the Condition of the Wounded and Sick in Armed Forces in the Field. Geneva, 12 August 1949.

Convention (II) for the Amelioration of the Condition of Wounded, Sick and Shipwrecked Members of Armed Forces at Sea. Geneva, 12 August 1949.

Convention (III) relative to the Treatment of Prisoners of War. Geneva, 12 August 1949.

Convention (IV) relative to the Protection of Civilian Persons in Time of War. Geneva, 12 August 1949.

Protocol Additional to the Geneva Conventions of 12 August 1949, and relating to the Protection of Victims of International Armed Conflicts (Protocol I), 8 June 1977.

Protocol Additional to the Geneva Conventions of 12 August 1949, and relating to the Protection of Victims of Non-International Armed Conflicts (Protocol II), 8 June 1977.

Convention on the Prohibition of the Development, Production and Stockpiling of Bacteriological (Biological) and Toxin Weapons and on their

Destruction. Opened for Signature at London, Moscow, and Washington, 10 April 1972.

Relevant International Statutes, Treaties, Charters, continued

Universal Declaration of Human Rights. (1948). GA. Res.217A III0, UN Doc A/810 at 71.

The Convention on the Prevention and Punishment of the Crime of Genocide 1948.

Convention on Prohibitions or Restrictions on the Use of Certain Conventional Weapons Which May be Deemed to be Excessively Injurious or to Have Indiscriminate Effects. Geneva, 10 October 1980.

Protocol on Prohibitions or Restrictions on the Use of Mines, Booby-Traps and Other Devices (Protocol II). Geneva, 10 October 1980.

Protocol on Prohibitions or Restrictions on the Use of Incendiary Weapons (Protocol III). Geneva, 10 October 1980.

UN Convention Against Torture and Other Cruel Inhumane or Degrading Treatment or Punishment 1987.

International Convention against the Recruitment, Use, Financing and Training of Mercenaries, 4 December 1989.

Convention on the Rights of the Child, 20 November 1989.

Convention on the Prohibition of the Development, Production, Stockpiling and Use of Chemical Weapons and on their Destruction. Paris, 13 January 1993.

Statute of the International Tribunal for the Prosecution of Persons Responsible for Serious Violations of International Humanitarian Law Committed in the Territory of the Former Yugoslavia since 1991, 25 May 1993.

Statute of the International Criminal Tribunal for the Prosecution of Persons Responsible for Genocide and Other Serious Violations of International Humanitarian Law Committed in the Territory of Rwanda and Rwandan Citizens Responsible for Genocide and other such Violations Committed in the Territory of Neighbouring States, between 1 January 1994 and 31 December 1994, 8 November 1994.

Rome Statute of the International Criminal Court, 17 July 1998.

Worst Forms of Child Labour Convention [182] 1999.

Optional Protocol to the Convention on the Rights of the Child on the Involvement of Children in Armed Conflict, 25 May 2000.

Agreement for and Statute of the Special Court for Sierra Leone, 16 January 2002.

Norms on the Responsibilities of Transnational Corporations and Other Business Enterprises with regard to Human Rights Agreement 2003.

Crimes of Aggression

At the end of World War I, the tolerance for waging aggressive war had dwindled. Nine treaties, as well as being established as customary *jus cogens* law, have substantiated crimes of aggression. One of the most significant of these is the Kellogg Pact of 1928 (General Treaty for the Renunciation of War) renouncing war as an instrument of state policy and condemned recourse to war for solutions to international disagreements. The Geneva Protocol of 1924 for the Pacific Settlement of International Disputes had also declared "war of aggression constitutes an international crime." In 1927, the Assembly of the League of Nations passed a unanimous resolution that declared war of aggression constitutes an international crime. The Sixth Pan-American Conference of 1928 (composed of twenty-one American Republics) also adopted a resolution stating that "war of aggression constitutes an international crime against the human species" (in opening statement of Supreme Court Justice Robert Jackson, 1945 [see Jackson, 1946]).

Crimes of aggression are considered to be the most destructive and destabilizing of all state crimes, according to the United Nations. In the words of the Nuremberg Charter, it is "the supreme international crime." The United Nations Charter specifically prohibits aggressive war under Article 2(4): All members shall refrain in their international relations from the threat or use of force against the territorial integrity or political independence of any state, or [behave] in any other manner inconsistent with the purposes of the United Nations. Despite the fact that precedence had been set for the definition of aggressive crimes during the International Military Tribunals of the Nuremberg defendants and in the General Assembly Resolution 3314 (XXIX) of December 1974, it continues to remain an irresolvable issue for inclusion in the crimes prosecutable by the International Criminal Court. The precedent definition was "the use of armed force by a State against the sovereignty, territorial integrity or political independence of another State, or in any other manner inconsistent with the United Nations" (United Nations General Assembly 1974 A/RES/3314[XXIX]).

International Human Rights Law

International humanitarian law and international human rights law are complementary. Both seek to protect the individual, yet in different ways. International Humanitarian Law (IHL) consists of both, humanitarian principles and international treaties aimed at constraining the affliction of combatants and noncombatants during international or noninternational armed conflicts. They protect persons or property that are affected by the conflict and limit states rights, within a conflict, to use methods and means of warfare of their choice. Thus, IHL applies in situations of armed conflict, whereas international human rights laws, or at least some of them, protect the individual at all times, in war and peace alike.

International human rights laws (IHRL) are primarily for peacetime and ideally apply to every individual. They are based on international rules versus international treaties or customs: soft laws. They are viewed as inherent entitlements solely based on being human. Their principal goal is to protect individuals from arbitrary acts that infringe upon these rights by their own governments, thus, primarily to protect people against state violations of internationally recognized (customary) civil, political, economic, social, and cultural rights committed against the state's own citizens. Human rights law does not deal with the conduct of hostilities. States are bound (if or when they have accepted these international rules or principles) by IHRL to bring together their domestic law with international obligations. These include the Universal Declaration of Human Rights, adopted by the UN General Assembly in 1948, the Convention on the Prevention and Punishment of the Crime of Genocide of 1948, the International Covenant on Civil and Political Rights of 1966, the International Covenant on Social and Economic Rights of 1966, the Convention on the Elimination of All Forms of Discrimination against Women of 1981, the Convention against Torture and Other Cruel, Inhuman, or Degrading Treatment or Punishment of 1984, and the Convention on the Rights of the Child of 1989. Criminal prosecution can occur for these violations; however, they must fall under violations of international crimes, such as crimes against humanity, genocide, or torture.

Political Repression

A common abuse of human rights law is the use of political repression by regimes in an effort to undermine political dissent and/or religious freedoms. International human rights law prohibits this specific form of state criminality. IHL requires governments to respect individuals' civil and political rights—such as their rights to free speech, fair trial, political participation, and religious freedoms. Additionally, the International Covenant on Civil and Political Rights (1966) and the International Covenant on Economic, Social and Cultural Rights (1966) provides a framework for state behaviors that are condoned. Examples of recent governmental political repression on its citizenry include the Malaysian government's detainment, without charge or trial, against peaceful political and Hindu rights activists. Many more people were killed and detained in the violent government crackdown on monks and other protesters in Burma (2007).

Customary Law

Customary laws are based on common and constant practices of states out of a sense of *opinio juris*—an ideal of natural law based upon legal obligation and principles. There is considerable judicial precedence and scholarly support that the rules within the Hague Convention (IV) of 1907 on the Laws and Customs of War on Land, the four Geneva Conventions of 1949, Additional Protocols I and II, and the Rome Statute reflect customary law. More specifically, acts including war crimes, genocide, crimes against humanity, piracy, slavery, and torture are considered to be within this paradigm of law. Nonetheless, the overarching body of customary law is less clear than those established by conventions. In part, this is because customary laws are created by traditions, norms, and declarations. For example, prior to the 1907 Hague Convention, the rules of war were considered customary laws as they developed out of state practices and a general belief of moral (legal) obligation (see 1874 Brussels Declaration; 1899 Hague I Pacific Settlement of International Disputes). However, with the development of the 1907 Hague Convention, these customary practices were codified, thus having status as both international public law and customary law.

Customary laws are said to develop out of general states' practices and a conviction within the international arena that such practices are required as a matter of law. State practices refer to a general, though not necessarily universal and consistent practice by states that formed from traditions. This practice is followed by a belief that such practices are out of a legal obligation, or *opinio juris*. While treaties bind only those states that have ratified them, customary law norms are binding on all states: a nonderogable rule (see International Court of Justice Article 38[1]). Ideally, this implies that customary laws are subject to universal jurisdiction. This can be accomplished by states exercising their jurisdiction in prosecuting an alleged perpetrator irrespective of where the crime was committed (see, for example, the Pinochet case). Nonderogable also means, ideally, that all states have the duty to prosecute or participate in extradition. But of greater significance is the fact no statute of limitation contained in the laws of any state can apply. Since customary law is seen as binding on all states, its scope and universality is often contested; nonetheless, the compulsory nature of customary law and general principles remain as the scaffold of international law. Historically, however, the fundamental principles behind customary laws were founded on willing state participation (Rothe and Mullins 2006).

Often customary laws become crystallized into treaties or statutes between states. Yet, unlike treaties, charters, and resolutions (which are codified laws and compelling for the signatory states), customary or *jus cogens* laws may or may not be *erga omnes*. *Jus cogens* refers to laws that are considered compelling on states. *Erga omnes* refers to laws that attain a status wherein they are compelling to all states regardless of their participation, or lack thereof, or reservations of the law. Furthermore, the evidence from *opinio juris* and state practice falls short of supporting the notion of customary law as mandatory, or *erga omnes*. Moreover, the principles of *jus cogens* (compelling law) and *erga omnes* (flowing to all) can often be conflicting. If a law is *jus cogens*, it should follow that it is *erga omnes*. When something is compelling to and for everyone, it would stand to reason that it should be expected for all. However, this is not always the case. An example of where customary law is not necessarily *erga omnes* is International Human Rights Law, which is morally compelling but not necessarily flowing to all. This is, in part, due to preexisting agreements that cover specific situations or refusal to participate in their recognition. In the case of Human

Rights Law, they are not applicable during a time of war, wherein these legal conditions are addressed by the Geneva Conventions that articulate similar principles within a theatre of combat. Specifically, International Human Rights differ in that they are a declaration of innate rights people are entitled to because they are human beings, irrespective of their citizenship, nationality, race, ethnicity, language, sex, sexuality, or abilities.

In general, international human rights are not considered customary international law or do not rise to the level of *erga omnes*; they are a Declaration. Simply stated, the Universal Declaration of Human Rights (UNDHR) is not a wholly binding treaty as it is a Declaration; nonetheless, several of the UNDHR provisions have the character of customary international law in that they are consistently applied by states. Additionally, human rights can become enforceable when they are codified as conventions, covenants, or treaties, or as they continue to become recognized as customary international law (see the Universal Declaration of Human Rights [UDHR], the International Covenant on Civil and Political Rights [ICCPR], and the International Covenant on Economic, Social and Cultural Rights [ICESCR]).

Chapter Summary

This chapter has thoroughly examined the basis of legality, or standards, for which we define these acts as forms of state criminality. I have limited the focus here to those most horrific acts that have been banned through multiple venues in international law. In other words, this chapter has focused on the legalistic components of the most common and harmful forms of state criminality. What is still needed is the contextual component for the crimes discussed in this section. As such, the following chapter provides content beyond the legalistic components or standards of the worst of the worst state crimes by providing detailed examples of the various offenses.

Notes

1. Raphael Lemkin's *Axis Rule in Occupied Europe: Laws of Occupation—Analysis of Government—Proposals for Redress* (Washington, D.C.: Carnegie Endowment for International Peace, 1944), pp. 79–95.

2. See also European Convention for the Protection of Human Rights and Fundamental Freedoms, Article 2(1); The American Convention on Human Rights, Article 4(1); the African Charter on Human and People's Rights, Article 4.

Chapter 3

A Glance into State Criminality

Civil wars, genocides, and crimes against humanity do not merely appear; they are produced by a complex intersection of historical, social, political, religious, economic, and cultural factors in a specific time and place. To fully understand the phenomena of state criminality, we must appreciate the basic forms that these events take. To do so, however, is not as straightforward as one might hope. For example, the broader contexts out of which these crimes emerge and the ways in which they are carried out vary according to time (history) and space (specific countries and/or involvement of external institutions). Before attempting to draw out any generalizations of the forms that state crime takes given specific conditions, it is important that we have a better understanding of the types of crimes discussed in chapter 2. Consequently, this chapter revisits the crimes listed in the previous chapter with specific examples of cases to better understand these acts.

Violations of International Criminal Law

Genocide

Rwanda

For months during the spring and summer of 1994, Rwandan Tutsis and many of their Hutu friends and family lived in abject terror as the *Interhawme* (militia) and regular citizens slaughtered hundreds of thousands of their fellow citizens. Beginning on the night of April 6, gangs of armed men went from door to door raping and killing those they referred to as *Inyenzi* (cockroaches), beginning what turned into one of the worst genocides of the twenty-first century (Mullins and Rothe 2008; Rothe, Mullins, and Sandstrom 2008). Calls to slaughter aired on national radio stations, barely coded in phrases like, "It is time to cut the tall trees," a reference to the Tutsis being generally taller than their Hutu counterparts. The world, well aware of what was happening, did nothing until June.

On October 1, 1990, the RPF made its first strike near the Rwandese border, opening fire on guard posts. The civil war had begun. While short-lived, the fighting lasting less than four weeks, it required the Habyarimana regime to protect itself and encouraged internal opposition groups to begin their struggle for recognition. The Habyarimana regime used the border skirmishes as an excuse to begin a crackdown on Tutsi within Rwanda; the so-called "Tutsi threat" was used to reestablish widespread support for the government that it hadn't seen since the onset of multi-parties and the democratization movement (Prunier 2005). Using the attacks, including the alleged attack on Kigali during October 4–5 as a pretext, a massive wave of arrests began. The arrests were not limited to RPF supporters, but instead targeted the educated Tutsis, Hutus in political opposition with the regime, foreign residents, and anyone else that had sent levels of discomfort to the political power elite. Propaganda was used to incite the population and instill loyalty to the regime. The Minister of Defense used the national radio to request the population to "track down and arrest infiltrators" (quoted in Prunier 1995: 109). This resulted in the mass killings of hundreds of defeated RPF who had taken refugee in the Mutara region. It turned out that the 350 "RPF" fighters were all regular Tutsi civilians. Additional violence ensued with over 500 houses burnt. The invasion had also rekindled strong fears in the Hutu MRND elite. These fears were translated into a mass recruitment drive for the Rwandese army. By November 1, 1990, the RPF headed back to Uganda to regroup in hopes of a later attack on Ruhengeri—a city in the northwest, near the Ugandan and Zairian (now DRC) borders where the largest Rwanda prison was located. Most inmates in the facility were held for political reasons and were thus an opportune target for a high-profile "liberation" attack. By early 1991, the RPF grew to over 5,000 men; by the end of 1992 they numbered nearly 12,000 (Prunier 1995). On January 23, 1991, the RPF carried out their attack on Ruhengeri, causing a ripple of panic throughout Rwanda. Their attack was a ready-made excuse for Habyarimana to arrest more civilians. The opposition pushed for quick political change, while the MRND hardliners began to see Habyarimana as being too soft (Mullins and Rothe 2008; Rothe et al. 2008).

By April 1992, negotiations with the RPF were in planning. The Foreign Minister, Boniface Ngulinzira, met with RPF leaders on May 24 in Kampala for a first round, announcing that direct negotiations would continue in Paris during June. Rumors that peace with the RPF would bring about large-scale demobilization created additional insecurity and outbreaks of disorder. This catalyzed a meeting between key opposition political parties (MDR, PSD, and PL delegates) and RPF leaders. Within days, massacres once again started and the hardliner fractions of the MRND were starting to take on an open defiance against Habyarimana. The *Amasau* (bullets) secret society was created within the army, which consisted of extremist officers who wanted to destroy the RPF, not share power with it. The creation of "Zero Network," a death squad based on the Latin America model made up of MRND militiamen supported by the Army, was implemented at this time. A new brand of extremism was emerging from the ranks of the old repressive order that wanted absolute power, even if that meant using absolute terror (Prunier 1995). It was at this time that Leon Mugesera also made a speech during a MRND party rally proposing a solution to the "Tutsi problem": "They belong in Ethiopia and we are going to find them a short-cut to get there by throwing them in the Nyabarongo River. I must insist on this point. We have to act. Wipe them all out" (Report of the Commission of Inquiry on Human Rights Violations in Rwanda 1992: 24–25). Sporadic violence continued in the early part of 1993. Extremist Hutu militiamen went on a murder spree that included torturing prisoners and burning homes for over a six-day period killing approximately 300 people, leading to the suspension of the Arusha Accords. On February 8, the RPF forces broke their end of the cease fire, beginning the February war. Meanwhile, hardliners in the presidential circles had lost complete faith in Habyarimana. They believed he should have reacted much stronger against the RPF attack in early February and they began to compile a list of "traitors." Once Habyarimana signed the Dar-es-Salaam ceasefire, the hardliners were outraged and issued a violent communication condemning the act. Shortly thereafter, Habyarimana was killed in a plane crash (Mullins and Rothe 2008; Rothe et al. 2008).

Almost within minutes after Habyarimana's plane was shot down, militia members set up roadblocks throughout the streets of Kigali. Militiamen and Presidential Guards instantly began house-to-house searches for anyone they had deemed an enemy, killing them on sight. Within days, the Commander-in-Chief Colonel Gatsinzi was removed from his position and replaced by General Augustin Bizimungu, a well-known extremist and supporter of the genocide plotting that had been occurring since 1992 (Prunier 1995).

At the onset of the genocide, victims were carefully selected and primarily slaughtered by Presidential Guards. By April 12, the fighting between the RPF and government troops turned into a full-fledged battle and the momentum increased across all of Rwanda, where civilian massacres had turned into a full-fledged genocide. The few foreigners paying attention to the events in Rwanda tended to confuse the RPF and Rwandan government war with the genocide, lending to false accusations that the RPF were the perpetrators of all the massive deaths and violence. The massacres spread as officials continued to incite anger and hatred, drawing on the ideology of Hutu supremacy. This facilitated the participation in the genocide by ordinary peasants. While the degree of participation varied from region to region and from individual to individual, a general pattern of widespread involvement of the Hutu population cannot be dismissed. The fear of not participating in the genocide was as much of an incentive as was the prevailing propaganda used to incite the violence from the onset. For example, testimony of one killer captured by the RPF stated, "I regret what I did. . . . I am ashamed, but what would you have done if you had been in my place? Either you took part in the massacre or else you were massacred yourself. So I took weapons and I defended the members of my tribe against the Tutsi" (*La Libre Belgique* 1994: 1). As the genocide continued, thousands of refugees attempted to escape. This amplified the numbers on the road, making them easy targets for waiting ambushes. Few places could offer shelter. Hospitals were no longer a safe haven for the wounded or those seeking shelter. Schools were no longer a refuge place, as Hutu teachers denounced Tutsi students to the militias or killed them themselves. A Hutu teacher told a journalist, "A lot of people got killed here. I myself killed some of the children. . . . We had eighty kids in the first year. There are twenty-five left. All the others, we killed them or they have run away" (Saint-Exupery 1994: 1).

The slaughter continued throughout April. Some areas saw the violence dissipate at the time, but only because nearly every Tutsi had been killed (e.g., Ruhengeri and Gisenyi). Other areas experienced continuous violence well into June (e.g., Kibungo, Southern Kigali., Butare, Kibuye, and Cyangugu). Nearly 80 percent of the killings, approximately 640,000 victims, were carried out between the second week of April and the third week of May. Mass graves were dug in some areas, while in others the bodies were left in the open or disposed of in riverbeds. Rivers, such as the Kagera, were filled with bodies, polluting the river and connecting lakes. Forty thousand bodies were picked up out of Lake Victoria, a runoff from the Kagera River, and were buried on the Ugandan shoreline. During the slaughter in Kigali, garbage trucks were brought in to remove the corpses. By mid May, at least 60,000 bodies had been picked up and buried. It was not until late May that the killings began to subside (Mullins and Rothe 2008; Prunier 1995; Rothe et al. 2008).

Genocidal Rape

The sexual assault of women within combat zones and occupied territories is one of the not-so-secret dirty elements pervasive within the history of warfare. In the post-colonial African context, rape has been as insidious as in any conflict (Mullins and Rothe 2008). Militia and regular army routinely rape women and girls once a village is taken; some of them are forced into marriages or held in sexual slavery for months or years at a time. When looking at the manifestation of rape in association with recent atrocities, there is an intensification of the nature and scope of sexual assaults on female civilian populations. The former Yugoslavia, Rwanda, Côte D'Ivoire, Central African Republic, Uganda, the Democratic Republic of Congo, and the Darfur region of Sudan have all produced incidents of widespread rape. Such a use of sexual assault is an orchestrated tactic of warfare. As has been reported both in Bosnia and in Rwanda, certain military units were tasked by their commanding officers with moving systematically through an occupied village and raping all the females they could find—part of the official battlefield tactics of the genocide. Women and young girls were often killed after being brutally raped. The genocide and violence in

Rwanda took on a form of racist sadism that was reaching nearly implausible extremes. A witness stated:

> If you looked, you could see the evidence, even in the whitened skeletons. The legs bent and apart. A broken bottle, a rough branch, even a knife between them. Where the bodies were fresh, we saw what must have been semen pooled on and near the dead women and girls. There was always a lot of blood. Some male corpses had their genitals cut off, but many women and young girls had their breasts chopped off and their genitals crudely cut apart. They died in a position of total vulnerability, flat on their backs, with their legs bent and knees wide apart. It was the expressions on their dead faces that assaulted me the most, a frieze of shock, pain and humiliation. (IRIN 2008)

Sexual assault as a means of instilling terror and humiliation in the locals is often a common practice. One victim recounted the following incident to a Human Rights Watch investigator: "I was raped by them in front of my husband. They held him down while they did it. I was released afterwards because my husband and children pleaded with them. . . . I was raped by more than three men. I cannot recall the exact number because I lost consciousness" (Human Rights Watch 2005c: 17). The village of Bukvu has been the location of repeated sexual atrocities committed by essentially every armed group active in the region. Countless reports of the "typical" elements of genocidal rape have emerged: families being forced to watch the rapes, gun barrels being used as tools of sexual assault and the pattern of moving into a neighborhood and raping every female found. Some attacks have taken on a much more brutal character: women had melted rubber dripped into their vaginas and onto their breasts; other women, after being raped, had their legs forcibly spread until their hips or upper legs fractured. Some women reported being raped while lying in the blood of their relatives who had already been killed (IRIN 2008).

As Bosnia and Rwanda witnessed horrific accounts of genocidal rape, Darfur has not been spared, as children are also raped or killed, and babies thrown against walls or rocks. Sexual mutilations of bodies are common, including the removal of females' breasts and men's penises. Testimony from a Darfur schoolgirl reported to Amnesty, "The Janjaweed entered my school and caught some girls and raped them in classrooms. I was raped by four men inside the school. When they left they told us they would take care of all us black people and clean Darfur for good" (Amnesty International Press Release 2005: 1). Other schoolchildren did not fare as well, as reports claim children were often raped and then thrown back into the building once the buildings were set on fire. Villages continued to be destroyed and people were forcefully displaced. Other testimony given to Amnesty International (Amnesty International Press Release 2005: 30) alludes to the mass rapes that occurred as a means of demoralizing survivors. He stated, "In February I left my home to flee 'exactions' [evacuations]. In the bush, I was intercepted by six Arabs; I tried to take my spear to protect my family, but they threatened me with a gun, so I stopped. The six Arabs then raped my daughter in front of me and my other children."

Human Rights Watch also stated that a thirty-five-year-old female interviewee told them that when the Janjaweed militia attacked her village, many of the residents gathered in the police station seeking protection. However, the civilians were held there while "militia selected young women for rape and men were shot and tortured if they protested" (Human Rights Watch 2005c: 3).

War Crimes and Crimes Against Humanity

Sierra Leone

The conflict in Sierra Leone occurred between 1991 and 2002, claiming some 75,000 lives and leaving scars on thousands more. The civil war, plagued by instability, corruption, and misrule as a result of power struggles to control Sierra Leone's rich diamond fields, was characterized by mass killings, mutilations, sex crimes, and other grave human rights violations. However, the war in Sierra Leone also had significant involvement of foreign governments and mercenary forces that provided support in exchange for lucrative contracts and mining concessions.[1] For example, the assistance of Charles Taylor's NPFL, and later Liberian government, included training, personnel, and considerable logistical support.

From the onset in 1991, the Revolutionary United Front (RUF) fought to overthrow the governments of both military and elected civilian regimes, citing corruption and oppression. In 1992, the All Peoples Congress (APC) President Joseph Momoh was overthrown during a military coup by Captain Valentine Strasser, whose National Provisional Ruling Council (NPRC) ruled until it was itself overthrown in 1996 by his deputy, Brigadier Julius Maada Bio. Multiparty elections were then held and Ahmad Tejan Kabbah became the new head of the Sierra Leone People's Party (SLPP). In May 1997, fourteen months after assuming power, President Kabbah was also overthrown in another military coup led by army major Johnny Paul Koroma, heading the Armed Forces Revolutionary Council (AFRC). Upon taking over the country, the AFRC suspended the constitution, banned political parties, and announced rule by military decree. It also ushered in a period of political repression characterized by arbitrary arrests and detention.

After the coup, President Kabbah and his government fled into exile in neighboring Guinea and began to mobilize international condemnation for and a response to the coup makers. The Kabbah government-in-exile and the AFRC/RUF signed an agreement on October 23, 1997, providing for the return to power of President Kabbah by April 1998. In March 1998, President Kabbah was reinstated as president and over the next several months was able to establish control over nearly two-thirds of the region including the capitals. However, once expelled from the capitals, rebels consolidated their positions in other parts of the country, gaining control of the diamond-rich Kono along with several other strategic towns and areas. By the end of l998, the rebels had gained the upper hand militarily and were in control of over half of the country. They then launched the January 1999 attack on Freetown. During the RUF occupation of Freetown, thousands of civilians were killed or suffered amputations as the militia made little to no distinction between civilian and military targets. According to Human Rights Watch documents, families were gunned down in the streets, children and adults had their limbs hacked off with machetes, and girls and young women were taken to rebel bases and sexually abused. It was not until February 1999 that the RUF/AFRC was driven out of Freetown. However, as they departed, they abducted thousands of civilians, who were used to carry looted goods and ammunition, forcibly conscripted into fighting, or used for forced labor; girls and women were used as sex slaves and forced to "marry" rebel husbands. As they moved eastward, the rebels continued to commit egregious human rights abuses, including killings and amputations. There was also an intensification of abuses by pro-government forces.

> The Sierra Leonean government caused numerous civilian casualties through helicopter gunship attacks during May and June 2000 against the RUF. . . . Abuses by both the government forces and the RUF caused the displacement of some 330,000 civilians from behind rebel lines . . . numerous cases of sexual violence were reported, including gang rape by Kamajor militiamen and commanders. (Human Rights Watch 2001)

On May 18, 1999, the Sierra Leonean government and the RUF signed another cease-fire agreement, effective May 24, 1999. Under the agreement, both parties were to maintain their respective positions and refrain from hostile or aggressive acts. Despite the latter peace effort, the Lomé Peace Accords of July 1999, the conflict reignited in May 2000 when the RUF took 500 UN peacekeepers hostage, renewing its offensive tactics against the government. Since the July 1999 signing of the Peace Agreement, many of the abuses listed above continued unabated: murder, mutilation, abduction, rape, massive looting and displacement of the civilian population, extortion, petty theft, and acts of intimidation. Attacks on villages around the towns of Port Loko, Lunghi, Kabala, and Kambia continued, causing massive displacement as thousands of civilians fled their homes. The situation continued with ongoing violence and thousands more civilians victimized. It was not until 2002, with the disarmament and demobilization phases declared completed, that the violence was subdued. By January 2002, 47,710 combatants had been disarmed and demobilized. On January 18, 2002, the armed conflict was officially declared to be over in a public ceremony attended by many dignitaries.

Torture

Abu Ghraib

After Saddam Hussein came to power in 1979, Abu Ghraib prison became a symbol of death and torture. Over 30,000 Iraqis were executed there; thousands more were tortured and mutilated, only to be returned to society as visible evidence to others of Saddam's power (American Enterprise Institute 2004; Kupelian 2004). A film of mutilation and torture carried out by Saddam's regime, released by the American Enterprise Institute (2004), depicted some of the horrors that occurred within the walls of Abu Ghraib. This included amputations of body parts, rape, the removal of tongues, and systematic beatings. Executions were routine at Abu Ghraib. During 1984 alone up to 4,000 prisoners were executed. The pattern continued until October 2002, when Saddam granted amnesty to most prisoners in Iraq, including those at Abu Ghraib.

Prior to the U.S. invasion of Iraq, Abu Ghraib was completely abandoned, leaving only the memories of the atrocities that occurred under Saddam's rule. After the fall of Baghdad, coalition forces needed a detention center for the growing numbers of prisoners. Abu Ghraib was chosen by Paul Bremer, administrator of the Coalition Provisional Authority. Less than one month after the invasion, April 2003, the Abu Ghraib prison complex was stripped of everything that was removable. Coalition authorities had the cells cleaned and repaired, floors were tiled, and toilets and showers installed, all in preparation to become a place of detention for Iraqi resisters (Danner 2004b). To Iraqis, the facility served in the national imagination as a constant reminder of past abuses that now coincided with the current occupation and abuses as suspected resisters or supporters of Saddam were taken away bound and hooded, often in the middle of the night (International Committee of the Red Cross 2004). Needless to say, the new use only played into the iconography of the prison within the Iraqi consciousness.

From the onset of the Iraq invasion, torture and cruel and inhumane treatment was practiced by U.S. forces. These practices intensified as the number of detainees continued to grow. In the summer of 2003, thousands of Iraqis were being detained, all loosely defined as suspected of crimes against the coalition or common crimes against Iraqis, or as high value detainees (Hersh 2004a). By this time, the use of torture and abuse had become a standard operating procedure. Contrary to reports that only a few rogue soldiers committed the abuses and torture, the systematic mistreatment and abuse was far more prevalent and included Central Intelligence Officers and the highly trained elite Special Access Program Forces. At the beginning of December, a confidential report was given to army generals that warned that members of the CIA and SAP forces were abusing detainees. The report, by Colonial Stuart Herrington, (commissioned by Major Barbara Fast), claimed members of a Special Operations Force had been abusing detainees throughout Iraq, including Abu Ghraib. While little to no public disclosure of the CIA's role in Abu Ghraib has emerged, one account speaks volumes of what the "other government agency" (OGA) was capable of.

Al-Jamadi, one of the CIA's "ghost" detainees, died in a prison shower room in a position known as "Palestinian hanging" during about a half-hour of questioning. "One Army guard, Sgt. Jeffery Frost, said the prisoner's arms were stretched behind him in a way he had never before seen" and he was surprised al-Jamadi's arms "didn't pop out of their sockets," according to a synopsis of his interview (Democracy Now 2005: 1).

Less than one month later, on January 13, 2004, the command at Abu Ghraib received a written notice from the International Committee of the Red Cross (ICRC) claiming abuse and torture had been witnessed by them during their spot visits. This included the systematic practice of keeping prisoners naked and bound in cruel positions. The ICRC Report (2004: 9) states "in Abu Ghraib military intelligence section, methods of physical and psychological coercion used by the interrogators appeared to be part of the standard operating procedures by military intelligence personnel to obtain confessions and extract information." Perhaps the most disturbing accounts by the ICRC include the abuse and torture of children at Abu Ghraib (the ICRC states that at least 107 children were being held in six facilities in Iraq, including Abu Ghraib) and the rape of female detainees. On this same day, Specialist Darby handed over to the Marine Corps Intelligence Department (MCID) a copy of a CD containing photos depicting abuses and torture when attention focused on detainee treatment. With these images that could not be denied, the Combined Joint Task Force 7 (CJTF-7), Central Command, Chairman of the Joints Chief of Staff, and the Secretary of Defense were all informed. However, it was not until April 29, 2004, that *60 Minutes II* on CBS aired the photos.

As testimonies from prisoners, military personnel, and investigative reports have shown, it was not a matter of a few rogue MPs on the night shift. In the case of Iraqi prisoners in U.S. custody, there is significant evidence that immediate superior officers were aware that prisoners were being tortured, and that these practices were not limited to the Abu Ghraib prison (see Jehl and Schmitt 2004c; Wilkinson and Rubin 2004; Zernike 2004a, 2004b). And as the torture memos and other internal state documents show, responsibility for these abuses does not stop with superior officers in Iraq, but goes right to the top of the Pentagon and the White House (Danner 2004a; Greenberg and Dratel 2005; Hersh 2004a; Kramer, Michalowski, and Rothe 2005; Rothe 2006).

As some have demanded, the chain of command, from the Executive Branch to Abu Ghraib, could be held accountable. Moreover, there is international precedent that those high in command are responsible for the policies and atrocities committed under their watch. As Cohn (2004) has observed, the well-established doctrine of "command responsibility," in both international law and U.S. military law, "provides criminal liability for commanders whose underlings commit war crimes. Even if the superior officer did not personally carry out the criminal acts, he would be liable if he knew or should have known of the conduct, yet failed to take reasonable measures to prevent or repress the criminal behavior." Nonetheless, international accountability failed to emerge.

State-Sponsored Assassinations

The United States and Israel

States often assassinate other heads of states or political figures. For example, the United States has been linked to the assassinations of Rafael Trujillo, Patrice Lumumba, Ngo Dinh Diem, and Mossadegh of Iran. In August 1960, the planning and preparations for the assassination of Patrice Lumumba, the leader of the Congolese independence struggle and critic of colonial oppression of Africa, were spearheaded by Frank Carlucci, tapped for the task due to his extensive governmental experience with the CIA and Pentagon during the Eisenhower Administration. "Investigations uncovered ample proof that the assassination of Lumumba was the direct result of orders given by the Eisenhower Administration, acting through the Central Intelligence Agency (CIA) and local clients financed and 'advised' by Washington" (Vann 2002). In 2002, the state released material that included an interview with Robert Johnson (the White House minute-taker under the Eisenhower Administration). In a meeting with security advisers in August 1960, Johnson recorded a discussion wherein Eisenhower ordered the CIA to "eliminate" Lumumba. Among the agents working in the Congo was CIA agent Frank Carlucci, who had spent several months befriending Lumumba. After the successful assassination of Lumumba by Carlucci, he went on to become National Security Advisor and Secretary of Defense in the Reagan Administration and, later, the chairman of the Carlyle Group (Vann 2002).

Israel openly uses state-sponsored assassinations against those whom the government deems a political or security risk. For example, on November 9, 2000, the Israeli government assassinated Hussein 'Abayat, firing a missile from a helicopter gunship. In the course of this assassination, two 52-year-old innocent women were also killed, 'Aziza Muhammad Danun and Rahma Rashid Shahin. This was the first of an escalated number of cases of targeted assassinations of Palestinians perpetrated by Israel in recent years. While chapter 2 provided the legal criterion prohibiting such uses, other scholars have suggested this form of state crime may provide an alternative to the mass numbers of "collateral damage" that is often the result of conflicts brought on to remove a regime, as such, potentially reducing victimization stemming from state crime.

Dr. Michael Bohlander (2008) discusses such a dilemma:

I wondered why it was that innocent Iraqi civilians would have to die in their tens of thousands because the Americans and their Allies thought it prudent to bomb the country's cities to rubble before they risked the lives of their own ground troops, and gambled on the very real dangers of destabilisation and ensuing sectarian violence, not to speak of the effects a destabilised Iraq would have on the whole region. None of these civilians had given any cause to be so treated. More to the point, I wondered why the cities had to be bombed at all. Could not the all-powerful United States have employed the services of its so-called "black-ops" specialists and simply assassinated Saddam Hussein and his top henchmen as the real (or perceived) root of the problem? Surely that was better than making all those innocent and helpless people suffer? [Others] will accuse me of proposing the unthinkable by tinkering with a fundamental legal principle that generally prohibits the assassination of Heads of State by other States, thereby allowing the use of the crime of murder to become an acceptable, if ultima ratio, instrument of international politics. . . . The question we have to ask ourselves is: What if we could give affirmative answers about operative capability for a black-ops strike and a positive prognosis for the wider societal consequences of such a course of action? In short, if we could do it, would we be allowed to do it, or even more drastically: Would we have to do it? (3)

If killing a Head of State can put a definite end to a serious danger to international peace and security caused by that Head of State, how can it be proportionate to respect international comity towards him but to prefer killing thousands of his innocent subjects to achieve the same aim? Does it really make a decisive difference whether he is a part of the operational chain of command, as, for example, Thomas Wingfield has suggested, or is it not enough that he holds de facto political power over the military? Do the actual circumstances of the assassination matter, i.e., whether it was done openly or treacherously or in a situation that did not (yet) warrant the initiation of hostilities in the conventional military sense? (4)

In the age of the often bemoaned asymmetric warfare and the war on terror, is there not a much more immediate moral asymmetry: If murdering a dangerous Head of State by using stealth or deception is unacceptable under international law, does that not leave us with the cynical conclusion that the people whom a lot of the humanitarian law of war is meant to protect in the first place, the civilians, are at the end of the day the ones who have to suffer the consequences after all? Does this not apply especially in scenarios where weapons of such immense destructive force are used, such as, for example, the bunker-breaking bombs used in the 2003 Iraq war, that any talk about surgical targeting and unintended collateral damage becomes absurd? Is it really better that thousands of innocent citizens die for the sake of one person, who may even be oppressing them, and are we really right to worry in such a context?

Would it not again be one of those international rules that apply to a multitude of smaller, weaker, poorer, or to put it bluntly, inconsequential countries, but not to the few big ones, and even among those not to each in equal measure? *Homo homini lupus—Hobbes locutus, causa finita?* (5)

Quoted from a working paper "Killing Many to Save a Few?—Preliminary Thoughts about Avoiding Collateral Civilian Damage by Assassination of Regime Elites" (2008).

Slavery

Côte d'Ivoire

The typical form of slavery is the forced trafficking of women and children. According to Human Rights Watch, the trafficking of persons is a tragic and complex form of human rights abuses. It is "the illegal and highly profitable recruitment, transport, or sale of human beings into all forms of forced labor and servitude, including trafficking into forced marriage" (Amnesty International 2008: 2). Common to all forms of slavery is the use of violence, overt or implied, and the requirement of either a failure of the state to maintain law and order or its complicity in allowing the practice to continue. Moreover, modern enslavement is a profit-making venture that has become a multi-billion dollar industry. According to the UN, profits for this form of human trafficking amount to approximately $7 billion a year (Anti-Slavery International 2007).

Due to the different forms of enslavement (i.e., sexual slavery, forced prostitution, domestic servitudes, child soldiers, debt bondage, forced labor, and infants as part of the commodity market for adoptions), the exact numbers of those that are currently being used as slaves is unknown. In Disposable People, Bales (2004) surveys the extant slavery in today's world and estimates that there are approximately 25 million people currently subjugated by governments, paramilitaries, organizations, and individuals capitalizing on the market of human bodies for sale. Unlike historical times where slaves were legally owned, current victims are bound by legal instruments such as contracts and debts and/or through force and violence. The International Labor Organization estimates that 2.45 million individuals have been trafficked for the purposes of free or cheap labor.

Case in point—the use of child and slave labor to man the cocoa farms of Côte d'Ivoire. The development of cocoa in West Africa has been linked to slavery and forced labor since the first commercial production in the late nineteenth century. Historically, slaves were transported from Angola to the islands of São Tome and Principe to work on the new cocoa estates. Similar cases of slavery and forced labor by both local chiefs and the colonial powers were widely reported on plantations in Côte d'Ivoire, Liberia, and Cameroon, up to the Second World War. After WWII, Côte d'Ivoire became the leading producer of cocoa. Slave labor for cocoa growers continues to be a problem to date. In part, this has been the result of larger international economic market demands and changes. Also, there have been large variations in the world market linked to farm development, pest control, and more markedly in the 1990s, these price changes were linked to the demands for economic "liberalization" or SAPs led by the International Monetary Fund (IMF) and the World Bank. Currently, there are approximately 600,000 cocoa farms in Côte d'Ivoire (Child Labor Coalition) with estimates of 15,000 children working as slaves on these farms.

Of those 15,000 children, it is mainly young boys between the ages of 12–16 that have been sold to farmers and forced to harvest the beans under inhumane conditions, including violence and extreme abuse. These children predominantly come from other countries, the largest supplier being Mali. Trade "agents" hang around bus stations looking for children that are alone or are begging for food, viewing them as easy and gullible targets; they lure the boys to travel to Côte d'Ivoire with them under pretenses of care and good employment. They are then sold to the highest bidder or to the farmer that paid the agent to bring children to his farm. Beyond the overworking, often 12 hours a day, the farmers do not pay the children nor are they feed properly; oftentimes they are allowed to eat corn paste as their only meal once a day. Children are locked up at night to prevent escapes. For example, Aly Diabate, born in Mali, was 11 years old when he was taken to a cocoa farmer. The slave trade agent had promised him that he would be helping his impoverished parents with the $150 he would earn if he came with him. Regretfully, this tactic was only a ploy as Ali soon found out.

He and the other children had to work 12-hour days in the cocoa fields. Aly, being only about four feet tall, was forced to carry bags of cocoa beans that were taller than he was, requiring other people to place the bags onto his head for him. Due to the weight of the bags, Ali would often fall down. As with other forms of enslavement, Ali's physical weakness, viewed as failure to work hard enough, was answered with a beating until he stood up and lifted the bag to continue on. To date, he still bears the scars left from the bike chains and cocoa tree branches that his "owner" used to punish him. Regretfully, Ali's case is not as severe as other children's situations, which have resulted in mutilations, starvations, and deaths. Nor is the use of slave labor a diminishing phenomenon.

Other forms of enslavement include the taking of children and/or women as plunder or property during a conflict solely for the purposes of raping them. During the Sierra Leone civil war, rebels routinely (along with governmental forces) abducted individuals for their pleasure. For example, Human Rights Watch, March 2000, reported that Fatmata, age 11, was one of three children abducted on January 25 when they'd gone in search of food and wood. She described her abduction, which lasted for nearly three weeks, to Human Rights Watch:

> We went to find wood and potato leaves in a village called Mathiaka . . . one of the men grabbed me, I got away but then more of them came and surrounded us. They beat me, hit me hard on the back of the neck with a gun and then later gave me a bushel of rice to carry to their camp in Rofurawa. The one who caught me made me pound rice and wash his clothes and he was the one who had sex with me. I begged him to let me go to my people but he said, "I'm going to have sex with you until they disarm us." I wanted so much to escape but I didn't know the bush around that place and he kept saying he'd kill me if I ever tried to get away. Some days I complained to his wife. She was so nice . . . she sympathized and said she too had been abducted. I was with them for twenty days. I was bleeding so much and still feel so weak. I'm only 11 years old . . . I haven't even seen my period yet.

Similar stories of children and women can be heard throughout the globe as the crisis of enslavement in various forms continues.

Child Soldiers

The use of child soldiers has been reported in over 33 ongoing or recent armed conflicts in almost every region the world. The practice of child "recruitment" results in atrocious consequences for the children, their families, and the communities. Denied a childhood and, more often than not, subjected to horrific violence, an estimated 200,000 to 300,000 children are serving as soldiers for both rebel groups and government forces.

Colombia (P,O)	Mexico (P,O)	Peru (O)
Russian Fed (O)	Turkey (O)	Yugoslavia (P,O)
Algeria (P,O)	Angola (G,O)	Burundi (G,O)
Chad (G)	Republic of Congo (G,O)	DRC (G,O)
Eritrea (G)	Ethiopia (G)	Rwanda (G,O)
Sierra Leone (all groups)	Somalia (all groups)	Sudan (G,P,O)
Uganda (G,O)	Afghanistan (all groups)	Iran (G,O)
Iraq (G,O)	Israel and OT (G,O)	Lebanon (O)
India (P,O)	Indonesia (P,O)	Myanmar (G,O)
Nepal (O)	Pakistan (O)	Philippines (O)
Solomon Islands (O)	Papua New Guinea (O)	Sri Lanka (O)
East Timor (P,O)	Tajikistan (O)	Uzbekistan (O)

G = governmental forces using children; O = Oppositional forces using children; P = Paramilitary forces using children

Their participation covers nearly all aspects of contemporary warfare, including direct combat, looting, recruiting other children, sexual slaves, and/or indentured servitude for militias or regimes. "They wield AK-47s and M-16s on the front lines of combat, serve as human mine detectors, participate in suicide missions, carry supplies, and act as spies, messengers or lookouts" (Human Rights Watch 2008b). Human Rights Watch has interviewed child soldiers in countries including Angola, Burma, Burundi, Colombia, the Democratic Republic of Congo, Lebanon, Liberia, Nepal, Sierra Leone, Sri Lanka, Sudan, and Uganda.

It is also significant that the first set of criminal charges issued by the ICC were allegations of the recruitment of child soldiers by Thomas Dyilo, the leader of one of the Democratic Republic of Congo's strongest militia groups. The DRC is not the only place in Central Africa where the abduction and pressing into service of children has become a central feature of militia life. Sierra Leone,

Central African Republic, and Uganda have also experienced widespread use of underage troops. In these locales, both boys and girls have been kidnapped and forced into service. While mainly assigned to the menial labor required of an armed group, e.g., fetching water, carrying supplies, and digging latrines, both males and females receive military training in the basic use of firearms. Additionally, the children are used as the front line of military engagements (e.g., the UPDF and LRA practices using child soldiers). For example, children may be used for direct combat to compensate for the weakened forces of a militia or a regime; they may be forced to walk across a field believed to be mined, to ensure that the adult men do not set one off. In firefights, the children are often used as a screen to protect the adults from gun fire. By placing the children in the front of a charge (or a defensive line), they will absorb much of the incoming fire.

These troops are viewed by the militia commanders as expendable. This is further seen in the generally brutal treatment the children receive at the hands of their new masters. When on a march, children who slow down, stumble, or fall are often beaten until they both get back up and resume the march at the speed desired by the commanders or collapse into unconsciousness (and death). Escaped children who have talked to Amnesty International, Human Rights Watch, and representatives of UNICEF have also indicated that they were deprived of food and water. Girls, while initially used as burden bearers and front line combatants, are given to soldiers, typically commanders, as wives once they hit puberty.

The use of child soldiers seems especially prevalent in long-term conflicts. Lengthier struggles will reduce the functional size of militias as troops are killed, wounded, or desert. In the decades-long conflicts seen in Uganda and the DRC, the militia have developed difficulties recruiting new members, especially if they make a habit of victimizing and terrorizing civilian populations. To fill out the ranks, paramilitaries use abduction and forced service to maintain their strength. For example, many of the child soldiers interviewed by Human Rights Watch that were abducted by the Lord's Resistance Army in Uganda reported that early during their confinement, they were forced to enact discipline upon their fellow abductees. Forced to march over long distances, children who fell, developed blisters on their feet, or otherwise voluntarily or involuntarily delayed the march were beaten, often severely. As often as not, the LRA soldiers forced other abducted children to carry out the beatings (Human Rights Watch 2003c, 2003d). Such experiences begin the process of desensitization and the normalization of deviance. Once they have had to beat their fellows, often kin or age-grade cohorts, then their ability and willingness to use violence against the citizens they will encounter on later raids is increased, or at least their resistance to such actions is reduced (as those who refuse to violently discipline their peers are beaten themselves).

Likewise, the Union Patriotic Congolese (UPC), one of the major militia groups involved in the ongoing civil war in the Democratic Republic of Congo, is also well known for its abduction of children for use as child soldiers. For example, in November of 2002, the UPC kidnapped the entire fifth grade at the primary school in Mudzi Pela; at Salogo they took all children over the age of 7. In 2003, the UPC claimed to have 15,000 active troops; locals suggested that at least 40 percent were child soldiers. Other witnesses have described a widespread practice at the start of the conflict where every Hema family had to provide either one family member to the UPC or a monetary payment in lieu of a person (Human Rights Watch 2003b, 2006a). As with the Lord's Resistance Army (see chapter 4), the UPC used children as frontline troops, human shields, and living land mine sweepers.

Children are desirable for a number of reasons. They are much easier to control than adults. Physically smaller and much easier to intimidate, they pose little threat to adult soldiers. Additionally, due to the plasticity of youth, children present the potential to be indoctrinated into the prevailing ideologies within the militia. It is much more likely that a child who hears the officer's propaganda will believe and internalize it as his or her own worldview, thereby creating a soldier loyal to the cause.

Crimes of Aggression

U.S. Invasion of Iraq

Kramer and Michalowski (2006) provided an extensive analysis of the U.S. instigated and led invasion of Iraq. According to the authors, the U.S. invasion of Iraq was a violation of the United Nations Charter and other forms of public international law, "making it a state crime of the highest order" (Boyle 2004; Falk 2004; Kramer and Michalowski 2005; Kramer, Michalowski, and Rothe 2005; Mandel 2004; Sands 2005; Weeramantry 2003). On the evening of the September 11, 2001 attacks and in following days, the Bush Administration advocated attacking Iraq immediately, regardless of the fact that there was no evidence linking Iraq to the events of the day (Clarke 2004; Kramer and Michalowski 2006). As soon as the Afghanistan war was underway, the U.S. began planning the invasion of Iraq (Clarke 2004; Fallows 2004). "The Bush Administration chose to risk invasion and occupation despite widespread concern around the world that this choice would result in more rather than less death, injury, and material destruction for Iraqis" (Kramer et al. 2005: 24). Throughout 2002, as plans for invasion of Iraq were underway, the Administration took measures to garner public support for the war, including attempting to tie together Iraq and the September 11 attacks. As noted by Kramer and Michalowski (2006), in the January 29th State of the Union Presidential Address, Bush "honed the focus of the 'war on terrorism' by associating terrorism with specific rogue states such as Iran, Iraq and North Korea (the 'axis of evil') who were presented as legitimate targets for military action." During the period of building up public support, the Administration exploited the political opportunities provided by the fear of additional terrorist attacks and the anger over 9/11. Bush (2002) stated that "we are in a conflict between good and evil, and America will call evil by its name. By confronting evil and lawless regimes we do not create a problem; we reveal a problem. And we will lead the world in opposing it." By linking Saddam Hussein and Iraq to the wider war on terrorism, the government was able to establish the idea that security required the ability to attack any country perceived to be directly or indirectly supporting terror.

The onset of the invasion of Iraq began with shock and awe bombings as ground forces made their way in. Days of concentrated bombing of Baghdad continued. In other areas of Iraq, resistance was significant. For example, stronger than expected resistance fighting continued in the southern port town of Umm Qasr, Nassiriya, and Basra. U.S, its allies, and Iraqi forces continued to suffer casualties in the face of stronger than expected resistance from Iraqi soldiers ("Day Four of the War" 2003). As the intense and often indiscriminate bombing continued, hundreds of civilian casualties also occurred. The high civilian death toll was the result of various military tactics and weapons. Ridha (2004: 1) demonstrates that indiscriminate "missile attacks caused scores of civilian deaths throughout Iraq without any discernable military gains." During the invasion, the widespread use of cluster bombs and numerous attempted "decapitation" strikes targeting senior Iraqi officials—often based on scanty or questionable intelligence—were responsible for the deaths of many Iraqi civilians. The World Tribunal on Iraq came to similar conclusions (Whitson 2004). Coalition forces also exposed Iraqi civilians to significant "collateral damage" through the deployment of napalm-like Mark 77 firebombs (Buncombe 2003; Ridha 2004), and the indiscriminate use of depleted uranium munitions that release dangerous radioactive debris in the short term and pose long-term environmental hazards to people exposed to uranium-contaminated soil or water (Michalowski and Bitten 2004).

As Iraqis watched the continued devastation of their country from the bombings, the U.S. further fueled resistance when on March 31, 2003, U.S. forces killed seven women and children at a checkpoint in southern Iraq. Less than 24 hours later, another civilian was killed while another was injured after troops fired on their car as it approached a roadblock ("Iraqi Civilians Killed at Checkpoint" 2003). The pattern of civilian deaths continued throughout April, as did the growing resistance. Once Baghdad was taken over by U.S. and allied troops, mass protests against the occupation began. On April 18, 2003, tens of thousands of Iraqis demonstrated against the U.S. occupation of Iraq in central Baghdad. Ten days later, as protests continued, U.S. forces fired on a group of Iraqi demonstrators near Baghdad, killing 13 people and wounding approximately 75 others. From the onset, the war on Iraq was illegal and can be considered a crime of aggression. Moreover, since that time, the U.S. has committed a multitude of war crimes, including restructuring the economic system, dismantling the Iraqi military, disposing of the existing governmental structure, conducting indiscriminate attacks against civilians, and using cluster and napalm-like bombs.

Human Rights Violations

Saudi Arabia

Concern of the systematic violation of human rights in Saudi Arabia rarely is discussed in the U.S.; however, it is well known by NGOs and other European countries that Saudi has a long and treacherous record for human right abuses. In nearly every sector of the society, there are reasons for concern: education, the press, freedom of speech and movement, the criminal justice system, religion, issues relating to gender and sexuality, and political freedom. For example, one can criticize the levels of secrecy and lack of internationally recognized standards of due process. There are often secret trials and executions, coerced confessions, prolonged incommunicado detentions, torture, flogging, amputations, other mistreatment during interrogation, and the death penalty for armed robbery, drug trafficking, rape, murder, and other offenses (Human Rights Watch World Report, 2003a).

A Saudi prisoner, released in 2002, told Human Rights Watch (HRW World Report 2003a: 1):

> Detainees were tortured, including beatings with sticks, whips, and electric cables; use of a revolving electric chair until the victim loses consciousness and begins to vomit; sleep deprivation for long periods, up to one week; and forcing the victim to stand on one leg and raise one arm for extended periods . . . prisoners were subjected to sexual harassment by threat or the actual practice [of] inserting an iron rod in the rectum.

Saudi courts inflict cruel, inhuman and degrading punishment, such as amputations of hands and feet for robbery, and floggings for lesser crimes such as "sexual deviance" and/or drunkenness. For example, alleged Saudi transvestites received prison sentences of six years and 2,600 lashes to be carried out in fifty sessions. In 2000, the right hand of a man was amputated for robbing pilgrims at Mecca's Grand Mosque. A court also ordered the removal of the left eye of Egyptian Abd al-Muti Abd al-Rahman Muhammad and sentenced him to an undisclosed prison term after he was convicted of throwing acid in the face of another Egyptian.

There is no religious freedom in Saudi Arabia for its citizens or foreigners who either live or visit the country. The state restricts the private construction of mosques or religious community centers. Christian residents are not permitted any public display of their faith, nor are there any Christian churches allowed. Females in Saudi Arabia face additional levels of discrimination: gender segregation in public places, unequal legal status with men, lack of freedom of movement, and inability to drive. Furthermore, in general, there is a lack of freedom of expression, including the press. The King Abdul Aziz Center for Science and Technology controls access to the Internet and routinely blocks sites it claims must be restricted for political or "moral" reasons. Nevertheless,

Saudi Arabia was elected in 1999 as a member of the UN Commission on Human Rights.

Political Repression, Killings, Forced Labor, and Displacement

Gulag

The term *gulag* was originally coined by Alexander Solzhenitsyn in *The Gulag Archipelago* (1973) to refer to a system of camps that existed in the Soviet Union from 1918–1956. The original use of these camps was to house criminals. However, the purpose of the camps changed under the rule of the Bolsheviks and Lenin. They began a system of prisons that were used as forced labor camps throughout the Soviet Empire designed to deter and destroy any resistance (political or ideological) to the Communist regime: the extreme of political repression.

The Gulag system of concentration camps grew vastly in size and violence under Stalin from 1924 to 1953. It had become a slave system used to provide labor surplus for the building of socialism and the massive move toward industrialization. This industrial growth included regions that were inhospitable and unfit for human habitation: North Russia, Siberia, and Central Asia. Projects included the White Sea-Baltic Canal and its expansion, the Moscow-Volga Canal, the Baikal-Amur railroad, and numerous hydroelectric stations. The prisoners were also used to extract coal, copper, and gold from mines, often working 18 hours a day with little to no food or clothing that could protect bodies from the extreme conditions (see Varlom Shalamov's *Kolyma Tales*, 1980).

Stalin constantly increased the number of domestic projects, which increased the need for more prisoners from the Gulag. Further, when labor was short in areas due to the high death tolls of those in the forced labor camps, Stalin would begin crossing off names of what is referred to as the "Black Book," thus giving them a death sentence. Not only did the camps serve as a system of forced labor for these and other projects, but they were used to remove and destroy political communist "enemies" that included religious leaders, Orthodox Christian believers, political opponents, economic opponents, and/or anyone Stalin believed was a threat to his power.

The oppression and numbers of those sent to the camps or killed outright occurred in waves. This included the waves of 1929–1930, 1937–1938, and 1944–1946. In the end, it has been estimated that approximately 20 million Soviet Union citizens lost their lives in these camps. The Gulag system has become a symbol of both tyranny and oppression that far exceeded the atrocities of the Nazis during WWII and an unspoken collective memory. Millions were imprisoned, forced to harsh labor, died of intentional starvation, or were killed execution style for being a "perceived" enemy of Stalin. The impunity and evil of the Soviet regime(s) created a nation of persecution, barbarism, and despotism behind the walls of Gulag camps. Moreover, it created a country that was filled with terror—as such, the gulag also served as a tool for state-sponsored terrorism against its own citizenry.

Chapter Summary

The goal of this chapter was to help familiarize readers with the categories of crimes discussed in chapter 2 by providing a few case examples. This was to bridge together the information regarding the legal standards for defining state acts as criminal and the international laws aimed at prohibiting such actions. While this chapter is not the final discussion of the types of state crime, it does lead to questions regarding the cost and extensiveness of such cases. The following chapter aims to provide some answers in regard to these issues.

Notes

1. Taken from Human Rights Watch Report (1999: 1): The 1992–1996 military regime (Captain Strasser's National Provisional Ruling Council: NPRC) contracted the South African-based private security firm Executive Outcomes in 1995 to protect the major diamond mining areas. Executive Outcomes remained involved in Sierra Leone until President Kabbah terminated its contract in 1996 as a condition of the 1996 Abidjan Peace Accord. The involvement of Ukrainian arms and ammunition suppliers began under the NPRC and intensified under Brigadier Maada Bio's government. During the January 1999 RUF offensive, armed white men were observed fighting alongside and giving orders to RUF forces. In April 1999, the ECOMOG force commander Felix Mujakperuo publicly accused the presidents of Liberia and Burkina Faso of supplying arms to the RUF by using Ukrainian registered aircraft and crews. The Sierra Leonean government has also contracted the services of several foreign soldiers and pilots, most of whom fly, man, and maintain the attack and transport helicopters currently being used by ECOMOG forces.

Chapter 4

Everyday Life and the Topic of State Crime

The topic of state criminality is not an everyday subject in the media, classroom situations, individual conversations, or in the political realm (especially here in the U.S.). Nonetheless, the extent of the costs and harms associated with crimes of the state far outnumber the combined costs and harms of all traditional criminality. This lack of attention does not just impact our everyday knowledge of events but also has an effect on our ability, as scholars of state crime, to research these crimes: methodological issues. As such, this chapter is divided into three sections: the presentation of these crimes in your everyday life (i.e., the media and university curriculums); types of harms and costs of state crime; and methodological concerns associated with studying these deleterious acts.

Everyday Interactions and the Topic of State Crime

Media Coverage

We are constantly bombarded with news. Some of this is relevant to our daily lives, while the majority we ignore as simply background noise. Indeed, news comes in all forms: interpersonal communications, the memos we receive in our mailboxes, and the daily paper delivered to our doorstep or available at newsstands. One of the many interesting aspects of the news business is the subjects the news media chooses to report on and how they are framed. It has been argued that this has a subtle effect on our perceptions of the world and the decisions we make (e.g., Barak 1994; Berger 1991; Hafez 2000; Herman and

Chomsky 1988; Hippler 1993; Hussain 2000; Mansfield-Richardson 2000; Mills 1968; Solomon 1990, 1992, 1999; Zupanov 1995).

According to Mansfield-Richardson (2000), the agenda-setting hypothesis states that if the media chooses to emphasize coverage of an event, issue, or area, then the public will deem it important and will in turn get excited about those events and issues. According to Hafez, the "agenda-setting hypothesis is based on the assumption that the media can have great impact on public opinion and on the agendas of public debates" (Hafez 2000: 34). This reinforces the media's role in formulating public opinion concerning world affairs, specifically state criminality. For example, Hippler (1993) found that media reporting changed public opinion of U.S. policy in Vietnam, Grenada, and Somalia by revealing the costs of American intervention to the general citizenry. As such, media coverage directly influenced public opinion, allowing it to act as a social constraint to existing policy and aiding in policymakers' support for military withdrawal of these countries. Yet, what does this say to the vast reduction of coverage of international events, much less state criminality, when this type of reporting has been reduced to the status of back page news? For example, Patterson (2000) found that between 1990 and 1998, U.S. television networks more than doubled the time devoted to celebrity and entertainment, disasters, accidents, and traditional street crime, while simultaneously decreasing the amount of coverage on international events. "Indeed, until the September 2001 attacks on the United States and the war in Afghanistan, international news almost disappeared from American television news" (2). According to Hoge (1997), coverage of foreign affairs in general decline from 45 percent of all stories in the 1970s to 13.5 percent in 1995 by network stations in the U.S. Other studies, including one by Livingston and Stephen (1998) also found a steady decline in international news by the broadcast television networks between 1972 and 1995.

In newspapers, international news coverage shrank from over 10 percent of nonadvertising space in the early 1970s to less than 3 percent in the 1990s (Hoge 1997). Similarly, international news in news magazines declined from 24 to 14 percent in *Time*, from 22 to 12 percent in *Newsweek*, and from 20 to 14 percent in *U.S. News and World Report* (Hickey 1998). In a study of 5,000 news stories taken from television, magazines, and newspapers, Patterson (2000) found similar patterns in content. The issue of sales often takes a priority over the content. This is reflected well in the statement made by Maynard Parker (1997), editor of *Newsweek*: "Featuring a foreign subject on the cover results in a 25 percent drop in newsstand sales." A similar statement was made by Mortin Zuckerman (1997), owner of *U.S. News and World Report*, who concurred: "The poorest-selling covers of the year are always those on international news" (quoted in Hoge 1997: 1). If editors perceive that the U.S. public does not care about specific issues, they will turn to other kinds of news or information to squeeze in between the advertisements (like entertainment and sports).

Further, due to the lack of specialization of reporters, when topics of state crime are covered, they often are done in a very brief manner and/or without an appreciation of the context and complexities of the case at hand, thus often providing misinformation. One such example has been the portrayal of the crimes against humanity and genocide that is occurring in Darfur that has been presented by the media as a civil war between the "Arabs" and "Blacks." Not only is this misinformation, but it ignores the role of the Sudanese government and their use of the Janjaweed (Arabs) as genociders. Additionally, coverage typically ignores the vast atrocities that are committed by the Sudanese military forces alongside the Janjaweed. Moreover, crimes of the state in developing countries are generally either under-represented in the mainstream media or they are distorted.

We can concur that crimes of the state are given relatively less attention than traditional street crime in the media, which has a direct impact on what citizens believe to be important issues. Additionally, the complexities involved in understanding, researching, and conveying the hows and whys of state criminality are ignored, with media coverage typically favoring brief and selective reporting. Nonetheless, there are sources available to find out information and/or for doing research on state crime. While problematic, these venues are at our disposal; the key is to know where to look. The following are a few suggested resources:

Media
Aljazeera http://www.englishaljazeera.net
Center for American Progress http://americanprogress.org
Daily World Headlines http://7am.com/weirdx/world
Dawn-Pakistan Newspaper http://www.dawn.com
Democracy Now http://democracynow.org
The Guardian http://www.guardian.co.uk.
The Independent http://www.independent.co.uk
The Morning Star http://morningstar.co.uk
Mother Jones http://motherjones.com
The Nation http://www.thenation.com

Alternative Sources
American Society of International Law http://www.asil.org
Amnesty International http://www.amnesty.org/
Crimes of War Project http://www.crimesofwar.org
Global Policy Forum http://globalpolicy.igc.org/
Human Rights Watch http://www.hrw.org/
International Court of Justice http://www.icj-cij.org
International Criminal Court http://www.icc-cpi.int/cases.html
International Criminal Law Network http://www.icln.net
International Criminal Tribunal for Rwanda http://www.ictr.org
International Crisis Group http://www.crisisgroup.org/home/index.cfm

FIDH— International Federation for Human Rights http://www.fidh.org
International Law Commission http://www.un.org/law/ilc/index.htm
International Red Cross http://www.icrc.org/
Interpol http://www.interpol.int
The Jurist http://jurist.law.pitt.edu/worldlaw/
Netherlands Institute of Human Rights http://www.law.uu.nl/english/sim
Office of High Commissioner for Human Rights http://www.unhchr.ch
Office of High Commissioner for Refugees http://www.unhcr.ch
Peace Palace Library http://www.ppl.nl
Special Court for Sierra Leone http://www.sc-sl.org
Supranational Criminology http://www.supranationalcriminology.org/
UC Berkeley War Crimes Studies http://warcrimescenter.berkeley.edu/
United Nations http://www.un.org
United Nations Office of Legal Affairs http://untreaty.un.org/ola-
    internet/olahome.html
United Nations Security Council http://www.un.org/Docs/sc/
University Centre for Humanitarian Law http://www.humanitarian-
    law.org/
Washington College of Law, War Crimes Research Office
    http://www.wcl.american.edu/warcrimes
Yale University: Avalon Project - Nuremberg War Crimes Trials
    http://www.yale.edu/lawweb/avalon/imt/imt.htm

Additionally, there are other forms of media that can provide insight into the vast types and occurrences of state criminality, namely film (Rothe and Ross 2007). There is a growing body of documentaries and Hollywood style movies centered on crimes of the state. This is good news for the dissemination of the topic; however, and most regrettably, documentaries on state crime are not the most likely to be seen at your local cinema or multiplex theatre. Additionally, the Hollywood films that do make it to the theatres or prime time television are more focused on entertainment than knowledge generating. Themes in these types of films typically involve multiple themes such as love, family, sex, drugs—the typical format of Hollywood entertainment. In these cases, the notion of the state crime remains dubiously buried within the overall message. Moreover, in most all Hollywood films (including the more recent *Blood Diamond*), there is a lack of framing the issue as a state crime, thus, intentionally or unintentionally, marginalizing the events, victims, and offenders of the actual atrocity. Nonetheless, they can serve as a means to raise the consciousness of this type of criminality, even if indirectly so, to where there may someday become more of a curiosity of crimes of the state and more discussion or questioning the overall silence that citizens and the media have comfortably accepted.

List of Documentaries of State Crime

- *Armenia: The Betrayed*—genocide
- *The Armenians*—genocide
- *The Armenian Genocide: Annihilation of the Armenian Population of the Ottoman Empire 1915–1923*—genocide
- *Back to Ararat*—genocide
- *Biography: Pol Pot Secret Killer*—genocide
- *Congo: White King, Red Rubber, Black Death*—genocide
- *Cry Freedom*—apartheid
- *Darfur Diaries: Messages from Home*—genocide
- *Death in Gaza*—illegal occupation, crimes against humanity, human rights violations
- *Everyone's Not Here*—genocide
- *The Forgotten Genocide*—genocide
- *Gacaca. Living Together Again in Rwanda?*—genocide, restorative justice, mass perpetrators
- *Gaza Strip*—illegal occupation, crimes against humanity, human rights violations
- *Ghosts of Rwanda*—genocide
- *Grand Imperial Strategy*—crimes of aggression
- *Heart of Darkness: The Democratic Republic of Congo*—crimes against humanity
- *Historic Atomic Bombs Testing Films DVD: Atom Bomb Test Explosions w/ WWII & Hiroshima History*—international humanitarian law
- *Horror in the East*—international humanitarian law violations, torture
- *Immortal Fortress: A Look Inside Chechnya's Warrior Culture*—war, political terrorism, torture
- *In Search of International Justice*—international social justice and controls
- *Inconvenient Truth*—crimes of aggression, international humanitarian law
- *Iraq for Sale: The War Profiteers*—crimes of occupation
- *Liberia: The Promised Land*—civil conflict, human rights violations, state interventions
- *Looking for Fidel*—political dissidents, human rights, political terrorism
- *Lost Boys of Sudan*—refugees of major conflicts
- *The Nazis: A Warning from History*—genocide
- *Peace, Propaganda and the Promised Land*—crimes of occupation
- *People on War: Even Wars have Limits*—international social justice, controls
- *The Road to Guantanamo*—torture
- *School of Americas*—torture, assassinations
- *School of Assassins*—political assassinations
- *Soldier Child*—child soldiers
- *Sometime in April*—genocide

- *Stalin: Man of Steel*—crimes against humanity, forced displacement, torture, slavery
- *Stolen Freedom: Occupied Palestine*—crimes of occupation
- *Uncovered—The Whole Truth About the Iraq War*—crimes of aggression and occupation
- *Wall*—crimes of occupation
- *Why We Fight–John McCain*—crimes of aggression
- *Zimbabwe: Countdown*—crimes against humanity

List of Hollywood Films

- *Ararat*—genocide
- *Blood Diamonds*—crimes against humanity, forced slavery
- *Hotel Rwanda*—genocide
- *Imagining Argentina*—forced disappearances, murder, political dissent
- *In the Name of the Father*—insurgent groups, political prisoners, Ireland CJ system
- *In the Time of Butterflies*—political murders, coups, conflict
- *The Killing Fields*—human rights, conflict, war
- *Lord of War*—illegal arms trade and smuggling
- *Nuremberg Trials: Judgment at Noon*—social justice, controls
- *The Official Story*—political prisoners, human rights, forced disappearances
- *Paradise Now*—terrorism
- *The Pentagon Papers*—war, propaganda, corruption, civil liberties
- *Salvador*—human rights, conflict, state sponsored terrorism
- *Savior*—genocide, crimes against humanity
- *Schindler's List*—genocide
- *Sophie's Choice*—genocide, victimization

For more details and discussion of these films, see Rothe and Ross (2008).

The University Setting and Student Awareness

The most prominent way in which students become aware of a field of inquiry is through courses they take and the textbooks used in that particular course. Textbooks serve various functions. One of the most important objectives involves framing the discussion in important academic disciplines by defining the boundaries for the inclusion and exclusion of appropriate discourse (Rothe and Ross 2007). Over the past two decades, criminologists have explored the basic content of introductory books in criminology and criminal justice (e.g., Tunnell 1993; Wagner 2006; Wozniak 2001; Wright 2000; Wright and Schreck 2000). Predictably, certain topics in the criminology/criminal justice curriculum are emphasized, while others are minimized. This is a crucial point that can have significant ramifications for students, scholars, and the field of criminology.

Introductory textbooks are often the first exposure students receive to any given subject matter. As such, these tools provide a framework for interpreting the field of criminology and criminal justice in both academic and practical/practitioner circles (Rothe and Ross 2007).

As one of the most devastating and costly types of crimes, state crime would seem an appropriate topic to somehow make its way into most, if not all, of the leading introductory textbooks on criminology. Within the most current and popular introduction to criminology texts, state crime receives minimal attention (see table 4.1). Of the eight leading criminology textbooks, three do not contain any discussion of state crime. Moreover, two of the other texts only briefly mention this subject within the context of state-sponsored terrorism. Of the remaining three texts, one included the topic under government crime; however, a portion of that referred to what state crime scholars call occupational crimes. Another text that mentioned state crimes referred to them as political crimes, thus leaving only one textbook that presented the acts as a state crime. Nonetheless, the examples of the latter were all presented to students under the broader heading of political terrorism. Additionally, none of the texts cover any of the state crime literature that has been produced in the last several years. All of the texts fail to provide a discussion of the etiological factors, any theory for understanding the complexities of state crime, or policy implications to reduce or control crimes of the state. Simply, these books (1) never include the subject of state crime within the larger umbrella of white-collar crime or as a separate field of study; (2) do not include a history of the criminological inquiry into crimes of the state; (3) omit any theoretical framework to address state crime, unlike the significant coverage given to theories that are supposed to explain traditional street crime; and (4) generally use similar or historic case studies like the Watergate break-in (1972) or the illegal sale of weapons in the Iran-Contra episode during the Reagan Administration (1980–88) when mentioning crimes of the state (whether directly as such or integrated as a form of terrorism or political crime). As such, when authors do cover this topic, they usually present a series of incidents or examples where state crime has occurred, failing to provide the contextual, theoretical, and historical factors associated with this subject (Rothe and Ross 2008).

Based on the leading criminology textbooks, it can be seen that the topic of state crime is highly marginalized compared to other topics, most notably traditional street crimes such as homicide or juvenile delinquency. There are relatively few courses focusing solely on state crime compared to those on juvenile delinquency, homicide, crime and the media, etc. This is not to say the subject matter is not being taught indirectly (i.e., a course on the Holocaust) or framed as a different subject (i.e., human rights); however, within criminology there is only a scant number of universities where a course specifically on state crime is listed in the catalogue and offered on a yearly basis. So then, how are students, leaving the university setting for the "real world" as lawyers, policy makers, or employees in other relevant sectors, able to grasp the severity and widespread nature of state crime? How are they to learn of the various forms of harms and costs of the worst of worst crimes? Most importantly, how can we effectively increase the levels of curiosity of these types of crimes to move beyond the complicit silence and/or lack of inquisitiveness when the topic of state crime is marginalized in media coverage and university settings?

Table 4.1. *Comparisons of Leading Textbooks' Coverage of State Crime*

Author of Text	Subject of State Crime	Chapter Topic of Inclusion	Reviews State Crime Literature
Glick	None	None	None
Schmalleger	None	None	None
Adler, Mueller, and Laufer	None	None	None
Conklin	Yes–21 words	Terrorism	None
Siegel	Yes–128 words	Terrorism	None
Titus Reid	Yes–2 pages	Government Crime	None
Beirne and Messerchmidt	Yes–11 pages	Political Crimes	None
Barkan	Yes–11 pages	Political Crimes	None

Adapted from Rothe and Ross (2008)

Costs of State Crime

David Friedrichs (2007: 122) rightly noted "that the worst crimes—in terms of physical harm to human beings, abuse of civil liberties, and economic loss—have been committed by individuals and entities acting in the name of the governments or the state." During the twentieth century, it has been suggested that 170 million people have been killed in "conflicts of a non-international character, internal conflicts and tyrannical regime victimization" (Bassiouni 1996). Since the beginning of the twenty-first century there have been hundreds of thousands more killed, maimed, tortured, displaced, and/or raped. For those who use a more expansive definition of state criminality, the costs and harms are even more insurmountable (see Green and Ward [2004] for this perspective).

However, the focus of this section will be on the costs and forms of harm from a legalistic standard. As discussed in chapter 1, using a social harm or analogous harm definition lends to nearly everything being able to be classified as a state crime given the right ideological position and dogma. As such, socially analogous harms, or those deemed social harms not prohibited by international or domestic laws, are omitted. Consequently, when we discuss harm here, we are referring to the harms, costs, and victimizations that have resulted from states violating domestic and international laws.

There are both direct and indirect harms and/or costs that are generated from crimes of the state. In other words, they can be immediate and easily seen, as in the case of genocides, crimes against humanity, and use of nuclear weapons; or there can be those that are indirect, such as environmental harms that are undetectable for years or indirectly destroy a country's social and economic fabric, as in the case of crimes of globalization. Other indirect costs include after conflict social controls, healthcare, morality rates, rebuilding a country or infrastructures, the pay of the "criminals," and a host of other expenses. Nonetheless, within direct and indirect harms, a basic typology of harms can be drawn:

- Environmental
- Physical
- Psychological
- Financial
- Cultural, Social, or Political

Environmental

Most often, when speaking about environmental crimes, it is corporations that are seen as the "criminals." This includes biopiracy, illegal dumping, illegal transportation of toxic waste, and many other types previously discussed. For example, this type of environmental crimes has cost nearly $31 billion USD annually, according to the United Nations Environment Program (2007). Environmental crimes are not a recent phenomenon or issue: clean-air laws were passed in England during the fourteenth century, where it was a capital offense to burn coal in London, and violators were executed (Kennedy 2003). In the U.S., up until 1870, a factory releasing even small amounts of smoke onto public or private property was found to be operating illegally.

As I noted in chapter 1, environmental crimes can also be committed by state-corporate collusion, state omission of legal obligations, or as a form of crimes of globalization (Friedrichs and Friedrichs 2002). Yet, we cannot ignore the fact that a significant amount of environmental crimes has been at the hands of government officials acting in the name or on behalf of the state. The most striking example is the nuclear production and the subsequent waste of materials (Kauzlarich and Kramer 1998).

As one example, the UK's nuclear waste clean-up program could cost tax-payers more than £70bn (Nuclear Decommissioning Authority [NDA] 2006). Additional costs linked to land contamination from the sites would drive the total to about £72bn. While not linked to nuclear radiation, the land contamination is a direct result of chemical storage and/or waste. Similarly, near Lake Ontario in Canada, an expensive and extensive cleanup has been undertaken. This includes the Canadian government's removal of more than 2 million cubic meters of uranium- and radium-contaminated soil from beneath homes, schools, and businesses (Canadian Press 2007). A similar cleanup of nuclear waste in the U.S. cost approximately $1,000 USD per cubic meter of soil that was removed for clean-up.

It has been noted that the largest, most complicated, and expensive environmental problem in the United States is the cleanup of nuclear wastes. According to Noyes (1995: 1):

> The U.S. Department of Energy (DOE) has approximately 4,000 contaminated sites covering tens of thousands of acres and replete with contaminated hazardous or radioactive waste, soil, or structures. In addition to high-level waste, it has more than 250,000 cubic meters of transuranic waste and millions of cubic meters of low-level radioactive waste. In addition, DOE is responsible for thousands of facilities awaiting decontamination, decommissioning, and dismantling.

The overall cost estimates for nuclear waste cleanup in the U.S. have been estimated to be between $200 and $350 billion.

Physical

There is no one good way to calculate the physical sufferings or costs that result from state criminality. While it is possible to estimate costs of physical harm in the form of structures (e.g., communities, villages, towns, or entire countries), to do so to the physical costs of humans is not only abstract but unrealistic. How do you reduce a person's life or limbs to a dollar amount? Along the same lines, to understand the totality of physical costs in the form of deaths or maiming does, to some degree, reduce human suffering to cold statistics. Yet, does having a count, even if imprecise, reduce the harms to one collective number, taking away from each individual's identity and pain? Or is it our only way to generate the numbers and physical costs of state crime, in cases of genocide, crimes against humanity, or war crimes? Additionally, we must consider that if there were no numbers or even range of numbers estimating the physical costs, we have effectively removed the sheer scale of the crimes. With this in mind, perhaps we can see that the scale of 170 million deaths at the hands of regimes is vast, while simultaneously recognizing that each of those individual lives mattered and was worth as much as our own.

Physical costs are not always immediate, yet does this mean they are not direct? For example, is there not a direct physical cost of genocide to all the surviving victims that lost entire families? Or do we count that as indirect and assume it to be solely psychological costs? As an example, a survivor of the Rwandan genocide, a Hutu teacher, married to a Tutsi, was forced to watch his pregnant wife be disemboweled and then had his child's fetus pushed into his face while being told to "Eat your bastard." Is there not a physical cost for him as well as deeply psychological cost? On the other hand, civilians die as a result of other countries intervening to stop conflicts. Do we consider these civilian deaths as part of the costs of the crimes against humanity or genocide that is occurring? Or are they separate as collateral damage? For example, when NATO forces began their bombing campaign to "free" Kosovo, 1,400 civilians were killed by air strikes.

In a direct sense, innocent children, women, and men have body parts removed from them in the middle of streets or in their homes, often for no other purpose but to leave a lasting message. As stated by Joseph Kone of the LRA militia in Uganda, "If you picked up an arrow against us we ended up cutting off the hand you used . . . You report us with your mouth, and we cut off your lips . . . You run from us we cut off your legs" (Kasibante 2006: 262). In another case, a Darfur refugee stated:

> The Janjaweed came to my house and asked me why I was not gone like the others. I said I had been in Mecca and I could not flee from a person. Then they shot me on my back. I fell. Then they cut my skin on the top of my head and my ears. Then they picked me up and threw me into the fire. They looted everything, the market, everything. They were as numerous as ants. (HRW, 2005b)

To what price or count of costs do we use to account for his or her physical harm? Others fall prey to the illegal use of cluster bombs, resulting in the loss of major body parts or in death. How can we tally such costs? What price or count should be assigned to women and young girls who have been physically harmed by multiple rapes, gang rapes, or years of sexual slavery? What price or tally should we use to count the multiple physical harms that are the result of people being tortured, starved to death, left dying in refugee camps, or forcefully displaced, losing not only their possessions, but often their lives in the process? For example, in 1972, Ugandan President Amin forced 60,000 Asians to leave the country and ordered a governmental expropriation of all their extensive property holdings, "including 5,655 firms, factories, and farms and U.S. $400 million in personal goods" (Human Rights Watch Report 1999b: 2). Other examples of state repression and torture include the massive mutilations and torture carried out by Saddam Hussein's regime: amputations of body parts, rape, the removal of tongues, and systematic beatings and executions—all were routine occurrences at Abu Ghraib. For example, during 1984, up to 4,000 prisoners, respectively, were said to have been executed. Regretfully, torture continued to a lesser extent under the U.S. control and occupation of Iraq.

Refugees seeking to stay alive often flee during the commission of state crimes, pouring into neighboring countries. Yet, what is typically believed to be humanitarian assistance in the form of refugee camps can often become extermination camps where additional or secondary physical costs occur. In Uganda, people were herded into camps by the Ugandan government for their own "protection," without food, health care, etc., for days at various locations, purportedly for screening. Many people died and human rights abuses were committed. Secondary physical costs continue to escalate if we consider the numbers of genocidal rape survivors that now battle AIDS as a result of the systematic rapes. For example, during the Rwandan genocide, women were intentionally infected with HIV as a part of the larger genocidal plan; others were unintentionally infected through the multiple rapes they endured; at least 175,000 women are now HIV positive as a result.

Perhaps the last thought we should take with us concerning the actual costs of state criminality is, how can we possibly combine loss of life, body parts, rape or torture victims, and the multitude of other physical costs into one large number and claim we know the cost of state crime? Regretfully, the true physical costs will remain a "doubly-doubly-doubly" dark figure that is really beyond what most of us could comprehend.

Psychological

When we discuss victims of traditional forms of street crime, especially violent crimes, we often consider part of the harm done includes psychological trauma. The same is true for victims of most state crimes. For example, a victim of rape usually always suffers psychologically. Imagine victims of genocidal rape that not only have been victimized by being raped or gang raped, but also have experienced, typically while witnessing, the deaths of intimate family members. A death of a loved one, no matter how it occurs, is emotionally and mentally trying. Yet, imagine family members being violently killed in front of you and walking the streets, seeing body after body of others that have been killed. Additionally, they are often left pregnant, diseased, and at times with mutilated breasts or other body parts as constant reminders. The psychological trauma of children who are forced to be child soldiers, beating, killing, or maiming others, can leave lifelong impacts on their mental health. Further, injury to the children while in captivity—the physical wounds, the psychosocial distress, the sexual violence—compound the trauma. Surely the extraordinary psychological suffering experienced by these victims needs to be taken into account also.

The psychological costs of being tortured, as with the other forms of serious state crimes discussed in this book, cannot be ignored. Such psychological and physical trauma leaves long-term issues. For example, Basoglu (2007: 1) reported that based on findings from interviews of 279 torture victims (from

Bosnia and Herzegovina, Republica Srpska, Croatia, and Serbia between 2000 and 2002) more than three-fourths (174) of them had post-traumatic stress disorder (PTSD) related to their torture, 55.7 percent (128) had current PTSD, 17 percent (39) were currently depressed, and 17.4 percent (40) had a past episode of major depression. On a similar scale, forced victims of trafficking for the purposes of sexual servitude or slavery also suffer from mental disorders. Farley et al. (2003) found that PTSD amongst victims was 68 percent, the same range as treatment-seeking combat veterans, in a study of women from nine countries.

Additionally, at a collective level, there is the financial cost that cannot be separated for their health and mental care, if they are fortunate enough to receive this. Imagine seeing your whole community killed or destroyed. Would this not have a psychological cost as well as physical and environmental? The trauma that the collective population goes through during and after the worst forms of state crime, namely genocide, crimes against humanity, war crimes, and aggression, is immense. In these conditions, the psychological effects on the brain can alter the way an individual thinks and lives. There is a collective level of fear and distrust that cannot be dismissed. Undue amounts of fear can cause secondary emotional problems.

Beyond the costs of mental care, rehabilitation, and other subsequent costs, the psychological trauma caused by state crimes, directly and indirectly, is often irreparable and can never be calculated into a formula to ascertain the "true" costs of the worst of worst criminals' actions.

Financial

The financial costs of state crime, as the other types of costs, far prevail over the costs of traditional crimes and even corporate crimes. If we consider the financial components, both direct and indirect, we have to take into account post-conflict infrastructure (e.g., village, towns, community centers, hospitals, schools, water or electrical systems, damaged oil refineries, bombed embassies, etc.); social control mechanisms (i.e., trials and appeals); finances for the atrocities (e.g., the covert funding for the war on Nicaragua or the purchase of arms in Rwanda); cleanup efforts (i.e., nuclear waste); restitutions; and the list goes on. Beyond this, there are hidden financial costs such as humanitarian aid donations, loans by international financial institutions for rebuilding, medical and psychological care for surviving victims, and medications for diseases that are a direct result of crimes of the state (e.g., HIV or malaria). From this brief discussion, it is a rather obvious point that it would be not only an arduous chore to attempt to generate a basic number for the financial costs of state crime, but one that could never be complete or reflective of the true costs. Nonetheless, to give some basic ideas, consider that, to date, costs to the U.S. for reconstruction efforts in Iraq is at $30 billion. The Congressional Budget Office estimates that by the end of 2010 the cost of the U.S. aggressive war will reach $600 billion (USCB 2007). Consider also the financial costs of intervening in a state crime. For example, it has been estimated that the NATO bombings cost $4 billion (with the U.S. share at $2.5 to $3 billion). Rebuilding efforts are estimated at $20 to $30 billion, costs to return the refugees to Kosovo is estimated at $422 million, and the costs of the refugees for the surrounding countries where they fled is estimated at $1 to $2 billion. As I noted, indirectly, there are post-healthcare and basic subsistence factors. For example, during 1995, the first year following the Rwandan genocide, international agencies were spending $1 million per day to provide basic food and public health services to 1.9 million externally displaced Rwandans (World Food Program 1996). In addition, the United States contributed an additional $256 million to relief efforts internal to Rwanda. (Other countries also provided much needed assistance.) What about the financial loss that is the result of massive population displacement and/or refugees that have fled, leaving behind unattended lands as many areas become unpopulated?

How long then do we consider post-conflict costs to be sure we have an accurate number? What about the financial costs of state-sponsored terrorism? For example, what amount would we apply to the building of the Gulag system in the USSR, or the railways that transported the prisoners there, or the pay for those employed at the supporting institutions? When we think of including the supporting systems and institutions, government workers, army forces, etc., the costs are insuperable to imagine or calculate.

Cultural, Social, and Political

Crimes of the state or other violators of international criminal law affect much more than the immediate victims. It is a crime against every individual in that country, and often in the surrounding states. It corrupts the whole social fabric as it prescribes a silencing of what happened by those that committed the acts as well as the rest of the society that sits by and does nothing (Levinson 2004). At the most primary level, state crimes affect political, cultural, and often traditional social systems' legitimacy. Often cultures are torn apart with massive levels of distrust and anger. Political systems can be totally obliterated by other countries or insurgency groups, or by the removal of a head of state committing such acts. For example, on April 10, 1979, Ugandan President Amin's seat in government abruptly ended when the Tanzanian forces and Ugandan militias successfully forced him to flee the country. Immediately after Amin's ouster, Ysuf Lule, Chair of the Uganda National Liberation Army's (UNLA) political arm, became the head of government. However, his rule lasted only sixty-eight days as he was perceived as having a pro-Buganda slant. As a result, the UNLA ousted Lule. He was replaced by Obote's former attorney general, Godfrey Binaisa—all of this in the span of a year (Mullins and Rothe 2008). Another example includes political repression used in an effort to maintain legitimacy, which has a significant cost politically, psychologically, and often physically for citizens. For instance, President Museveni repressed all political opposition in an effort to maintain control of the government under "Operation North" and created an information blackout, during which governmental forces committed additional atrocities on the population.

Traditional social institutions, including religion, can be jeopardized. Take, for example, the post-genocide era in Rwanda and the near collapse of the Catholic churches due to the role of that institution and many of its clergy. On the other hand, state crime can result in other forms of criminality that reach the levels of violations of international law resulting in the manipulation of traditional cultural or social institutions that have collapsed. For example, in Uganda, the Holy Spirit Movement (HSM) was a revitalization movement in that it attempted to recreate the universe and a moral order disintegrated by broader events that were occurring under the brutal and corrupt Museveni regime. The HSM was renamed the Lord's Resistance Army, led by Joseph Koney, who is wanted by the ICC for a multitude of charges including maiming, the use of child soldiers, and rape. There is also the damage that extends into all forms of a country as reconciliation is often a long and tedious process. During the interim, the cultural and social fabric of these places is indeed not only in jeopardy but also has long-term costs that range from the individual to the state level.

Having briefly examined the different forms of harm, namely physical, psychological, financial, environmental, and cultural-social-political, it is clear to see that the costs of these crimes come in various forms. Additionally, what we find is that they are not able to be categorized into singular types. Simply, they often go hand-in-hand. In an effort to solidify the idea of the vast harms and costs, I have taken the subfields or hybrid forms of state crime and attempted to show the various elements typically at play in each: state-corporate crime, political crime, crimes of aggression, and the worst of the international crimes.

State-Corporate Crimes

From the illustrations in chapter 1—Halliburton and war profiteering, the crash of ValuJet, and the wholesale looting and illegal exporting of the Democratic Republic of Congo's resources—state-corporate crime includes heavy economic costs. While it would appear that economics is the leading cause, let's think about the physical costs as well. For example, in the case of the ValuJet, innocent passengers were killed, all in the name of profit and a state agency that failed to do its job (Mathews and Kauzlarich 2006). In the case of the DRC, Uganda, Rwanda, and transnational corporations, hundreds of thousands have been enslaved, tortured, and/or received cruel treatment in forced working conditions in the mines (Mullins and Rothe 2008). The case of Halliburton was not just economic either; instead, there have been political and social costs, including the very legitimacy of using private corporations in conflict and the complicity of the state bringing into question issues of legitimacy (Rothe 2006). Other cases of state-corporate crime share these same characteristics: the Firestone tire debacle (Mullins 2006), the Imperial Chicken fire (Aulette and Michalowski 1993), the Challenger explosion (Kramer 1992), and the collusion between the German state and corporations in the Holocaust (Friedrichs 2000; Mathews 2006); all had very real physical as well as economic costs. On the other hand, as I previously noted, corporations contracted by the state for nuclear weapon productions have had large environmental costs. Of course, there is the physical as well through the testing on human subjects, the dumping of wastes, unprotected workers, and the actual use of the weapons in Hiroshima and Nagasaki.

Crimes of Globalization

The example used in chapter 1 for crimes of globalization was the Rwandan genocide and the role of IFIs (Rothe, Mullins, and Sandstrom 2008). I have also used Rwanda in several other examples throughout the other chapters. Taking this particular crime into account, all possible types of harm can be identified: physical, psychological, financial, environmental, and social-cultural-political. Other noted cases of crimes of globalization include the Senegalese *Le Joola* ferry sinking (Rothe, Muzzatti, and Mullins 2006). In this case, the costs encompassed economic, physical, financial, and social-cultural-political aspects. In response to imposed SAPs, the Senegalese government was forced to cut spending in many areas, including its ferry programs, which were central to transportation in the country. Especially in light of the geographic location, governmental cuts mandated by the IFIs caused a lack of alternative travel. This had a direct impact not only on citizens' ability to trade, get products, and obtain services, but also on the upkeep and return of the Le Joola to open waters with only one of the two functioning engines wherein it capsized, resulting in 1,863 passengers' deaths—the second largest maritime disaster. Another example of crimes of globalization was the IFI-financed dam in Pak Mun, Thailand (Friedrichs and Friedrichs 2002). In this case, the types of costs included the financial, environmental, and social. For example, the dam resulted in a loss of livelihood for rural fisherman, resulted in environmental damages to the waterway, and led to the social disintegration of some communities that were once reliant on the river. Based on research of such cases, we once against find that each case has multiple types of costs, and each case reaffirms the significantly high price of state criminality in any form.

Political Crimes

The key types of political crimes that this text focuses on as state crime include political and economic corruption, state-sponsored terrorism, and assassinations. While trying not to be repetitive, once again we see that the types of harms can include financial, physical, and social-cultural-political. What may be missing from this list is the environmental. As the example in chapter 1 noted, the political and economic corruption in Zimbabwe did indeed have political costs including damaged public trust and confidence, and the erosion of legitimacy of the regime; social costs due to the mass displacement campaign; financial costs to the economy of Zimbabwe and the Congo; and physical costs, albeit indirectly, through the use of forced labor and/or child labor in the mines. As with most forms of government corruption, there will be political harms and costs. On the other hand, state-sponsored terrorism typically has physical, psychological, and social-cultural-political ramifications. There is the immediacy of fear that is often generated into the public's psyche and, more times than not, physical harm in the form of life itself or the infliction of severe pain, torture, or maiming. As will be discussed in later chapters, the U.S.-sponsored war with the Contras on the Sandinista government in Nicaragua created a paramilitary that thrived on public, civilian terrorism. In this case, thousands died, others were tortured, and infrastructures were damaged: a culture of fear was created all in the name of regime change. There are also state-sponsored assassinations that result in the death of the one being targeted, but also of innocent civilians caught in the wrong place at the wrong time. This has been the case with Israel's use of assassinations in Palestine and the United States' use of assassinations in the war on terrorism (e.g., Pakistan targets). Here again we have the physical costs. When used as a widespread or common governmental tactic, fear and often social and cultural upheavals are created. There is also a level of governmental legitimacy being questioned by other state political leaders, NGOs, and, often-times, the state's own citizens.

Genocide, Crimes against Humanity, Crimes of Aggression, and War Crimes

Genocide, crimes against humanity, and crimes of aggression are not only the worst of the worst forms of state criminality, but they also have the gravest harms and costs. Whether we are talking about the genocides by the Nazis, the Yugoslavian government, Rwandan regime and Interwhawme, Sudanese government and Janjaweed, we can trace the multiple types of costs for each incident—environmental, physical, psychological, financial, and social-cultural-political. I have included here crimes of aggression. We cannot ignore the criminality that stems from states taking it upon themselves, by deploying a global authority, to "uphold" human rights and freedom by force. As we will see in later chapters, these international crimes have various motivational and opportunity factors, yet each and every one of them are filled with such pain and costs, immediate and long-term, for the victims, the perpetrators, the society, and the world at large.

Whether we try to make neat categories to attain the true cost of state crime by using types of harms or types of crimes, we have the same problem. The costs are too significant, intertwined, short- and long-term, and often hidden with indirect measures. Thus, it seems the task of finding an even semi-precise accounting of the costs and harms of state crime is beyond the scope of our ability and perhaps due to the harmful nature of our imagination as well. Knowing this then, how can we best get an idea of the totality of state crime? It is with this in mind that I turn to the following section on methods and methodological issues.

Methods and Methodological Issues

Key issues with studying crimes of this magnitude include: (1) access to materials, (2) availability of resources, (3) availability of victims' accounts, and (4) an

understanding of the totality of the event. However, prior to specific methodological issues is the basic decision of what type of method to choose. This, of
course, is dependent upon what questions one is seeking the answer to (e.g.,
issues associated with victimization and/or their needs, how or why the crime(s)
occurred, deterrence or controls, and a host of other potential topics). With all
these variables and issues that surround the study of state crime, this section is
divided into two subsections: one focusing on common methods, and the second
centered on methodological issues or barriers to the field of inquiry.

Methods

To date, the majority of research on state crime has looked at definitional and
conceptual issues, typically through the detailed examination of selected cases
of state crime (or more frequently state-corporate crime): the case study method.
As with any field, such work is the foundation on which understanding is built.
Case studies are typically considered a form of qualitative methods. Qualitative
methods are used to interpret observations; to discover underlying meanings in
relationship of phenomenon; to consider the subjective nature of actions, attitudes, beliefs, individual preferences, backgrounds, and social perspectives; and
to explore social meanings. The quintessential characteristic of case studies is
that they strive towards a holistic understanding of systems of action: interre-
lated acts engaged in by the actors in a specific social time and space (Feagin,
Orum, and Sjoberg 1991). In general, strengths of qualitative methods include
the ability to gain a more in-depth insight into individuals, their actions, beliefs,
or social reality; observe people in their own environment; observe subjective
interpretations often hidden in quantitative measures; observe body language;
and obtain unexpected information that may surface within the process of the
method itself, hence the researcher can investigate it further. Thus, the case
study approach can address processes over time, identify the interplay of meaningful actions and structural contexts, and interpret the unintended and intended
outcomes in social transformations (Skocpol 1984).

A case study method is not a style of data gathering or an analytical tech-
nique; it is a methodological approach to research. Case studies emphasize detailed contextual analysis of a limited number of events or conditions and their
relationships. This method incorporates a systematic gathering of information
about specific phenomena to allow for an effective understanding of how or why
the event(s) occurred. Robert K. Yin (1984: 23) has defined the case study
method as an empirical inquiry "that investigates a contemporary phenomenon
within its real-life context; when the boundaries between phenomenon and context are not clearly evident; and in which multiple sources of evidence are used."

There are different ways to gather and analyze data sources for case studies.
To mention a few, there is the use of archival data (historical), primary data
(firsthand accounts or legal documents), interviews, observations, ethnographic
work, and surveys (see "Historical Case Study Methods," p. 87). Content analy-

sis is also a viable option for case studies (with a quantitative or qualitative approach). Typically, however, using the case study method involves using different approaches together and collating information from several sources, also called triangulation. This can include using nongovernmental organization reports, United Nations Human Rights Commission Reports, other scholarly sources, and newspaper accounts (although this presents other problematic issues if used alone, yet can be used in combination with several other sources). Essentially, this includes combining many pieces of data to obtain (1) a more holistic view of the crimes, (2) some sort of "truth" through confirming and reconfirming information via several sources, and (3) repetition wherein you can feel confident you have received all available information.

Case studies are an important building block in the field of state crime and in the broader area of white-collar crime. Despite the wealth of excellent case studies, little has been done to provide an overall assessment of the full extent of our knowledge or to construct a conceptual context that allows us to compare and contrast existing studies. Nonetheless, there are some things that simply cannot be done within this approach. As such, we should not ignore the importance of using comparative methodologies. Using a comparative approach is an important direction for understanding the specific crimes (i.e., traditional rape and genocidal rape techniques) using extant theoretical tools at our disposal. We have a whole body of criminological research aimed at understanding "street" crime that can be useful not just as a tool of integration, but for understanding similarities and differences of the types of crimes (Rothe et al., 2008).

Historical Case Study Methods

Historical Case Study method is usually regarded as strong in validity though not necessarily reliable. The notion of reliability is at risk due to the inherent danger of subjective and speculative interpretations that cannot be completely controlled for. Archival information contains several innate flaws (Berg 1998). Examples of this include missing elements in official documents or missing portions of such documents. For this reason, any research utilizing archival data is subject to receiving or obtaining only partial information. This then limits what can be analyzed. The other side to this limitation is the researcher's decision of what to examine or what information is sought after in archival collections. The process of sedimentation of archived information also limits this study. The sediment in archives is the result of people defining certain materials (and excluding other material) as "worth keeping" in archival situations (Hill 1993). This includes primary sedimentation, in which individuals or organizations create, save, collect, or discard material. The deposit of archived information is then reliant on what is "deemed" as relevant information. This puts archival data at risk for incomplete or subjective access (Hill 1993). Other limitations include the

> compartmentalization of social agencies and organizations that contribute to
> the complex nature of assessing the intent, impact, and social context of the
> event (pertinent if using the historical case study for more than an individual
> life account).

Typically quantitative approaches concentrate on measuring or counting through collecting and analyzing numerical data and applying statistical tests. The overarching goal is to provide a generalized understanding of patterns, correlations, and causation among variables (Babbie 1998). Quantitative researchers generally do not interact with the research subjects and assume objectivity. For example, typical units of analysis include groups of individuals, community, counties, and states. Relying on the accuracy of official data as well as self-reports of surveys, the researcher must interpret the statistics accurately. The data, instrument, and analysis are guided by a predisposed notion of findings, thus risking omitting significant variables (issues of spuriousness). While the issue of generalizabilty is a goal of many quantitative studies, this is not necessarily feasible if using this approach for studying state crime. There are other significant obstacles associated with quantitative analysis, especially for explaining state crime: complexities making it difficult to incorporate all variables, access to data, lack of databases in general, issues associated with relying solely on victimization surveys, and several more. These will be discussed in more detail in the following section.

Methodological Issues or Barriers to Overcome

A key issue associated with the study of state criminality, no different than traditional street crime, is knowing the actual numbers of victims and perpetrators (Bijleveld 2007). As we know with street crime, there is a dark figure. Yet, criminologists attempt to get beyond this and obtain estimates that are more reflective of crime by using, though imperfect, the multiple venues available (self-report surveys, the U.S.'s National Crime Victimization Survey, and the British Crime Survey are well known examples). However, with international crimes, this dark figure is a "doubly-dark figure" (Bijeveld 2007: 4).

In part, this can be due to a state's unwillingness to disclose the information for multiple reasons, victims' desires to remain silent, lack of survivors, lack of pre-conflict census data, lack of post-conflict citizenry data, significant population displacements, and a score of other variables. As such, criminologists must attempt to use multiple methods to make the doubly-dark figure of the crimes, at best, a dark figure of the crimes. The important task of counting the precise number of victims remains a laborious task, yet not only is it important but it also speaks to the difficulty of quantitative methods for these types of crimes. For example, the death toll in Darfur has been estimated to be between 60,000 and 160,000, according to Deputy Secretary of State Robert B. Zoellick. However, the Coalition for International Justice[1] reports estimates near 400,000. The number of victims from the genocide in Rwanda is estimated to be between 500,000 and 1,000,000. The mortality rate of Pakistanis, due to the conflict in 1971, varies by a three-fold variation, between 1 and 3 million, and estimates of the death toll in Congo between 1964 and 1965 varies ten-fold (Bijeveld 2007). As you can see, such figures display enormous variance, leaving several problems. Such margins lend to the figures becoming "at best a mere statistic" (Bijeveld 2007: 4). With these margins, the figures can also be trivialized or can make it even easier for the perpetrators to use the uncertainty to dispute estimates as "overstatements" or "imprecise."

Further, finding a sound method to obtain these statistics is important for prosecution and could include not only direct killings, rape, looting, and infrastructural destruction, but also deaths caused indirectly by specific groups. As Bijeveld (2007: 6) noted:

> For Congo it was estimated that mortality due to preventable causes such as malnutrition and infectious diseases was many times the so-called "direct mortality" . . . famine and other preventable disasters are often used by governments as a cheap and efficient way to get rid of certain segments of the population. To establish this pattern is necessary to document and understand the patterns of gross human rights violations, as well as to be able to assess in what ways the scale of the damage could have been mitigated and can be mitigated in similar circumstances in the future.

There are various forms that can be used to obtain statistics, no different than those used for traditional street crime, namely, victim surveys. These have been used for estimating mortality. Yet, in situations of these types of crime, significant portions of the population may have fled the country or may reside in refugee centers abroad, making it more difficult to account for the double-dark figures; or, if entire families were killed, mortality would be underestimated. An additional barrier to obtaining exact numbers or using victimization surveys is the inability to often go to the regions affected if the conflict is ongoing. Security issues can affect access to areas and thus the representativeness of the total numbers of victims. Further, some victims may not be willing to open up and share their experiences; this is particularly the case with victims of genocidal rape.

Another barrier to studying crimes of the state is that there are often not funds available from standard funding sources for this type of work. While these are problems, they are not insurmountable ones (Mullins and Rothe 2008). This can be even more significant for studying crimes of the state than other marginalized topics within criminology (e.g., privatization of prisons, critical criminology topics including cultural criminology). Obtain hands-on data, administering surveys, collecting interviews from victims or offenders, and attending court sessions in the Netherlands (ICC, ICTR, ICTY), etc., can be extremely costly endeavors that most researchers cannot afford. As such, the limitations for grant monies can significantly affect the type of research on state crimes we do, as well as limit access to primary data.

Chapter Summary

Information on crimes of the state is out there. The problem is knowing where to look and how to find it. The goal of this chapter was to provide a glance into how and where to find this information with the hope that by introducing a few of the most common barriers and constraints associated with knowing about and/or studying crimes by the state, you will look beyond them and search out cases through international news sources, legal documentations, transcripts from court proceedings, and documentaries, or even by asking about crimes of the state directly in courses. The other goal of the chapter was to show the extensiveness of and various types of the costs and harms involved. Indeed we are talking about the worst of the worst criminals and crimes known to mankind. The next step that is necessary to understand the complexities involved in state criminality is to turn to theory. After all, it is said that theory is like a light switch: use it and it will illuminate all corners of the room.

Notes

1. The Coalition for International Justice is a Washington-based nongovernmental organization that was hired by the United States Agency for International Development to try to determine whether the killing in Darfur amounted to genocide. The Coalition also concluded that 142,944 people may have been killed by government forces or allied militias, which were the main groups ravaging the civilian population.

Chapter 5

Integrated Theory of
International Law Violations

This chapter reviews the main criminological theoretical explanations that can be used to address key catalysts of state crime. A discussion of integrated theories that aid our understanding of how and/or why these acts can occur follows. As was pointed out in previous chapters, the standard used for defining state crime is through the use of international law. As such, the chapter concludes with a presentation of the most systematic and complete integrated theory to date: Integrated Theory of Violations of International Criminal Law.

Traditional Criminological Theories

Many traditional criminological theories have guided policies and our understandings of crime. However, as most criminologists have long ignored the worst types of crimes, those discussed in this text, relatively little attention has been given to the value of these theories for addressing violations of international criminal law. Moreover, while many of the criminological theories may well provide insight into juvenile delinquency, robbery, burglary, etc., standing alone, or as individual theories, they have serious shortcomings. Nonetheless, this does not mean we should reinvent the wheel. Instead, we need to recognize the value of contributions that do exist. As such, the chapter begins with an overview of those relevant criminological theories for understanding the worst of atrocities, state crimes, each in their own limited capacity.

Rational Choice Models

Rational choice models are typically associated with the classical school of criminological thought. The underlying assumption of human nature of the classical school, and shared by rational choice theories, is that humans are calculative rational beings with abilities to reason. Individuals make rational choices after a cost-benefit analysis: the doctrine of rationality. This was based on the hedonistic assumptions of human nature wherein individuals are pleasure seeking animals that need their appetite to be constrained by regulations—perceived pleasure (criminal act) outweighing the pain (punishment). While the classical school viewed humans as free-willed, later developments recognized limitations to this. Alterations to the belief in complete free-willed beings include the concepts of bounded volunteerism and/or bounded free will, meaning individuals have free will but that freedom is constrained due to their life position and environment.

Cornish and Clarke (1986) developed one such version of rational choice theory. This theory assumes that offenders act after a rational decision-making process that includes (1) the initial choice to become involved, and then (2) the decision whether to commit a criminal act. The key differentiation to the classical school of thought is the inclusion of bounded rationality. Simply stated, bounded rationality views the decision-making process as guided by incomplete or inaccurate information. This is due to social factors and individual estimates of the perceived costs and benefits.

Cohen and Felson (1979) further developed the rational choice theory to include choice constrained by opportunity. The elements of routine activities include a motivated offender (a given), suitable targets (opportunity), and capable guardians (operationality of control). This follows Cornish and Clarke's concept of bounded rationality but illuminates the situational factors. While rational choice theory is often viewed as a theory of victimization, Cohen and Felson provided three key catalysts that are indeed relevant to all crime, including crimes of the state and other violators of international criminal law.

Along the lines of rationalization is the concept of techniques of neutralization. Sykes and Matza (1957) presented concepts of neutralization and justification that include (1) denial of responsibility, (2) denial of injury, (3) denial of victim, (4) condemnation of the condemner, and (5) appeal to higher authority. These techniques can best be understood in terms of the simple process of rationalizing one's own behavior, whether in response to cognitive dissonance, as a precondition to acting, or other factors; it is a process of rationalization. Such processes can be prior to an act, aiding a cost-benefit analysis, or post-action to minimize a person's behaviors.

Deterrence Models

Directly related to rational choice models are theories of deterrence. This perspective varies significantly from using informal deterrence—shaming (see
Braithwaite 1989a; Paternoster and Simpson 1996), to formal deterrence
(Cornish and Clarke 1986; Bachman et al. 1992). However, there are common
basic assumptions and central concepts of these deterrence models. In essence,
all deterrence theories are models of obedience. This is based on the assumptions of human nature and the core concepts of the classical school of thought.
General deterrence results from the threat of punishment, to deter from the first
offense. Laws are believed to affect general deterrence by their educative component, habitulating (patterned recognition), and their moral component (setting
standards for right and wrong). Specific deterrence is aimed to prevent recidi-
vism or future criminal acts by the offender.

Deterrence based on extant laws should be more promising for actors committing crimes that constitute violations of international criminal law than those
committing traditional street crime being deterred by laws due to the social
integration and position of most potential offenders (Rothe and Mullins 2006a).
As street crime and white collar crime research has shown, social location
and position strongly influence deterrence (see, for example, Berk et al. 1992;
Paternoster and Piquero 1995; Paternoster and Simpson 1996; Piquero and
Paternoster 1998; Stafford and Warr 1993). Those actors most likely to be
involved in these types of crimes would seem to be those who are most influenceable by law.

Control Theories

Controls have also been used to explain traditional street criminality. Tittle's
(1995) Control Balance Theory was based on the premise that the amount of
control to which an individual is subject, compared to the amount of control he
or she can exercise, will determine the probability of deviance occurring. Tittle
recognizes that constraints/control constitute inhibitors of actions. In other
words, control is not conceptualized as a complete prevention but as a means by
which actions can be limited: "control incorporates the idea of barriers, or constraints" (143). The concept of control ratio reflects the degree of control that is
available to be used relative to the degree of control that is exerted over the
individual. He states that "[t]he key variables, control ratio and deviant motivation, are at least structurally or situationally linked, and are perhaps largely
determined by structural or situational variables" (Tittle 1995: 166). According
to Tittle, constraints are the probability (or perceived probability) that potential
control will be exercised. According to this model, the leading factor in power
holders' (elites and professionals) deviance is the amount of control that is or
can be exercised relative to the amount of control exerted over them: "Behavior
is influenced by the likelihood and magnitude of anticipated controls (sanctions,

limitations, on future conduct, and so on), that is, that people's actions can be and typically are curtailed, partially curtailed, by anticipation of the likely controlling responses of others" (Tittle 1995, 185).

As such, the state would be viewed as having a high probability of deviance due to the degree of control abilities being unbalanced.

Disorganization Theories

Disorganization theories are typically associated with the Chicago school of thought. Here the shared underlying assumption of individuals is based more on the blank slate perspective, or a socially constructed view of human nature. Crime causation is viewed in terms of social causation. For example, the fast changing occurrences in demographics, agriculture, industrialization, immigration, urbanization, and a newly formed social class all aided the Chicago school's concept that certain effects were occurring from the cultural and societal changes. Namely, the fast-changing cultural and social organization was viewed as related to causes of crime. The rapid changes would damage the existing set of normative controls, leading to the breakdown of consensus to "dissensus" (Mullins and Rothe 2008; Rothe and Mullins 2008). The disorganization that occurs would have two manifestations: (1) long-term leading to reorganization, and (2) short-term resulting in deviance. As such, community traits were linked to crime (Shaw and McKay 1942).

Sutherland took concepts out of the Chicago school of thought and focused on what he called "differential social organization." He paired cultural conflict, occurring due to the social disorganization, with a lack of harmonious social influences, with the idea that individuals learn patterned criminal behavior. As such, Sutherland contributed to the significance of recognizing the larger social structure while simultaneously introducing individual behavioral catalysts (Mullins and Rothe 2008).

Bursik and Gramsik (1993) and Sampson and Raudenbush (1999) built on Shaw and McKay's model of social disorganization by introducing the concept of "collective efficacy": defining a neighborhood in terms of its ability to maintain order amongst the residents. This efficacy can exist only when mutual trust and cohesion of the community are linked to shared intervention of neighborhood social control. Other factors outside of the local residents' control also affect social disorganization and the efficacy of informal control sanctions including the cognitive landscape, socioeconomic status, residential mobility, heterogeneity, and urbanization.

In essence, these models view disorganization as a result of structural barriers that affect the development of formal and informal ties that would promote the ability to solve common problems when communities lack informal mechanisms of social control, or exhibit ineffectual levels of collective efficacy; crime rates increase due to the lack of community self-organization. Essentially a control theory of crime, this work points out that indicators of concentrated disadvantage are largely responsible for a community's inability to act collectively.

Anomie Theories

A related, yet separate, concept to social disorganization is anomie. The depiction of human nature is two-fold for this orientation: on the one hand, human nature does not exist without society, and yet, humans have an insatiable appetite that needs to be controlled or regulated by society. Additionally, deviance arises as a consequence of discontented human desires. There are two main concepts as to how and why these discontented human desires happen and how and why they lack fulfillment.

The first conceptualization of anomie is attributed to Emile Durkheim and later to Robert Merton. In the Durkheimean sense, anomie refers to a societal condition where rapid social change has had mass communal effects that lead to normlessness in a structure that has a lack of social constraints or regulation. Such rapid social change occurred through the transition from an organic to mechanical society. Merton picked up on Durkheim's concept of egoistic anomie, where a value has been placed on the unrestricted pursuit of individual desires, and extended it into a theory of deviance.

Merton's classic structure-strain theory is also of relevance. While often presented as one theory, anomie/strain, Merton proposed two separate theoretical concepts: anomie, which works at the structural level, and strain, which operates at the individual level. Merton's focus was not on rapid social changes, nor did he rely on the underlying assumption that human appetites were insatiable. Instead, Merton saw norms as creators of these insatiable appetites. Anomie is viewed as the result of high emphasis on cultural goals with low emphasis placed on institutionalized norms to achieve these goals. Simply, the social structure has an inherent contradiction between the expected aspirations (cultural goals) and obtainable legitimate means to achieve these culturally emphasized goals. As such, the intrinsic value of following norms is meaningless, anomie, without the attainment of the goals. In other words, the unequal social structure, anomic conditions, acts as a constraint to achieve the goals through legitimate means, which brings a contradiction that can lead to strain. According to Merton, strain occurs when attempts to achieve culturally emphasized goals and expectations are unattainable, either due to blocked goals or means. Individuals then may respond several ways to this strain: conformity, innovation, ritualism, and rebellion. In the case of criminality, the blocked goals lead to strain and the response is that of an innovator.

96   *Chapter 5*

Learning Theories

Learning theories share certain assumptions of human nature and their relation
to the social environment in which they exist in. The assumption here is that
individuals are shaped, and can be reshaped, by specific environments and/or
conditions. The process of normal learning generates criminal behavior no different than any other knowledge. As such, the key to these theories is the process of learning and the subsequent content of what is learned. Perhaps the most
well known scholar associated with learning theories, also known as the founder
of the field of white-collar crime, is Sutherland (1939, 1948, 1949). As noted by
Sutherland (1949: 300), "Any person can be trained to adopt and follow a pattern of criminal behavior."

Sutherland's Differential Association theory contains nine postulates that
serve as the framework for the process of learning criminal and noncriminal
behaviors:

1. Criminal behavior is learned
2. It is learned in interaction with others during communication.
3. Learning occurs within intimate personal groups.
4. The learning includes techniques, motives, drives, attitudes, and rationalization.
5. The direction of motives is derived from the definition of law perceived
   as favorable or unfavorable.
6. Delinquency occurs because of excess of favorable definitions over non-
   favorable.
7. Associations vary in time, frequency, priority, intensity, and duration.
8. The learning process to criminality is no different than any other learning process.
9. Criminal behavior is an expression of general needs and values; it is not
   explained by those needs and values, as noncriminal behavior is an expression of the same needs and values.

Through these processes, individuals learn how to define their environment,
favorable or unfavorable attitudes, and specific behaviors.

Akers (1977) developed a social-psychological social learning theory
wherein (1) deviant behavior is learned through operant conditioning; (2) the
behavior is learned nonsocially and through social interaction, vis à vis reinforcements; (3) the major part of deviant behavior is learned in groups that control the major source of reinforcements; and (4) the learning of techniques, attitudes, and avoidance is a function of reinforcers. The social reinforcements,
then, provide the basis for involvement in criminal and deviant behavior. Additionally, these reinforcements, positive or negative, are necessary conditions for
both deviant acts and conforming behaviors.

Criminologists have also long been interested in the behavioral norms and values seen as unique to the streets. Since the mid-twentieth century, scholars have identified and explored a subculture that permeates specific social networks. More recently, work done by the likes of Elijah Anderson (1990, 1999), Neal Shover (Shover 1996; Shover and Henderson 1995; Shover and Honaker 1992), and Richard Wright (Wright and Decker 1994, 1997) resurrected the notion of a street-based subculture. In such environments, social actors are driven by demands for instant gratification to engage in violent and property crime. Such environments also lend to providing fertile ground for specific learning process as was noted by other scholars of learning theories. Additionally, subcultural theories can be seen as having relevancy in socially disorganized environments wherein they may arise in response to the larger structural conditions and provide an alternative set of values that become internalized through socialization (Mullins and Rothe 2008).

Organizational Theories

The notion of examining organizations in the context of criminal behaviors dates back to Sutherland's work on white-collar crime. Organizational theories, however, were not included in criminological literature until the late 1970s through the mid 1980s. It was then some criminologists began to incorporate ideas from organizational sociologists' research (Ermann and Lundman 1982; Gross 1978; Schrager and Short 1978; Vaughn 1982, 1983). In the 1970s, the organizational sociologists argued that social scientists needed to move beyond focusing on the individuals who make up an organization and to recognize that the aggregate whole "functions as an entity" (Hall 1987, quoted in Kauzlarich and Kramer 1998: 7). Moreover, they are capable of actions that affect a community (Perrucci and Potter 1989). Such recognition brings the relevance of incorporating organizational theories into the realm of criminology given that, if organizations affect a community, criminogenic organizations would also affect a community. Moreover, "there are social structures that cannot be reduced to the actions of particular individuals and that, therefore, have to be explained in different terms" (Browning et al. 2000: 132).

Since corporate crime is organizational crime, any explanation calls for an organizational level of analysis. After all, organizational goals, organizational structure, and organizational environments are the major organizational factors that influence the commission of corporate crimes (Kramer 1982). As such, it was argued that organizations, as social actors, "can and should be the primary focus of analysis in state and corporate crime" (Kauzlarich and Kramer 1998: 9). Gross noted that "there is built into the very structure of organizations an inherent inducement for the organization itself to engage in crime" (Gross, quoted in Kauzlarich and Kramer 1998: 145). Further, organizations are strongly goal-oriented[1] and concerned with performance, while governing norms may be weak or absent (anomie). These goals may be blocked internally or externally (e.g., standard operating procedures or codes of conduct) and as such cause strain. Broader theories of organizational behavior and corporate offending highlight certain structures that may develop in bureaucratic environments where goal attainment is pushed to an "any means necessary" degree. Certain organizations further reinforce instrumental rationality within decision-making processes (see Perrow 1986; Weber 1946) that can enhance the perceived value of criminal behaviors and reduce the perceived harm of the same act. Cultures can develop within organizations or subunits that can motivate criminal endeavors (see Sutherland 1949). The very nature of complex organizations provides a host of opportunity-producing elements. Bureaucracies can maintain levels of secrecy with respect to how their resources are utilized; external actors need not know what was done within the organization or by whom. Information may also be hidden from other organizational actors, including those who are actually carrying out elements of the criminal activity. Due to internal organizational structures of information control, the ability of external agencies to obtain information on the nature and dynamics of these decision-making events heighten criminal tendencies (Rothe and Mullins 2006c).

Phenomenology and Everyday Knowledge

The foundation of phenomenological studies assumes that the only phenomenon social scientists can be sure of is that we are conscious, thinking beings and therefore all studies should be centered on any phenomenon as it is consciously experienced, free from all preconceptions or causal ideas. The acceptance of any causal links, deterministic theories, or of preconceived concepts as "truth" or "real" as a reality all of its own would be a contradiction to the fundamental assumptions of phenomenology. The phenomenological work of Berger and Luckmann (1967: 4) suggested that knowledge is "the relationship between human thought and the social context within which it arises." Objective reality is defined as the reality of everyday life that appears to be objectively real or a given to the individuals that live within it. To understand the process of subjectivity, Berger and Luckman rely on the processes of socialization: internalizing the objective reality of others as one's own reality. Simply, reality is objectively real through a subjective process of socialization. This process of socialization then reifies the existing "objective" reality. Phenomenology relates to criminology through the process of the phenomenologically influenced sociology of deviance. Thus, crime is viewed as a social phenomenon that is created and enacted through a process of social interaction. This perspective is also important when we consider how state criminality often eludes the label of "crime" due to its position and access to power and political resources.

Summary of Traditional Criminological Theories

Standing alone, each of the theories reviewed fails to explain state criminality in whole. As noted by Enloe (2004: 22), "Something does not cause every single thing. For an explanation [reduced to one cause] to be useful, a great deal of human dignity has to be left on the cutting floor." In other words, by limiting ourselves to one strand of thought to explain something as complex as state criminality, we would forfeit many significant variables and be guilty of reductionism. It is for this reason that we need to move beyond one specific theory toward integration to allow a more complete explanation of crimes of the state.

Integrated Theories

Integrating theoretical models generally take three forms: (1) by piecemealing existing theories to address one level of analysis or phenomena, (2) by incorporating different theoretical models (within one field of the social sciences or in culmination of fields) to address a phenomena at all levels of analysis, and (3) by using different theories from different disciplines—an interdisciplinary approach (Barak 1990). I suggest the latter two types of integration are necessary and must be combined. Moreover, the idea of one overarching paradigm for a specific field of social sciences is in and of itself misleading. A paradigm should not be viewed as a privileged theoretical stance but instead as a set of shared assumptions regarding human nature and the social structure that presently dominates a field. From this, orientations or approaches evolve to explain specific phenomenon.

While some criminologists have ventured into integrating traditional theories, there is still a general belief that integrating different fields or different theories at the individual level or structural levels is enough to provide answers to the most complex forms of crime. Yet, due to the complexities of state crime, utilizing theories that explain only the individual level processes, that of organizations, controls, or external precipitating conditions, is bound to overlook the intricacies of such cases and provide no additional guidance for future understandings of atrocities or the ability to foresee potential situations prior to becoming full-blown violations of international criminal law. While this may be an acceptable form of integration for some, I believe that an analysis of phenomena that has such complexities as time-space, history, culture, politics, ideology, and economics must include an integrated model that addresses all levels of analysis: the structural to the individual(s) involved in the crimes. Integration is the most viable path forward for theorizing the types of crimes I seek to address here. First, to ignore extant theory is to be forced to reinvent the wheel. Such a posture is not only myopic in that it ignores decades of established theorizing and theory testing, but it is arrogant in its rejection of what has come before.

After all, decades of research have established that certain phenomena are related to crime commission. The job then of an integrationist is to provide an underlying framework (and set of assumptions) that makes sense of empirical reality. Perhaps most relevant to the development of the integrated theory is the theoretical framework by Kauzlarich and Kramer (1998), which built upon earlier work by Kramer and Michalowski (1990), which presented an integrated model of state offending that explored motivation, opportunities, and controls at three levels of analysis: the interactional, organizational, and the cultural-structural level. Moreover, their model integrates components of several traditional criminological theories that fall short by themselves in addressing state/corporate crime. For example, Kauzlarich and Kramer utilize anomie and strain, rational choice, differential association, routine activities, political economy, and organizational models. Kauzlarich and Kramer discuss how motivation is affected by one's socialization within that environment, the social meaning given to his or her behavior, an individual's goals, and issues of personality such as personal morality and obedience to authority. Borrowing from Sykes and Matza (1957), they include techniques of neutralization as a variable of control. At the organizational level, Kauzlarich and Kramer draw heavily from organizational theorists. As Kauzlarich and Kramer argue, organizational crime depends on two other factors—availability of illegal means and the social control environment that fosters organizational crime (146).

Organizational opportunities are said to include instrumental rationality, role specialization, and task segregation, while controls include a culture of compliance, reward structure, safety and quality control procedures, and effective communication processes. At the structural or institutional level of analysis, the major social institutions and social structure are included, particularly the political and economic institutions and their interrelationship. Kauzlarich and Kramer (1998: 146) suggest the primary assumption of that perspective is that the very structure of corporate capitalism provides the impetus toward organizational crime, thus becoming crimes of capital (Michalowski 1985). They further propose that the political economy perspective stresses the shaping and/or constraining influences of the broader historical structure of a society as a factor of organizational behavior. This includes factors such as the culture of competition, economic pressure, and performance emphasis under the catalyst of motivation. Also needed is the availability of legal and illegal means, blocked goals, and access to resources that are included under opportunities. Controls at the structural level are said to include international reactions, political pressure, legal sanctions, media scrutiny, and public opinion.

While I find this to be a useful model, it fails to adequately incorporate the increasingly international nature of state criminality, and especially cases that do not involve typical Western capitalistic-based forms of state crime (Rothe and Mullins 2006a). Further, as it stands in the works cited above, it is more of a theory that allows illumination of cases, instead of empirical prediction and testing. Having said this, the value of an integrated theory is only such if it is manageable and/or useful for explaining crimes. After all, "everything is not the cause of some one thing" (Enloe 2004: 22). The following section presents an integrated theory of international criminal law violations that expands upon the previous work of Kauzlarich and Kramer (1998) by Rothe (2006), refined by Rothe and Mullins (2006a, 2007a, 2008) and Mullins and Rothe (2008).

An Integrated Theory of International Criminal Violations

With the complexities of these crimes, it is necessary to examine catalysts and inhibitors at all levels of analysis. In doing so, the integrated theory combines insights from criminological and sociological theory presented earlier in this chapter that help to explain the multiple levels at play within each specific case. Any given incident of international crime is a product of a myriad of social forces that come together in the production of the event in question. Thus, attention must be given to specific time-space. Global political and economic conditions are one variable that makes these crimes more or less likely, provides tensions and contradictions for countries to navigate, and presents problems for state actors to resolve—either criminally or legally. Contextualization of such acts is essential to understand both the idiosyncrasies of an individual event as well as the patterns that emerge in the phenomena as a whole.

Moreover, any given crime is a product of multiple catalysts and forces; to fully elucidate a singular occurrence, one must examine a number of factors at multiple levels of analysis. Consequently, this theoretical model recognizes the necessary catalysts of motivation, opportunity, constraints, and controls for each of these levels. As such, it contains both breadth and depth. Such analytical acuity allows a precise pinpointing of key forces and how they interact within a specific criminal event or context (see table 5.1).

Except for recent work on crimes of globalization (see Friedrichs and Friedrichs 2002; Rothe, Muzzatti, and Mullins 2006; Rothe, Mullins, and Sandstrom 2008), most organizational criminology, including state crime, has ignored the social forces and incipient social structures occurring within the international realm in favor of focusing on a state itself or specific political economic systems. Further, when the international arena is taken into account, it is done so in a rather simplistic manner, resting upon a highly idealized and reified account of globalization (Whyte 2003). While an international context may be assumed, it is not fully specified or conceptualized in how it influences decision making at the state level. Whatever occurs at the supra-national level is perceived as a state-level influence. State policies are viewed as inevitably market driven as such; the focus is limited to the dynamics of a global and capitalistic economy, most notably, U.S.-centered. However, the institutional elements and context of a state, its economic, political, cultural, and historical environment, is distinct from and often exhibits forces in contradiction with those elements at the international level. These forces may influence the nature of social forces within a state's macro-level structure, but can also exert their own unique influences. Any given state, and the social structure it represents, will be the product of long-term historical contingencies and forces that necessitate an examination of

Chapter 5

Table 5.1. *Integrated Theory of International Criminal Law Violations*

International Level	Motivation	Opportunity	Constraints	Controls
	Political interests	International relations	International reaction	International law
	Economic interests	Economic supremacy	Political pressure	International sanctions
	Resources	Military supremacy	Public opinion social movements	
	Ideological interests	Complementary legal systems	NGOs and INGO	
			Oversight/ economic institutions	
Macro Level	Structural transformations	Availability of illegal means	Political pressure	Legal sanctions
	Economic pressure or goals	Control of information	Media scrutiny	Domestic law
	Political goals	Propaganda	Public opinion	
	Ethnogenses	Ideology/nationalism	Social movements	
	Anomie	Military capabilities	Rebellion	
Meso Level	Organizational culture and goals	Communication structures	Internal oversight	Codes of conduct
	Authoritarian pressures	Means availability	Communication structures	
	Reward structures	Role specialization	Traditional authority structures	
Micro Level	Strain	Obedience to authority	Personal morality	Legitimacy of law
	Socialization	Group think	Socialization	
	Individual goals and ideologies	Diffusion of responsibility	Obedience to authority	Perception of reality of law application
	Normalization of deviance	Perceived illegal means	Informal social controls	
	Definition of the situation			

For previous versions see Rothe and Mullins (2009), "Toward a Criminology for International Criminal Law: An Integrated Theory of International Criminal Violations." *International Journal of Comparative and Applied Criminal Justice,* vol. 33; Mullins and Rothe (2008), *Power, Bedlam, and Bloodshed: State Crime in Africa.* Peter Lang Publishing; Rothe and Mullins (2008), "Genocide, War Crimes and Crimes Against Humanity in Central Africa: A Criminological Exploration," in R. Haveman and Allette Smeulers (Eds.), *Towards a Criminology of International Crimes.* Antwerp: Intersentia; Rothe and Mullins (2006), *Symbolic Gestures and the Generation of Global Social Control: The International Criminal Court.* Boston: Lexington, p. 213.

factors more traditionally referred to as macro-level forces. Broader cultural, political, and economic factors in play at a given time and space can, to a greater or lesser extent, produce a given crime.

A related, yet separate, concept to social disorganization is anomie. Unlike Kauzlarich and Kramer (1998), I use anomie in the Durkheim sense. While no longer applicable to conditions of rapid social change envisioned by Durkheim, the transition from mechanical to organic society, the relevance of anomie understood in these terms can be seen with conditions left by abrupt colonial departures or coups, often dismantling entire sets of socio-political structures. Not only do such events rearrange governmental structures, but the organization of economic ownership and production are reconfigured as well (Mullins and Rothe 2008). Weak institutions produce a vacuum of formal and informal social control. On the other hand, Durkheim and others such as Colvin and Cullin (2004) have recognized that overregulation can also create criminogenic environments at the state level. For example, history has shown that overregulated states have resulted in terrible atrocities such as the Soviet Gulag system. Further, the vast literature on the Holocaust points to the hyper-centralization of power during the Nazi regime as both motivation and facilitation of the genocide at all levels of analysis.

Since state crimes and other violations of international criminal law are committed within an organizational structure (states, paramilitaries, militaries, etc.), one must explore factors at play within the organization itself. While the Kauzlarich and Kramer (1998) model incorporates elements of organizational theory, it is limited to highly bureaucratic institutions or those based on capitalistic profit-generating tendencies. As corporate crime researchers have shown, some organizations are much more criminogenic than others. For example, in this model and as suggested elsewhere (Rothe and Mullins 2008; Mullins and Rothe 2008), many of these types of crimes are committed by militias and paramilitaries that do not fit into the organizational model conceived by many organizational theorists. The social processes and a broader conception of organizational cultures is essential in understanding these crimes. Further, looking beyond the capitalistic notion of organizational structures as corporate entities, within certain organizations the presence of a reward structure does not ensure compliance; instead, it creates the very criminogenic tendencies that scholars have believed reduce or control criminality (Mullins and Rothe 2008). A case in point is the reward structure allotted to the Janjaweed by the Sudanese government, mainly in the form of promised goods from looting, including the livestock of the Darfurians.

A separate body of criminological theory emphasizes the influence of social disorder within immediate residential environments as having powerful criminogenic effects. Typically referred to as social disorganization theory (see Shaw and McKay 1942; Bursik and Grasmick 1993), this line of theorizing suggests that when communities posses a diminished capacity to create and enact informal mechanisms of social control, or exhibit levels of low collective efficacy, crime rates increase due to the lack of community self-organization. In the absence of legitimate forms of social organization, illegal organizations—or at least groups that engage in persistent criminal behavior—proliferate to provide social structures and opportunities absent due to broader conditions of institutional failures. Here, widespread social disorganization is most readily apparent in producing militias (Mullins and Rothe 2008).

There is also a need to include aspects of associational and social learning theories (e.g., Akers 1977; Sutherland 1939) and core elements of symbolic interactionism and phenomenology (e.g., perceptual aspects and definition of the situation) to understand these phenomena. The idea of learning criminal behaviors through socialization is relevant not only in organizational settings but also in a larger cultural setting. Again, cultural elements discussed above come to bear—both in the broader sociocultural sense and organizational cultures into which the individual has been socialized. Certain organizations may inculcate actors into broader ideological beliefs that facilitate violating laws; day-to-day interactions provide ample opportunity for the transmission not only of criminogenic value systems but also of neutralizations to excuse such behaviors.

As noted, Akers' (1977) social learning theory is also relevant to the study of state crime at the meso and interactional levels. This model is useful combined with Sutherland's Differential Association for providing an understanding in some cases. For example, as seen with child-soldiers who are forced to commit atrocities, the process of stimuli presentation—negative and positive—is routinely used to ensure obedience. Child soldiers are motivated/rewarded with personal praise, social inclusion, drugs, and valuable items. They are also brutally disciplined, or forced to carry out beatings on their peers as both punishment and conditioning. Further, new child recruits are trained and socialized into the militia by their peers.

Merton's (1938) classic structure-strain theory is also of relevance. For example, through years of political turmoil and marginalization, many militia groups enact alternative means to accomplish political capital, including coups and/or insurgencies that are directly related to the atrocities this theory aims to explain (e.g., LRA in Uganda or the Darfur insurgency that sparked the Sudanese government's harsh military response and collusion with the Janjaweed).

In line with the majority of traditional criminological theories, this integrated theory does not ignore the influence of individuals and individual decision makers in explaining criminality. All acts require that a singular social actor make a decision and produce an act. In any crime involving state, militia, or paramilitary actors, orders to carry out the activities must be developed, agreed upon, and enacted. Within a bureaucracy as complex as a polity, this involves not one, but a multitude of social actors in a number of organizational positions. Structure clearly frames action and thought, channeling human behavior toward certain outcomes and away from others; it defines possibilities and molds goal structures. Social actors respond to stimuli within their environments, yet exercise individual choice in decision-making processes based on any number of variables. While individual agency is indeed modified or even extremely constrained by the social conditions present within any complex organization, no bureaucratic actor is a mere automaton. Individuals carry with them pre-established cultural and ideological visions. Such a lens influences how they evaluate information, create policy objectives, and direct organization activities to the realization of those policies. More essentially, at the top levels of power, agency can often be fully revealed and active. While indeed processes like groupthink can come into play, original decisions, directives, and directions must be established through some form of agentic decision-making process. While such individual predilections and predispositions are often overlooked, it must be acknowledged that the perpetrators and the decision makers in these cases possess agency. They are not automatons blindly responding to socio-political forces, but rather lively social actors who often wield large amounts of social power and institutional authority that can be brought to bear in the commission of a crime (Rothe and Mullins 2006a).

With this in mind, the issue of goal attainment is as relevant to individual goal seekers as it is to organizations. Further, to believe or hope at all that deterrence can be an effective mechanism for those most likely to commit international crimes, I do assume a bounded rationality is held by actors. Having said this, I do not reduce all decision-making or agency to that of bounded rational actors. Nor do I agree with many works that presume rational choice answers all; in these cases, the meanings of rational have become nearly all inclusive, making the empirical usefulness and testability futile. After all, when you have a hammer, everything around you starts to look like a nail. I also agree with Almond (1990: 1) when he stated that using rational choice "may lead to empirical and normative distortions, unless it is used in combination with the historical, sociological, anthropological, and psychological sciences."

State crime scholars have also identified external and internal controls on the behavior of states (see Ross 1995, 2000). External controls have been defined as those that lie outside of the specific state apparatus and are imposed on the state itself. Internal controls are those that arise within the state and are directed against itself, such as previously discussed domestic laws and self-regulation. These controls can be tangible (i.e., the firing of an agent) or symbolic (i.e., an official statement of denial or a promise to investigate). Internal controls are broadly conceived of as restrictions placed on state agencies by themselves or other state agencies. The United Kingdom's establishment of a Royal Commission on Police Procedure and a Police Complaints Board in response to police brutality (Ross 2000); the passing of the Parliament of Canada Act and the Canadian Security Intelligence Service Act; the Zorea, Blatman, and Karp Commissions in Israel; and campaign finance reform laws in Japan (Rothe and Mullins 2006a) are all examples of such internal controls. Suggested external controls *within* the state have included media organizations, interest groups, and domestic nongovernmental organizations (NGOs). External controls located outside of the state would include the United Nations (UN), the World Court

(WC), the International Criminal Court (ICC), and, potentially, other states. As internationally sanctioned bodies, these organizations hold the power to apply sanctions to states that either violate international law or are overly abusive of their own citizens. However, the ability to back up sanctions with coercive force is limited to members who are willing to volunteer the necessary force to act in the organization's name. It is for this reason that U.S. violations of international law regarding nuclear weapons have gone unsanctioned (Kauzlarich and Kramer 1998). Also, economic organizations such as the World Bank (WB), the International Monetary Fund (IMF), and the World Trade Organization (WTO) represent potential controls on criminal states through the manipulation of financial assets, trade agreements, and trade sanctions. However, as other scholars have noted, these same institutions may directly or indirectly create the criminogenic conditions that lead to these types of atrocities (Friedrichs and Friedrichs 2002; Rothe, Muzzatti, and Mullins 2006; Rothe, Mullins, and Sandstrom 2008). While this research has provided valuable insight into controls and constraints, I believe these are not conceptually interchangeable.

Phenomenologically, a constraint differs from a control in that it is an inhibitor or barrier that occurs *at the onset of* or *during* an illegal action. This constraint can act as a complete blockage to the act, or it can act as a restraint that inhibits or causes the actor(s) to find alternative means to crime enactment. For example, structural constraints can act as a tool for conformity via the narrowing of options and/or motivations. Thus, one option or type of option that is open to actors may be viewed as not worth doing or may not be within the actor's practical consciousness (or mutual knowledge). A control, on the other hand, is a formal mechanism meant to block in full an illegal action or ideally hold accountable through prosecution, sanctions, or some form of social justice postcriminality. Having briefly reviewed some of the key contributions to our proposed integrated theory, I now turn to what I believe is a comprehensive tool that can aid the systematic study and explanation of the worst crimes known to humanity.

The Four Catalysts

Motivation

Unlike some criminological theories that assume motivation is either mundane or unimportant (e.g., most control, routine activities, and deterrence theories), especially for the crimes examined here, I feel motivation is a crucial theoretical component. The assumption of motivation being consistently present, and as such irrelevant to consider, can be linked back to the classical school perspective, wherein human nature is perceived as hedonistic. While I agree with key postulates of Routine Activities Theory, the elements of a motivated offender, suitable targets (opportunity), and capable guardians (operationality of control), and the concept of bounded rationality that illuminates situational factors, I do not agree that "criminal inclination is a given and . . . [we need to] examine the manner in which the spatio-temporal organization of social activities helps translate their criminal inclinations into action" (Cohen and Felson 1979: 589). Rather, motivation is an essential variable to be explained. The complex psychological, social, and cultural factors (as well as interactions among these factors) that produce motivations are not so easily dismissed; the drive to genocide or mass atrocity is inherent in all human cognitive processes that merely need to be controlled (Mullins and Rothe 2008; Rothe and Mullins 2006a, 2008, 2009).

Those theories that assume motivation tends to resort to simplistic explanations that take for granted the rewards of crimes are self-contained and self-evident. However, especially for genocide, war crimes, and crimes against humanity, the acts are not necessarily inherently rewarding, nor do they necessarily involve hedonistic tendencies or other seemingly innate human psychosocial drives. If they were, such widespread criminal atrocities would be much more common than they are, especially considering the dearth of controls on such behaviors.

Motivation is the constellation of the general and specific drives that lure and entice a given organization and/or organizational actor toward offending. Motivation itself, however, should not be construed as the same as *Mens Rea,* the mental state or degree of fault which an actor held at the relevant time (Blaskic Appeals Chamber Decision 2005, ¶694). Motivation is a force that drives or is the desire to commit a crime. Simply, the intent of an action is not the same as the motivating factors that are applicable at multiple levels of analysis; intent is specific at the individual psychological level. Specific motivating forces can include the enhancement and/or maintenance of political power, personal or organizational economic gain, access to valuable natural resources, religious factors, or revenge. Often, these factors interact with others to create more intensely motivated populations. General motivations, while often linked to specific, can include factors such as political marginalization of a specific group or party (e.g., colonial powers often marginalized a portion of the population, giving specific preferential treatment to one group). In turn, this can result in specific motivating factors including political or economic gain. Further, ethnic divisions that were created by either colonial or post-colonial authorities can lead to specific motivation including revenge and/or the destruction of the reified "dehumanized other" (Mullins and Rothe 2008; Rothe and Mullins 2008). Additionally, it must be acknowledged that while I identify general (or modal) motivation factors, there can also be a wide variety of motivations individually within a criminal group (Smeulers 2007).

Opportunities

Opportunities are those social interactions where the possibility for a crime to be committed emerges and presents itself to a motivated offender (see Felson 1998). While all the motivation in the world may be present, without opportunity there cannot be a commission of a crime. Further, just as Cloward and Ohlin (1963) stated, the presence of legitimate and illegitimate opportunity must be taken into account. This is especially true given the use of international law as a standard for defining the criminality.

As an example at the macro-level, being a state strongly enhances the ability to create and capitalize upon criminal opportunity. Even the poorest countries have tremendous amounts of human and financial capital to draw upon for crime commission. On the other hand, the desirability of drawing upon illegal means will be even more tempting when legal means of accomplishing the goals are absent, blocked, or constrained. Further, the inaction of local or international bystanders will also facilitate the generation of opportunity (see Grunfeld 2007). On the meso-level, opportunity for specific actors is affected by the larger culture and/or state structure. For example, in the case of the Sudanese genocide, the opportunity for the Janjaweed to commit the crimes against humanity thus far has been provided by the el-Bashir regime's collusion. The opportunity for the LRA to commit atrocities and continue in a 20-year-long conflict was largely been created by the direct economic and social support of the Sudanese government, as well as their de facto control of the northern hinterlands.

Constraints

Constraints are those social elements that stand to potentially make a crime either riskier or less successful; offenders must navigate around a constraint. I envision these as taking several forms, including what other scholars have defined as controls: international reactions, political pressures, public opinion, international social movements, oversight from agencies such as the United Nations, political pressures, media scrutiny, and socialization. Simply, a constraint differs from a control in that constraints are not expected to fully control or block state or organizational criminogenic behaviors, nor do they act to penalize violators. Instead, by definition they serve as potential barriers before or during an act (Rothe and Mullins 2006a). Nonetheless, states are often in unique positions to both navigate around extant constraints and/or to neutralize the power they represent. For example, Sudan was able to circumvent the constraints NGO's represented by curtailing the ability of aid workers to effectively monitor the regime's activities or have access to civilians that provide testimony of the abuses. Additionally, states can attempt to neutralize international pressures by rhetorically framing the events in question as "insurgent activity" and/or cases of general banditry by militias. When organizations are sponsored by the government, they are effectively freed from potential constraints of the population or foreign involvement. Having said this, a constraint's ineffectiveness does not negate its presence. Minimally, additional actions are required by the criminal actor that led to additional costs, be they real or opportunity. Further, the power of constraints to stymie criminal actions can be enhanced by examining how states negotiated prior constraints. It must also be noted that, as a constraint, a latent effect may well be that the potential constrainer may not only be unsuccessful, but may also become a victim or may be re-victimized through the process (Rothe and Ross 2008). For example, figure 5.1 demonstrates the potential paths of a constraining mechanism (excerpt from Ross and Rothe 2008).

Figure 5.1. *Paths of Attempts to Control*

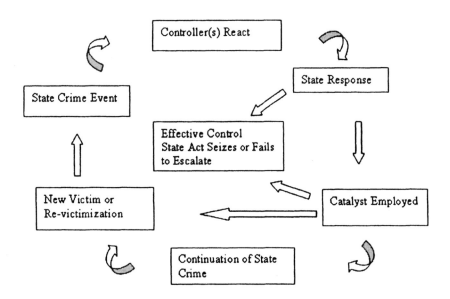

Controls

A control is a *complete* blockage to an act or when a criminal penalization is ideally inevitable after the fact. This means that conceived criminal action will not occur and, if it does, ideally there will be legal repercussions. Unlike constraints, I view controls as institutions that have the ability to stave off or prevent entirely the criminal action or to ideally address such violations as an after-the-fact mechanism in the form of accountability. With any type of offending, this typically is in the form of formal social controls such as laws and/or regulations that can act as deterrents or provide accountability, punishment, or sanctions.

As a control, laws are indeed present and, as was noted by Rothe and Mullins (2006c, 2007a) and Mullins and Rothe (2008), deterrence based on extant laws should be more promising for actors committing state crimes than that of traditional street crime due to the social integration and position of most potential offenders. As street crime and white collar crime research has shown, social location and position strongly influence deterrence (see, for example, Berk et al. 1992; Paternoster and Piquero 1995; Paternoster and Simpson 1996; Piquero and Paternoster 1998; Stafford and Warr 1993). Those actors most likely to be involved in these types of crimes would seem to be those who are most influenceable by law. On the other hand, the work of Tittle (1995) suggests that the social positions and general practices of militia leaders would not be as likely to be deterred by the law due to the levels of power and control they wield. Consequently, deterrence could potentially serve as a control only if continued prosecutions for these types of crimes occur via the International Criminal Court (ICC). For example, the ICC claims that its indictments have simultaneously reduced the violence within Northern Uganda and compelled the LRA back into peace talks (Agirre 2007). Further, such controls can also be nationally generated but locally implemented (e.g., the gacacas in Rwanda [see Havermen 2007]).

Causal Logic

While the discussion above identifies and describes key etiological factors functioning at all levels of analysis, in and of itself, it does not specifically identify and discuss "causal" relations. In order to build a thoroughly predictive model, Mullins and Rothe (2008) have specified and detailed such relationships. The chart presented in figure 5.2 has a slight variation of that causal relationship.

To elucidate the causal relationship among the important catalysts discussed above, Mullins and Rothe have drawn upon the idea of nodes of interconnection (Tittle 1995). Following Control Balance Theory, they proposed that the various elements of theoretical significance examined above come to influence social structure and behavior through points of intersection (e.g., the boxes numbered 1–4 in figure 5.3). While the important theoretical issues operate at multiple levels of analysis, at the end of the day, so to speak, a crime is still committed by an individual social actor(s) once a decision to offend has been made.

Crimes have multi-level causes and, in many cases, the social actor is a member of an organization; nonetheless, the specific criminal action is still individualized in its commission after, albeit bounded, a decision. Thus, one should examine the aggregate effects of a catalyst at the different levels of analysis above the micro level as they come together to create a social force that works to affect the decision-making process of whether or not to offend—the decision-making "moment" or monad. While it is possible, for example, to identify motivational forces at all four levels of analysis, functionally, they all produce or enhance the motivation within individuals (Mullins and Rothe 2008).

The opportunity point of intersection represents combined forces that govern the presentation or perception of opportunities to engage in violations of international criminal law. This is viewed as a set of combined opportunities, filtered through individual perception. The intersection of motivational relationships is similarly conceived. As constraints (and controls) tend to exist externally of individuals, Mullins and Rothe (2008) conceive of all four levels of analysis combining in effect to create a singular constraint intersection and a singular control intersection. They see constraints as not influencing motivation or opportunity directly but rather as reducing the perceived strength of the motivation and/or opportunity, thus affecting the monad of decision making and subsequent offending. While constraints and controls either block offending behavior or at least reduce or alter enactment patterns, they do not necessarily reduce motivational factors.

Figure 5.2. *Causal Model*

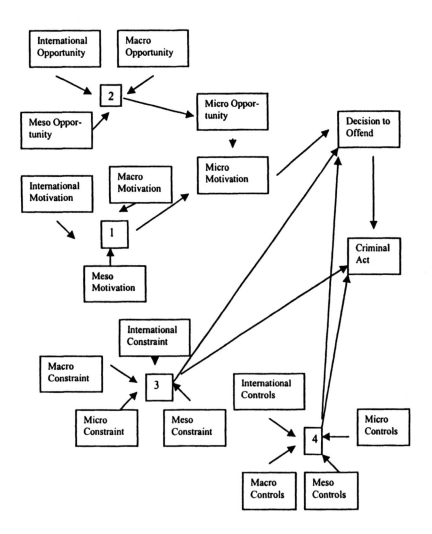

Revised Chart from Mullins and Rothe 2008; Rothe and Mullins 2009

Figure 5.3. *Causal Logic Model with Integrated Theory Variables*

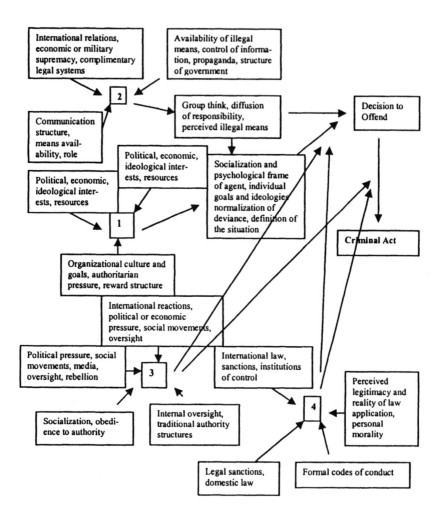

See also Rothe and Mullins 2009.

Chapter Summary

This chapter has focused on theoretical explanations for understanding state crime. The overall premise guiding this section is that traditional criminological theories have much to offer for our understanding of the worst crimes and criminals. However, standing alone, each has barriers for a complete understanding. While I do not claim that a true, complete understanding will ever occur, an integrationist approach provides the best option due to the complexities and multiple forms that undergird these crimes.

Notes

1. These include operative goals, subunit goals, and managerial goals.

Chapter 6

State Crimes by Types of Government: Democratic

Behind the ostensible government sits enthroned an invisible government owing no allegiance and acknowledging no responsibility to the people. To destroy this invisible government, to befoul the unholy alliance between corrupt business and corrupt politics, is the first task of the statesmanship of the day.

Theodore Roosevelt, 1906

There are a variety of forms of state criminality, as has been pointed out in previous chapters. As noted by Barak (1991: ix), "state criminality knows no economic, ideological, or geographical boundaries . . . it can be found in the Eastern and Southern as well as the Western and Northern Hemispheres." Nonetheless, when we look at the various examples already given in previous chapters, a theme begins to emerge. Simply, "the nature, patterns, or seriousness of state crime will not necessarily be the same for all types of state formation" (Barak 1990: x). Consequently, the following two chapters attempt to draw out this matter more clearly by delineating crimes of the state by types of government using a comparative approach. After all, we do know that the comparative approach has proved fruitful for understanding the types of governments that are more likely to participate in torture. Additionally, autocratic regimes have been more likely to engage in severe repression of oppositional groups, lending to crimes against humanity, human rights violations, and genocides (Harff 2005). Keeping this in mind, this chapter draws from the "typical" forms of state crime and common structural and enactment patterns associated with federal republics (those with more than one-party systems), democracies, and parliamentary governmental structures. It is also important to note that some of the literature on types of state regime consider parliamentary and republic governments as democratic institutions, thus making clear distinctions between these specific three forms problematic and subjective. After all, is not Britain a democratic society yet also classified as parliamentary? Therefore, the three state structures are presented together in an effort to illustrate some overall commonalities compared to other types of regime compositions.

The Democratic, Parliamentary, and Republic Multi-Party States

Of the 192 countries, 132 are said to fit into the categories of democratic, parliamentary, and republic forms of government. It must be noted though that such classifications vary according to who defines the governmental structure; also, most governments contain characteristics of, or are classified as, more than one form of rule. For example, the U.S. is considered a democracy, yet more clearly is a federal republic where the people elect representatives to make laws. China, on the other hand, is considered an authoritarian or communist state, yet calls itself the People's Republic of China. Some countries labeled as republics are one-party ruled, thus not fitting into the category of republic as defined in this chapter. Further, any typology will have exceptions—those that do not fit in such classifications. Although almost half of the countries are considered democracies, the number of "full democracies" is relatively low with a mere 28 qualifying and with twice as many, or 54 states, that are rated as "flawed democracies," according to the 2007 Economic Intelligence Report (Kekic 2007). Nonetheless, the states discussed in this chapter are typically the most empowered countries in the world—economically, politically, and militarily. Of the remaining 85 states, the EI Report states that 55 are authoritarian and 30 are considered to be hybrid regimes and will be discussed further in the following chapter.

The countries listed as full democracies by the EI Report include by ranking: Sweden, Iceland, Netherlands, Norway, Denmark, Finland, Luxemberg, Australia, Canada, Switzerland, Ireland, New Zealand, Germany, Austria, Malta, Spain, United States, Czech Republic, Portugal, Belgium, Japan, Greece, United Kingdom, France, Mauritias, Costa Rica, Slovenia, and Uruguay.

The types of crimes that are committed by full democracies, parliamentary, or federal republics have historically been through indirect or covert means (state-sponsored assignations and terrorism; funded, supported, or initiated coups or insurgencies; counter-insurgencies; covert or low-intensity warfare; violation of sanctions including arm embargoes [in collusion with corporations], and/or renditions); and, perhaps more significantly, have been enacted against other countries and their citizenry, typically without the consent or knowledge of their citizenry. As noted by Barak (1991: 5), "Low intensity warfare is designed not only to defend empire against rising challenges from the poor but also to conceal from [their] citizens the unpleasant consequences of empire" (see the illustration below of the U.S. dirty war on Nicaragua).

Democratic states, republics, and parliamentary states also participate in assassinations of heads of states. Recall from chapter 3 the examples given and the poignant argument put forth by Michael Bohlander on the moral dilemma of assassinations versus the death of innocent civilians caught when states attempt to remove or kill a leader of a sovereign country or strong opposition to the extant administration. With the ideology that "killing a man is murder unless you do it to the sound of trumpets" (Voltaire, quoted in Elibron Quotations), states have indeed violated international laws prohibiting such actions since World War I. Consider the recent (2006) case where "Former KGB officer Alexander Litvinenko, who passed away late last week from what many intelligence officials have indicated they believe to be a state-sponsored assassination, was likely the victim of the Russian Foreign Intelligence Service, Sluzhba Vneshney Razvedki (SVR)" (Alexandrovna 2006: 1). Allegations of the United States' involvement in assassination plots against officials in Cuba, Vietnam, the Congo, the Dominican Republic in the 1960s, and Chile in the 1970s are also examples of political assassinations and/or attempts to assassinate. Of course, the states discussed here readily deny or have denied until such involvement is proven.

Similarly, the types of governmental structures discussed here have had a long history of initiating or facilitating coups or sponsoring by proxy insurgencies and counterinsurgencies. After the assassination of Kennedy in 1963, the CIA's use of covert operation programs or SAPs increased on a dramatic scale (Vidgen 1995). For example, the United States' intervention throughout Central America dates back to the 1800s and the Monroe Doctrine; few countries were as extensively and repeatedly intervened in as Nicaragua. During the twentieth century, the United States exerted its dominance over Nicaragua by direct-armed intervention from 1912–1925 and 1926–1933, through the client dictatorship of the Somoza regime from 1936–1979, and in an effort to delegitimize and remove the Sandinista government from 1980–1990. Each of these periods reflects geopolitical and ideological interests of the United States. (For more details see the following illustration.)

The U.S. Dirty War in Nicaragua

Nicaragua became a test case of the Reagan Administration for using low intensity warfare to reinstate U.S. power, domestically and internationally, that had been weakened from the Cold War and U.S. actions in Vietnam. For example, the first foreign policy issues acted on by the incoming Reagan Administration involved Nicaragua. These included policy initiatives such as economic isolationism; creating, solidifying, and supporting the Contras indirectly and directly; and militaristic covert interventions.

Early in 1981, U.S. economic assistance to Nicaragua was terminated and the Reagan Administration began anti-Sandinista paramilitary training in Florida, California, and Texas (Walker 2003). Economic isolationism also included using the position of the U.S. in the World Bank and Inter American Development Bank to stop all multilateral and bilateral loans for Nicaragua.

The first "Presidential Finding on Central America," submitted to Congress March 9, 1981, set the stage for the $19 million to be used for clandestine assistance of anti-Sandinista paramilitary groups. In December 1981, Reagan made official his intentions to dismantle the government of Nicaragua with the signing of a Directive 17 granting the CIA $19.8 million to create a paramilitary force in Honduras to aid in the execution of the covert war.

By the start of 1982, "Project Democracy," the official name given to the mission by the Administration, was underway. The U.S. payrolled paramilitary force (Contras) targeted objects (e.g., bridges, oil refineries, cement plants, clinics, daycare centers, and other infrastructures) as well as persons (e.g., civilians, health officials, educators, and public officials). By 1982, the Contra forces had built up to 4,000 persons. Seeing their covert activities as semi-successful, the Reagan Administration proclaimed, "the Sandinistas are under increasing pressures as a result of our covert efforts" (National Security Council Document 1982: 84). What was projected to the Congressional oversight and the general population of the U.S. (using the Contras to pressure and harass the Nicaraguan government) was different than the realpolitik wherein the Contras were being used to conduct vicious attacks on small villages, agricultural co-ops, civilians, children, and any force deemed necessary by the CIA and NSA (National Security Force) to overthrow the Sandinista regime. As noted by then CIA Director Stansfield Turner (1985, quoted in Chomsky 2002), the policy had become "terrorism, as State supported terrorism."

During the latter part of 1982, there was an increase in Contra activities and joint military adventures between the U.S. and Honduras (one of the locations of the U.S. military base where the Contras are trained, funded, and supplied). These actions were embedded in the earlier policy of economic and political isolationism, including the Administration's attempts to end loans to Nicaragua through political pressure and its weight in the international finance institutions including the World Bank (WB) and International Monetary Fund (IMF), political pressure on Western European governments to support the Contras, and verbal public attacks against the Sandinista government, all in an effort to isolate Nicaragua diplomatically from other states. In October 1983, U.S. Army counterinsurgency specialist John Kirkpatrick created a 92-page manual for the CIA called Psychological Operations in Guerilla Warfare. The manual outlined the most efficient means to (1) assassinate civilians, (2) use selective force against civilian leaders that are pro Sandinista, (3) use fear and terror to win the hearts and minds of the peasantry, and (4) use soft targets such as healthcare facilities and other social structures. The manual was cleared and approved by CIA officials at Langley Headquarters, where 2,000 copies were then ordered and over 200 distributed to the FDN (Nicaraguan Democratic

Federation—a branch of the Contra forces) to be used in training the Contras.

The CIA continued to use their agents as well as a specially trained force of "unilaterally controlled Latino assets" (UCLA) that were contract operatives (i.e., mercenaries) from Salvador, Chile, Argentina, Honduras, Bolivia, and Ecuador. The CIA and UCLA operations included deploying floating gunfire simulators offshore to aggravate tensions amongst the Nicaraguan Army guarding the coastal installations. While such practices had been ongoing over the past two years, the formal legitimization and standard operating practices acted to enhance the scope of attacks. For example, during September 1983, the CIA conducted direct attacks on Nicaraguan ports at Puerto Sandino and sabotaged an underwater pipeline. In October 1983, the CIA and UCLA attacked the largest Nicaraguan port with grenades and mortars (igniting 3.4 million gallons of fuel, killing over 100 civilians, and causing evacuations of 25,000) (Walker 2003). The Reagan Administration did not stop at these sabotorial types of attacks. In June 1983, three U.S. diplomats were implicated in an assassination plot against the Nicaraguan Foreign Minister, Father Miguel d'Escoto (Dixon and Jonas 1984).

In December 1983, Reagan approved the National Security Council (NSC) proposal to escalate the operations against the Nicaraguan government. This included an intensification of attacks against their ports, power plants, bridges, and other infrastructures (Walker 2003). The NSC's policy marked the beginning of several forthcoming years that were wrought with webs of secrecy and intensified violence. By the end of 1983, the estimated costs of attacks against Nicaragua amounted to over $2 billion; mass infrastructure damage resulted in a state of emergency being called in Nicaragua. Over 300 rural schools were forced to shut with over 53 teachers killed. In addition, there were 800 civilians killed, 715 wounded, 37 individuals "disappeared," 433 kidnapped, and over a dozen health facilities destroyed (Dixon and Jonas 1984).

The following year, 1984, was witness to continued devastation in Nicaragua. Contra attacks against the Nicaraguan regime continued by air and sea. Additionally, other arenas were beginning to pay the price for the Administration's policies and war, including internal U.S. and international politics. In January 1984, a crew on board a U.S. helicopter violated Nicaraguan airspace while setting the stage to expand the Contra base in Honduras and scoping soft and hard targets for future air raid. In response, the Nicaraguan government shot down the helicopter. In fulfillment of Reagan's December 1983 approval for the CIA to mine Nicaragua's harbors in January and February of 1984, the Atlantic and Pacific harbors were mined with underwater explosives packed with 300-pound C-4 explosives (Walker 2003). As noted by United States District Court for the Southern District of New York Decision No. 86 Civ. 2500 (1986: 1), "the Central Intelligence Agency [CIA], with the approval of the President, manufactured the mines and supervised and directed their placement, and that it carried out these acts in a negligent, malicious or wanton manner."

By the end of the Reagan Administration's term, the damage done to Nicaragua was staggering, yet the goal of replacing the Sandinista regime, President Ortega, was never accomplished. Between 1980 and 1987, the death toll stood at approximately 31,290 Nicaraguans, with an additional 20,681

casualties and 120,324 citizens displaced, including approximately 7,852 or-
phans. The economic devastation caused by the U.S. role and support of the
Contras was estimated at roughly $4 billion (Burns 1987).

State-sponsored terrorism is common to all types of governmental structures. However, the means to which it is done is drastically different. Three
different ways that states can engage in the use of terror are:

- Governmental or state terror
- State involvement in terror
- State sponsorship of terrorism

The first category is the one typically associated with government structures
such as military juntas, authoritarian regimes, dictatorships, communism, theocracies, one-party republics, and totalitarian regimes. Governments terrorize their
own population to control or repress. These actions are usually a part of the
formal policy of the regime and use official state institutions including the judiciary, police, military, paramilitary groups, or other government agencies. On
the other hand, when we talk about state-sponsored terrorism by democratic,
federal republics, or parliamentary governments, we need to note that it is typically carried out by proxy or using deep covert methods—state involvement in
terror and state sponsorship of terrorism. Consider that, since WWII, many
states have used covert activities for the pursuit of state or individual interests.
For example, the French have been accused of having their police covertly acting in Spain and sponsoring the GAL (antiterrorist liberation group) death
squads in their war against the leftist and Basque separatists. In Spain, numerous
groups such as the Guerrilleros de Cristo Rey, Batallón Vasco Español, Antiter-
rorismo ETA (ATE), and Grupos Antiterroristas de Liberación (GAL), alleged
to consist of Spanish police and funded with secret money, violently attacked
suspected members of the ETA (Vidgen 1995).

States have long used "puppet" terrorist organizations to act on behalf of the
sponsoring state, thus allowing an administration to effectively wage a low-
intensity war against rivals without risking discovery or political backlash. As an
example, the U.S., along with French intelligence, assembled from all over a
mercenary army of approximately 100,000, drawing from the most militant
sectors they could find, namely Islamic fundamentalists including bin Laden, to
oppose the Russian occupation of Afghanistan. They were trained, armed, and
organized by the CIA and others to fight a holy war against the Russians, which
they did and eventually won. Of course, this relationship has indeed resulted in a
backlash for the U.S., as this same al Qaeda group the U.S. created and supported is now labeled as a terrorist group. Additionally, states have used covert
means to commit terrorist acts. Consider that, in 1987, France confessed to per-

p:trating an act of terrorism. In 1985, secret service agents working under the Foreign Intelligence Service (DGSE), headed by Defense Minister Charles Hernu, destroyed the Greenpeace Rainbow Warrior ship that was believed to be used to hamper French nuclear tests in the Pacific Ocean. The ship was destroyed under the orders of the French government (Wolfreys 2000).

Beyond the sponsorship or creation of puppet terrorist groups or the destruction of goods to initiate fear, the forms of states discussed in this chapter have sponsored terrorism by supplying military goods. The U.S. has, for example, "sold billions of dollars worth of arms and ammunition to client states all over the world; those countries have used these munitions for state terrorist activities" (Friedrichs 1996b: 136). Friedrichs notes that, in the early 1980s in El Salvador, "well over 10,000 people were murdered in a single year by government forces supported by the United States and as many as 70,000 may have been kidnapped and tortured to death" (136). The U.S., via the CIA, has also funneled support to "corrupt totalitarian leaders it viewed as supportive of U.S. interests." In turn, the supported dictatorships have actively committed state terrorism upon their own population (see also chapter 7 for discussion of Pinochet's rule of terror).

The exceptions to the crimes committed by these types of governmental structures that are typically done covertly include the crimes of aggression, torture, and war crimes that are directly against other states and their citizenry. On the other hand, oppression of segments of society or repression of civil disobedience against one's own population has been used involving surveillance, harassment, homicide, and imprisonment. However, the scale or magnitude and severity are markedly different than oppression and repression by other forms of governments. Furthermore, this is not to say that democratic governments do not violate human rights; however, such violations are of a different nature than the types of regimes that will be discussed in the following chapter. For example, in the case of democratic, parliamentary, or republic governments, human rights violations are typically in the form of reducing civil liberties and/or not recognizing to the full capacity these fundamental rights versus regimes that provide little to no civil rights from the get-go. Take the case of Germany, where the freedom of peaceful assembly and association is alleged to be guaranteed by the Universal Declaration of Human Rights. Yet, on October 28, "more than 300 police officers raided homes and meeting places of suspected neo-Nazi groups in Schleswig-Holstein" (U.S. Department of State Country Reports on Human Rights 2004: 3). During 1961, thousands of Algerian protesters took to the streets in France to demonstrate against a curfew in force in Paris. Over 200 Algerians were beat to death, shot, or drowned, and over 10,000 were interned and arrested. Another 50 were summarily executed in the Prefecture de Police courtyard (Wolfreys 2000). The U.S. has also committed human rights violations in the form of oppression and repression of civil disobedience (surveillance, harassment, homicide, and undue imprisonment).

The crime of aggression is indeed most likely to be associated with democratic, parliamentary, and federal republics—the highly empowered capitalistic countries. As discussed in chapter 3, the recent 2003 invasion and occupation of Iraq by the U.S. and UK is indeed such an example where a country invades a sovereign state to attain their economic, military, and political interests. Other U.S. military ventures include the invasion of Grenada (1983) and Panama (1989), the Gulf War against Iraq, and the bombing of Tripoli and Benghazi in Libya in 1986, which "have been condemned in various quarters as illegal or criminal" (Friedrichs 1995: 127). In the course of war, these types of governments also commit their fair share of war crimes (see chapter 2 for detailed discussion of these acts). For example, the U.S. was accused of deliberate, systematic, and large-scale bombardment of civilian targets, dwellings, villages, dams, dikes, medical establishments, leper colonies, schools, churches, pagodas, and historical and cultural monuments during the Vietnam War, including its actions in Cambodia (see chapter 8 for a discussion of these charges from the Russell International War Crimes Tribunal).

Consider that during the U.S. aggressive war against Iraq during the Gulf War, G. H. Bush and his administration

> flew 110,000 air sorties against Iraq, dropping 88,000 tons of bombs, nearly seven times the equivalent of the atomic bomb that destroyed Hiroshima. 93% of the bombs were free falling bombs, most dropped from higher than 30,000 feet. Of the remaining 7% of the bombs with electronically guided systems, more than 25% missed their targets, nearly all caused damage primarily beyond any identifiable target. Most of the targets were civilian facilities. (The Commission of Inquiry for the International War Crimes Tribunal for Iraq 1991: 3)

While torture is considered to be a war crime, it is also a crime in and of itself (see chapter 2 for the legal definition and relevant treaties). We may tend to think that democratic governments do not torture, especially given that democracy is often used as the model form of government for promoting human rights, freedom, and liberty. Yet, make no mistake, the countries with this type of government do indeed practice the use of torture (see example in chapter 3 of the U.S. torture that occurred in Abu Ghraib). As noted by Darius Rejali (2008: 1), "Historically, of course, torture has always happened in democracies. The Greeks and Romans, the Renaissance republics, all—even Britain, France and America were torturing in their colonies well before World War II." The U.S. has used torture as an integral part of its war on terrorism post 9/11/2001 (for a detailed discussion of the U.S. use of torture in Guantanamo, Afghanistan, and Iraq, see Rothe 2006 and Rothe et al. 2008). To relate to the types of torture used, consider the following testimonies from three torture victims who had been in Abu Ghraib:

Detainee #151365

I entered Abu Ghraib 10 July 2003 . . . they put me in a tent and then brought me to the Hard Site. The first day they put me in a dark room and started hitting me in the head and stomach and legs. They made me raise my hands and sit on my knees; I was like that for four hours. Then the interrogator came and he was looking at me while they were beating me. Then I stayed in this room for 5 days, naked with no clothes . . . they replaced the Army with the Iraqi police and after time they started punishing me in all sorts of ways. And the first punishment was bringing me to room one, and they put handcuffs on my hand and they cuffed me high for 7 to 8 hours. They kept me this way on 24, 25, and 26 October. The following days they put a bag over my head, and I was without clothes and without anything to sleep on. In November they started a different type of punishment, where an American Police came in to my room and put the bag over my head and cuffed my hands and he took me out of the room into the hallway. He started beating me, him and 5 other American Police. Some of the things they did was make me sit down like a dog and they would hold the string from the bag and they made me bark like a dog. And the policeman was tan color because he hit my head to the wall. When he did that the bag came off my head and one of the police was telling me to crawl in Arabic, so I crawled on my stomach and the police were spitting on me and hitting me on my back, my head, and my feet. It kept going on until 4 in the morning. The same thing would happen in the following days. And I remember one of the police hit me on my ear; then the police started beating me on my kidneys and then they hit me on my right ear and it began bleeding and I lost consciousness. The American Police put red woman's underwear over my head and then tied me to the window in my cell with my hands behind my back until I lost consciousness. When I was in Room #1, they told me to lay down on my stomach and they were jumping from the bed onto my back and my legs, others were spitting on me and calling me names and they held my hands and legs. Then two officers tied my hands to the door while laying down on my stomach. One of the police was pissing on me and laughing. He released my hands and I went and washed and then the soldier came back into the room and the soldier's friend told me to lie down, so I did that. And then the policeman was opening my legs, with a bag over my head, and he sat down between my legs on his knees and I was looking at him from under the bag and they wanted to do me because I saw him and he was opening his pants, so I started screaming and other police starting hitting me with his feet on my neck and he put his feet on my head so I couldn't scream. They left and the guy with glasses comes back with another person and he took me out of the room and they put me inside the dark room again and they started beating me with the broom that was there. Then they broke the glowing finger and spread it on me until I get on to the floor. And one of the police he put a part of his stick that he always carried inside my ass and I felt it going inside me about 2 centimeters. And I stated screaming and he pulled it out . . . and the two American girls that were there when they were beating me, they were hitting me with a ball made of sponge on my dick . . . one of the girls was playing with my dick . . . And they were taking pictures of me during all these instances.

Detainee #151108

They stripped me of all my clothes, even my underwear. They gave me woman's underwear . . . and they put a bag over my face. One of them whispered in my ear "today I am going to fuck you" and he said this in Arabic. Whoever was with me experienced the same thing. This was on October 3 or 4, 2003 . . . when they took me to the cell an American soldier and his rank was sergeant I believe he called me faggot because I was wearing woman's underwear and my answer was no . . . And they forced me to wear this underwear for 51 days . . . and most of the days I was wearing nothing else. I faced harsh punishment from Grainer. He cuffed my hands with irons behind my back to the metal of the window, to the point my feet were off the ground and I was hanging there for about 5 hours just because I asked about that time because I wanted to pray. And then they took off my clothes and he took the female underwear and he put it over my head. After he released me from the window, he tied me to my bed until before dawn. He prohibited me from eating food. They took pictures of everything they did to me. . . . I don't know if they took a picture of me because they beat me so bad I lost consciousness after an hour or so. They did not give us food for a whole day and night. Now I am talking about what I saw. They brought three prisoners naked and tied them together with cuffs and they stuck one to another. I saw American soldiers hitting them with a football and they were taking pictures. I saw Grainer punching one of the prisoners right in his face very hard . . . and the American soldiers told to do like homosexuals (fucking). I saw . . . fucking a kid, his age would be about 15. The kid was hurting very bad and they covered all the doors with sheets. Then when I heard the screaming I climbed the door because on top it wasn't covered and I saw who was wearing the military uniform putting his dick in the little kid's ass and the female soldier was taking pictures and that was in cell #23. On the North side, I was right across from it on the other side, they put sheets again on the doors and they cuffed one prisoner in room 1, they tied him to the bed and they were inserting the phosphoric light in his ass and he was yelling for God's help . . . used to get hit and punished a lot because I heard him screaming and they prohibited us from standing near the door when they do that. Not one night for all the time I was there passed without me seeing, hearing, or feeling what was happening to me.

Detainee #150422

First they tortured the man whose name is Anjid Iraqi. They stripped him of his clothes and beat him until he passed out and they cursed him and when they took off his head I saw blood running from his head. They took him to solitary confinement. The evening shift was sad for prisoners. They brought three prisoners handcuffed to each other and they pushed the first one on top of the others to look like they are gay, when they refused they beat them up until they put them on top of each other and took pictures of them. They beat up an Iraqi whom they ordered to stand on a food carton and they went pouring water on him and it was the coldest of times. When they tortured him they took gloves and they beat his dick and testicles with the gloves and they handcuffed him to the cell door for a half day without food or water. After that they brought young Iraqi prisoners and tortured them by pouring water on them from the second floor until one of them started crying and screaming saying my heart. They brought six people and they beat them up until they dropped to the floor and one of them his nose was cut and the blood was running from his nose and he was screaming but no one was responding. The doctor came to stitch the nose and the Grainer asked the doctor to learn how to stitch and its true the guard learned how to stitch. After that they beat up the rest of the group until they fall to the ground. Grainer beat up a man . . . and he was beating him until he gotten almost crazy . . . and after they put him in his cell for four days they were pouring water on him and he couldn't sleep. They hanged him and he was screaming but no one helped.

(Testimonies recorded in the Taguba Report and cited in Rothe 2006)

The British army had also been accused of torture when they detained members of the Irish Republican Provincial in 1971. They were said to have used methods that included sensory deprivation, prolonged wall standing, hooding and "deprivation of food, water, and sleep" (Ross 1995: 13). The French army also has been charged with using torture and murder in Algeria between 1954 and 1962. As explained by then General Paul Aussaresses, director of the French secret service in Algiers, over 3,000 prisoners that were considered to have "disappeared" had in reality been executed. He also revealed that torture and murder were an integral part of France's war policy.

While not synonymous with torture, the practice of covert renditions of prisoners is also regrettably an all too common phenomenon. Take, for example, that prior to September 11, 2001, U.S. covert practice of rendering detainees abroad as well as interrogating them in secret did indeed exist (e.g., Guatemala 1984–1986); however, post September 11, 2001, the practice surged (Rothe 2006). It is now known that over 100 individuals have been detained as ghost detainees: those being secretly detained without being recorded or identified to any MP or MI personnel, essentially disappeared persons (Hersh 2004a). The Central Intelligence Agency secretly operated covert and illegal prisons for "terrorist" suspects in multiple locations including Egypt, Poland, and Romania from 2003 to 2005. A recent article in *The New Yorker* by Mayer (2005) titled "Outsourcing Torture" revealed details about how the G. W. Bush Administration embraced the use of renditions. Several other press reports detail the CIA's use of its fleet of Gulfstream V and Boeing 737 jets to secretly transfer detainees to states around the world, where they will be tortured. Take the case of Mr. Arar, discussed by Senator Patrick Leahy (2005: 1):

Mr. Arar, a Canadian and Syrian citizen, was stopped by immigration officers at John F. Kennedy International Airport in September 2002 as he attempted to change planes on his way home to Canada from Tunisia. He claims that he was interrogated by an FBI agent and a New York City police officer, and that he was denied access to a lawyer. He further claims that he repeatedly told U.S. officials that he feared he would be tortured if deported to Syria. After being detained for nearly two weeks in a federal detention center in New York, Mr. Arar was transferred by U.S. authorities to Syria and held at the Bush Administration's request. Mr. Arar claims that he was physically tortured during the first two weeks of his detention in Syria, and that he was subjected to severe psychological abuse over the following 10 months, including being held in a grave-like cell and being forced to undergo interrogation while hearing the screams of other prisoners.

If we take into account the hybrid forms of state crime, state-corporate or crimes of globalization, we can see that they too are more often than not closely correlated with parliamentary, democratic, or republic regimes (with more than one-party system), or, as other scholars of state crime have suggested, crimes by the capitalist state (Barak 1991). After all, it has been argued that since modernization, democracy and capitalism have been interlinked and are viewed as inevitably linked as one. According to Dahl (1998: 166), "Democracy and market capitalism are like two persons bound in a tempestuous marriage that is driven by conflict and yet endures because neither partner wishes to separate from the other." Dahl suggests that capitalism and democracy are so tightly enmeshed because laissez-faire capitalism requires government intervention in the form of regulatory laws and policies to ensure a working market economy; thus, state and capital have a common interest and goal. Dahl continues to note that the need to intervene in economic conditions by states creates an environment where economic decisions override morality and politics, inevitably inflicting harm on some people. "The historical record is clear: in all democratic countries, the harm produced by, or expected from, unregulated markets has induced governments to intervene in order to alter an outcome that would otherwise cause damage to some citizens" (Dahl 1998: 175). While not causally linked, it is the case that all the countries listed above as full democracies are indeed capitalistic in their mode of production. Nonetheless, a democratic government structure may be sufficient for capitalism but not necessary. Consider that Chile under Pinochet's military junta rule (see chapter 2) was also a capitalistic economy. Pinochet, with counsel of U.S. economists and international financial institutions, implemented laissez-faire, free-market, neoliberal, and fiscally conservative policies, where market forces guided most of the economy's decisions (Klein 2007). Yet, the crimes committed by Pinochet were typical with the forms of government including military juntas, authoritarian, dictatorships, and communism (forced disappearances, torture, imprisonment, human rights violations, and crimes against humanity).

Nevertheless, as noted by Michalowski (2008), whether it is the U.S. invasion and occupation of Iraq or the Russian counterinsurgency in Chechnya, modern corporate states stand quite ready to commit modern atrocities in their pursuit of power, that is, to kill, maim, and orphan tens of thousands of civilians. Pilots and other warriors in service of capitalist states, as well as the citizens who support them, have been convinced that the only way to preserve their society is to push the button or pull the trigger that will turn civilians by the hundreds into dead "collateral damage" (Collins and Glover 2002; Rothe et al. 2009). It has been suggested that states, in an effort to defend the interests of the elite class, will, "if necessary, systematically break either its own laws or those of another country" (Wolfreys 2000: 142). As noted by Heinz Dieterich, the material debasement of "the majority of Latin American peoples is an inevitable consequence of the current capitalist accumulation model" (quoted in Barak 1991: 10). Similarly, "the accumulation and expansion of capital, and the preservation and extension of its conditions of existence, remain the major determinants of domestic and international state activities in societies with capitalist economies" (Pearce 2003: xi). The dominance of transnational corporations comes into play in the more egregious cases of state crimes of the past decades and is often more in line with opportunistic profit taking than any central role in motivating or facilitating mass criminal atrocities. For example, recent examinations of illegal mineral expropriation in the Democratic Republic of Congo (DRC) during and after the Second Congolese War highlight the role that transnational corporations and international marketplaces (i.e., the Swiss FreePort system) played in facilitating Rwanda and Uganda's theft of Congolese gold from the Ituri region of Orientale Province (see Mullins and Rothe 2008; Rothe and Mullins 2006). However, it should be noted that these companies did not directly encourage the conflict or even the massive human rights violations and crimes against humanity committed in the region. The corporations were simply taking advantage of existing disorder and violence and worked in collusion with such regimes, militias, and/or paramilitary forces. Moreover, environmental crimes, as noted in chapter 1, are most likely to be a form of state-corporate crime and are centered on profit-venturing efforts and often protected by states.

As previously noted, one of the more common crimes committed by democratic and capitalistic states, especially in collusion with corporations (state-corporate crime), is the illegal trade of arms—violating trade embargos (Green and Ward 2004). Consider that the U.S. and Britain, in collusion with major weapons manufacturers including British Aerospace (BAe) and Lockhead Martin, were core to the arming of the Indonesian army's occupation of East Timor. As Jackson (2001: 45) stated, "the U.S. supplied over 90% of the weapons used by the Indonesian military in the invasion of East Timor." Then in 1996, the British government awarded BAe an additional trade agreement that included a large shipment of Hawk 16 fighter aircraft and arms. As noted by Green and Ward (2004: 40), the occupation of East Timor by Indonesia, which was secured and armed by the U.S. and Britain, "resulted in the deaths of 200,000 East Timorese, representing a quarter to a third of the overall population."

Britain and British companies were also implicated in the breaching of the arms embargo on Sierra Leone to facilitate Sandline International's role in Sierra Leone. As noted by Human Rights Watch (1999a), the "involvement of Sandline stirred controversy as its sale of arms and ammunitions to President Kabbah, with the approval of the UK government, appeared to constitute a violation of the embargo, which the UK had been instrumental in bringing about." The same practice occurred when Dresser, Inc., a subsidiary of Halliburton, did substantial business with Iraq from 1997 through the summer of 2000, closing

$73 million worth of deals with Saddam Hussein at a time when such dealings were prohibited by international trade sanctions. Many of these contracts occurred under the United Nation's oil for food program through joint ventures with the Ingersoll-Rand Company via subsidiaries known as the Dresser-Rand and Ingersoll Dresser Pump Companies. Although Cheney claimed that Halliburton divested itself of the subsidiaries in 1998, as soon as the company learned of the trading in violation of U.S. legislation prohibiting business ventures while Iraq was under sanctions by the U.S. and the UN (Kristof 2005), the firms continued trading with Baghdad for over a year past the time of Cheney's initial "awareness" (Rothe 2006). In 2002, the U.S. Securities and Exchange Commission investigated a bribery case involving Halliburton and Nigeria. Halliburton admitted that its employees paid a $2.4 million bribe to a government official of Nigeria for the purpose of receiving favorable tax treatment in violation of the U.S. Foreign Corrupt Practices Act and the convention adopted by the Organization for Economic Cooperation and Development prohibiting bribe-giving in the course of commercial transactions.

While, indeed, political corruption occurs in these types of state structures as well, it is of a different form and extensiveness that occurs, as will be illustrated in the following chapter. If you recall from chapter 1's discussion of the various types of state criminality, there are two main forms of corruption: political corruption, which includes the rigging of electoral processes and/or lack of transparency; and economic corruption, which includes misusing state funds, receiving kickbacks, or using black market monies. When we limit the discussion of corruption to the types of governmental structures discussed in this chapter, we see that the lack of transparency and the rigging of electoral process have indeed occurred. Take, for example, the 2004 scandal of G. W. Bush's second-term election and accusations that the Republican Party had rigged several state voting outcomes. Consider also the general lack of transparency of the government that has occurred in the U.S. recently through increased legislation and executive orders. Recall also the example used in chapter 1 for state-corporate crime with Halliburton's war profiteering and the connection to Vice President Dick Cheney (for a more detailed analysis of the case, see Rothe 2006). Similarly, David Shayler, a former British Intelligence agent, became a whistle-blower in 1997 when he revealed rampant corruption within both arms of the British intelligence agencies, domestic and foreign. Part of the allegations included linking the British government with a payment of $160,000 to an Islamic militant group after a failed assassination attempt on Colonel Mu'ammar al-Qadhafi of Libya. The figure on page 129 (figure 6.1) illustrates the level of corruption with a list of the top twenty corrupt states and the twenty least corrupt countries.

It should be noted that corruption, as defined by Transparency International (2008), includes what I have termed *occupational crime*. As such, the levels of state corruption, an agent of the state committing acts of corruption on behalf of the state, would be slightly less but is still reflected in the chart.

Figure 6.1. *Levels of Corruption*

Top 20 Corrupt States			Top 20 Least Corrupt States		
Rank		Score	Rank		Score
180	Somalia	1.0	18	Belgium	7.3
178	Iraq	1.3	18	Japan	7.3
178	Myanmar	1.3	18	USA	7.3
177	Haiti	1.4	16	Ireland	7.7
176	Afghanistan	1.5	16	United Kingdom	7.7
173	Chad	1.6	14	Germany	7.9
173	Guinea	1.6	14	Norway	7.9
173	Sudan	1.6	12	Austria	8.1
171	DRC	1.7	12	Hong Kong	8.1
171	Equatorial Guinea	1.7	11	Luxembourg	8.3
166	Cambodia	1.8	9	Australia	8.7
166	Kyrgyzstan	1.8	9	Canada	8.7
166	Turkmenistan	1.8	7	Iceland	8.9
166	Uzbekistan	1.8	7	Netherlands	8.9
166	Zimbabwe	1.8	5	Finland	9.0
158	Angola	1.9	5	Switzerland	9.0
158	Azerbaijan	1.9	4	Singapore	9.2
158	Burundi	1.9	1	Denmark	9.3
158	Congo Republic	1.9	1	New Zealand	9.3
158	Gambia	1.9	1	Sweden	9.3

The previously discussed criminal acts by states are most commonly associated with democratic, republican, or parliamentary forms of government. While such commonalities do suggest a theme for the type of crimes by the state, there are also other structural factors that are familiar to these types of political apparatuses.

Other Structural Commonalities

Beyond the typology for types of regimes and crimes committed, a common central theme runs through each of the crimes discussed here regardless of the type of regime: capital accumulation or capital maintenance—social, economic, or political. The term *capital* is being used here to put an emphasis on conflicts and the power function in societies. Social, economic, and political capital consists of resources in the larger social struggles that are carried out in different social/political arenas and can be used to produce or reproduce inequality. The two most common structural variables of the types of crimes committed by these regimes are global economics and the nature and direction of power. As noted by Green and Ward (2004: 186), "In some forms of state crime we can see a very direct relationship between political economy and the motivation of the perpetrators." After all, global economics involve more than ensuring domestic economic or short-term stability. As rightly stated by Barak (1991: 275), the pursuit of state interests and subsequent criminality is often the result of "long range goals of controlling natural resources, labor and markets of other countries." This was true dating back to the expansionism of colonial holdings and remains so today, though the form is different.

Global economics has indeed factored into many of the crimes that are committed by democratic, republic, or parliamentary states that also have capitalism as their economic mode. Whether we are talking about state crime, state-corporate crime, or crimes of globalization, the economy is a significant factor, most notably as a form of capital accumulation that lends to additional political accumulation. Whether through the implicit support of corporations, the direct use of corporations (e.g., private warriors or for profit mercenaries), or international financial institutions that are backed by these types of governments, multiple examples can be given of the collusion that results or enables state criminality. As stated by Green and Ward (2004: 186), "transnational financial institutions play a significant role in the encouragement of state crime." Kramer (2006) also suggested that when dealing with highly capitalized and empowered countries, nearly all state crime can be considered a form of state-corporate crime.

Along the same lines is the desire to become or remain a global power. This was true when colonial empires were started and remains so today given that economic expansion under the protection of powerful guns continues to be justified in terms of delivering civilizing benefits, never in the name of what it is—imperialism (Michalowski and Kramer 2006). As Michalowski and Kramer (2006: 310) rightly noted:

> Throughout the late eighteenth and nineteenth centuries U.S. leaders sought to expand America's economic horizons through both acute and chronic applications of force, including enslavement of Africans, expropriation of Native lands in the name of "manifest destiny," the invasion of North African states to protect U.S. trade interests in that region, the claim of North and South America as an exclusive American sphere of economic and political influence (the Monroe Doctrine), the expansionist war with Mexico, and the use of American warships to ensure Asian trading partners.

If we look at Britain, we see similar acts of state crime during its extensive history of expansionism through force. For example, the Kenya Human Rights Commission (KHRC), in February 2008, filed a representative lawsuit against the British government in the British High Court on behalf of the survivors of the Mau Mau war for independence for "personal injuries sustained [by the survivors] while in detention camps of the Kenya Colonial Government, which operated under the authority of Britain between 1952 and 1960" (Wanyeki 2007).

The nature and direction of power is also relevant to the types of state criminality and, perhaps more importantly, to the tools with which they commit such acts. Along with the distribution of power is the need for political stability and legitimacy. The need for government legitimacy is especially important for how heads of state actualize their crimes. In other words, the very need for legitimacy and political stability will determine the path taken if the administration is determined to commit a state crime. It is these "means" or ways that I will next address.

Common Means to Accomplish State Criminality

When it comes to democracies, parliamentary governments, or multi-party republics, several common themes emerge as to the means used to commit such crimes in the post-colonialist era. As we will see in chapter 7, there are some that are common to all forms (otherizing, military threats and the use of fear), but those that are used most frequently with the government structures discussed in this chapter include the use of political, economic, and/or military threats by proxies and/or through covert or secretive means.

Covert operations can include using military and/or nonmilitary sources for assassination of foreign officials, regime change, destruction of civil or political property and institutions, subversion of elections, disinformation campaigns, state-sponsored terrorism, and illegal weapons sales. Consider that the United States has waged covert warfare around the world, including Afghanistan, Albania, Angola, Burma, Cambodia, Chad, Chile, China, Costa Rica, Cuba, Dominican Republic, El Salvador, Grenada, Guatemala, Honduras, Hungary, Indonesia, Iran, Laos, Lebanon, Libya, Nicaragua, North Korea, South Korea, Syria, Thailand, Vietnam, and Zaire. The example on page 117 of the U.S. war on Nicaragua is an excellent example of states using covert means to accomplish political, ideological, and economic interests via illegality. The U.S. war on Nicaragua was carried out covertly and by using proxies: the Contras. Proxies also include the use of private corporate warriors (for a more detailed discussion, see Singer 2004). Additionally, countries, including the U.S. and Britain, have secretly used illegal arms exports to embargoed regimes, thus acting covertly and using these other states or insurgencies within them as proxies to accomplish the goals of the sponsoring state. Take, as an example, the case of Britain, the U.S., and East Timor (Green and Ward 2004: 41):

> In December 1975, after U.S. Secretary of State Henry Kissinger returned from Jakarta, having given Suharto the green light to invade East Timor, he called his staff together and discussed *how a congressional ban on arms to Indonesia could be circumvented.*. "Can't we just construe a communist government as self-defense?" he asked. Told this would not work, Kissinger gave orders that he wanted arms shipments secretly started again in January.

If we recall one of the larger scandals under former President Reagan, the Iran/Contra affair, the U.S. acted in the same way by selling illegal arms to Iran for additional funding of the Contras. For example, in September 1985, the U.S. shipped 408 missiles to Iran as part of the secret "arms for hostages" deal; a day later, Benjamin Weir was released (in early 1986, 4,000 more missiles were shipped to Iran through Israel). Through a multifaceted web of international bank accounts, arms brokers, corporate fronts, and shipping companies, the CIA and Pentagon special operations sustained the flow of arms, cargo planes, ships, safe houses, communications gear, and other supportive aids to the Contras. In November 1986, the Administration was publicly exposed for their illegal sales of arms to Iran in return for U.S. hostages in Lebanon (Caruthers 1991).

The use of political, economic, and/or military threats is also common means for accomplishing state criminal activities. These can be direct threats of interventions or coercive means. As an example, consider that President G. W. Bush coerced the United Nations Security Council into an unprecedented series of resolutions, finally securing authority for any nation in its absolute discretion by all necessary means to enforce the resolutions against Iraq, when there was a counterforce acting to constrain the Administration when it wanted to conduct its illegal war on Iraq. To secure votes, the U.S. paid multi-billion dollar bribes, offered arms for regional wars, threatened and carried out economic retaliation, forgave multi-billion dollar loans (including a $7 billion loan to Egypt for arms), offered diplomatic relations despite human rights violations, and in other ways corruptly exacted votes, creating the appearance of near universal international approval of U.S. policies toward Iraq (International War Crimes Tribunal for Iraq 2007). Former President Reagan used coercive means and political pressure on international financial institutions and other countries in an effort to economically marginalize Nicaragua—economic strangulation.

The process of otherizing is also used, generally along with propaganda. Unlike the way in which the regimes mentioned in chapter 7 have used the otherizing in the form of ethnic or racial identities, the government structures discussed in this chapter typically label them as threats (communists) or outright evil. Recall President G. W. Bush's State of the Union address, where he labeled countries as the axis of evil, and terrorists as evil doers. Two weeks after September 11, Bush stated to the FBI, "The people who did this act on America, and who may be planning further acts, are evil people. They don't represent an ideology; they don't represent a legitimate political group of people. They're flat evil. That's all they can think about, is evil."[1] This statement was meant to support the Administration's decision to act, even if illegally, and/or to generate fear of these "others." Fear is indeed a key tool that states use to justify and neutralize their behaviors. While other forms of government use fear directly to ensure compliance (see chapter 7), the democracies, parliamentary governments, or republics use fear to garner support or as an ideology for the greater good. The following quotation sums up this connection well:

> Of course the people don't want war. But after all, it's the leaders of the country who determine the policy, and it's always a simple matter to drag the people along whether it's a democracy, a fascist dictatorship, or a parliament, or a communist dictatorship. Voice or no voice, the people can always be brought to the bidding of the leaders. That is easy. All you have to do is tell them they are being attacked, and denounce the pacifists for lack of patriotism, and exposing the country to greater danger.

Herman Goering at the Nuremberg Trials (1947: 278–279)

The use of ideology as a tool is omnipresent in the many examples cited in this text, whether it is promoted through straight propaganda or as a national identity and/or obligation, nationalism, values, or a moral stance, i.e., a free world—spreading democracy or human rights. Ironically, the above methods generally are presented as a way to ensure peace: peace through warfare, covert or overt. As Barak (1990: 279) rightly stated, "the Orwellian notion of peace through state-perpetrated warfare has certainly been a difficult process to shake." Also noted by Roy (2004: 56), "Democracy has become Empire's euphemism for neoliberal capitalism." Moreover, the highest stated value of democracy, liberty, has become what Gramsci (1995: 242) once anticipated: "a practical instrument of government used as an ideology to pursue international self-interests disguised as a human value."

Conclusion

This chapter has endeavored to draw out some common themes or patterns associated with specific forms of governments: democratic, parliamentary, or multi-party republics, which are also based on a capitalistic economy and typically highly empowered—politically, militarily, and economically—or, as Wallerstein (1974) noted, the core countries. As with all types of state crime, the motivational force is the attainment or maintenance of capital: social, economic, or political. However, this chapter has emphasized that the types of crime committed and the ways or tools used to carry out their criminality can be delineated by types of government structures. While this chapter has focused on the most powerful countries and their criminality, the following chapter will explore the typical crimes and means by which they are enacted by autocracies, dictatorships, communist governments, military juntas, theocracies, and one-party republics.

Notes

1. The statement is an excerpt from remarks made by Bush to the FBI on September 25, 2001, in a larger discussion of the Patriot Act. Excerpt reprinted in G. W. Bush (2003), *We Will Prevail* (p. 22). National Review Books.

Chapter 7

State Crimes by Types of Government: Non-Democratic

The history of power politics is nothing but the history of international crime and mass murder (including, it is true, some of the attempts to suppress them).

Karl Popper

While democratic, parliamentary, and multi-party republics have indeed committed massive numbers of state crimes, in general these have been carried out covertly, by proxy or indirectly. Yet, when it comes to other types of government, as discussed in this chapter, the crimes committed by agents in the name of or on behalf of the state are not only more direct but also, per case, larger in scope and have the intent of doing massive systematic harm or death to a significant portion of the population under their rule as well as to neighboring state populations (Mullins and Rothe 2008). For example, the civil war in the Congo twice became a location for a major conflict involving most central and eastern African countries, such as Uganda, Rwanda, Burundi, Chad, and others, who sent troops to support various factions and to loot local natural resources including its human population (i.e., slave labor). The conflict between the Ugandan government and the Lord's Resistance Army has long carried into Chad and Sudan. The Central African Republic has been destabilized by the warfare in Sudan, the DRC, and Uganda (Mullins and Rothe 2008). Additionally, if we consider that almost 40 percent of the world's population lives under authoritarian rule, a significant portion of humanity is subject to being victimized by the worst forms of state crimes (Kekic 2007).

Following is an illustration of the extensiveness of crimes of the state by the various forms of government. While these are but a few examples, they do help to draw out a common theme or forms of state criminality that can be associated in part with the type of regime or governmental structure. Essentially, a pattern of massive human rights violations, crimes against humanity, and/or genocides are most likely to come out of countries that have a one-party system; a military junta regime; and communist, autocratic, dictatorial, or theocratic form of government. This is not to say that such types of regimes or governments are sufficient for these crimes to be committed. After all, making such a claim removes all agency from the acting heads of state. Nonetheless, such arrangements are conducive to these types of state criminality, given the predispositions of the leaders; the economic, cultural, and political situations within the country; the role of religion; and other factors including an "otherized" population and/or histories of colonialism.

Examples of Genocide, Crimes against Humanity, and Widespread Human Rights Violations: 1955–2002

Afghanistan 1978–1992: Communist coup results in political purges of ruling circles followed by Soviet invasion. Widespread Mujahedeen rural insurgency provokes Soviet and Afghan government tactics of systematic terror, destruction of villages, and execution of prisoners. Under the Taliban regime, massive human rights abuses were committed against women in particular.

Algeria 1962: In the wake of independence from France, Algerian militants attacked Europeans and Muslim civilians who collaborated with French colonial authorities.

Angola 1975–1994: Both National Union for the Independence of Angola (UNITA) rebels and Popular Movement for the Liberation of Angola (MPLA) led government forces and perpetrated destructive campaigns and atrocities against civilians.

Argentina 1976–1980: The military staged coup and declared state of siege. Death squads targeted subversives for disappearances, kidnappings, torture, and murder.

Bosnia 1992–1995: Muslim residents of Bosnia were subject to "ethnic cleansing" measures including destruction of property, forced resettlement, execution, and massacres by Serb and Croat forces seeking union with Serbia and Croatia.

Myanmar (Burma) 1978: To secure the border region, regular military units supported by militant Buddhist elements depopulated Arakanese Muslim communities in Western Burma by oppression, destruction, torture, and murder.

Cambodia 1975–1979: Khmer Rouge initiated the restructuring of society with massive deaths by starvation, deprivation, executions, and massacres of supporters of the old regime, city dwellers, and ethnic and religious minorities (particularly Muslim Chams).

Chad 1982–1990: Under President Hissene Habre, vast atrocities were committed including human rights violations, general repression, and massive deaths.

Chile 1973–1976: In the wake of a military coup, supporters of the former regime and other leftists disappeared or were arrested, tortured, exiled, and summarily executed.

China 1959; 1966: Army and security forces suppressed counterrevolutionary elements of society, including Tibetan Buddhists, landowners, and supporters of former Chiang Kai-shek regime. During 1966, under condonement of the military and with the consent of the Party faction, Red Guard youth gangs targeted a wide spectrum of society for arrest, harassment, re-education, torture, and execution.

Cuba 1959–1999: Under Fidel Castro there have been massive human rights violations that have included imprisonments, death, torture, and general repression.

El Salvador 1980–1989: In the face of widespread insurgency, military, security units, and death squads killed, imprisoned, and harassed suspected leftists among clergy, peasants, urban workers, and intellectuals.

Equatorial Guinea 1969–1979: Unsuccessful coup attempts triggered a violent and sustained crackdown on all political opposition, including ethnic-Bubi separatists on the island of Fernando Po (now known as Bioko).

Ethiopia 1976–1979: Army, internal security units, and civilian defense squads massacred political and military elites, workers, students, bureaucrats, and others thought to oppose the revolutionary regime.

Guatemala 1978–1990: Military government used anti-subversive anti-guerrilla campaigns with indiscriminate use of death squads against suspected leftists and indigenous Mayans. The killings became systematic and widespread after July 1978.

Iran 1981–1992: To consolidate the Islamic revolution, the government violently suppressed dissident Muslims and rebel Kurds and selectively executed prominent Baha'is. There were also widespread human rights abuses committed against its citizenry.

Iraq 1963–1975; 1998–1991: To suppress repeated rebellions for independent Kurdistan in northern Iraq, the government engaged in large-scale massacres. Beginning in 1988, military and security forces launched the Al-

Anfal campaign of indiscriminate destruction across Iraqi Kurdistan to neutralize Kurdish guerrillas. Measures included gassing, massacres, disappearances, forced resettlement, and demolition of villages.

Israel 1948–1949; 1967–2008: The Israeli occupation of Palestinian territory has resulted in violations of human rights and has been considered as committing crimes against humanity based on the seclusion of Palestinians, which has resulted in extremely high levels of poverty and unemployment, and has fueled the ongoing cycles of violence against Israelis.

North Korea 1948–1994: The North Korean government has systematically used repression and torture, and has committed human rights violations as well as crimes against humanity. It has been estimated that 1.6 million died as a result of purges and concentration camps.

Rwanda 1963–1964, 1994: Local Hutu officials orchestrated vengeance attacks against Tutsis following cross-border incursions by Tutsi rebels. During 1994, the now well-known genocide occurred resulting in the deaths of approximately 800,000 Tutsi and some Hutu moderates.

Sri Lanka 1989–1990: Government unleashed military and police death squads against the citizenry.

Sudan 2003–2008: Government begins program to eliminate insurgency by using the Janjaweed to carry out its genocidal intentions against the Darfurians. At the time of this writing, the genocide continues.

Uganda 1971–1979; 1980–1986: After General Amin seized power through a coup, he systematically exterminated political opponents and personal enemies. Tribes closely associated with his predecessor also were targeted for destruction. Amin's regime was ousted by the Tanzanian invasion in April 1979. Beginning in 1980–1986, with the overthrow of Amin, former Prime Minister Obote took control of the government. Political and tribal rivals of Obote were targeted by army and armed bands.

South Vietnam 1965–1975: Government military and paramilitary forces engaged in killings, reprisals, and bombardments against villagers supporting Viet Cong.

Yugoslavia 1998–1999: Serb militias backed by Yugoslavian armed forces targeted ethnic-Albanians to counterinsurgency and cleanse Kosovo of Albanians.

Zimbabwe 1982–1987: The Robert Mugabe regime committed vast levels of corruption, oppression, and other forms of human rights abuses against its citizenry.

Taken in part from Barbara Harff (2008), *Annual Data on Cases of Genocide and Politicide, 1955–2006.* Compiled for the U.S. Government Political Instability Task Force (formerly known as the State Failure Task Force).

Consider that totalitarian/communist regimes that ruled in Central and Eastern Europe during the last century and in some cases into the twenty-first century have been characterized by massive violation of human rights (recall previous discussions on the Gulag as case in point, and see figure 7.1 for estimations of victims by the former communist USSR) (White 1998).

Figure 7.1. *Victims of Former USSR 1917–1987*

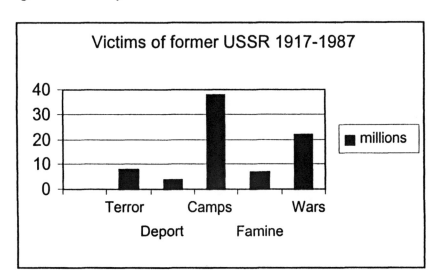

Besides the former Soviet Union, communist regimes include or have included countries such as Afghanistan, Albania, Angola, Benin, Cambodia (Kampuchea), China, Congo, Cuba, Ethiopia, North Korea, Laos, Mongolia, Mozambique, Vietnam, South Yemen, and Yugoslavia (Council of Europe Parliamentary Assembly Committee 2005: 1). A few estimations of numbers of individuals that have been killed by communist regimes, according to the Council of Europe Parliamentary Assembly Committee (2005: 3), consist of: Afghanistan, with over 1.5 million civilians killed; Cambodia, with 2 million victims; China, estimated at 65 million; North Korea, at 2 million; and Vietnam, with another 1 million civilians killed by the state. Consider the following continents also: Africa, with 1.7 million victims; Eastern Europe, with over 1 million victims; Latin America, low-figured at 150,000 civilians; and the former Soviet Union, at approximately 20 million victims.

The most typical or common types of crimes committed by communist regimes include the use of individual and/or collective executions of the general population that are considered political opponents or threats to regime power; starvation of mass portions of the population in consequence of requisitions, as a

political weapon or a means to discard civilians; concentration camps or imprisonment for slave labor or as effective incapacitation for segments of the "trou-
ble" population; torture; mass assassinations and/or deportations; and genocides.
Other typical violations of human rights include restrictions of freedom of
movement, freedom of religion, discrimination of employment, education, and
access to resources often resulting in poverty and/or exclusion. Take Cambodia,
as a case in point. Between 1975 and 1979, approximately 1.5 to 2 million Cam-
bodians died from starvation, overwork, torture, and/or execution. In essence,
over 20 percent of the entire Cambodian population lost their lives in the Khmer
Rouge revolution due to state-organized violence.

Countries that consider themselves republic or even democratic but consist
of a one-party rule have also committed vast numbers of state crimes that are
similar in nature to communist regimes (see figure 7.2). One-party systems are
often the result of decolonization (Mullins and Rothe 2008). This is usually
because the party had a dominant role in the country's liberation, independence
struggles, or the result of military takeovers or other forms of government coups.

Figure 7.2. *Countries Under Single Party Rule between 1945-1995*

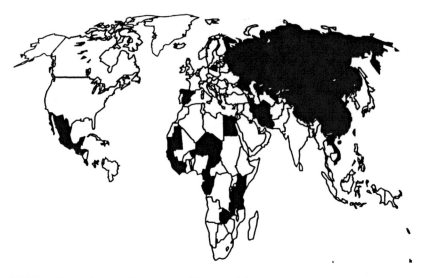

This has been the case in many African and Latin American states that had been
subject to either colonialization or years of coups and counter-coups. Examples
of countries under a one-party system that are not considered communist here
include: Eritrea (People's Front for Democracy and Justice); North Korea Dé-
mocratic People's Republic of Korea (Korean Workers' Party leads the Democratic Front for the Reunification of the Fatherland); Lao People's Democratic
Republic (Lao People's Revolutionary Party leads the Lao Front for National

Construction); Syrian Arab Republic (Baath Party leads the National Progressive Front); Turkmenistan (Democratic Party of Turkmenistan); Vietnam Socialist Republic of Vietnam (Communist Party of Vietnam leads the Vietnamese Fatherland Front); Algeria (National Liberation Front); Egypt (Arab Socialist Union); Iran (Rastakhiz Party); Iraq (Baath Party); and Uganda (National Resistance Movement/Party).

Consider that most African territories were quickly transformed from utterly subjugated regions into sovereign, independent states that had to figure out how to maintain themselves and their peoples. As such, coups and counter-coups became common practice and typically resulted in one-party regimes or military junta rule. Military coups d'état, whether instigated as a response to a corrupt regime, ethnic hostility and disenfranchisement, or driven by a powerful charismatic leader, these movements usually result in a one-party state under the control of a single, populist leader and his coquetry of kin and allies. The dictators and their group of social elite allies often see the state as a personal source of wealth and comfort. Often coups are initially welcomed by citizenry, as they bring stability and temporary socioeconomic order. Yet, in most cases, these regimes became thoroughly corrupt and violent toward resistance in the population. For example, the reigns of Mobutu Sese Seko in the Congo (which he renamed Zaire), Milton Obote and Idi Amin in Uganda, and Charles Taylor in Liberia were all characterized by the use of the country's resource reserves as personal enrichment enterprises for the sociopolitical elites (Mullins and Rothe 2008). Harsh programs of disappearances, extralegal executions, and other crimes against humanity were par for the course in the former administrations. The violence and corruption of such regimes ultimately led to their own deposal by subsequent coups, which typically then set up their own one-party state or maintained a military junta rule (see figure 7.3). Take, for example, Argentina, between 1976 and 1983, where thousands of people were secretly kidnapped and tortured in hundreds of detention centers throughout the country. Consider that over 10,000 people were murdered by the military regime that took control with widespread national and international support of their efforts in the coup d'état to combat leftist guerrillas.

Theocracies, states ruled by or subject to religious authority, have also resulted in massive violations of human rights (e.g., Afghanistan, Iran, Israel, and Saudi Arabia). As is often the case, theocracies are often self-labeled as democracies or parliamentary systems when processes of elections are carried out. However, democratic processes are generally circumvented by the theocratic government structure, thus guised as democratic yet in realpolitik remains theocratic (Ben-Yuda 2007). As an example, in the Iranian 2008 election, the slate of candidates approved shows that reformists have been permitted to stand for only a minority of the seats, and therefore factions close to Supreme Leader Ayatollah Khamenei will win a majority. Reformist candidates are on the ballot in only about 106 out of the 290 districts. According to Human Rights Watch (2008c) candidates competing for 290 seats in the republic's eighth parliament must

Figure 7.3. Countries under Military Rule 1945-1995

submit to evaluations by both the Interior Ministry and an unelected body of 12 religious jurists known as the Guardian Council. So while there appears to be an electoral process, it is guided and dictated by religious factions and beliefs.

To provide a few examples of how religion is used in determining civil and legal decisions, let's review a February 2008 case in Iran. According to Iran's Islamic Penal Code, "immoral" relationships such as those between men and women who are not married may be subject to criminal punishment. Three individuals accused and convicted of adultery (based on the husband's testimony) were sentenced to death by public stoning. The Supreme Court of Iran upheld the ruling based on the Islamic Penal Code of Iran that allows execution as a punishment for adultery, and allows it to be carried out by stoning (Human Rights Watch 2008a). As another example, Saudi Arabia conducted massive arrests that sent hundreds of Islamist opponents to prison in 1994. More recently in Saudi Arabia, during the first part of 2008, 57 men were arrested in front of a shopping mall in the holy city of Mecca. The country's religious police arrested the men for behavior that allegedly included flirting, dancing to pop music, and wearing improper clothing. The Commission for the Promotion of Virtue and the Prevention of Vice (referred to as the muttawa) runs the religious police, who are charged with enforcing Saudi Arabia's strict Islamic lifestyle. Its members patrol public places to make sure women are covered and are not wearing makeup, the sexes don't mingle, shops close five times a day for Muslim prayers, and men go to the mosque and worship. Common abuses by theocratic states are a general lack of recognition of human rights, especially for females (these are especially dominant in theocratic countries that uphold Islamic law wherein a woman's testimony is worth one half that of a man's); routine detentions; torture of detainees or political dissidents; lack of freedom of expression or movement; and overall discrimination.

Authoritarian states are often categorized as either a communist, theocratic, military junta rule, or one-party republics (see figures 7.2 and 7.3). Take, for example, the following list provided by Kekic (2007) in the U.S. Economist Intelligence Unit Report to the CIA.

List of Authoritarian Regimes

Afghanistan, Algeria, Angola, Azerbaijan, Bahrain, Belarus, Bhutan, Burkina Faso, Cameroon, Central Africa Republic, Chad, China, Comoros, Congo Brazzaville, Cote De Ivory, Cuba, Democratic Republic of Congo, Djibouti, Egypt, Equator Guinea, Eritrea, Gabon, Guinea, Guinea Bissau, Iran, Jordon, Kazakhstan, Kuwait, Laos, Libya, Mauritania, Morocco, Myanmar, Nepal, Niger, Nigeria, North Korea, Oman, Pakistan, Qatar, Rwanda, Saudi Arabia, Sierra Leone, Sudan, Swaziland, Syria, Tajikistan, Togo, Tunisia, Turkmenistan, Uzbekistan, Vietnam, Yemen, and Zimbabwe.

As I have previously noted, the structure or type of government is an important variable for predicting what type of state criminality is most likely to occur based on the given form of the state political apparatus. For example, the forms of government discussed in this chapter are more likely to be associated with:

- Genocides (see chapter 3 on the Rwandan genocide);
- Genocidal rape (the cases of Rwanda, Yugoslavia, and Darfur discussed in chapter 3);
- Crimes against humanity (e.g., case of Sierra Leone in chapter 3);
- Slavery (see the case of Côte d'Ivoire in chapter 3);
- Child soldiers (see list of countries in conflict that have been alleged to use child soldiers, in chapter 3);
- Political corruption (see the case of Zimbabwe in chapter 1);
- Human rights violations (see example of Saudi Arabia in chapter 1);
- Forced labor, displacement, and disappearance (e.g., Argentina and Chile); and
- State-sponsored terrorism committed against their populations (e.g., former USSR, Chile, and Argentina).

While the type of regime structure is neither necessary nor sufficient by itself as a predictor of state criminality, it is correlated with the type of crime. However, other variables are correlated with such propensities along with, of course, the agency of the particular head of state or regime. Simply, is the very structure of an authoritarian, totalitarian, dictatorial, communist, or theocratic regime enough that such crimes by the state will most likely occur? I believe the answer is no. As I have suggested elsewhere in this text, the issue of agency and specific time/space and societal conditions can act as inhibitors, even if a state is so structured and a head of state is prone to commit such acts. The motivation of the actor is not enough, nor is the form of government by itself. As such, the following section deals with other common structural variables that have also been present in the majority of cases of state crime that are committed by governments that are ruled in the various forms discussed in this chapter.

Other Structural Commonalities

As noted in chapter 6, capital accumulation is a central theme that runs through each of the crimes discussed here: capital accumulation or capital maintenance. Social, economic, and political capital are resources in the larger social struggles that are carried out in different social/political arenas and can be used to produce or reproduce inequality. Whether it is a head of state, leading political players within a regime or region, militia, or paramilitary, the interest or desire to attain some form of social capital is omnipresent. For example, the LRA's stated reason for overthrowing the Musevini regime is to socially, economically, and politically empower the Acholi region. The stated reason for the Hutu genocide on the Tutsis was to maintain political, social, and economic capital. The systemic corruption in Zimbabwe is to attain political, economic, and, in some cases, social capital. The Gulag was used by Stalin to maintain political capital and the drive for additional political and economic capital. Having stated this, let there be no mistake; while capital accumulation, in some form, is behind the initial decision-making process, it by no means can explain subsequent actions or the conditions that allowed such criminal activities to occur. An abundance of other variables must come into play. According to Harff (2005: 2), five factors are predictors in genocide or crimes against humanity:

1. **Prior genocides and crimes against humanity:** A dichotomous indicator of whether a genocide or politicide has occurred in the country since 1945;
2. **Political upheaval:** The magnitude of political upheaval (ethnic and revolutionary wars plus regime crises) in the country;
3. **Ethnic character** of the ruling elite: A dichotomous indicator of whether the ruling elite represents a minority communal group;
4. **Ideological character of the ruling elite:** A belief system that identifies some overriding purpose or principle that justifies efforts to restrict, persecute, or eliminate certain categories of people;
5. **Type of regime:** Autocratic regimes are more likely to engage in severe repression of oppositional groups.

I concur that these variables are indeed relevant. The terminology I have used elsewhere discussing these same factors include the importance of space (prior history), political stability, ethnic divisiveness, agency of the head of state or regime, and type of governmental structure. However, there are other structural factors that play as an important of a role as these.

For example, global economics, social and/or political instability, socially disorganized environments, illegitimate or weakened regime, economic collapse or highly indebted to foreign powers, ethnic tensions and/or socially constructed divisions, and postcolonial conditions are key structural conditions that undergird most of these crimes. Global economics needs little explanation. Whether that be the attainment of a larger global economic market, the drive to corner a particular market (as is typically the case with forms of state-corporate crime and crimes of the state committed by federal republics, democracies, or parliamentary systems), or the fluctuations or collapses in specific commodity markets that have drastic effects on national and local economies (i.e., Rwanda and the coffee collapse), thus affecting the state social, economic, and political instability, the need to examine economic issues at the global level is real. Compared to Western, and many Asian, economies, those of central Africa are less diversified, which amplifies the influence of the drop in value of a given product on the economy as a whole. Such circumstances are typically a holdover result from the colonial period, where dominating powers set up colonial economies to be focused on the exportation of one or two commodities back to the "motherland." For many African states, essential participation in international markets required maintenance of the old colonial cash-crop economies. For example, both Rwanda and Côte d'Ivoire suffered substantially due to the collapse of international coffee markets. As the price of coffee beans fell, peasants in the rural areas found their primary source of economic revenue tighten; states received less tax monies from this now debilitated sector of the economy. Such global forces enhanced local criminogenic factors experienced both by individuals in the poorer areas and the politicosocial elites. Additionally, by the 1960s and 1970s, many of these countries found themselves enmeshed in debtor relationships with institutions of international finance—the World Bank Group (WB) and International Monetary Fund (IMF) and the states that head those organizations (Mullins and Rothe 2008; Rothe and Mullins 2008).

As with the global level, state economic conditions are key to criminogenic environments that are conducive to state criminality. For example, when state economies are overly controlled by foreign investors and/or the global market, they are typically heavily indebted, reliant upon the decision making of commodity market leaders or foreign investors that often result in additional economic, political, and/or social upheavals. When drastic fluctuations occur or when a commodity is forced to crash for economic gain of those in control of the market, weak economic states find themselves in dire conditions socially and economically. This, in turn, can result in overall instabilities, coups, or additional forms of state repression to offset the chaos or disorder brought about by the larger economic conditions. Further, transnational corporations are often directly involved in black market and/or illegal export and importing of state resources (e.g., Democratic Republic of Congo), which leads to further conditions of instability, triggering domestic responses that can result in adding motivational fuel to state criminality.

As noted, the notion of specific time, or history of a country, is relevant. This must take into account beyond the time period of the previous genocides or crimes against humanity that have been committed. This should include considering the traditions, culture, practices, forms of rule, and past foreign interventions. A historical past of colonial rule is one of the factors to consider. While again not a sufficient condition, historical experiences of colonialism can be relevant. This is especially true if we consider the type of authority or rule the colonial powers held over the territory, how they dismantled their governing structure, how independence was won, and if the colonial powers created ethnic identities, religious or cultural practices, and/or divisive authority structures favoring specific populations. As such, the specific experiences of a country's past, including that of colonial rule, can have very different outcomes. For example, the cases currently under investigation at the International Criminal Court share a similar history of colonial rule (e.g., Uganda, the Democratic Republic of Congo (DRC), Chad, and the Sudan). However, such historical conditions did not result in consistent post independence outcomes. Uganda's transition to independence was relatively peaceful, given that it inherited a stable economic and political structure. Contrarily, the Democratic Republic of Congo tore itself apart in regional revolution within days of Belgium granting her independence. Nonetheless, there are commonalities of post-colonial rule.

The nature and direction of power is also relevant as the previous discussion of types of governmental structures showed. Along with the distribution, or lack thereof, power is the factor of political stability. This is related to both government legitimacy and a regime's ability to govern without extreme forms of repression. After all, control, especially given heavily centralized control with no balances or checks, provides ample opportunity for the state or state actors to engage in criminal behaviors. Nonetheless, a regime with power can maintain political stability, even if it is done by means of repression and the use of fear. It also is important to recognize that, where central political authority has collapsed, contending groups generally will make rival claims to the state authority, which can create further instability and lead to conditions of additional oppression, targeting of opposition groups, and/or economic and social instability in the form of military coups or counter-coups. The seeds of discontent and insurrection are often sown by the processes that bring temporary stability, especially in the cases of coups, and can be the very mechanisms of violations (state oppression) to maintain newly-found political, social, and economic capital. As previously noted, the history of central African political conflicts is filled not only with coups d'état, but counter-coups designed to remove despots from power (Mullins and Rothe 2008; Rothe and Mullins 2008), which brought about temporary stability but quickly turned into another regime that committed its own share of crimes, sewing the seeds for further insurgency movements. Take for example Chile's experience. General Pinochet (1973) received support of many people, political parties, and other countries immediately after he led a successful coup against the Allande regime, as it was believed that the dictator- ship (military junta) of Pinochet would restore the status quo as it had been before 1970. It was not long before these supporters realized that the new regime had different objectives, including the repression of all left wing and center political forces, solidifying their concentration of political power.

On the other hand, weakened regimes are often unable or unwilling to gov- ern or control the country for fear of replacement or outright inability to do so. Yet, a country unable to adequately police or subdue a paramilitary force in its hinterlands creates a gap of institutional control that simultaneously provides motivation and opportunity for the rise of organized criminal activity, lending to environments of social disorganization. In response, repression is often used to gain quick and/or hard control by the increasingly weakened regime or that of a replacing political force (e.g., military junta). Furthermore, heavily centralized or autocratic states often benefit only a portion of the population and can quickly become corrupt, using the states' resources for their personal gain and that of their kin and allies (e.g., Amin and Obote in Uganda or Habyarimana in Rwanda).

Scholars of genocides and other war crimes have long pointed toward the "otherizing" effects of ethnic polarization and dehumanization as facilitating violence in general and widespread lethal violence in particular. If minority groups are targeted for severe political or economic discrimination, the risks of genocide or crimes against humanity against those groups are increased. This otherizing has typically been manifested through constructed ethnic or racial divisions. After all, a central element within atrocity-producing environments is a set of intense ethnic rivalries and tensions often focused on capital attainment, be it political, social, or economic. Just as colonial powers dehumanized the peoples of Africa to legitimate colonial domination, ethnic groups dehumanized each other, facilitating political and economic subordination as well as wanton violence and destruction (e.g., Rwanda Hutus). Whether this ethnic otherizing was created by former colonial powers or as a political tool to gain control of a state, as was the case with the divisions between the "Arabs" and the "Furs" in Sudan and Darfur, the result creates conditions conducive to a regime eliminat- ing or repressing that particular group to maintain political, economic, and/or social capital. This was the case in the creation of the ethnic identities of the Arabs and the Blacks in Sudan, which later came to be significant in the Suda- nese government's use of the Janjaweed in committing the genocide and crimes against humanity.

As an example, by the 1968 Sudanese elections, the Umma political party had separated into two: one supporting Sadiq and the other Sadiq's uncle Imam al-Hadi. Darfur was a staunch supporter of the Umma party and, as such, it became the battleground between the two parties. To gain support, Sadiq, after calculating that demographics would favor the Fur and other "African" tribes, made an alliance with the leader of Darfur leaving his uncle with the "Arab" tribes. As part of the electoral tactics to gain political support, they exaggerated a kind of racial-cultural rhetoric that had started to grow from the years of economic favoritism out of Khartoum for the North. This encapsulated the promotion of an ideology (Prunier 2005). The "African" electorate was told that if Darfur had been marginalized and neglected, it was the fault of the Arabs. The Fur, Masalit and Zaghawa eagerly accepted this belief given that historically their presence and representation was absent from the power center of Khartoum; however, the marginalization had not really been racial or cultural, rather it was regional. Nonetheless, the Arab discourse offered a hope for the Arabized tribes to be co-opted into the "Arab elite" ruling group, which had historically remained at the center of political power (Prunier 2005). The political manipulation of these divides began to take on more than a symbolic meaning; it set the stage for later ethnic politics and violence. The ideology of an ethnic superiority has been a factor in multiple cases of state crime. As Prunier (1995: 59) noted, egalitarian racial ideologies are buttressed by an elitist and secretive authoritarian government that facilitates the conditions to commit the worst of the worst forms of state crime.

Beyond the typology of forms of government and a few other common structural conditions such as power distribution, economic conditions, political and/or social stability, or presence of ethnic divisiveness, there are also common enactment procedures that are used by the types of regimes discussed in this chapter. Simply, from these conditions we have explored above, we can draw on common enactment procedures. These include the use of nationalism, religion, ethnoism or racism, propaganda, militarization, and/or fear to create or enable an environment conducive to a state's criminality.

Common Enactment Tools

While regimes and/or paramilitaries utilize unique and case-specific tools to accomplish their goals, there is a pattern to the means in which they do this that is linked to the type of governmental system and other conditions. The process of otherizing is not done overnight. Instead, it is done by using certain procedures to ensure it is crystallized within a society. As previously noted, this can be done in the form of political separation (one party superiority to the others), linguistic differences (as in the case of the Arabs in Sudan), geographic placement (those in closest proximity to the centralization of power), and even religion.

Historically speaking, religions have been used as one of the main tools in the creation of otherizing and/or ethnic divisiveness. This has been especially the case in genocides. After all, "the primary driving force leading to genocide is not the pathology of individuals organizing and committing the genocide, but the pathology of the ideas guiding them" (Anzulovic 1999: 4). Ervin Staub (2003: 353) suggests that ideologies are "almost always a part of the genocidal process." Ideologies aid in the creation of the "other." Religion has offered theological, moral, and mythical groundwork for genocides (e.g., Bosnian Muslims and Croatian Serb genocides); religious institutions have knowingly and actively created ethnic, social, political, and economic divisions favoring groups of civilians over others that have led to genocides (e.g., Rwandan Tutsis). Organizational actors and leaders (e.g., clergy) have frequently been active participants in the carrying out of mass slaughters (e.g., Hutu attacks on Tutsis and the Holocaust of the Jews). While the relationship between these social phenomena is complex and often nuanced, the interconnection is undeniable. This is not to suggest that religion in and of itself is a necessary cause of genocide, as genocidal programs have been carried out without a specifically religious framework (e.g., Stalin's purges, the Khmer Rouge, Russia's slaughter of the Circassians in the mid nineteenth century). Further, religion is not a sufficient cause either, as even where it is a central motivating factor, other etiological factors are present (e.g., Kosovo and Serbia; the Jewish slaughters that occurred adjunct to the crusades) (Rothe and Mullins 2008).

Religion and the Croatian Genocide of the Serbs

In 1941, Germany declared war against Yugoslavia, quickly becoming the victors and occupying the territory. Yugoslavia was then divided up between Germany and its allies, and Croatia became an independent state. The "Independent State of Croatia" (NDH) was proclaimed "Ustashe" and headed by Ante Pavelic in alliance with the German Nazi Party. The first task of the regime was to eliminate Serbian Orthodox Churches. Soon thereafter, the Ustashe began a policy of forced conversion to Catholicism and extermination of Serbs living in Croatia. The Serb identity was based on a religion/national basis; as such they could be forcibly assimilated as Croats. This involved "forced conversions of the Serbs to Catholicism and subsequently the establishment of a 'Croatian Orthodox Church'" (Hoare 2004: 2). Those who refused to be converted, and often even those that had undergone forced conversion, were brutally slaughtered, tortured, and/or sent off to concentration camps. A large number of clergy were assassinated and religious institutions were destroyed. Additionally, a series of concentration camps was created in the Croatian territory where Serbians, Jews, and Roma were forced to work all day long, eventually dying of starvation or plainly executed (Rothe and Mullins 2008).

The genocide of the Croatian Serbs has become known as the Ustashe Genocide of 1941–1945. An estimated one million men, women, and children along with most of their clergymen were killed and their churches destroyed, with the full support of the Roman Catholic Church, Vatican, and clergy (Paris, 1990). The genocide of the Serbs was implicitly supported by Archbishop Stepinac as he called on all Catholics and churches to support the Croatian leader and his policies during the genocide. Pope Pius XII also fully supported the regime, elated by the mass waves of conversion to

Catholicism, while fully aware of the ongoing genocide. Additionally, Franciscan clergy actively participated in the killings in camps and in the streets. Further, through the support of the Vatican, Pavelic and others in his regime were provided an escape out of Croatia and Europe to safe havens, thus allowing them impunity for the systematic genocide that occurred.

Bosnia and Herzegovina Genocide of the Bosnian Muslims

The genocide of the Bosnian Muslims was the first case since the Holocaust to be tried in an international venue: the International Criminal Tribunal for the Former Yugoslavia (ICTY). During the late 1980s, Slobodan Milosevic vied for political power using nationalism and religious hatred as his platform—similar to efforts used by the Nazi regime and Hitler. He reignited historical accounts of the Ottomon rule and mythology to inflame longstanding but hidden tensions between Serbs and Muslims in the independent province of Kosovo. At this time, Orthodox Christian Serbs living in Kosovo were the minority of the population and often made unfounded claims that they were being abused by the Albanian Muslim majority, fueling growing tensions. Milosevic then turned his attention to Croatia. Recall that during World War II, Croatia was a pro-Nazi state led by Ante Pavelic, and the Serbs living in Croatia as well as Jews had been the targets of widespread massacres. In 1991, the new Croatian government, which was reviving fascism, began enacting discriminatory laws that targeted Orthodox Serbs, and once again flew the Ustasha flag. Milosevic's military forces invaded Croatia in July 1991 under the premise of "protecting" the Serbian minority. After the fall of Vukovar, the Serbs began the first of a series of mass executions that killed hundreds of Croatian males.

Less than one year later, Bosnia was recognized as an independent state by the U.S. and European countries. Milosevic's response to Bosnia's declaration of independence included the well-known attack on Sarajevo, the capital of Bosnia. As the Serbs gained ground, "they began to systematically round up local Muslims in scenes eerily similar to those that had occurred under the Nazis during World War II" (United Human Rights Council 2006: 1). The killings continued throughout 1993, operating under the leadership of Radovan Karadzic, President of the proclaimed Bosnian Serb Republic. In all, over 200,000 Muslim civilians had been systematically killed and approximately 2,000,000 had become refugees.

While the genocide was the result of several catalysts, including nationalism, culture, ideology, and politics, it was also both motivated and justified by Christianity. The historical consciousness of the battle of Kosovo, where the Serb Prince Lazar was killed leading to the defeat of Serbia and the 500-year rule of the Ottoman Empire, served as a contemporary mythological tool to equate Bosnian Muslims as "Christ-Killers." In art, drama, and literature, Lazar has been portrayed as Christ, including a now famous portrait of the last supper where Lazar is surrounded by his knights, including the traitor who gave his battle plans to the Turks. The depiction is a replica of Christ's last supper with his disciples, including Judas. The death of Lazar was the focus of an annual ritual celebration (Vidovdan Day).

On the 600th anniversary of Lazar's death, Serbian President Slobodan Milosevic used the occasion for political purposes to seize absolute power in Yugoslavia, speaking of the past battle and suggesting future battles to come by Serbia as the defender of Christian Europe against Islam. The day of celebration, mythical memories, and Milosevic's speech generated and fueled long-standing myths of fear and hatred of non-Christians (Turks). Serb nationalists have claimed that Slavic Muslims had betrayed their heritage and as such were labeled as Turks. As such, they were Christ killers. Here religious identity served as a racial transformation that was used to support the genocide of Bosnian Muslims. By 1992, the rage manipulated by political leaders through the use of Kosovo ritual and religious symbolism was transformed into a genocidal program in Bosnia-Herzegovina (Sells 2001).

Religious symbols, rituals, ideologies, and mythologies were used politically to create the conditions for the attempted extinction of Bosnian Muslims by Serbian National/Christians (Sells 1996). The religious mythology of Lazar was combined with several years of political manipulation by the army, religious nationalist militias, and the media. Not only did religion play a significant role in creating the conditions for the massacres, but Serbian Bishops were also involved. They were one of the three core bases of support for the militias carrying out the genocidal policies. Often the planning for the genocide was organized in Serbian Orthodox churches. Bishop Atanasije wrote that Slavic Muslims were primitives; nationalists claimed they had a defective gene rendering them incapable of reason (Sells 2001).

The Serbian Orthodox Church was central to the genocide. Religious leaders would hold ceremonies to mark the successful cleansing of towns once the Serb Muslims had been killed. In all, over 1,400 mosques were destroyed; Bosnian graveyards were eradicated. Approximately 400,000 were killed, and an estimated 20,000–50,000 Bosnian Muslim women were raped by Bosnian Serb soldiers in a systematic campaign of ethnic cleansing (Rothe and Mullins 2008).

Another common tool or enactment procedure used to carry out massive human rights abuses, crimes against humanity, and/or genocide is the use of rape. After all, rape and/or genocidal rape have long been used as a tool of terror and of population elimination. This is especially true when there are existing conditions of ethnic divisiveness and/or general repression of the female population given cultural and social practices of sexual discrimination. Additionally, due to the high rate of HIV/AIDS in many of these countries, rape serves as a transmission episode and the inevitable death sentence that the disease brings.

In the case of the types of regimes discussed in this chapter, rape is often used as an organized military tactic of terror and/or a means of accomplishing genocide to (1) generate fear in subdued population, (2) humiliate the population (both men and women), (3) derogate women (spoilage of identity), and (4) create a cohort of mixed-ethnic children to maintain the domination. Derogation and identity spoilage of the rape victims are another set of key motivators behind genocidal rape events. Again, due to strong strains of patriarchy within these cultures, unmarried women who have been raped are typically no longer looked upon as potential wives—the rape has destroyed their marital desirability. Further, they can also, in turn, be shunned by family members and have nowhere to turn for survival. Such women will either starve or live the rest of their lives in highly marginal social positions (e.g., begging, prostitution, etc.). Such conditions are genocidal as they increase the overall death toll related to the genocidal event, even if indirect and down the line. In raw terms, this is the removal of women from the breeding population and prevents a population from recovering from a genocidal event. Whether it be militias (LRA or the Janjaweed) or governments (Ugandan, Sudanese, Rwandan, or former Yugoslavian), rape was/is a common mechanism used in the context of conflict. The following quote taken from a surviving victim in the ongoing genocide in Darfur illustrates the intertwinement of ethnic otherizing and the use of rape: "The Janjaweed entered my school and caught some girls and raped them in classrooms. I was raped by four men inside the school. When they left they told us they would take care of all us black people and clean Darfur for good" (Amnesty International Newswire 2005: 1).

Sexual assault is also used as an orchestrated tactic of warfare. As has been reported both in Bosnia and in Rwanda, military units were tasked by their commanding officers with the duty of moving systematically through an occupied village and raping all the females they could find.

Nationalism is another tool that is often used to create the conditions conducive to crimes by the state. This is particularly an attractive tool for weak governments as a means of legitimizing the government, when the state is at its weakest. New governments have repeatedly turned to the ideology of nationalism in order to unify the state amidst the mayhem of its near anarchic condition. Nationalism is also often used to revive or create a common identity and consciousness that is all too often used to exclude minorities, create a collectivity to ban against the others, and/or rekindle past hatred or conflicts between political groups. Politicians are most effective in manipulating the masses when they are able to draw on preexisting sentiments. For example, nationalism, in the form of ethnic nationalism, was used by the Hutu to incite anger against the Tutsis in the pre-genocide buildup.

The opposition parties have plotted with the enemy to make the Byumba fall to the *Inyenzi* [cockroaches]. . . . Any person who is guilty of acts aiming at sapping the morale of the armed forces will be condemned to death. What are we waiting for? . . . and what about those accomplices who are sending their children to the RPF? Why are we waiting to get rid of these families? We have to take responsibilities into our own hands and wipe out these hoodlums. . . . The fatal mistake we made in 1959 was to let them [Tutsi] get out. . . . We have to act. Wipe them all out. (FIDH Rwanda quoted in Prunier 1995: 172)

Another example includes the use of nationalism to isolate and persecute the Roma in Romania, where violence, persecution, and discrimination toward the Roma were clearly linked to the rise and influence of nationalism. Likewise, the social construction of a nationalism in Sudan based upon Arab unity reinforced the sense of alienation among groups that did not geographically, historically, linguistically, or traditionally identify with an Arab identity. This was further reinforced by the position of the government and its economic and social preference for the Arab solidarity and identity associated with northern geographic areas and Khartoum. Ethnic and/or cultural identities, initially abstract ideological political categories, became reified into powerful social forces. When regimes are structured along the lines of a theocracy, even if partially democratic, nationalism becomes intertwined with the particular religion, increasing its potency to be used for justifications for oppression, human rights violations, or crimes against humanity.

A nationalistic ideology, along with the promotion or creation of ethnic divisions, is often carried out through state propaganda. As such, the use of propaganda to carry out or commit a state crime is commonplace. Take, for example, Rwanda, wherein propaganda was used to incite the population and instill loyalty to the regime. This came in the form of the Hutu manifesto, pamphlets, and radio dissemination. The Minister of Defense of Rwanda used the national radio to request the population to track down and arrest infiltrators, or the insurgent Tutsi movement, thus playing on nationalism and the ethnic divisions that had been created in the past. A similar practice has occurred in Darfur. According to an August 2004 document seized from a Janjaweed official, the "execution of all directives from the President of the Republic [of Sudan] was necessary . . . [and the militia should] change the demography of Darfur and make it void of African Tribes." It continued with a general encouragement to "kill, burn villages and farms, terrorize people, and confiscate property from members of African Tribes and force them from Darfur" (Kristoff 2005: 2). Adolf Hitler was a master in the use of propaganda to raise the public's hatred of non-Aryans and their loyalty to himself and the Nazis—nationalist identity. As noted by Charles Cozic (2008: 1),

To get the people to fight for their respective rulers' interests, the politicians and warlords stoke ethnic hatred through propaganda about invented atrocities committed by the other side. Then the same characters go out and actually commit atrocities in supposed retribution for the atrocities they claimed were done by their opponents. The cycle of violence and murder then escalates and develops a life of its own.

Fear is another common tool used to subdue populations, to ensure the general population partakes in the crimes committed by the state, to maintain their rule via force, or to continue the ongoing ethnic hatred or nationalistic sentiments. The fear of not participating can be as much of an incentive to aid in the commission of the crime as the prevailing propaganda used to incite the violence from the onset.

The internal contradiction that affected many of the general peasants can be seen by this testimony. Based on fear that they would be viewed as Tutsi sympathizers and killed, the internalization of the dominant discourse of a Tutsi threat drove ordinary men and women to become genocidiers. Fear and intimidation can also be the very tool used by the state to commit atrocities on the population: once paralyzed by fear, a regime ensures there will be little or no insurgency or political dissidents, thus enabling the government to commit human rights abuses and other crimes. As an example, let's again turn to Chile under the military dictatorship of Pinochet. Pinochet managed to ensure his legitimacy, power, and continued position as head of the state by using methods to control the population and quell any opposition. He repressed the people by imprisoning, abducting, or exiling whomever he considered to be a threat, not even distinguishing between children and adults. If arrested, they were taken to camps and tortured by electrocution, the removal of fingernails, beatings, immersion in liquids, burning by cigarettes, sexual abuse, and psychological torture. Chileans were all affected by the repression, including the overwhelming sense of fear that was a pervasive part of everyday life. Pinochet used this fear to stop people from opposing him and, as such, maintained his power. Fearmongering is also a key mechanism used to legitimate and/or overshadow illegal or illegitimate governmental action. Moreover, heightening general levels of fear can be used simultaneously with other measures including nationalism, ethnic hatred, foreign intervention, or a vast array of other tools at the disposal of a regime.

An additional commonality is the presence and noteworthy role of bystanders in every instance of these crimes. "Third parties at the state and international level are the focal point for the prevention of gross human rights violations, because the perpetrator is unwilling and the victim is unable to prevent or stop the atrocities" (Grunfeld 2007). The understanding of why anyone would remain a direct bystander during the commission of such state crimes is indeed tied to the above mentioned factors—propaganda, fear, and nationalism—and is, of course, dependent upon other structural factors previously discussed. Grunfeld (2007: 2) suggests that the role of the bystander "is the most decisive factor when the conflict or the human rights violations have reached a stage of repression and coercion." This includes the inaction of other states, international institutions of control, citizens, and others who, through their complicity or "ignorance," supported or aided, directly or indirectly, the perpetrators of the crimes.

Conclusion

This chapter has endeavored to draw out some common themes or patterns associated with specific forms of governments. I began with the presentation of governmental structures most associated with direct violence against a state's own citizenry: autocracies, dictatorships, communism, one-party republics, and theocracies. Indeed, these very forms of government have routinely been identified as having a greater incidence of state crime than the types of state structures discussed in chapter 4 (Ross 2000: 3). Additionally, the chapter attempted to show how historical, economic, social, political, religious, and ethnic identities are directly involved in the forms that state crimes take, as well as the means in which they are carried out. Yet, the goal is not to provide the end-frame discussion of such state crimes, but rather a point of departure for discussing potential controls of such behaviors.

Chapter 8

International Controls for Crimes of States and Other Violators of International Criminal Law

After having explored the various types of state criminality and the theoretical tools for understanding the "hows" and "whys," the next step is to examine the extant controls and constraints against these types of criminal acts. The most salient control for crimes of the state is international law. While chapter 2 introduced the legal component of the most serious crimes a state and/or paramilitary can commit, the notion of international criminal laws as a control mechanism requires us to explore the mechanisms that can be used. For this reason, this chapter will examine the history and efficacy of the laws as a deterrent. Moreover, recent years have been marked by some major new initiatives for international institutions of social control: to bring perpetrators of state crimes to trial, such as International Criminal Tribunals on genocide in Bosnia and Rwanda, as well as the establishment of the permanent International Criminal Court (Mullins, Kauzlarich and Rothe 2004; Rothe 2006; Rothe and Mullins 2006a). Further, as will be discussed in this chapter, there is variation in accountability and responsibility under international laws for states versus individuals. As such, this chapter focuses on international social controls in the form of those established tc deter (i.e., law) and the institutions that hope to be both a general deterrent and a venue for prosecuting violators (states or individuals): the retributive justice mechanisms.

International Law

International law does indeed have a long history; however, it is only in recent years (relatively speaking) that it has become a regular feature of modern political life (Sands 2005). The second half of the twentieth century marked significant developments within the codification of public law (including the codification of criminal liability for individuals who violate public law). International rules now codified as criminal law provided a framework for judging and prosecuting individual behavior and state actions, and, in theory, an end to impunity (Sands 2005). Moreover, as a control mechanism, the extant laws are more promising for actors committing state crime than that of traditional street crime (Rothe and Mullins 2006a).

International criminal law is composed of substantive law and procedural law. The substantive law is the body of rules indicating what acts amount to international crimes, elements required for them to be considered prohibited, and under what conditions states must prosecute or bring to trial those accused of violating such laws (Cassesse 2002a). International criminal law is a branch of public law. Public law is best defined as the body of law that comes from treaties, charters, protocols, resolutions, and customary law. It was only after World War II that new categories for international crimes developed. These included crimes against humanity and genocide. Before proceeding, it should be noted that there now exists a "hierarchy" among these crimes as they pertain to prosecution and penalty: crimes against humanity, genocide, and war crimes (Politi and Nesi 2004). Genocide is the "official" worst crime, crimes against humanity are secondary, and war crimes are the lowest on the scale. Interestingly, the first two imply state responsibility, while the latter implies individual responsibility. International criminal law is a "hybrid branch of law: it is public international law impregnated with notions, principles, and legal constructs derived from national criminal law, human-rights law, and customary laws" (Cassesse 2002a: 19).

International Humanitarian Law

International humanitarian law and international human rights law are complementary. Both seek to protect the individual, yet in different ways. International humanitarian law (IHL) consists of both humanitarian principles and international treaties aimed at constraining the affliction of combatants and noncombatants during international or non-international armed conflicts (war crimes). They protect persons or property that are affected by the conflict and limit the states' rights, within a conflict, to use methods and means of warfare of their choice. Thus, IHL applies in situations of armed conflict, whereas international human rights law (IHRL), or at least some laws, protect the individual at all times, in war and peace alike. IHL aims to protect people who do not or no longer take part in hostilities. The rules embodied in IHL impose duties on all parties to a conflict. These are based on the Geneva Conventions (listed at end of this section), which define the fundamental rights for civilians and combatants that are injured, ill, or captured during a "war" of international or internal nature. All actors involved in a conflict are bound by these international laws. This includes states and individuals (individuals at all levels may be criminally charged for "grave breaches" of the Geneva Convention, the additional Protocol I, and for other violations of the laws and customs of war); thus, these are also "war crimes." War crimes have been delegated to individual responsibility, even if under collusion between state crime and individual crime.

International Human Rights Law

International Human Rights Law (IHRL) is primarily for peacetime and applies to every human being. They are based on international rules versus international treaties or customs. These laws are viewed as inherent entitlements based solely on being human. Their principal goal is to protect individuals from arbitrary acts that infringe upon these rights by their own governments; thus, they primarily protect people against state violations of internationally recognized (customary) civil, political, economic, social, and cultural rights committed against the state's own citizens. Human rights law does not deal with the conduct of hostilities. States are bound (if or when they have accepted these international rules or principles—the soft laws) by IHRL to bring together their domestic law with international obligations. These include the Universal Declaration of Human Rights, adopted by the UN General Assembly in 1948; the Convention on the Prevention and Punishment of the Crime of Genocide of 1948; the International Covenant on Civil and Political Rights of 1966; the International Covenant on Social and Economic Rights of 1966; the Convention on the Elimination of All Forms of Discrimination against Women of 1981; the Convention against Torture and Other Cruel, Inhuman, or Degrading Treatment or Punishment of 1984; and the Convention on the Rights of the Child of 1989. Criminal prosecution can occur for these violations; however, they must fall under violations of international crimes such as crimes against humanity, genocide, or torture.

The Laws of the Air, Sea, and Space

The laws of the sea are one of the oldest disciplines in international law. The League of Nations Conference for the Codification of International Law (1930, The Hague) dealt with the breadth of the territorial sea. Parts of treaties or conventions also guide the laws of sea (Geneva Convention for the Amelioration of the Condition of Wounded, Sick, and Shipwrecked Members of the Sea). Nonetheless, the next directly related significant developments occurred with the United Nations Conferences on the Law of the Sea (Geneva 1958 and 1960), which accentuated a need for a generally acceptable Convention on the law of the sea. This resulted in the United Nations Convention on the Law of the Sea (UNCLOS) (1982). The UNCLOS states the area of the seabed, ocean floor, subsoil, and its resources are the common heritage of mankind, irrespective of the geographical location of states. The Conventions includes the banning of pollution and dumping: (1) the introduction by man, directly or indirectly, of substances or energy into the marine environment, including estuaries, which results or is likely to result in such deleterious effects as harm to living resources and marine life, hazards to human health, hindrance to marine activities, including fishing and other legitimate uses of the sea, impairment of quality for use of sea water and reduction of amenities; (2) any deliberate disposal of wastes or other matter from vessels, aircraft, platforms or other manmade structures at sea. The law of space started with the United Nations Committee on the Peaceful Uses of Outer Space (COPUOS) in 1958. The Outer Space Treaty (1967) was later elaborated on, resulting in the 1979 Moon Agreement wherein the international use of the moon and the exploration of its resources are addressed. There are other treaties that cover both space and sea, for example, the Treaty Banning Nuclear Weapons Tests in the Atmosphere, in Outer Space and Under Water (1963). The public international air laws relate primarily to laws and agreements governing aviation. These include the Treaty on Open Skies (Helsinki 1992), The Protection of Civilian Populations against Bombing from the Air in Case of War, the Warsaw Convention (1929), the Montreal Convention (1999), and the historical Hague Rules of Ariel Warfare (1923). These laws, unlike the criminal laws discussed previously, are for states and as such would have a different institution of control handling violations.

State or Individual Criminal Liability

Similar to the arguments once used against categorizing corporations as criminals (see chapter 1), the notion of state criminal liability has been infused in a definitional quagmire. After all, as with corporations, if there is no ass to kick or soul to damn, how can we prosecute a state? As noted during the Nuremberg Trials: "Crimes against international law are committed by men, not by abstract entities, and only by punishing individuals who commit such crimes can the provisions of international law be enforced." Yet, as we will see, there are different institutions that address violations of the state and those of individuals. However, this is not to say that criminal liability cannot be extended to the state or that the culpability is an either-or situation. For example, Articles 9 and 10(10) of the Nuremberg Trials mention the criminal liability of an organization (state), as does the 1996 Draft Articles on the Law on International Responsibilities of States (adopted by the United Nations International Law Commission (Articles 5–15). The latter holds that imputing to a state an international violation of law committed by one of its apparatus amounted, in principle, to concentrating responsibility on the public official. The precedence of the Treaty of Versailles, 1919, also holds accountable the Heads of State. The former held that individuals criminally responsible were not solely judged in place of the state; the state of Germany was also held liable and ordered to pay compensation as a result of its criminal activities. On the other hand, the punishment of a state's official could constitute the means of satisfaction that an injured state is entitled to. Yet, this is considered separate from other obligations, such as reparations by an offending state. As we will see, under the Rome Statute of the International Criminal Court (1998), while having jurisdiction over individuals, the state is not alleviated from its obligations or liability. The Rome Statute, Article 25 (1, 2, 3, and 4) Individual Criminal Responsibility states:

(1) The court shall have jurisdiction over natural persons pursuant to this Statute.
(2) A person who commits a crime within the jurisdiction of the Court shall be individually responsible and liable for punishment in accordance with this Statute.
(3) In accordance with this Statute, a person shall be criminally responsible and liable for punishment for a crime within the jurisdiction of the Court.
(4) No provision in this Statute relating to individual criminal responsibility shall affect the responsibility of States under international law.

Article 4 ensures that the Court's exclusion of state responsibility is not precluded from customary international law or treaties obligations. Additionally, crimes of aggression at this time fall under state responsibility (Cassesse 2002b). War crimes, on the other hand, have been delegated to individual responsibility.

Summary of International Laws

No doubt international law has a long history and is embedded in multiple treaties, charters, and conventions. Moreover, the codification of international criminal law has not only made great strides but is now represented in the crimes under the International Criminal Court's jurisdiction. As such, having a solid body of international law is not a problem per se. The failure of international law to serve as a deterrent is the result of the lack of effectual enforcement mechanisms. After all, states that hold vast economic, military, and political power within the international arena and have long ignored international law as a frame for their behaviors if it conflicted with their foreign policy interests. Thus, there is no realistic threat of prosecution for many forms of state crime. When law is viewed as irrelevant or illegitimate, it obviously no longer holds a deterrent value. Likewise, international treaties are structured in such a way that reservations may be attached to them by states, which undermines the original intent of a treaty. Further, since the international system of control is based on a complimentary system, meaning states willingly accept jurisdiction, many types of crimes go unpunished. To suggest policies that would strengthen the enforcement of international law as an effective deterrent, we must turn to institutions that are capable of such actions. No different than domestic laws associated with traditional street crime, laws need be enforced through a formal criminal justice system. I now turn to the extant international institutions.

International Institutions of Control

The Hague Peace Conference of 1899 was the first real initiative to create an international oversight body for state disputes. The Conference resulted in the Permanent Court of Arbitration, which was established in 1900 and began operating in 1902. In 1907, a second Hague Peace Conference was convened. The Conference confined itself to recommending that states should adopt a draft convention for the creation of a court of arbitral justice as soon as agreement was reached. Although the proposed court never materialized, the draft enshrined certain fundamental ideas that served as a guide for the drafting of the Statute of the Permanent Court of International Justice (PCIJ) (International Court of Justice 2007).

By 1919, the first international political organization developed as an attempt to organize and encourage interstate relations and peaceful settlement of international disputes (Rothe and Mullins 2006a). The League of Nations was formed with the purpose of unifying an international arena composed of sovereign states with divergent political interests, economic interests, cultural disparities, religions, state practices, and traditions (Carty, 1991). Article 14 of the Covenant of the League of Nations gave the Council of the League responsibility for formulating plans for the establishment of a Permanent Court of International Justice (PCIJ). Although the Permanent Court of International Justice was brought into being through and by the League of Nations, it nevertheless was not a part of the League. In particular, a member state of the League of Nations was not by this fact alone automatically a party to the Court's Statute. The outbreak of the war in 1939 had serious consequences for the PCIJ, having its last public sitting on December 4, 1939. The judges of the PCIJ all resigned in January 1946.

The end of World War II brought new alliances and fresh attempts to generate and legitimate an international institution designed to foster peaceful cooperation among countries. In 1945, representatives of fifty states assembled in San Francisco, USA, to develop the charter of an international organization to maintain peace and security called the United Nations (UN) and to dissolve the failed League of Nations. This included the establishment of the International Court of Justice (1946) at the Session of the United Nations General Assembly and Security Council. In April 1946, the PCIJ was formally dissolved, and the International Court of Justice came into existence. With the development of the UN, international relations and law began to take on a fundamentally different character (Rothe and Mullins 2006a, 2006c). By the 1950s, "there existed an embryonic global constitutional order, with rules that remain in place to this day" (Sand 2005: 10).

And indeed, even though a short link has been drawn between the Nuremberg trials and The Hague (ICTR and ICTY), there have been two periods wherein visions and principles of international criminal justice formed:

> First, the time after Nuremberg till the end of the 1980s where "realpolitik seemed to negate the principles of responsibility and accountability declared at Nuremberg" (Cooper, 1999, 11). [Secondly], the sometimes euphorically observed serial collapse of authoritarian states, eventually symbolized by the fall of the Berlin Wall at November 11, 1989, produced, what could be called, a "window of universalistic utopia" where under the headline of "transitional justice" human rights standards of the western world should become not only guiding but binding for the rest of the world. It was the period where the ad hoc tribunals and other hybrid courts were created. (Eweld 2008: 2)

Exploring the issue of the ability of intergovernmental bodies to act as control agents is important, even if these agencies have had a historically poor record of enacting control. The UN, the World Court, and the new ICC are uniquely positioned to act as global dispute resolution agents. While possessing a clear mandate, these organizations have no real authority or ability to use coercive force. Where these institutions have been successful in taking the role of dispute resolvers, Western industrialized powers provided their armies as enforcement mechanisms—and tend to do so only when they have had a distinct self-interest in the outcome. The UN peacekeeping mission, and the Serbian war crimes trials at the World Court, is case in point. Little real social control was enacted during the Bosnian phase of Serbian-led genocide. However, when this pogrom was extended to Kosovo and it became clear that Serbian aggression was not going to be limited to its immediate neighbors and could destabilize the entire region, the UN and the U.S. stepped in using military power to enforce compliance with UN resolutions. Moderately distant from the rest of Europe and the world, the early genocide went unsanctioned until it endangered south central European stability. Geographic proximity eventually compelled action. Similar genocides in Rwanda generated no military responses, only UN "talk" due to the country's social, economic, and geographical distance from the industrialized West (Rothe and Mullins 2006a). Nonetheless, their existence as potential controls merits attention, especially if we are to consider policies that could potentially address the weaknesses in each. The following subsections address each of these institutions, their roles, and their structure in relation to their ability to act as controls.

United Nations

In 1945, representatives of fifty countries met in San Francisco at the United Nations Conference on International Organization to draw up the United Nations Charter. By October 1945, the Charter of the United Nations had been ratified by fifty-one countries including China, France, the Soviet Union, the United Kingdom, and the United States. The creation of the UN also dissolved the failed League of Nations. The mission of the UN was said to represent the principles of a higher moral and legal authority based on social justice, control, and universalism—the legitimation of which would require creating a collective identity and consciousness—the same need seen in state formation requiring the development of nationhood: the reification of nationalism (see Brubaker 2004). Attaining international social control and collective security became primary in international political agendas (Rothe and Mullins 2006c). This trend is reflected in the opening statement of the UN Charter:

> WE THE PEOPLES OF THE UNITED NATIONS DETERMINED to save succeeding generations from the scourge of war, which twice in our lifetime has brought untold sorrow to mankind, and . . . to establish conditions under which justice and respect for the obligations arising from treaties and other sources of international law can be maintained . . . to unite our strength to maintain international peace and security.

When states become members of the United Nations, they are agreeing to accept the obligations of the UN Charter. According to the Charter, the UN has four purposes: to maintain international peace and security, to develop friendly relations among nations, to cooperate in solving international problems and in promoting respect for human rights, and to be a centre for harmonizing the actions of states. As such, the UN's successes and failures are correlated to the cooperation of its member states. As stated by Secretary General Trygve Lie (1946), "The United Nations is no stronger than the collective will of the nations that support it." Nonetheless, during the first decade of its existence, a legitimization crisis plagued the UN. Member states refused to meet their financial obligations (thereby creating a tenuous operating budget) and questioned the very validity of the UN (UN Annual Review 1954). Over the next few decades, the UN saw significant strides in increased memberships, new state formations (due to the end of colonialism), and the development of human rights laws. By the end of the Cold War, the UN had grown significantly, incorporating new state members, and hundreds of subcommittees and nongovernmental organizations.

Structure and Function of the UN

The United Nations has six main organs: The General Assembly (GA), the Security Council (SC), the Economic and Social Council, the Trusteeship Council, and the Secretariat (seated at UN Headquarters, New York). The sixth organ is the International Court of Justice (ICJ) (seated at The Hague, Netherlands).

The UN also has over fifteen other agencies, multitudes of programs, and more than thirty affiliated organizations, known together as the UN system (i.e., World Bank). The General Assembly is composed of all member states, each with one vote for decisions related to international peace, new statehood members, and the UN budget. At this level of decision making, a two-thirds majority is needed for approval. The Security Council, which has been highly critiqued for its structure, carries the power in its decision making over the General Assembly. In the SC, there are fifteen members, of which five are permanent— China, France, the Russian Federation, the United Kingdom, and the United States. The other ten country delegates are elected by the General Assembly for two-year terms. Decisions in the SC require nine "yes" votes for approval of an issue. A decision cannot be taken if there is a "no" vote or a veto by a permanent member, which significantly reduces actions of the SC, especially given the realpolitik of international relations and state interests. Its only means of empowerment for its controlling tools, such as imposing economic sanctions or ordering arms embargos, is based on state compliance of all members. Nonetheless, the UN was responsible for formulating the Universal Declaration of Human Rights (1948) and over eighty conventions and treaties that help protect and promote specific human rights.

The potential for the UN as an institution of social control, however, is rather limited. For example, only the Security Council under Chapter VII of the UN Charter has the authority to enforce measures to "maintain or restore international peace and security." These enforcement mechanisms or social controls are often estranged or merely public symbolic shaming efforts, especially given the power of the SC members. For example, Kofi Annan (September 2004), Secretary General of the UN, had little power but to publicly denounce the U.S. invasion of Iraq, calling it illegal. Other symbolic controls included Annan's statement on September 24, 2004, that cited the torture of Iraqi prisoners by U.S. forces as an example of how fundamental laws were being "shamelessly disregarded." As such, the power of control at the UN is often used only on less empowered or weak, failing governments. As previously noted, the UN could potentially order sanctions. Mandatory sanctions are also used to apply pressure on states to comply with Security Council objectives. Such objectives may include interstate or intrastate peace when diplomatic means fail. The range of sanctions include comprehensive economic and trade sanctions and/or more targeted measures such as arms embargoes, travel bans, or financial or diplomatic restrictions. Other targeted sanctions involve the freezing of assets (which the U.S. has used against alleged terrorist groups) and blocking the "financial transactions of political elites or entities whose behavior triggered sanctions in the first place" (UN 2001: 2). However, the structural limitations placed on the sanctions committee are great, as the Security Council must approve any sanctions. As such, with the power of veto of the Council, it is highly unlikely sanctions would be put on the U.S., China, Russia, France, the United Kingdom, or their close allies (i.e., Israel, due to the close relationship with the U.S., or the limited sanctions placed on Sudan due to China's growing presence in that country).

Thus, to empower the United Nations to where it could act in situations beyond the political interests of states and their allies would require a restructuring of the powers of the Security Council and/or enhancing the powers of the General Assembly: providing one vote per state member and allowing democratic decision making for applying sanctions (Rothe and Kauzlarich 2008). This is particularly true if they are to truly represent the catalyst for world peace (Mullins and Rothe 2008). For the UN to address these types of issues, it must require states to move beyond symbolic gestures of aid and/or intervention and create a full-time international force that is large enough to meet such demands and be given an agenda beyond humanitarian aid (e.g., as was the case in Rwanda where UN peacekeepers were left underpowered and stood by witnessing the ongoing genocide). However, the UN must do so in a neutral capacity without the considerations of political, economic, and ideological interests of key members. This can be reduced only by restructuring the Security Council.

International Court of Justice

The International Court of Justice (ICJ), seated in The Hague, is the principal judicial organ of the United Nations. It was established in June 1945 by the Charter of the United Nations and began work in April 1946. The first case entered was the *United Kingdom v. Albania*, May 1947. The sources of law that the Court can apply include international treaties and conventions in force, international customs, general principles of law, and judicial decisions (or precedent decisions). The Court has two functions: (1) to settle legal disputes submitted by states, and (2) to give advisory opinions on legal questions. The settlement of legal disputes can occur through mediation, the intervention of a third party to allow states to resolve their dispute and arbitration; the dispute is submitted to the decision or award of an impartial third party resulting in a binding settlement. Mediation and arbitration preceded judicial settlement. Simply, the ICJ is a court for state arbitration, not for addressing individual criminality. Court proceedings are instituted in one of two ways:

> 1) [T]hrough the notification of a special agreement: this document, which is of a bilateral nature, can be lodged with the Court by either of the States parties to the proceedings or by both of them. A special agreement must indicate the subject of the dispute and the parties thereto. Since there is neither an "applicant" State nor a "respondent" State, in the Court's publications their names are separated by an oblique stroke at the end of the official title of the case, e.g., Benin/Niger;
> 2) [B]y means of an application: the application, which is of a unilateral nature, is submitted by an applicant State against a respondent State. It is intended for communication to the latter State and the Rules of Court contain stricter requirements with respect to its content. In addition to the name of the party

against which the claim is brought and the subject of the dispute, the applicant State must, as far as possible, indicate briefly on what basis—a treaty or a declaration of acceptance of compulsory jurisdiction—it claims the Court has jurisdiction, and must succinctly state the facts and grounds on which it bases its claim. At the end of the official title of the case the names of the two parties are separated by the abbreviation "v." (for the Latin *versus*), e.g., *Nicaragua v. Colombia.* (International Court of Justice 2007)

By signing the UN Charter, a member state of the UN is ideally supposed to also comply with any decision of the Court in a case to which it is a party. Objections can be raised in an effort to prevent the Court from delivering judgment on the merits of the case (the respondent state may contend, for example, that the Court lacks jurisdiction or that the application is inadmissible). The Statute makes provision for other cases where the respondent state does not appear before the Court (as the U.S. has done in the past) because it rejects the Court's jurisdiction. In such cases, the Court must satisfy itself that it has jurisdiction. For this reason, the jurisdiction of the court is applicable only if the States involved have accepted its jurisdiction. The U.S. withdrew from the ICJ shortly after it was found responsible for several illegal acts against Nicaragua (1984) (Rothe 2006). Exceptions to the Court's mandate for consensual jurisdiction can occur by "virtue of a jurisdictional clause, i.e., typically, when they are parties to a treaty containing a provision whereby, in the event of a disagreement over its interpretation or application, one of them may refer the dispute to the Court" (International Court of Justice 2005: 1).

The ICJ (2007) is composed of 15 judges elected to nine-year terms with the following distribution—Africa, 3; Latin America and the Caribbean, 2; Asia, 3; Western Europe and other States, 5; Eastern Europe, 2—which corresponds to that of membership of the Security Council. The Court has always included judges of the nationality of the permanent members of the Security Council. The president and the vice-president are elected by the members of the Court every three years. To date (January 2008), the ICJ has entered 136 cases of state complaints.

The ICJ lacks the ability to enforce its rulings; it must rely on the United Nations Security Council (UNSC) for issues of noncompliance. Simply, if parties do not comply with the Court's decision, they can be taken before the Security Council for enforcement action. However, if the judgment were against one of the permanent five members of the Security Council or its allies, any resolution on enforcement would be vetoed. This occurred, for example, when Nicaragua brought the issue of the U.S.'s noncompliance before the Council. Furthermore, if the Security Council refuses to enforce a judgment against any other state, there is no alternative method of forcing the state to comply. It should also be noted that the ICJ is able to require only monetary reimbursements or restitution; it is not a criminal court. As such, any policy solutions that could address the weakness of the ICJ would have to include the restructuring of the power of the Security Council in relation to the ICJ decisions and enforcement. Additionally, the ICJ could be empowered with the authority to freeze state assets and/or monies to retrieve any monetary awards made by the court for states that have been victimized by another state (Rothe and Kauzlarich 2008).

International Criminal Tribunals

International tribunals have been used to address past atrocities, including those committed by the German Nazis and Japan during WWII. Yet, it was nearly a half century later before key international tribunals were used again—the International Criminal Tribunals for Yugoslavia and the International Criminal Tribunal for Rwanda. It is the latter two that will be the focus of this section.

ICTY

The International Criminal Tribunal for the former Yugoslavia (ICTY) was established under Chapter VII of the UN Charter, by the United Nations Security Council, Resolution 827, 1993, in response to the serious violations of international humanitarian law committed in the territory of Yugoslavia between 1991 and 1993. The ICTY is seated in The Hague in the Netherlands. The mandate of the ICTY is to prosecute and try four clusters of offenses: grave breaches of the Geneva Conventions, violations of the laws or customs of war, genocide, and crimes against humanity. Unlike the ICJ, the Tribunal is able to address only crimes of natural persons (not states). Nonetheless, the ICTY filed the first indictment against an acting head of state, Slobodan Milosevic, for crimes committed while he served in his formal capacity as head of state. Other individuals that are high-ranking members of the political and military offices have also been indicted.

The Court has sixteen permanent judges, elected by the United Nations General Assembly for a four-year term, and a maximum of twelve ad litem judges. The statute guiding the functions of the Court draws from both the civil law and common law systems and as such, elements of the adversarial and inquisitorial procedures are incorporated. Trials can begin only when the accused is physically present before the Tribunal (another key difference from the ICJ, where the court may proceed without the presence of a state party to the dispute). As of the end of 2007, the ICTY employed 1,173 staff members from eighty-two different nationalities.

While there are significant issues with the ICTY (i.e., costs, ineffective victim redress, location, etc.), it cannot be denied that the Court has contributed significantly to the ability of international institutions of control (Law and the International Criminal Court). For example, it has expanded the boundaries of international humanitarian and other forms of international criminal law by setting landmark precedent decisions. Namely, it

1. [E]xpanded upon the legal elements of the crime of grave breaches of the Geneva Conventions of 1949 by identifying the existence of an international armed conflict, and also the extended and exact definition of protected persons under the Conventions.
2. [N]arrowed the differences that are perceived between the laws or customs of war applicable in internal and in international conflicts.
3. [I]dentified a general prohibition of torture in international law which cannot be derogated from by a treaty, internal law or otherwise.
4. [A]dvanced international humanitarian law pertaining to the legal treatment and punishment of sexual violence in wartime.
5. [S]pecified crucial elements of the crime of genocide, in particular the definition of the target of such a crime, a group or part of a group of individuals.
6. [M]ade determinations that crimes against humanity can be committed not only as part of, but also just during an armed conflict, thus identifying a wide scope of protection.
7. [S]pecified the definitions of enslavement and persecution as parts of crimes against humanity.
8. [C]larified that formal superior-subordinate relationships are not necessarily required for criminal responsibility.

(International Criminal Tribunal for Former Yugoslavia Annual Report 2007)

ICTR

Like the ICTY, the International Criminal Tribunal for the Prosecution of Persons Responsible for Genocide and Other Serious Violations of International Humanitarian Law Committed in the Territory of Rwanda was established by the UN Security Council, under Chapter VII of the Charter of the United Nations, and the Rwandan citizens responsible for genocide and other such violations committed between January 1994 and December 1994 (Statutory Instrument 1996 No. 1296). Unlike the ICTY, the ICTR is seated in Arusha, United Republic of Tanzania. The UN detention facility, composed of fifty-six cells, is also located within the Arusha complex.

The Court consists of two trial chambers and an appeals chamber, the prosecutor, and registry. The first trial began in January 1997. As of April 2007, the tribunal handed down twenty-seven judgments involving thirty-three accused. Just as with the ICTY, there are significant issues with the ICTR (i.e., costs, ineffective victim redress, location, etc.), but it cannot be denied that this Court has also contributed significantly to the ability of international institutions of control (Law and the International Criminal Court). For example, it has expanded the boundaries of international humanitarian and other forms of international criminal law by setting landmark precedent decisions. Namely,

1. The Akayesu case, as discussed in chapter 2, was the first to interpret the definition of genocide as defined in the Convention for the Prevention and Punishment of the Crime of Genocide (1948).
2. The Chamber also defined the crime of rape. It underscored the fact that rape and sexual violence constitutes genocide in the same way as any other act of serious bodily or mental harm, as long as such acts were committed with the intent to destroy a particular group targeted as such.
3. The guilty plea and subsequent conviction of Jean Kambanda was the first time that a head of government was convicted for the crime of genocide.

At the date of this writing, both the ICTY and ICTR are attempting to reach the completion strategy stated by the UNSC, Resolution 1503 (2003) wherein all trials be completed by 2008 and all appeals heard by 2010.

Summary of International Tribunals

The value of the ICTY and the ICTR cannot be understood just in terms of "retribution" for the victims of the genocide. They have contributed significantly to the extant body of law. Indeed, even the Court's weaknesses have led to an enhanced system of international control: the Rome Statute of the International Criminal Court. However, the tribunals are ad hoc systems of justice that have proven to be very costly and filled with compromises resulting from the multiple legal systems that are often mixed to achieve international cooperation for trying individuals accused of the worst atrocities of mankind. Due to their ad hoc nature, the tribunals for Yugoslavia and Rwanda proved to be more than challenging. In part, this was due to the costs associated with the tribunals, the complexities of reaching consensus on the procedures, and the veto power of the Security Council that allows for a selectivity of cases that would be eligible for international tribunals (Bassiouni 1999). Of course, there have been other complexities unique to each of the tribunals discussed in this chapter, including the ways in which victims' needs are addressed, inclusion of those wishing to be a witness or to testify, geoproximity of the Court, and/or the use of experts in testimony.
Nonetheless, at this time they are the only potential venue for post controls in situations where a state is unwilling to prosecute its own actors for atrocities or to submit themselves to the jurisdiction of the International Criminal Court. With the precedent set by the Pinochet case, which established and/or reinforced (1) universal jurisdiction of International Criminal Tribunals (ICTs), and (2) heads of state as responsible actors, future ICTs may be the only viable alternative for holding accountable certain state leaders who participate in such crimes. The recognition of this possibility by the G. W. Bush Administration reinforces the notion that such an outlet can have the potential to be a control if other states were willing to challenge the economic and military superpower. For example,

fear of an ICT prosecution was formally discussed within the State Department. The FBI warned several former U.S. officials not to travel to some countries, including some in Europe, "where there is a risk of extradition to other nations interested in prosecuting them." And as Senator Helms (June 2002: 2) noted:

> [T]his year for the first time we have seen an international criminal tribunal investigate allegations that NATO committed war crimes during the Kosovo campaign. In addition, a month ago, in May, NATO Secretary General Lord Robertson submitted to a degrading written interrogation by a woman named Carla Del Ponte, chief prosecutor of the Yugoslavia War Crimes Tribunal.

While there have been other forms of international tribunals, namely Peoples Tribunals, they have not matched the precedence, accomplishments, or recognition of the ICTY and ICTR. Furthermore, the latter type of tribunals were not formed by the UN; instead they were constructed by international lawyers and citizens out of a specific state (these will be discussed further in the following chapter), for example, the World Tribunal on Iraq and the Citizen's International Criminal Tribunal for Afghanistan (*The People v. George W. Bush*). While this tribunal found President Bush guilty of war crimes resultant to U.S. attacks against Afghanistan in 2001 (ICTA 2004) as a nonempowered ad hoc tribunal composed of independent lawyers and citizens, it did not have a large enough impact publicly or politically to constrain future policies of the Administration (Rothe 2006). Regardless of the potential for future ICTs to address crimes by state leaders, paramilitaries, or militias, the likelihood is rather small, especially given that the International Criminal Court is now a fully functioning permanent Court whose mission it is to end all impunity.

The International Criminal Court

The history of proposals to establish an ICC to address conflicts within international society spans 126 years (for a detailed history of the Court's development, see Rothe and Mullins 2006a). The issue of jurisdiction was a major constraint that inhibited the previous attempts to establish an ICC and remained a major contention in the development of the Rome Statute. This is due to several factors. Jurisdiction is the root of the contradiction between international relations (international society as it is) and the ideology or ideal type of international society presented in principle (the *ought*, not the *is*, of international relations). This includes the current composition of international society (independent sovereign states based on self-governing and ultimate authority) and the principles or ideology for consensus, common values, goals, and interests (Rothe and Mullins 2006a, 2006c). Nonetheless, on June 15, 1998, the end of decades of work to establish an ICC and the commencement of a five-week Diplomatic Conference resulted in the Rome Statute of an International Criminal Court. The proposed Statute opened for votes on July 18, 1998; 120 delegations voted in favor of the Rome Statute, 7 voted against, and 21 abstained. Those opposed to the Rome Statute included India, Iraq, Israel, Libyan Arab Jamchiriya, Qatar, China, and the U.S. The final vote represented the end of years of efforts to establish a Statute for an ICC, and the Rome Statute was put forth, requiring that sixty states become signatories to the treaty by December 31, 2000 (Article 126) for the Statute to enter force. That goal was far exceeded with 139 state signatories at the closing date. The International Criminal Court became a reality on July 1, 2002, with more than 120 states attending the final Preparatory Commission meetings. As of October 17, 2007, 105 countries are states parties to the Rome Statute of the International Criminal Court. Out of them, 29 are African states, 13 are Asian states, 16 are from Eastern Europe, 22 are from Latin America and the Caribbean, and 25 are from Western Europe and other states (International Criminal Court 2007). "The ICC is a court of last resort. It will not act if a case is investigated or prosecuted by a national judicial system unless the national proceedings are not genuine, for example, if formal proceedings were undertaken solely to shield a person from criminal responsibility. In addition, the ICC only tries those accused of the gravest crimes" (International Criminal Court 2007: 1). Further, unlike the UN or the International Court of Justice, the ICC addresses crimes of individuals versus states. In contrast to the ICJ, the ICC is not a court of arbitration; it is a fully embodied criminal court.

Structure and Function

The ICC, seated in The Hague, Netherlands, consists of 105 states forming the Assembly of States Parties (ASP) to the Rome Statue. The Assembly of States Parties is the management oversight and legislative body of the International Criminal Court. It is composed of representatives of the states that have ratified and acceded to the Rome Statute. The Assembly of States Parties has a main Bureau, consisting of a president, two vice presidents and eighteen elected members for a three-year term (International Criminal Court 2007). The ASP's role is to decide on items such as the adoption of normative texts and the budget; and the election of the judges, the prosecutor, and the deputy prosecutor(s). According to Article 112:7 of the Rome Statute, each state party has one vote and every effort has to be made to reach decisions by consensus, both in the Assembly and the Bureau. If consensus cannot be reached, decisions are taken by vote.

The International Criminal Court consists of four chambers: (1) the Presidency; (2) Judicial Court (an Appeals Chamber, Trial Chamber, and a Pre-Trial Chamber); (3) Office of the Prosecutor; and (4) the Registry. Each of these plays a significant role in the Court's processes. The Presidency is an elected office serving terms of three years and holding responsibility for the administrative duties of the Court, excluding the office of the Prosecutor. The Presidency coordinates and seeks the concurrence of the Prosecutor on all matters of mutual concern. The President serves a six-year term on the Appeals Court. The First and Second Vice Presidents serve nine-year terms on the Trial Division. The judges composing the Presidency also serve on a full-time basis. The President and First and Second Vice Presidents are elected by an absolute majority of the sixteen judges of the Court.

The Registry is solely responsible for the administrative and nonjudicial aspects of the Court and for creating a Victims and Witness Unit providing protective and security measures for witnesses, victims, or others at risk due to testimony given to the court. More specifically, the Registry is responsible for the administration of legal aid matters, court management, victims and witness matters, defense counsel, the detention unit, finance, translation, building management, procurement, and personnel, and it serves as the channel of communication between the Court and states, intergovernmental organizations and nongovernmental organizations (i.e., Amnesty International, Doctors Without Borders).

The functions of the Judicial Court are divided into chambers, which allows the judges to be on more than one chamber if it serves the functioning of the Court in a more efficient manner. The Appellate Chamber is exempt from this, as an appellate judge is prohibited from serving on other chambers (Article 39, Rome Statute). All the judges are nationals of states parties to the Rome Statute. The Presidency, acting on behalf of the Court, can propose to increase the number of the judges, if it is considered necessary and appropriate. The Registry then will circulate the proposal to all states parties for final discussion by the Assembly of States Parties. The judiciary of the Court is composed of three divisions: Pre-Trial Division, Trial Division, and the Appeals Division. The Appeals Division is composed of the President and four judges; the Trial Division—Second Vice President and five judges; and the Pre-Trial Division—the First Vice President and six judges.

The Office of the Prosecutor is a separate division of the Court with the responsibility for the investigation of referrals on crimes covered by the ICC. The Prosecutor has full authority over the administration of the Prosecutorial Division (Article 42, Rome Statute). Cases brought to the ICC are handled independently by this office, unlike the system used by the United Nations' Security Council where there must be joint agreement to charges brought forth against individuals for crimes covered under international laws and treatises. The Rome Statute provides that the Office of the Prosecutor acts independently; a member of the Office of the Prosecutor must not seek or act on instructions from any external source, such as states, international organizations, NGOs, or individuals (International Criminal Court 2007). A state may refer cases to the Prosecution, or the Prosecutor can initiate the investigation based on information of a crime being committed within the jurisdiction of the Court (Articles 14 and 15, Rome Statute). In addition to state party and Security Council referrals, the Prosecutor may also receive information on crimes within the jurisdiction of the Court by individuals or nongovernmental organizations.

Having learned from the past and from witnessing one of the fundamental weaknesses of the ad hoc tribunals (ICTR and ICTY), the Rome Statute created two independent institutions: the International Criminal Court (ICC), for prosecuting those responsible for these crimes; and the Trust Fund for Victims, for helping victims of these crimes. It was recognized that prosecution (or retribution) is only one component of justice. The role of the Trust Fund for Victims is to advocate for and to assist the most vulnerable victims of genocide, crimes against humanity, and war crimes. As noted by the Court, "It is impossible to fully undo the harm caused by these most serious crimes. It is however possible to help survivors regain their dignity, rebuild their families and communities, and regain their place as fully contributing members of their societies."

The Trust Fund for Victims is composed of a Board of Directors and Secretariat. It began its operations in early 2007. The Trust Fund can work during three periods: at the end of a prosecution of ICC crimes (Court-ordered reparations), during a prosecution where victims of the crimes may have critical needs (the fund can provide immediate assistance, healthcare), and/or before or in the absence of a prosecution.

The crimes that are subject for prosecution under the Rome Statute are defined in Article 5, which lists the crimes within the jurisdiction of the ICC: crimes of genocide, crimes against humanity, war crimes, and crimes of aggression (still to be defined by the Assembly of State Parties). While these acts are both customary and criminal offenses, the ability of the ICC to penalize all who offend is limited. For example, the ICC is limited in its investigative reach, making it unable to subpoena any state or its records. While the Court may request a warrant or subpoena, the Prosecutor and the Court lack an empowered policing agency to ensure the enforcement of either request (Articles 54–58). However, on December 22, 2004, a cooperation agreement between the Offices of the Prosecutor and the International Criminal Police Organization (INTERPOL) was signed establishing a framework for cooperation between the two agencies. The agreement enables the Office of the Prosecutor (OP) and INTERPOL to exchange police information and criminal analysis and to cooperate in the search for fugitives and suspects. The agreement also gives the OP access to INTERPOL telecommunications network and databases (Rothe and Mullins 2006a).

Currently, the ICC is conducting investigations on situations in the Democratic Republic of Congo, Uganda, Central African Republic, and Darfur. To date, eight arrest warrants have been issued at the request of the Prosecutor. The current (January 2008) cases are as follows: DRC—*The Prosecutor v. Thomas Lubanga Dyilo and Germain Katanga*; Uganda—*The Prosecutor v. Joseph Kony, Vincent Otti, Okot Odhiambo and Dominic Ongwen*; Central African Republic—no cases at this time; Darfur, Sudan—*The Prosecutor v. Ahmad Muhammad Harun and Ali Muhammad Ali Abd-Al-Rahman*. Of these cases, three have been referred to the Office of the Prosecutor by the states and the UNSC has referred one (Darfur).

Summary of ICC

The Rome Statute suggests it has jurisdiction over the most serious crimes, but realistically the Court has limited jurisdiction. For example, its jurisdiction is inclusive only of a state party to the treaty or by agreement of a state not a party to the Statute. The criteria listed in Article 12 for the exercise of jurisdiction requires a state to become a party to the Statute or to accept the jurisdiction of the Court if the crime occurred on that state's territory, its vessel, or aircraft; or if the accused is a national of the state (Article 12, a–b). No person can be held liable by the Court unless the crime occurred within the jurisdiction of the Court. First, compliance by a non-party state is highly unlikely, and noncompliance can act as a detriment to the ability of the ICC to be an effective measure of international justice. Secondly, the alternative route to the ICC would be for the UN Security Council to unanimously recommend the case to the prosecutor for investigation. Again, with the veto power of the UNSC, recommendations would be highly unlikely to include major powers or their allies (e.g., Israel and the United States) (Rothe and Mullins 2006b; Rothe and Kauzlarich 2008). However, the ICC is a project in process—legitimating of the institution does not come with a treaty's ratification but with the long process of action. It is through the successful addressing of the initial cases that the ICC will become more and more legitimate and thus more and more powerful (Rothe and Mullins 2006a, 2006b). Nevertheless, as noted by Ambos and Stegmiller (2008: 190):

> [T]he establishment of the ICC and the operation of the fundamental principle of complementarity had a strong positive impact on national legislation for the prosecution of international crimes. In many countries reforms were adopted or initiated in the context of the ratification of the ICC Statute and the insertion of special legislation on international crimes now complements the domestic criminal law. One of the most significant results of the establishment of the ICC is, therefore, the increase of the potential of national prosecution of international crimes.

Militia leaders and heads of state frequently scoff at investigators working for Amnesty International or Human Rights Watch who suggest that what they are doing could lead to the leaders' imprisonment. They see impunity; they perceive themselves as the only legal order extant in the countryside. One of the strongest results of ICC prosecutions will be to disabuse them of such notions. This appears to be currently playing out, as a key member of the Prosecutor's office of the ICC has preliminarily stated that the issues of arrest warrants for the conflict in Uganda and Congo have resulted in a reduction of violence, especially noted in the context of the Ugandan civil war (Agirre 2007). For the ICC to truly be an effective agent of social control, it must be given universal jurisdiction. This can happen if the Rome Statute can be recognized as customary law, as it would be elevated to the status of universal jurisdiction, or through the restructuring of the treaty (Article 127). Further, the Court must be empowered with its own policing agency to ensure state compliance. As the case of Darfur has shown, the el Bashir regime is not going to willingly hand over itself or key Janjaweed leaders. Nor are countries like the United States going to surrender sovereignty or hand over past or present state leaders to the court or a third party that is a member of the Rome Statute. Moreover, the Court must ensure that it remains neutral in the case selection process. As has been noted with Uganda, the Court's public statement for investigations and arrest warrants for the Lord's Resistant Army leaders was done standing alongside the Ugandan president, who has also been accused of these same violations. To ensure legitimacy, the Court must maintain an objective stand in its investigations and announcements.

Chapter Summary

This chapter has presented the fundamental mechanisms of international controls against crimes of the state. In doing so, I attempted to provide enough of an in-depth overview to provide a general understanding of each institution (Law, UN, ICJ, ICTY, ICTR, and the ICC), along with some of the barriers that have reduced their ability to be an effectual control. Nonetheless, there are those that argue that these international systems are problematic simply due to the fact that they are systems of retribution more than social justice. For example, Cobban (2007) suggests that the long-term interests of societies that experience this magnitude of atrocities may best be served by utilizing amnesty, reconciliation, and reintegration versus the formal social controls, retributive model, established by the international political community. Others, such as Vanspauwen et al. (2008), have argued that the adversarial nature of trials provides little contribution to explaining the causes of mass violence and represents only one side of the "coin of justice." The "truth" that is revealed during the process of these trials is fragmented facts. Moreover, the raison d'être of the retributive form of "justice," or the courts, is to establish criminal responsibility of perpetrators. Moreover, "prosecuting and punishing perpetrators and removing them from the society is nothing but a symptomatic response to violent conflicts" (Vanspauwen et al. 2008: 4). Finally, it has been suggested that reconciliation is always dismissed in these processes; they are not structured to restore relationships between people. Nonetheless, the courts may have reconciliatory effects, either at the individual or collective level.

When looking at the literature on social controls and social justice, we are left with the feeling that there is a dichotomy between the Western formal legal process that, according to Cobban (2007), has failed to address the needs of society and victims, and that of the more successful forms of social justice (amnesty, in particular). This may be shortsighted, as societies may require, in specific cases, a multitude of responses, including a formal international social control approach along with a state-level form of social justice, be they gacaca,[1] truth and reconciliations, or amnesties. There are levels to social justice, which, in a broad sense, should include finding truth about the past and events and calling into account the offenders (Huyse 1996; Kritz 1995). Both are absolutely crucial to break through the walls of impunity and to move toward a culture of accountability and social justice (Mathews 2002; Minow 1998). After all, historically we have seen that impunity for heads of state has prevailed, thus preventing any potential for deterrence—Stalin killed millions but was never charged with any crime; the Pol Pot regime slaughtered over 1 million innocent civilians but never saw the inside of a prison cell; and Idi Amin and Raoul Cedras comfortably retired without any ramifications or accountability for their actions. With this in mind, the following chapter will address the various forms of controls at the state level, including restoration, truth and reconciliation, gacaca, amnesties, and domestic laws.

Notes

1. The *gacaca* is a customary system of community hearings used to resolve local disputes. Post-genocide, the gacaca tribunals were legally established judicial bodies that allowed the vast numbers of perpetrators to be better served than using the formal state legal system. Moreover, the trial of those alleged to have participated in the genocide takes place within the communities in which the offenses were committed.

Chapter 9

Domestic Controls:
Sole Mechanisms and/or Complements
to International Instruments

Control over state crime is the strongest at the international level. At the other levels of analysis, effective controls cannot be reasonably analyzed with a broad brushstroke. For example, domestic legal sanctions and laws vary from state to state, and as such, any internal responses to past or occurring forms of state criminality would necessarily have to take into account the specific country's needs, especially those in transitional capacities (Rothe and Kauzlarich 2008). Additionally, effective responses and post controls need to be varied enough to incorporate the vast types of crimes. For example, international prosecution for the Rwandan genocidaires has been highly problematic when considering the scope of participants. The vast numbers of offenders created massive infrastructure problems for the state. In response, gacacas were set in place to address the crimes and to achieve reconciliation at the local levels (Haverman 2007). States also may often need to incorporate systems of amnesty and/or truth and reconciliation commissions, or rely on traditional cultural or spiritual redresses to address offenders in certain cases. Case in point, the situation in Uganda and the use of children by the LRA presents a challenge for addressing the atrocities they have been forced to commit as they are returned to their communities; here reintegration is key more than formal controls. As was pointed out in chapter 8, at times international controls may not provide the best or sole solution for the local level or communities. After all, in post-conflict situations, peace is the most desired commodity. However, peace depends "not only on the absence of war but also on the existence of both justice and truth, with both justice and truth dependent on the other" (Amnesty International 2007). As such, responses may need to be more than what is typically thought of as systems of accountability. For this reason, this chapter explores core domestic controls and various formal responses to crimes of genocide, war crimes, crimes against humanity, human rights abuses, and/or extensive corruption, aimed at reconciliation, accountability, and restoration.

> As for what is called the law of nations, it is clear that without any real sanction these laws are only illusions that are more tenuous even than the notion of natural law. The latter at least addresses itself to the hearts of individuals, whereas decisions based on the law of nations, having no other guarantee than the utility of the one who submits to them, are respected only as long as those decisions confirm one's own self-interest.

Domestic Laws

As with any social phenomena, the social construction of what constitutes a criminal act is continuously re-defined; behaviors are either legitimized or de-legitimized in public and legal discourse arenas. As many scholars have pointed out, these processes are influenced by existing politico-social power structures. When the state commits acts they would view as intolerable or illegal by others (genocides, crimes against humanity, repression, war crimes, or corruption), they generally label them "legitimate," a "positive" violence, or justified by the greater good. The state can also, due to its very position, legitimize certain violence as a means of social control. In other words, the process of defining values and norms in the legitimation (or lack thereof) of behavior is a key role of the state political apparatus. Simply, while a state's domestic laws, ideally, can serve to control its actions, due to the unique position of a government as a self-regulator and lawmaker, it is in the position to create or nullify laws governing it (Rothe 2006). Nonetheless, most all international treaties, charters, or statutes require that states' domestic laws conform through legislation or constitutional changes to the international standard a state has agreed to comply with.

For example, the U.S. War Crimes Act of 1996 and the Expanded War Crimes Act of 1997 were created and passed in response to the development of the Rome Statute of the International Criminal Court being developed during the early and mid 1990s. The U.S. Torture Statue (18 USC 2340) is the domestic codification of the Convention against Torture and Other Cruel, Inhumane or Degrading Treatment of Punishment (ratified by the U.S. in 1994). The Uniform Code of Military Justice (UCMJ) is the code that subjects all military personnel to criminal responsibility for acts such as Article 93—Cruelty and Mistreatment. The above were all legislated to bypass potential international legal responsibility (especially from the ICC) by ensuring the domestic procedures and laws were in place. This does not mean they need be used, but the state can argue that, as a sovereign, it has the means and legislation to prosecute those accused, thus negating the need or ability of international intervention. Simply, the legislation enforced the state's position that, as a sovereign state, it could and would domestically prosecute its own citizens for breaches of international war crimes that were to be included in the Rome Statute of the International Criminal Court.

On the other hand, states, due to their unique position, can ensure impunity at the local level for participants of state-sanctioned violence and criminality. For example, during the ongoing genocide in Darfur, the Sudanese government ensured the Interim Constitution for Sudan (Article 60), ratified July 6, 2005, which contained a provision granting immunity from prosecution to the president and vice president of the Republic of Sudan. Similarly, Article 92 granted immunity to members of the National Legislature. Again, this was a strategic move to ensure impunity for the genocidiers, complicit and implicit, at the state level. Thus, if the regime were overthrown or dismantled, the Constitution afforded them legal protection from prosecution. A new law, The Immunity Law, was executed in Burundi, granting temporary immunity to political leaders who returned from exile. It was approved by the National Assembly in August 2003: "The temporary immunity covers crimes with a political aim committed from 1 July 1962 (Burundi's independence) to the date of its promulgation (27 August 2003)" (IRIN 2003). This piece of domestic legislation has come under much scrutiny by international leaders, organizations, and citizens of Burundi, as it contradicted the Arusha accord for peace and reconciliation law. Moreover, it grants amnesty for those "who planned the crimes," while those who executed the orders were to remain in custody.

This is not to say that a country should never consider or implement amnesty or immunities. It can indeed be one mechanism that achieves reconciliation and restoration; nonetheless, when such laws are put in place to grant impunity for state leaders without the larger goal of restoration or support of the peoples, such acts are an additional abuse of political power and become a "legalized tyranny" or create "the legal criminal." Further, it is this type of action by state leaders that has reinforced the need for an international institution of control that can indeed intervene in cases where states either cannot or are unwilling to prosecute those accused of violating international criminal law.

Legalised Tyranny

by Lord Johan Steyn

History has shown that majority rule and strict adherence to legality is no guarantee against tyranny. Hitler came to power by democratic vote. Moreover, in Nazi Germany, amid the Holocaust, pockets of the principle of legality (for what it was worth) sometimes survived. In Nazi Germany, defendants sentenced to periods of imprisonment before the Second World War were left alone during the terms of their sentences. Only when their sentences expired did the Gestapo wait for them at the gates of the prisons and transport them to the death camps. So even in Nazi Germany an impoverished concept of legality played some role. The role of judges in this period is, of course, part of the Nuremberg story. But at or after Nuremberg, nobody had any doubt what torture is. That at the highest levels the United States Administration has recently persistently tried to water down what is torture is deeply depressing for our times.

In the apartheid era, millions of black people in South Africa were subjected to institutionalised tyranny and cruelty in the richest and most developed country in Africa. What is not always sufficiently appreciated is that by and large the Nationalist Government achieved its oppressive purposes by a scrupulous observance of legality. If the judges applied the oppressive laws, the Nationalist Government attained all it set out to do. That is, however, not the whole picture. In the 1980s during successive emergencies, under Chief Justice Rabie, almost every case before the highest court was heard by a so-called "emergency team" which in the result decided nearly every case in favour of the government. Safe hands were the motto. In the result the highest court determinedly recast South African jurisprudence so as to grant the greatest possible latitude to the executive to act outside conventional legal controls.

Cited in the Asian Human Rights Commission (AHRC), May 10, 2006

Domestic Law and Civil Remedies

Most governments have similar laws that govern traditional street crimes such as murder, kidnapping, and larceny, and many of them treat any offender from any country as the same as one of their citizens. As such, these laws act in a way to allow a citizen of another country to seek redress in the offenders' state(s) of citizenship. For example, in the U.S. there is the Alien Tort Claims Act (ATCA). Its origins date back to the first Judiciary Act of 1789, which created the U.S. court system. It provides that "the district courts shall have original jurisdiction of any civil action by an alien for a tort only, committed in violation of the law of nations or a treaty of the United States" (National Law Journal 2004: 1). The ATCA grants U.S. courts jurisdiction in any dispute where it is alleged that the "law of nations," or international laws, are broken (Rothe 2006). As an example of the Tort Act for noncitizens to use as recourse against U.S. citizens, in June 2004, a Supreme Court ruling upheld the core principles of the 1789 Alien Tort Claims Act (ATCA). As such, potentially, individuals abused and tortured at Abu Ghraib (and in the war on terrorism in general) would be entitled to bring a civil suit against the U.S. for alleged abuses. This would include being able to sue corporations whose employees took part in the systematic abuses and torture. Such is the case with CACI International and Titan, who are named as defendants in a suit filed in Federal District Court in Washington, D.C. under the

Alien Tort Claims Act, on behalf of four Abu Ghraib detainees. The Center for Constitutional Rights (CCR) and the Philadelphia law firm of Montgomery, McCracken, Walker and Rhoads filed a second lawsuit (a class action suit) on June 9, 2004, in federal court in San Diego. This action also utilizes the Alien Tort Claims Act (ATCA), along with the 5th, 8th, and 14th Amendments to the U.S. Constitution (Rothe 2006).

Another component of domestic laws is their ability to try noncitizens for crimes committed within their territory or, in some cases, committed in one country by a national of another country—enforcement by third countries. In other chapters, I have used the Pinochet case as an example of state-sponsored terrorism and as later coming to set international legal precedence. This was the result of enforcement by a third country, most notably Spain. Baltasar Garzon, the Spanish judge who initiated the successful prosecution of General Pinochet, also secured the detention in Mexico of the Argentine torturer Ricardo Miguel Cavallo, who is now awaiting extradition to Spain for his trial. Additionally, the Belgium Parliament empowered Belgian courts to exercise jurisdiction over war crimes and breaches of the Geneva Convention committed anywhere in the world by a citizen of any country (Hitchins 2001). According to Hitchins (2001: 1):

> The Netherlands, Switzerland, Denmark, and Germany have all recently employed the Geneva Conventions to prosecute war criminals for actions committed against non-nationals by non-nationals. . . . The British House of Lords' decision in the matter of Pinochet has also decisively negated the defense of "sovereign immunity" for acts committed by a government or by those following a government's orders. This has led in turn to Pinochet's prosecution in his own country.

Yet, this is another case where we must be cognizant of states' interests in using their authority to pursue foreign nationals, citizens, or even heads of state. For example, in September 2000, Zimbabwe's President Robert Mugabe (whom we discussed in chapter 3) visited the U.S. to attend the UN Millennium Summit. Prior to his arrival, he had been served with summons of appearance for a lawsuit that had been lodged, alleging that he had organized assassinations, torture, rape, terrorism, and other acts of violence to reduce or control his political opposition (state repression). Yet, the U.S. State Department submitted an official "suggestion" to the court claiming that Mugabe was entitled to head-of-state immunity in U.S. courts. Further, they noted that putting President Mugabe on trial would be incompatible with U.S. foreign policy goals and interests—an example of the realpolitik involved, even in the implementation of laws and justice. Nonetheless, domestic law and civil remedies can act as enforcement mechanisms or controls for those beyond its borders as well as for those within. Such types of recourse are indeed an alternative to the newly formed ICC or to relying on the long and arduous task of creating an ICT through the United

Nations. Moreover, they afford protections to the accused typically not provided in domestic military tribunals.

Beyond this, there are generally laws within each state's legal system that prohibit these types of behaviors, some stronger than others, especially given the position of a state to legitimate or even decriminalize its actions. Luckily, such cases are not the dominant ones. Again, at this point we are talking about the presence of laws, not the enforcement of them. Additionally, due to the vast array of domestic laws, it would be beyond the scope of this chapter to identify and discuss them in detail. Nonetheless, as an example, consider the following: Sweden criminalized genocide with a special domestic law in 1964 and war crimes are penalized through a legal norm. On the other hand, Finland and Poland cover genocide and war crimes within the general Finish and Polish penal codes. In Finland and Sweden, crimes against humanity can be punished only as ordinary offenses. In order to prosecute war crimes in Finland, Poland, and Sweden, a reference to international treaty and customary law is deemed necessary. Austria has a special national provision covering only the crime of genocide. Croatia, Serbia, and Montenegro penalize not only genocide but also war crimes as special offenses; yet, crimes against humanity are not codified separately and are prosecuted as ordinary criminal offenses. When looking at domestic laws in Spain, Ivory Coast, France, and Italy, national prosecution systems also differ. Heterogeneity is the key word regarding "national prosecution of international crimes." Canada, on the other hand, has enacted an independent "Crimes Against Humanity and War Crimes Act," which penalizes the worst of the worst state crimes—acts of genocide, crimes against humanity, and war crimes—and relies on customary international law. In Israel and the United States, crimes against humanity can be punished only as an ordinary criminal offense, while acts of genocide are explicitly covered. In China, violations of international criminal law can be prosecuted only as ordinary offenses. The legal situation in domestic jurisdictions is quite heterogeneous and the prosecution of international crimes is very limited in many countries' legal systems (Ambos and Stegmiller 2008).

Military Tribunals

Domestic military tribunals are not to be confused with the international tribunals discussed in chapter 8. The war-crimes trials at Nuremburg and Tokyo were not military tribunals; they were ad hoc tribunals like the International Criminal Tribunals for the Former Yugoslavia and Rwanda. Moreover, domestic military tribunals have been called, often interchangeably, military commissions, tribunals, court-martial or war courts, court of inquiry, and common law war courts. To give an idea of the history behind these types of courts, consider that British precedents for using them date back to around 1650. They were used in the U.S. during the Civil War by President Lincoln; in this case, the tribunals were also used for civilians in the spring of 1865. They were also used during the Indian

Wars to try Native Americans. Throughout history, the support for and/or criticism of use of military tribunals has waned and waxed according to different political and ideological stances of administrations. The current G. W. Bush Administration has reinstituted using the Courts to address civilians as well as those they deem "enemy combatants," which has been a highly controversial decision. Interestingly, the U.S. has consistently criticized other countries for using the same type of redress (e.g., Burma, China, Colombia, Egypt, Malaysia, Peru, Russia, and Turkey).

With these caveats in mind, it is important to note that military tribunals can serve as a last resort mechanism when a country will not prosecute its own people that have committed atrocities in that country or another. For example, the trials against Argentinian and Chilean leaders in Spain were instituted for this very reason. The Derechos News Service (1998: 2) noted that

> [I]n 1996 the Progressive Union of Prosecutors decided to file criminal complaints against the Argentinian and Chilean military for the disappearance of Spanish citizens in those countries. . . . On June 28th, [1996] Judge Garzon ruled that the court had jurisdiction to investigate the facts denounced by the popular action and to prosecute any of the crimes committed by the accused and others responsible for the crimes.

In October 1998, upon hearing that Pinochet was present in England, the popular action asked the court to interrogate Pinochet about his role in Operation Condor and requested that he and other Chilean military be charged for the disappearance and kidnappings of civilians. Another group of Chilean relatives of the disappeared asked the judge to charge Pinochet and other leaders with genocide, terrorism, and torture. On October 16, Garzon ordered the arrest of Pinochet, issuing an international arrest order. On November 3 of that year, Garzon issued an extradition order for Pinochet, setting worldwide legal precedence for a military tribunal for a head of state by another state, thus showing universal jurisdiction for the crimes of genocide. As noted by the BBC (1999: 1), because there was "no real prospect of Pinochet being tried in Chile or any international tribunal, Spain's extradition request was the only vehicle for the emplacement of the rule of law in these matters." The power of this mechanism to be an effective control is direct but also indirect, through the perception of those that have committed such atrocities and violated international criminal law that a military tribunal could be initiated to prosecute their actions. For example, fear of military tribunal prosecutions was formally discussed within the U.S. State Department. The FBI has warned several former U.S. officials not to travel to some countries, including some in Europe, "where there is a risk of extradition to other nations interested in prosecuting them" (Rothe 2006: 248). Henry Kissinger is sought for extradition for violations of international law, and as such he does not leave the U.S. without assurances of not being extradited. Moreover,

> Secretary of State Colin Powell demanded that Belgium change its war crimes legislation in order to halt a case against Powell, George Bush senior, Vice President Dick Cheney, and former U.S. army commander Norman Schwarzkopf for committing war crimes during the 1991 Gulf War. Washington fears a similar lawsuit is about to be made against George W. Bush for human rights violations and civilian deaths in the current war. (Michaels 2003: 1)

Other examples include countries prosecuting Rwandese genocide suspects under their national jurisdictions: a Swiss military court arrested a genocide suspect in 1996 and tried him between July 1998 and April 1999; a Belgium Crown Court (*Cour d'Assises*) tried four individuals for war crimes and human rights violations from April to June 2001; and the Canadian government put into use two federal immigration tribunals to try a Rwandan accused of genocide, but the federal court halted his deportation proceedings in April 2001 (Amnesty International 2002a). It is with this in mind that military tribunals can produce positive results and can act as a much larger control than a country's own military forces or individuals caught committing such crimes on the soil of another state.

Special Domestic Courts

Beyond a state's existing criminal justice institutions, temporary special courts have also been convened to address violations of international criminal law by agents of the state (or post heads of state administrators). The use of these special courts can provide an alternative to or act as a complement to international tribunals (e.g., East Timor, Kosovo, Bosnia, Serbia, and Croatia). These local justice mechanisms operate under state law, although there can be an international component. Nonetheless, they are considered domestic courts and differ from other hybrid forms of domestic/international as in the case of Sierra Leone that will be discussed later in this chapter. For example, there has been a transfer of cases from the ICTY to local Bosnian courts. In this case, the temporary or ad hoc court serves as an "internationalized" war crimes chamber of the Bosnian State Court system. The War Crimes Chamber, established in Sarajevo in March 2005, handles cases of serious war crimes that were transferred from the ICTY, as well as war crimes cases initiated locally (Human Rights Watch 2006b). Additionally, it will continue to handle war crimes cases after international involvement has been phased out. According to Almiro Rodrigues, judge at the War Crime Chamber in Bosnia and Herzegovina,

> [T]he Chamber is vital for the process of reconciliation in Bosnia . . . the prosecution of war crimes suspects on home soil has a far more positive effect on reconciliation than the dispensation of "distanced" justice in a forum such as the ICTY. It is important the perception of justice being done in accordance with the traditional maxim "justice must not only be done, but seen to be done." Such a perception becomes far more prevalent if a domestic, rather than an

alien, judicial mechanism, dispenses justice. Moreover, it forces Bosnian society to confront the truth of its recent past in a very practical and real sense. (Rodrigues 2006: 3)

Similar initiatives have been carried out in Serbia and Croatia to help alleviate the financial and economic burden on the ICTY.

In response to the atrocities committed in the Kosovo conflict during 1999, panels known as "Regulation 64 Panels" were instituted to adjudicate war crimes cases. At the time of this writing, the Regulation 64 panels have conducted more than two dozen war crimes trials, which resulted in the indictments of Milos Jokic and Dragan Nikolic for genocide. Additionally, the trial for Milorad Trbic began in November 2007, in which he was being charged with genocide. In March 2000, the UN Transitional Authority for East Timor created a judicial system of district courts for East Timor, which included a Serious Crimes Panels. In the case of East Timor, the Dili District Court has exclusive jurisdiction over genocide, war crimes, crimes against humanity, murder, sexual offenses, and torture, for crimes committed between January and October 1999 (UN Office for the Coordination of Humanitarian Affairs, IRIN 2008). Similarly, an "Extraordinary Chambers" was created in Cambodia to address the crimes committed by the Khmer Rouge between 1975 and 1979. The Chamber is mandated to try those responsible for genocide, crimes against humanity, and other crimes defined by the Cambodian law (murder, torture, religious persecutions, destruction of cultural property in armed conflict, and violations of the Convention of Vienna on the protection of diplomats). Nonetheless, as we will see with other special courts, the Chamber has been unable to hold accountable those that orchestrated the atrocity. For example, Pol Pot, the regime's leader, died in 1998, and Ieng Sary is politically protected against prosecution through his self-proclaimed 1996 amnesty. Successful indictments, however, do include two senior Khmer Rouge leaders: Ta Mok, 75, alias "The Butcher"; and Kang Kech Eav, widely known as Duch, who managed the S-21 prison where many of the executions occurred (UN Office for the Coordination of Humanitarian Affairs, IRIN 2008).

While these types of specialized courts have contributed to accountability in cases that would have been yet another example of impunity, they do have many practical barriers to their success. Additionally, as I previously noted, in some cases these special courts are convened by a government in response to international political pressures and serve as nothing more than a symbolic, hollow gesture. For example, on June 14, 2005, Sudan opened a Special Court to try alleged war criminals in the ongoing genocide campaign against the Darfurians; however, as Amnesty International noted, the establishment of such a court was reminiscent of past governmental inquiries into the atrocities and represented a tactic to avoid prosecution of regime members by the ICC (Amnesty International 2005). After all, the announcement of the creation of Special Courts came one week after the Prosecutor of the ICC announced the opening of investigations into the war crimes and crimes against humanity committed in the Darfur

region. Additionally, according to the Constitution, a provision was implemented granting immunity from prosecution to the President and Vice President
of the Republic of Sudan as well as members of the National Legislature. To
date, the Special Criminal Court has handed down several verdicts; however,
none of the cases were related to the conflict in 2003 or 2004, nor did any verdicts convict any high level officials. Thus, it remained a symbolic gesture by
the el-Bashir regime to ensure impunity to those that orchestrated the genocide
(Mullins and Rothe 2007).

Hybrid System—Sierra Leone

The middle ground between international tribunals and wholly domestic courts
has been called "hybrid tribunals." The special courts mentioned in the previous
section are often grouped in this category; however, I view them as separate
since they are able to continue without international involvement and rely heavily on domestic law and participation of local prosecutors and other agents of a
criminal justice system. However, the hybrid tribunals in the case of Sierra
Leone consist of international and domestic judges but, more importantly, an
international prosecutor, Desmond de Silva, appointed by the UN Secretary-
General (May 2005). The hybrid system for Sierra Leone is a jointly adminis-
tered court by the United Nations and the Sierra Leone government (UN Resolution 1315, August 14, 2000). The Special Court was created by a treaty between
the United Nations and the Sierra Leone government in response to the devastating conflict that occurred between 1991 until 2002, which was characterized by
massive human rights abuses committed by all warring factions. It is mandated
to try only those who bear the greatest responsibility for war crimes and crimes
against humanity committed in the territory of Sierra Leone between 1996 and
2002, leaving the rest of those that committed such acts to the country's Truth
and Reconciliation Commission (UN Office for the Coordination of Humanitarian Affairs [UNCOH], IRIN 2008). As of January 2008, eleven people have
been indicted by the Special Court via three separate trials; they were charged
with war crimes, crimes against humanity, and other serious violations of international humanitarian law (rape, sexual slavery, conscription of children into an
armed force, and attacks on UN peacekeepers, among others). Although individually charged, they have been grouped into three separate trials: the Revolutionary United Front (RUF) trial, begun in July 2004; the Civil Defense Forces
(CDF) trial, commenced in June 2004; and the Armed Forces Revolutionary
Council (AFRC) trial, begun in March 2005. According to the UNCOH (2008:
1), "The single most well known person indicted by the Special Court is the
former Liberian President, Charles Taylor, accused of backing the civil war in
Sierra Leone by providing arms and training to the RUF in exchange for diamonds."

The advantages of a hybrid system of justice, as used in Sierra Leone,
include the following: it tends to avoid allegations that it is partisan, as the judi-

cial body is composed of a mixture of domestic judges and international ones; it is less costly than "pure" international ad hoc tribunals; it is more transparent than a domestic military tribunal; there is less of a cost burden on the state involved, which is often going through massive reconstruction efforts (political, economic, and social); it is international enough that head of state immunity would not apply; and it has the ability to carry out an extensive outreach to disseminate information about the court through video, radio, and discussion. Nonetheless, such tribunals are often unable to hold accountable all individuals involved and are often seen as incompatible with larger restorative justice measures. The latter two points were core to the formation of other alternative domestic measures taken to address state crime, including the gacaca trials, truth and reconciliation commissions, and amnesties.

Systems of Accountability, Restoration, and Social Justice

In the aftermath of state crimes that leave countries ripped apart, accountability is only a small part of the countries' needs. Additionally, a state is often in a state of transition. In such cases, there must be controls that serve as transitional justice mechanisms that can provide restorative aspects as well as accountability as known in the Western model of social justice. The best examples include the Truth and Reconciliation Commission in South Africa, the gacaca in Rwanda, Amnesty in Mozambique, or a combination of nonformal or ad hoc judicial mechanisms of conflict resolution (Hayner 2001; Villa-Vicencio 2000). Such mechanisms are considered a valuable and complementary tool to civil or state or international criminal courts because of their strong emphasis on truth, reparation, and reconciliation (Christie 2001; Vanspauwen, Parmentier, and Weitekamp 2007, 2008).

Gacaca Trials-Rwanda

In response to the 1994 genocide, the Rwandan government wanted to hold accountable the massive numbers of genocidaires through prosecution in an effort to end the impunity that had long characterized the Rwandese political culture. To do so, it passed special domestic legislation: Organic Law No. 08/96 (1996), which established specialized genocide chambers in the Courts of First Instance and Organic Law No. 40/2000 (2001) for the creation and implementation of the *gacaca* (Amnesty International 2002a). The gacaca is a hybrid system that merges customary practice with a Western, formal court structure. Historically, the gacaca were a customary system of community hearings that were used to resolve community disputes such as land or inheritance rights, or marital disputes. These were informal, ad hoc in nature, and led by community elders (*inyangamugayo*). By creating approximately 10,000 gacaca throughout the country, the Rwandese government transformed this traditional mode of conflict resolution in order to try the more than 800,000–1,000,000 genocide suspects that are overfilling the country's prisons. Thus, the new tribunals are formal legal judicial bodies that hear three of the four categories of genocide and crimes against humanity. The categories are meant to distinguish between the various degrees of individual responsibility and they carry different penalties:

> The first category includes leaders and organizers of the genocide, persons who abused positions of authority, notorious killers who distinguished themselves by their ferocity or excessive cruelty and perpetrators of sexual torture [to be heard at the ICTR]. Category 2 includes the perpetrators of or accomplices to intentional homicides or serious assaults against individuals that led to their death. Category 3 contains persons guilty of other serious assaults against individuals, while category 4 covers persons who committed property crimes. (Amnesty International 2002a: 2)

The gacaca courts hear charges only for crimes that fall into categories 2–4. These courts are located in the local communities and try those persons alleged to have participated in the genocide within the regions where the offenses occurred. The government claims that these community-style hearings, where the members themselves serve as witness, judge, and party, more effectively ventilate the evidence, establish the truth, and bring about reconciliation than what had been achieved previously by either the specialized genocide chambers of the Rwandan courts or the ICTR. As noted in by Fatuma Ndangiza (2004: 1) of the National Unity and Reconciliation Commission, "Most of the perpetrators who have confessed, when they are taken to the communities to tell what they did, they ask for forgiveness." The estimated cost of the gacaca system totaled approximately $1.03 million by the end of 2007. Yet, as of January 1, 2008, approximately one million people accused of involvement in the 1994 genocide had appeared before the courts, where more than 800,000 were tried. Apart from a legal system, gacaca is much more. It is a social process:

> It is a cultural phenomenon with historical roots; it is a psychological phenomenon as part of a complex of ways to overcome the mental aftermath of the genocide; it is a political phenomenon, bridging gaps (or widening them) between political opponents, or as an alleged mechanism for the minority in power to suppress the majority of the population, to give just some examples of ways to approach the *gacaca*. Maybe the least important therefore is to consider the *gacaca* as a legal system. (Haverman 2007: 3)

When these types of courts are convened and trials are carried out in a fair manner, and where judges exclude themselves from personal cases, they can be an effective alternative for delivering justice to the victims and survivors of the genocide as well as to the perpetrators. Yet, as with any other system of control we have explored here, when they fail to deliver justice fairly, they can lose legitimacy and weaken efforts to end impunity. Nonetheless, they are strong alternatives to impunity and, in many cases, a practical solution in transitional situations.

Truth Commissions

Since 1974 with the Commission of Inquiry in Uganda, there have been nearly two dozen truth commissions in various regions around the world with varying degrees of structure and success.

Truth Commissions

Country	Date of Commission	Time Period Covered
Uganda	1974	1971–1974
Argentina	1983–1984	1976–1983
Uruguay	1985	1973–1982
Uganda	1986–1995	1962–1986
Philippines	1986	1972–1986
Nepal	1990–1991	1961–1990
Chile	1990–1991	1973–1990
Chad	1991–1992	1982–1990
El Salvador	1992–1993	1980–1991
Sri Lanka	1994–1997	1988–1994
Haiti	1995–1996	1991–1994
Burundi	1995–1996	1993–1995
South Africa	1995–2000	1960–1994
Guatemala	1997–1999	1962–1996
Nigeria	1999–2001	1966–1999
Uruguay	2000–2001	1973–1985
Panama	2001–2002	1968–1989
Sierra Leone	2002	1991–1999
Ghana	2002	1966–2001

Source: United States Institute of Peace, www.usip.org/library/truth.html

---

Generally, these commissions are established to report on human rights abuses over a certain period of time in a particular country or in relation to a particular conflict. The overarching goal is allow victims, their relatives, and perpetrators to give evidence of human rights abuses, providing an official public forum for their accounts and a historical record of the atrocities that occurred. Additionally, there has been a concerted move, headed by the United Nations, toward establishing truth commissions as a complementary tool together with restricted amnesty limited to those "least responsible" for crimes. The following subsection provides a few examples and a brief overview of some of the more well-known truth commissions. This is then followed by a discussion of amnesties.

South Africa Truth and Reconciliation Commission

The Truth and Reconciliation Commission (TRC) was established by the 1995 Promotion of National Unity and Reconciliation Act to investigate crimes committed during the apartheid era in South Africa, from March 1960 until May 1994. Specifically, the commission was charged with finding the extent of and recording human rights violations committed by the state and the insurgent groups as a part of the institutionalized apartheid, recommending reparations, and overseeing the amnesty given to those who admitted their crimes. The amnesty component was limited to those who made full disclosure of all the relevant facts relating to acts associated with a political objective committed in the course of the conflicts of the past. Chaired by Archbishop Desmond Tutu, hearings began in April 1996. Upon completion of the TRC in July 1998, the commission received over 7,000 applications for amnesty and rejected more than 4,500 of the applications, granting approximately 125 amnesties. It heard testimony from over 21,000 victims of apartheid. Findings include that "[t]he state, in the form of the South African government, the civil service and its security forces, was, in the period 1960–94 the primary perpetrator of gross violations of human rights in South Africa and, from 1974, in southern Africa" (*Truth and Reconciliation Commission Final Report*, Section 5, 2003). This included the head of state and chair of the State Security Council, Botha, for facilitating a climate in which gross violations of human rights "could and did occur and as such is accountable for such actions." The charges brought by victims included the deliberate, unlawful killing and attempted killing of persons opposed to the policies of the government; the widespread use of torture and other forms of severe ill treatment; and the forcible abduction of individuals who were residents in neighboring countries.

In the cases where amnesty was denied or not sought by the defendants, prosecution could be considered wherein evidence found by the commission could be handed over to prosecutors. The hope of the commission was to contribute to reconciliation in South Africa's divided society by providing a venue for truth. Nonetheless, very few political leaders or leading white civilians came forward to apologize or accept responsibility for their role. Mathatha Tsedu, the political editor of South Africa's most popular black newspaper, *The Sowetan,* said, "Black people are the sufferers here . . . they saw the TRC as a mechanism to try to deal with that pain. . . . White people have so much to hide about what they have been doing all along and they saw the TRC as some kind of witch hunt and therefore didn't go" (cited in BBC News 1998: 2). Additionally, many victims and their accounts were not taken into consideration or heard because they were not "victimized enough," according to the Mandate. Only victims of gross human rights violations were defined as victims in the TRC Act. As such, the victims that were omitted from this process felt their rights and feelings had been neglected and justice was not gained. In this respect, it is important to consider the distinction between individual and collective victimization, direct and indirect, to better address the needs of both groups without sacrificing one over the other (Vanspauwen et al. 2007, 2008). This may well mean using a combination of mechanisms to reveal truth, accountability, community restoration, and social justice.

Sierra Leone Truth Commission
Beyond the hybrid court of Sierra Leone, the country created a truth commission under the auspices of the National Forum for Human Rights for the purpose of creating an impartial historical record of violations and abuses of human rights and international humanitarian law related to the armed conflict in Sierra Leone, from the beginning of the conflict in 1991 to the signing of the Lomé Peace Agreement. Its purpose was to address impunity, to respond to the needs of the victims, to promote healing and reconciliation, and to prevent a repetition of the violations and abuses suffered (Truth Commission Charter 2000). The commission was composed of seven commissioners, four Sierra Leoneans (selected through a process managed by the Special Representative of the UN Secretary-General) and three international commissioners. The commission was composed of four units: legal and reconciliation, administrative, information management, and public outreach. The commission was to report on the nature and extent of the violations and abuses; the context in which the violations and abuses occurred; and whether those violations and abuses were the result of deliberate planning, policy, or authorization by the government, group, or individual. This was to contribute to helping the victims restore their dignity and promote reconciliation by providing the victims an opportunity to give an account of their victimization, giving special attention to the subject of sexual abuses and to the experiences of children within the armed conflict. Further, the truth and reconciliation commission worked alongside the international criminal tribunal and the Special Court for Sierra Leone. In all, the commission collected 7,706 statements of Sierra Leoneans, living in Sierra Leone and/or as refugees in Gambia, Guinea, and Nigeria. This significantly contributed to the understanding of the scope of atrocities that had occurred during the conflict and the involvement of the various fraction groups. As a "truth" finding or fact-finding venture, and based on the information presented in table 9.1, the commission did provide a basis for understanding and a tool for reconciliation for the victims.

Table 9.1. *Counts and Proportions of Violations and Victims by Violation Type*

Violation Type	Percent of Violations	Count of Violations	Percent of Victims	Count of Victims	Ratio Violations Per Victim
Forced Disappearance	19.8	7983	41.6	6241	1.28
Abduction	14.8	5968	36.4	5456	1.09
Arbitrary Detention	12	4835	29.3	4401	1.1
Killing	11.2	4514	30.1	4514	1
Destruction of Property	8.5	3404	21.5	3231	1.05
Assault	8.1	3246	19.9	2977	1.09
Looting	7.6	3044	18.4	2761	1.1
Physical Torture	5.1	2051	12.8	1917	1.07
Forced Labor	4.6	1834	11.2	1675	1.09
Extortion	3.2	1273	7.7	1149	1.11
Rape	1.6	626	3.9	581	1.08
Sexual Abuse	1.2	486	3.2	474	1.03
Amputation	0.9	378	2.2	336	1.12
Forced Recruitment	0.8	331	2.2	324	1.02
Sexual Slavery	0.5	191	1.2	186	1.03
Drugging	0.1	59	0.4	57	1.04
Forced Cannabalism	0	19	0.1	19	1
Total		40,242		14,995	

Source: Sierra Leone Truth and Reconciliation Commission Database: Appendix 1: 11

Truth and Reconciliation Commission of Chile

In 1988, President Augusto Pinochet lost a referendum that triggered democratic elections for the first time in decades. Once Patricio Alywin was named the new head of state in 1990, the government created a truth commission to illuminate the past atrocities of the Pinochet government. The truth commission, known as the Rettig Commission, was composed of representatives from both Pinochet supporters and his opponents. The primary task was fourfold: to establish a complete picture and the extent of human rights violations that had been committed under the Pinochet regime, to gather evidence and victim identifications for the purposes of possible reparations, and to recommend legal measures in an effort to ensure deterrence and end the impunity that had long-served the previous regime. Specifically, it was to investigate and provide a written record of "disappearances after arrest, executions, and torture leading to death committed by government agents or people in their service, as well as kidnappings and attempts on the life of persons carried out by private citizens for political reasons" (cited in Brahm 2005: 1). Despite the severe political restraints placed upon it (e.g., limited mandate and stifled cooperation), the commission investigated 3,400 cases of death and reached definitive conclusions on all but 641 and investigated 2,920 cases of disappearances and identified 2,298 victims of military abuses during Pinochet's rule (Human Rights

Watch 1999b). It attributed 95 percent of the crimes to the military. While the commission did not name perpetrators, provisions were made that they would be made public in 2016 (Quinn 2001). Once the commission had completed its work, it submitted the findings to the government. The report called on the state and all of society to acknowledge and accept responsibility for past crimes. The commission's report later came to be a significant contribution to the finding of facts for Spain's request for extradition and charges against Pinochet.

Victims of Human Rights Abuses Provided by the Report of the Chilean National Commission on Truth and Reconciliation

Victims of government agents or persons at their service:

Numbers of those killed:

In war tribunals	59	2.8%
During protests	93	4.4%
During alleged escape attempts	101	4.8%
Other executions and deaths by torture	815	38.5%
Disappeared after arrest	957	45.2%

National Commission on the Disappeared of Argentina

As with the other truth and reconciliation commissions, the National Commission on the Disappeared for Argentina (CONADEP) was created in 1983 as a tool for truth-telling and to chronicle the events and cases that occurred. As such, the commission's report would not determine responsibility of those named as having had part in the mass numbers of the disappeared. The commission was structured with five departments: the Depositions Department, Documentation and Data Processing, Procedures, Legal Affairs, and the Administrative Department. The commission presided over hearings of thousands of cases of abduction, disappearance, torture, and executions in which they compiled over 50,000 pages of documentation. As a result, they recommended that the Argentina courts process the investigation and verification of the depositions received by this commission for potential prosecutions. CONADEP was able to present evidence comprising 1,086 dossiers that proved the existence of secret detention centers and provided a partial list of the disappeared as well as a list of members of the Armed Forces and Security Forces mentioned by victims as responsible for the serious crimes. This resulted in nine members of the former junta being prosecuted in trials. Without such a process, quite possibly the junta members would have escaped accountability in any form. Additionally, the historical record of the numbers of victims and their voices were documented at a time the public needed a collective recognition of the past events (United States Institute of Peace 2008).

The Commission on the Truth El Salvador

The conflict in El Salvador lasted twelve years (1980–1991) and resulted in a mass number of deaths and other violations of human rights. During July 1992, the Secretary General for the United Nations began an effort to create the Commission on the Truth for Salvadorians. The commission was charged with examining the systematic atrocities committed by the state armed forces and members of insurgent groups that inflicted individuals and the communities as a whole. The mandate of the commission defined their function as to

> [h]ave the task of investigating serious acts of violence that have occurred since 1980 and whose impact on society urgently demands that the public should know the truth. "The Parties recognize the need to clarify and put an end to any indication of impunity on the part of officers of the armed forces, particularly in cases where respect for human rights is jeopardized. To that end, the Parties refer this issue to the Commission on the Truth for consideration and resolution.

The Commission was given two specific powers: the power to make investigations and the power to make recommendations. The latter power is particularly important since, under the mandate, the Parties undertake to carry out the Commission's recommendations.

Unlike other truth commissions discussed, the Salvadorian commission was comprised exclusively of international staff. This was due to the ongoing involvement of the UN on the peace process as well as the domestic legal, political, and economic conditions that were the result of the conflict.

As with the other TRC's discussed in this chapter, the Commission on the Truth registered more than 22,000 complaints of serious acts of violence. Of those, nearly 60 percent were for extrajudicial executions, over 25 percent involved victimization through enforced disappearances, and nearly 20 percent were complaints of torture (United States Institute of Peace 2008). Of these reported cases, the commission found that approximately 85 percent of the cases of violence were attributed to agents of the state, paramilitary groups working with or for the state, and death squads. On the other hand, of all the complaints registered, only 5 percent were attributed to the insurgent group, The Frente Farabundo Martí para la Liberación Nacional (FMLN). With the numbers of complaints that had been heard and verified, the commission was limited in its recommendations for prosecution. As noted by the TRC report,

The question is not whether the guilty should be punished, but whether justice can be done. Public morality demands that those responsible for the crimes described here be punished. However, El Salvador has no system for the administration of justice which meets the minimum requirements of objectivity and impartiality so that justice can be rendered reliably. (*Truth Commission Report* 1993)

Consequently, they were limited to naming the accused. Furthermore, five days after the report was issued, the government passed legislation granting amnesty to those named in the report. The end-result of the nine-month work of the commission and involvement of the mass victims was the revelation of some truth, but no accountability for perpetrators.

Amnesties

States have used a wide variety of types of amnesty to address crimes of the state and other violators of international laws (e.g., paramilitaries and/or militia groups). These are often combined with truth and reconciliation commissions, as in the case of South Africa where amnesty accompanies only full truth disclosures or conditional amnesty. In other cases, such as the Democratic Republic of Congo, the amnesty covers political assassinations but not war crimes that were committed during specific times. In other cases, amnesties are used for political purposes to achieve peace, as in the case of Mozambique, or as a means to allow impunity after individuals have been named as perpetrators by truth commissions (i.e., El Salvador). Amnesty laws may be a precondition for peace negotiations by one or more of the forces involved in a conflict or may form the central corpus around which a fragile peace is built. In other situations, they serve as a form of reintegration into the community, often through a combination of culturally-specific traditions. For example, traditional healing mechanisms, such as purifying those involved in a civil war, made it possible, after the purification, for links to the past to be severed and the individual to be reintegrated. Additionally, in Mozambique, the term *reconciliation* is used to refer to forgetting the past and being tolerant. Together, the fact that Mozambique experienced a civil war along with these community-level traditions allowed amnesty to succeed to the degree it did. In other cases, such as Uganda, amnesty is being used to reintegrate the mass numbers of child soldiers that have escaped and are returning to their communities. Here again, traditional rituals are used to "purify" the child's sins at the same time informal amnesties are granted.

Perhaps the best way to "judge" whether amnesty would be a legitimate and solid response to state criminality is to use the following criteria by Naqvi (2003): if amnesty is limited to achieving the objectives of securing peace and initiating or furthering reconciliation; if it is accompanied by other measures such as truth commissions, investigatory bodies, or lustration; if it is the result of negotiation between the outgoing and incoming regimes or of a peace deal brokered; and if it applies to lower-ranking members of armed forces or insurgent groups considered least responsible. While amnesties are generally frowned upon by Western models of criminal justice and/or nongovernmental organizations promoting accountability, they can serve as a tool for collective forgiveness in cases where entire communities were victimized and in situations of large-scale participations of atrocities. However, when amnesties are used for the purposes of granting impunity to a select few or regime leaders, they serve no grander function as a mechanism for reintegration or restoration. In these cases, amnesty allows a state to judge its own case, violating the general principle forbidding self-judging, and is unlikely to be considered a valid mechanism of control under international law (Naqvi 2003).

Impeachment

Impeachment is a process of removing heads of state that hold security of tenure; the official cannot be removed from his or her office except in exceptional and specified circumstances. It is a formal process that is governed by nearly every country's constitution or laws and is equivalent to a criminal indictment. Typically, impeachment serves to remove the person(s) from office; however, this may not always be the case. While all laws, regulations, and other systems of controls are politicized, impeachments are particularly vulnerable to misuse and manipulation by other or competing party members. Nonetheless, it is a control mechanism that can be used to address crimes committed by a regime and/or parts of an administration. While less tenable than other forms of control, it is a viable mechanism for reacting to and controlling state criminality.

Impeachments are not a new phenomenon, though they are rather rare. The United States has had two presidents impeached: Presidents Johnson (for violating the Tenure of Office Act) and Clinton (for perjury and suborning perjury), though neither was removed from office. The process of impeachment against President Nixon by the House Judiciary Committee was ended when he resigned before the house voted. In 1992, the Peruvian Congress voted to impeach President Fujimori and to remove him from office, naming the Second Vice President as new head of state. Fujimori's impeachment was in response to a general fear of dictatorship rule due to his attempt to dissolve Peru's Congress, to suspend the Constitution, and to detain lawmakers that were primarily the opposition Apra Party. During 2004, South Korea experienced the country's first presidential impeachment when President Roh Moo-hyun was removed from office on the grounds of illegal electioneering and incompetence. Other examples include President Banisadr of Iran, who was impeached during 1981 by the Iranian Parliament, Brazil's President Collor de Mello in 1992, President Pérez of Venezuela in 1993, and President Grau of Paraguay in 1999. There have also been some social and political calls for the impeachment of President George W. Bush and Vice President Cheney.

Impeachments can be an effective means for removing or shaming leaders' behaviors; yet, they are limited in addressing the scope of many state crimes. They cannot address larger structural problems that often accompany or predate the more widespread and atrocious forms of criminality, nor are they effective for addressing entire governmental structures that participate in these forms of crime. It is the latter that has been addressed through processes of lustration.

Lustration

The term *lustration* is derived from Latin, meaning to purify ceremonially (Merriam-Webster Dictionary). As a control mechanism, it is a tool, created by special legislation, to effectively remove a segment or political party from holding political and/or civil offices that committed abuses under a past regime. States that undergo extreme transitional circumstances are often facing multiple challenges for restoration and some form of justice for past abuses. This is especially the case for state crimes that are the result of systematic or institutionalized abuses by vast bureaucracies, where a significant portion of the population is implicated through acts of omission or commission rather than direct actions of regimes. The various forms lustration has taken have been dependent on a state's history and the nature of transitions, ranging from soliciting information, to investigating, trying, and disqualifying from office those most complicit with the past regime. Lustration has most notably been used in countries that have dealt with a legacy of abuse under communism in post-Soviet Eastern Europe. In these cases, states have adopted some form of practice of lustration that excludes from political offices for various time frames former communist party functionaries and those who collaborated with secret police forces (Brahm 2004). Nonetheless, lustration has occurred in other contexts, including the U.S.-led de-Baathification in Iraq after the 2003 invasion and occupation.

Out of the context of communist countries, post-communist countries adopted lustration laws, with Czechoslovakia as one of the first. In October 1991, former Party officials, members of the People's Militia and members of the National Security Corps, were barred from holding a range of elected and/or appointed positions in state-owned companies, academia, and the media for five years. In 1990, Hungary held its first free elections in forty years, in which the Communist Party, the Hungarian Socialist Party, was defeated. In March 1994, the Hungarian Parliament adopted a lustration law subjecting 12,000 "officials" to a screening process to determine whether they had collaborated with the former Secret Police (e.g., members of Parliament and government, ambassadors, army commanders, chiefs of police, career judges, district attorneys). If found to be collaborators, they were barred from political or state-owned civil jobs. Albania also practiced lustration against former communist party members. In Lithuania, the government declared in 1991 that former KGB employees and collaborators could not hold local or national government posts until 1996.

The few cases listed above illustrate how lustration is commonly used to remove a political, ethnic, or religious party that oppressed other segments of society during its rule. Nonetheless, lustration practices do not come without their own political ramifications and abuses. Some observers have suggested that, while there is nothing wrong with this practice in principle, it has often been implemented in a sub-par fashion by entangling the innocent (Brahm 2004). Furthermore, it is not a magic panacea for addressing past abuses or attaining social equilibrium—nor is it necessarily effective for restorative justice. Such a move, as is the case with most attempts to use lustration, is guided by the assumption that former officials and collaborators would undermine a new democratic system, which may not be the case at all (Boed 1999). This can be seen with the U.S. initial (Coalition Provisional Authority) implementation of a de-Baathification program. A formal policy and law was then implemented by the new Iraqi government barring all Baathists from holding government, military, and police positions. Since that time, however, the U.S. has demanded that the former members of Saddam Hussein's Baath Party, whom the U.S. military recruited into Iraq's internal security forces, keep their positions. In the case at hand, lustration efforts, which targeted numbers of innocent civilians as well, were supported primarily because of political and economic interests for a new regime and may have contributed to the ongoing civil strife and ethnic divisions occurring in Iraq.

Coup

A coup d'état is the overthrowing of a government to replace a branch of the government—typically the head of state—with either a new civil or military government. A coup is different than a revolution in that a coup results in a change in power from the top-replacing key leading government personnel without transforming the overarching political system. If successful, the past head of state or displaced regime members surrender to the opposition, acknowledge their topple, or take exile in another country, and the force(s) that orchestrated the coup is then legitimized in some fashion, even if only self-proclaimed.

Coups date back centuries and in many areas of the world, since the modern state, have been a regular political occurrence—in various Latin American countries during the nineteenth and twentieth centuries, and as a routine practice in many African states post-colonial rule. For example, as was pointed out in previous chapters, the Ugandan government is not only the product of post-colonial political forces but the end result of series of coups and counter-coups. In some countries, domestic law or constitutions may provide a legal mechanism for overthrowing the government. For example, the U.S. Declaration of Independence states that, to secure these rights, "Governments are instituted among Men, deriving their just powers from the consent of the governed—That whenever any Form of Government becomes destructive of these ends, it is the Right of the People to alter or to abolish it, and to institute new Government." As worded, this could provide the legal means for a coup, but also a revolution due to the wording "to alter or abolish." Nevertheless, a coup in the U.S. is far from likely to happen.

The use of a coup to displace a corrupt or abusive regime can be a practical solution to a country's security and social fabric, minimizing victimization that may occur in a civil conflict. However, coups have been used all too often to carry out another state's political or economic interest. In these cases, what occurs is additional state criminality on the part of the initiating state (e.g., the Reagan Administration's efforts to overthrow the Sandinista government, or when displaced heads of state retreat into the countryside [or cross into a neighboring state], regroup, and resurface as a militia group, which was the case when Obote fled Uganda to return years later for a second term as head of state or the RPF in Rwanda—see chapter 8). In other cases, one coup leads to another harsh or criminal head of state replacing the head in power, thus solving nothing, just replacing actors. As a form of post control, a coup, like lustration efforts, can have more negative than positive effects. Such tactics should be carefully considered and measured by the "true" intentions of those orchestrating the overthrow.

Chapter Summary

This chapter provided brief reviews of domestic controls, including some of the hybrid or innovative ways states have attempted to address massive past crimes. Undoubtedly, some are more problematic than others. For example, domestic laws do little in the form of deterrence for state actors when or if they can re-define their behaviors as legitimate, necessary, or for the greater good. For this reason, except for mechanisms such as coups, criminal heads of states or leaders of agencies within regimes most often must be held accountable by external controls, typically other states, as was the case with the increased use of domestic courts, or by international institutions. Other forms of control have looked beyond just accountability to try to address issues of restoration or restorative justice. This has included efforts such as the hybrid tribunals, truth commissions, and, in some cases, conditional or blanket amnesties as a means of social healing. As I noted in the introduction of this chapter, controls at this level must take into account the specific country's needs, especially those in transitional capacities. Additionally, effective responses and post-controls need to be varied enough to incorporate the vast types of crimes and the extent of the type of government that is in place. As a closing thought, we must also be cognizant that most all types of social control have risks and can pose latent consequences. This is no different at the domestic level than it is for international controls where issues of power, politics, and intervening states' interests often come to bear on the effectiveness or ineffectiveness of responses. Additionally, in every case, no mechanism of social control can serve as a form of justice for all. In other words, there will always be underlying factors to each system that can be easily critiqued, and there will be those victims and perpetrators who feel whatever control was enacted did not succeed in a justice for all.

Chapter 10

Constraints for State Crime

In chapter 7, I discussed how constraints are not expected to fully control or block state or organizational criminal activities. Instead, by definition (Rothe and Mullins 2006a, 2008), they serve as potential barriers before or during an act. While, indeed, conceptualized constraints (e.g., media, nongovernmental organizations, or social movements) may on occasion fully block or stop crimes of the state, they are, by their very nature, nonformal, typically lacking empowerment mechanisms, and as such they should be viewed as potential impediments. These distinctions have resulted in a common oversight or misunderstanding by scholars of state crime in that these constraints, when failed, have been perceived as opportunities. Indeed, it may be the case that they further facilitate acts by not blocking them as would be expected by the extant controls; however, the opportunity to commit such acts was already present. Thus, whether something or someone should be viewed as a constraint should not be dependent upon its success; instead, the mere presence or activities of this mechanism should be taken into account, recognized for any impediment it may or may not have served. It is only through this acknowledgment that effective policies can be implicated, based on knowing the degree to which a constraint failed or succeeded in limiting a state's criminality.

This chapter will focus on some of the most commonly conceptualized and present constraints, as has been noted in the examples throughout this text. This includes exploring those at the international and domestic levels. Having said this, we must acknowledge that such divisions are rather arbitrary. Unlike formal controls of states and the international systems of control, constraints often work in a dialectic process. In other words, nongovernmental agencies may be actively working in a state and serve as a facilitator of information to the international political arena, media, and other relevant sources. Likewise, international media accounts or UN reports may generate domestic responses. As such, the following sections may combine some of the key international and national constraint mechanisms, including the media, showing the interrelatedness that often occurs, yet still drawing distinctions between the international and domestic.

International

The integrated theory of state crime and other violators of international criminal law suggested that constraints at the international level included international reactions, political pressures, public opinion, non-governmental organizations and social movements, and oversight agencies. Yet, each of these mechanisms is a result of more subtle actions by key agencies or actors. For example, an international reaction is rather broad and ambiguous, yet such abstractness allows for a multitude of various sources creating such reaction. The same is true with public opinion. For example, international reactions and public opinion can stem from the work of non-governmental organizations such as Amnesty International, International Red Cross, or Human Rights Watch, or from the media. Political pressure can come from these sources as well as other states, citizens' tribunals, NGOs, or as a result of public opinion or other general negative reactions. The category of oversight can include the non-formal pressure by institutions and key members such as the United Nations or international financial institutions (i.e., World Bank Group or the International Monetary Fund). With this in mind, a brief discussion of core organizations or bodies that facilitate the catalysts of constraint listed in the theory (see chapter 7) is presented along with several examples.

Nongovernmental and Intergovernmental Agencies

The theoretical model suggests that nongovernmental bodies can act as a constraining mechanism. Within the scope of NGOs, there are several different international organizations that fit the definition: Doctors Without Borders, Amnesty International, and Human Rights Watch. Each of these has been discussed in the previous chapters under specific case examples of state crime. Nonetheless, it seems fitting to present a brief overview of the main organizations, along with a brief example or two of their roles in constraining crimes of the state.

Doctors Without Borders (DWB or MSF) was established during 1971. It is the first non-governmental organization that provided emergency medical assistance and made a commitment to being bearers of witness to the predicaments of the people it assists, including those under grave circumstances of state criminality. It is an international network that has sections acting in nineteen countries. Mostly comprised of doctors and nurses, the volunteers raise concerns of their patients, solicited and unsolicited, with governments, the UN, other international organizations, and the media. This involves writing and disseminating reports on conditions, including those civilians face in the cases of government-sponsored atrocities, such as violations of international humanitarian law they have witnessed—from Chechnya to Sudan. For example, a recent report, *Forgotten Crises* (Doctors Without Borders 2007), documenting the ten most underreported humanitarian crises, was distributed to the following media outlets in an effort to gain U.S. political and public outrage.

1. NPR—All Things Considered
2. WBUR-Boston (NPR)—Here and Now
3. KPCC-Los Angeles (NPR)—AirTalk
4. KCPW-Salt Lake City (NPR)—Midday Utah
5. WNYC-New York (NPR)—The Leonard Lopate Show
6. KZYX-Northern California (NPR, PRI)—Forthright Radio with Joy LeClaire
7. Democracy Now
8. *Sacramento Bee*: Editorial: At Year's End, a Global Agenda for Compassion

Other examples include the Doctors Without Borders report that was given to other international organizations and media groups showing that DWB treated 1,292 rape survivors in Beni, Kayna, and Rutshuru in the DRC in a very short period of time, bringing attention to the massive abuses of women in the region. They have drawn attention to the aftereffects of the genocidal rapes that occurred in Rwanda that left women and young girls with HIV, AIDS, and other sexually contracted diseases, leading to yet another cultural, social, and economic crisis.

Amnesty International (AI) is also a worldwide nongovernmental movement of people that crusade for human rights. It began campaigning in 1961 and currently has more than 2 million members and is active in approximately eighty countries. AI states its mission is "to conduct research and generate action to prevent and end grave abuses of human rights and to demand justice for those whose rights have been violated." Amnesty tries to do this by exerting influence on governments, political bodies, companies, and intergovernmental groups (UN or the ICRC). This is done by promoting public demonstrations, vigils, and letter-writing campaigns; holding awareness concerts; lobbying governments; and carrying out appeals and petitions to governments. Amnesty is active in undertaking mass interview accounts of crimes against the population. Most recently, it provided reports, documenting through interviews, the extensive nature of rape in Rwanda; mass amputations in Northern Uganda by the Lord's Resistance Army; and crimes in Darfur, where genocide continues to take place along with the systematic rape and mutilations of young girls, boys, women, and men (see Mullins and Rothe 2008). Likewise, AI monitors and reports on governmental oppression of highly empowered countries, including the U.S. and the UK.

Human Rights Watch is also dedicated to protecting the human rights of people around the world while simultaneously acting as a mouthpiece for those silenced by their own governments or militia groups during conflicts or government-sponsored political oppressions. According to HRW, they

> stand with victims and activists to prevent discrimination, to uphold political freedom, to protect people from inhumane conduct in wartime, and to bring offenders to justice . . . hold abusers accountable . . . challenge governments and those who hold power to end abusive practices and respect international human rights law.

In its World Report 2008d, Human Rights Watch discusses oppression and human rights situations in more than seventy-five countries, including atrocities in Chad, Colombia, the Democratic Republic of Congo, Ethiopia, Iraq, Somalia, Sri Lanka, Sudan, Burma, China, Cuba, Eritrea, Libya, Iran, North Korea, Saudi Arabia, and Vietnam, and the abuses in the "war on terror" (committed by France, Pakistan, the United Kingdom, and the United States, among others). Along with nongovernmental bodies, there is also The International Red Cross and Red Crescent, established in 1859, which is considered an intergovernmental organization as it is the guardian of international humanitarian law in times of conflict. As such, it is the "keeper" of the Geneva Conventions and the principles and laws that ensure prisoners and civilians are afforded the rights accorded to them by IHL and customary law. It is the now the world's largest humanitarian network, with activities in almost every country—the Geneva-based International Committee of the Red Cross (ICRC), the International Federation of Red Cross and Red Crescent Societies (the International Federation), and National Societies in 186 countries.

The ICRC's latest report (2007) noted that it was a year "marked by acute violence in countries such as Iraq, Sudan, Somalia, Afghanistan and Sri Lanka." ICRC operations ranged from rapid response in the case of sudden or worsening crises, such as those in Lebanon, Sri Lanka, and Somalia, to ongoing emergencies, such as those in Chad, the Central African Republic, and Colombia. During 2006, ICRC expenditure reached its highest level in half a century, with over 40 percent going to Africa. The report highlighted the issue of internal displacement as one of particular concern to the ICRC given that, during 2006, ICRC assisted nearly 3.5 million displaced people in nineteen countries. Recall that international humanitarian law prohibits the displacement of civilians during conflict and, as guardians of the laws of war, the ICRC attempts to ensure respect and adherence to the rules, preventing civilian displacement and the consequences thereof. As noted by Jakob Kellenberger, the president of the ICRC, "One of the ICRC's top priorities is to improve respect for the law—in particular by reminding the parties to armed conflicts of their obligations. It is then up to the belligerents themselves and all the States party to the Geneva Conventions to demonstrate the necessary political will to apply and enforce the law."

By using a combination of methods, from on-the-ground aid to documenting abuses by governments and paramilitaries and disseminating them throughout the world to international organizations like the UN, media outlets, other NGOs, other states' governments, and their own websites, these organizations (DWB, HRW, Amnesty, and ICRC) all attempt to constrain ongoing atrocities through exposure, documentation, and/or direct involvement. However, as many of the cases discussed throughout this book have noted, their efforts, while laudable, have had relatively little impact on crimes committed by states. Nonetheless, we should not minimize the impact they have, and even if they do not block or stop such crimes, their documentations, witnessing, and voices have proven to be of help for generating political and public outcry that has resulted in some other forms of intervention in crisis that had been silenced or ignored.

Media

The media has long been characterized as the watchdog of governments. The concept of the media watchdog—the media as a controller of government—is one of the oldest beliefs in journalism. Such a belief can be traced back to Edmund Burke, in late eighteenth-century England, when he referred to the media as a "fourth estate"—the political power possessed by the press of that time, with the same power of control as the other three "estates" in the then-British realm: Lords, Church, and Commons. From this time, the idea of the press as the "fourth estate" or watchdog was considered to be an independent check on the activities of the government (Ibrahimi 2007).

Of course, the current views of the media as a fourth estate or watchdog are based on media organizations that operate in democratic environments. The expectations for state-owned media as a constraint is very different in that they are the mouthpiece for the government, heavily censored, and often used to ensure government ideologies and citizen compliance. Censorship works like a muzzle on the watchdogs: the "dog" cannot bark or bite, thus no threat. Nonetheless, speaking in general terms, the media can act as an effective constraint, especially now that there is a barrage of available media sources that reach beyond states. In an ideal setting then, media can expose the predations of a government in a way that nothing else can do and, in that regard, can expose crimes of the state that have been silenced at the state level through censorship, propaganda, isolationism, and other catalysts at a state's disposal. International media sources have drawn global attention to many cases of state crime that have sparked public and political outrage, then impacting or enabling other constraint mechanisms to also put pressure on governments. For example, with the atrocities that are currently playing out in Africa (Uganda, Sudan-Darfur, DRC, and Côte d'Ivoire), BBC, Africa News, and the Integrated News Integration Network run by the UN Office for the Coordination of Humanitarian Aid have reported thoroughly and frequently about these events to garner international political support to end the ongoing crimes. They have staff on the ground in these countries and report events to the rest of the world. As with the NGOs, though, this information is not enough to compel action.

Nonetheless, without these international media outlets, it is possible that the world's citizenry would know nothing of the ongoing crimes against humanity and genocides in many parts of the world. Why? Because many states use their own media to place countermessages into the international discourse, creating debates out of the reporting of facts and presenting alternative realities for international consumption. Both the el Bashiri regime in Sudan and the Museveni regime in Uganda have actively produced counterdiscourses that, while they carry seemingly little currency over all, do seem to add just enough legitimacy to the positions they advocate to delay and/or weaken international responses to ongoing situations and/or delegitimize external claims of events within the countries. In these cases, it is imperative that external news sources reveal what is occurring within these states while governments continue to oppress, kill, disappear, loot, torture, or imprison for purposes of death or silence.

Other examples of media exposing state crime include the exposing of torture that was committed by U.S. forces before and at Abu Ghraib. On April 28, 2004, pictures of abuse and torture of Iraqi detainees at Abu Ghraib prison by U.S. military were first released by the CBS network and *The New Yorker*, showing a hooded man—naked on a box, arms spread, with wires dangling from his fingers; pyramids of naked bodies; a line of naked men posed as if masturbating; and a man on a dog leash. These images instantaneously spread around the world as the collective representation of Abu Ghraib. U.S. citizens were confronted with the reality of their government's involvement in the use of state-sanctioned torture. The images of abuses and torture that came out of Abu Ghraib left nothing for the symbolic imagination to elaborate or deny. Instead, they presented a literal fact of the image and what it represented (Stein 2004). Until the images surfaced in the media, the suppression of visual information regarding military operations had kept invisible to the public and those high in the echelon of political ranks the devastation due to war or state covert activities. Yet, even before the infamous release of those images, international media raised concerns over the U.S. treatment of detainees. *St. John's Telegram* of Newfoundland ("Human Rights Watch Call on U.S." 2002) ran a story on December 30, 2002, that stated: "U.S. officials who take part in torture, authorize it, or even close their eyes to it, can be prosecuted by courts anywhere in the world." Additional coverage of the issue occurred in the *Ottawa Citizen* (2003), titled "Fear of Terrorism Is No Excuse to Flout Laws." During October of that same year, reports of Iraqi detainee abuse and cruel and inhumane treatment at Abu Ghraib also surfaced. An article by *The Gazette* in Montreal (2003: A18), stated: "Situation doesn't meet rights standard . . . this is wrong." Random reports continued to appear within the international media months before the images were released by the mainstream U.S. media. In March 2004, the ONASA News Agency (2004) ran a 473-word article decrying abuse and torture by U.S. forces. However, even with political or public negative reactions, disapproval does not necessarily change the situation. In the cases of the invasion of Iraq and the use of torture as a means of intelligence gathering, public and political reactions failed to restrain the Administration's policies.

Beyond traditional media outlets, broadcasters working for a specific television channel or corporation, there are also international reporters that are "without borders" (RWB), who actively attempt to hold all types of governments accountable, whether a state's media is failing or unable to reveal situations. For example, Reporters Without Borders has asked Somali authorities to release two journalists while simultaneously condemning the interim government for flagrant violations of press freedom, suggesting it is the second most dangerous place for journalists, after Iraq, to report and reveal the truths of on-ground activities.

Citizens Tribunals

> *We are not judges. We are witnesses. Our task is to make mankind bear witness to these terrible crimes and to unite humanity on the side of justice in Vietnam.*

> In *Bertrand Russell War Crimes Tribunal on Vietnam*, 1971

The first people's or citizens' tribunal is often attributed to the Bertrand Russell War Crime Tribunal on Vietnam, during 1967, which occurred in two sessions: the first in Stockholm, Sweden, and then in Copenhagen, Denmark. Seven years later, the Russell Tribunal II on Latin America was established (1974), and held in Brussels (1975) and Rome (1976), dealing predominantly with government crimes in Brazil and Chile. Since 1979, thirty-three people's tribunals have taken place throughout the world (Whitney 2008). While names of the tribunals vary to some degree (e.g., citizens' tribunals, people's tribunals, or world tribunals), their goal remains the same: To bring truth to light. As Falk (2005: 1) pointed out, these tribunals "proceed from a presumption that the allegations of illegality and criminality are valid and that its job is to reinforce that conclusion as persuasively and vividly as possible."

Citizens' or people's tribunals are typically created by key members of civil society (lawyers, judges, key witnesses, and/or nonprofit agencies) in response to perceived crimes committed by a government, be it theirs or another. Moreover, such tribunals are generally perceived to be the sole means by which truths can be revealed and a collective and historical account is created that may well differ from those posited by the government or its agents under scrutiny. These organizations are a culmination of legal proceedings (non-formal relative to domestic or international criminal justice systems but based on and exercising full legal processes), public forums for speaking "truth," and a symbolic gesture of condemnation of a government's criminal actions that may otherwise escape legal and/or public scrutiny (Schuler 2007). As such, the issue of legitimacy is often brought into question. If a tribunal is not viewed as legitimate by civil society, it runs the risk of being portrayed as a charade versus a tool for revealing truths or creating a historical account of the criminal act(s). Nonetheless, citizens' tribunals can serve as an important milieu for raising issues to a more visible level than other forms of constraint mechanisms, notably the media or other states. This has been viewed as the foundation of self-legitimating of the tribunals. As noted by Francois Houtart, President of the Tribunal of International Opinion (TIO) on forced displacement in Bogota, the tribunal's legitimacy "derives from the visibility it gives to crimes against humanity, especially those perpetrated or neglected by states. The tribunals represent the ethical conscience of humanity expressed through distinguished personalities in the judicial world, from scientific, religious, artistic, and political fields" (quoted in Whitney 2008: 1).

This is especially the case for highly empowered countries that are able to avoid the ramifications of formal controls; tribunals held by other countries are often the only option for factual revelations or creating a collective or historical account. Having said this, it should be noted that in a similar situation, a tribunal directed "against the government of the host country would be strictly prohibited" (Schuler 2007: 1). Nonetheless, there are an abundance of tribunals to draw from that have attempted to serve as witnesses to truths perceived to be hidden or falsified by governments in face of public outcry or formal legal culpability. For example, the Concerned Citizens Tribunal (CJP) was a citizens' tribunal headed by Justice V. R. Krishna to conduct a probe into the violence in Godhra and other areas of Gujarat. As a result of the tribunal, a three-volume report, *Crime Against Humanity*, has been cited as the most important document documentation of the Gujarat violence and has received extensive print and electronic media coverage, both domestic and international (Concerned Citizens Tribunal 2002). The following examples illustrate recent or ongoing tribunals that have been convened in an effort to draw international attention and pressure to ongoing atrocities and crimes committed by governments.

The International Citizens' Tribunal for Sudan

In the Trial Chamber

New York, November 13, 2006

Prosecutor v. Omar Hassan al-Bashir

Judgment

The International Citizens' Tribunal on Sudan hereby pronounces judgment on the defendant, Omar al-Bashir, President of Sudan.

The principal crimes listed in the Indictment, Crimes Against Humanity, Genocide, and Violations of the Laws and Customs of War, are the main elements of the joint criminal enterprise directed by the defendant. The acts of subordinates by which the defendant and his associates carried out the enterprise run the gamut from mass murder to rape to pillage to enslavement. The span of time during which these acts were committed covers sixteen years, from 1990 to the present. The scenes of these crimes ranged over much of the territory of Sudan, from the villages of the Beja people in the East to the towns of Darfur in the West, from the homes of the Dinka and Nuer in the South to the mountain habitats of the Nuba peoples in the center. For a longer span of time than in any other case in modern history, Sudan has been subjected to serial genocide, serial crimes against humanity, and serial war crimes.

Two guiding motives intertwine to drive the joint criminal enterprise described at this Tribunal. First, President Bashir and his partners in the enterprise have acted to insure that the central regime, installed in a military coup in 1989, maintained and expanded Khartoum's grip on the country's resources, both political and economic. Second, this regime has sought to exterminate, uproot, and reduce to desperate conditions the non-Arab peoples of Sudan while suppressing non-Arab cultures and in other ways promoting the Arabization of the country. Obsessed with the need to have their status as Arabs recognized, the leaders of Bashir's regime have spread their own distorted notion of Arabism, given special privileges to Arabs migrating to the country, forced abducted non-Arab Dinka children to take Arab names, imposed their own intolerant version of Islam, and promoted a racist Arab-supremacist ideology incompatible with mainstream Arab traditions elsewhere.

In their actions and policies during their sixteen-year rule, Omar al-Bashir and his associates have written a primer for tyranny. They have been like a plague of locusts upon the Sudan. To provide a setting for their crimes, they have done the following:

1. They have practiced policies of "divide and rule," setting one opposition group against another with consummate skill. They have then used agreements with one group, such as the North-South Comprehensive Peace Accord of September 2005, as hostages to prevent any attempts to interfere with their depredations elsewhere, especially in Darfur.

2. They have exploited and distorted the Islamic notion of jihad, mobilizing Muslims to carry out attacks on civilians and armed formations by representing such actions as holy war. The attacked populations were often Muslims themselves; but applying their own distorted theology, the al-Bashir regime claims that these people are "not true Muslims."

3. They have tightly controlled access to areas in which their criminal activities were underway, such as the Nuba Mountains, and now Darfur, turning away reporters by visa refusals, arrests, and threats of harm or death.

4. They have rendered humanitarian operations all but impossible in many areas, subjecting aid organizations to delays, financial exactions, and terror.

5. They have disguised their crimes as "counterinsurgency" operations to suppress "terrorism," "tribal clashes," or "ethnic disputes" over land and water.

6. They have systematically distracted and deceived the United Nations and the Organization of the Islamic Conference and have so distorted the truth, that several U.N. Resolutions even called upon the al-Bashir regime to disarm the Janjaweed militias when, in actuality, these militias were directly armed by the Sudanese government and carried out their attacks with Sudanese government bombing and air raids.

7. They have mastered the art of playing for time, producing strategic delays and postponements enumerable times, while hundreds of thousands of people die, and millions of refugees are forcibly displaced from their homes.

8. They have enlisted the aid of global oil companies who fear losing their investments if the al-Bashir regime is overthrown.

9. In response to threats to bring them before the International Criminal Court (ICC), they have instituted sham judicial apparatuses, including the Darfur Special Court and the Judicial Investigations Committee, in an attempt to preclude jurisdiction by the ICC.

10. They have sponsored phony conferences on counterterrorism while at the same time cooperating with international terrorists.

11. They have dominated policy making by regional organizations such as the African Union while manipulating, subordinating, and abusing its manifestly incapable uniformed monitoring forces in Darfur, and ensuring that the African Union force lacks the mandate to prevent the murders and rapes being committed against innocent civilians in Darfur.

To allow crimes such as those in the Indictment to go unnoticed and unpunished is to grant justification to those who argue that a centralized, Arab-dominated state in Sudan is better than a "failed state," however destructive of pluralism and tolerance. But who defines failure? And who judges whether life in a failed state can be better than one in a repressive state, where all central institutions seem operational but citizens are neither free nor safe? The Bashir regime has employed indiscriminate armed force to impose a single identity, a single religion, and a single set of institutions upon the whole of Sudan. The cost has been millions of human lives.

When challenged by peoples it has neglected or harassed, the Sudanese government has consistently provided an unequivocal response: unrestrained, genocidal attacks by aircraft and ground forces upon civilians. Not to denounce the crimes listed in the Indictment, crimes of which President Bashir is the leading perpetrator, is to reject the seriousness of the threat posed by Sudan's genocide to the variety in the world's mosaic of independent cultures. The crime of genocide, after all, encompasses more than killing or forced deportation. It includes any grave threat to the survivability of a culture. The imposition of Arabic in Darfur, supported by serious penalties for the use of an indigenous language like Fur, is only one instance of this assault upon a culture.

In the case of Darfur, African cultures partly dependent upon symbiotic exchanges between non-Arab farmers and Arab herdsmen in a functioning multicultural society have been destroyed by the attacks ordered from Khartoum.

To Bashir's primer on how a criminal regime can succeed in its projects, successfully defying the United Nations as well as the initiatives of individual governments, committing crimes against humanity in an atmosphere of fear and impunity, this Tribunal must present a counter-primer.

The supreme test of a government is its ability to align itself with internationally accepted standards of justice. If justice is the first condition of humanity, the goal that distinguishes human society from that of animals in which only the strong rule and no one recognizes rights, then the Bashir regime must be held accountable to justice. Currently accountable only to the narrowest of Sudanese Arab elites, the members of the joint criminal enterprise described in this trial have so far benefited from impunity, but they have not tasted justice.

Since the members of the Khartoum regime whose crimes have been examined at this trial have shown no indication that they will bring themselves to justice, it is the responsibility of others to do so. Those of us who fail to take that step risk becoming, in the eyes of history, collaborators with that criminal government.

Sudan's double identity as an Arab regime and an African regime, its membership in both the Arab League and the African Union, suggests the first places that judgment should be rendered. When a member of a family misbehaves, it is the duty of other family members to bring the miscreant into line. The Arab family has steadfastly refused to call Sudan to order. It has failed to call for Bashir's judgment for mass murder under the sacred laws of Islam. Indeed it has placed obstacles in the way of sanctions and his general refused to allow stories and statements critical of Sudan to appear in its press.

The United Nations has not been much more forthright or forceful. It has passed many resolutions with high-sounding words, but has failed to enforce them. When a deviant member of the family of nations flouts, indeed revels in the abandonment of the most basic norms of human decency, is there really justification in evoking the excuse that protocol requires the permission of that same arrogant and defiant entity to accept U.N. peacekeepers in its territory? When that family of nations, in its majesty assembled, declares its responsibility to protect citizens of any country whose human rights are being violated, can it consider its responsibility a serious matter if it requires the consent of the violator to stop the crimes? Are the boundaries of countries—boundaries now being crossed by Sudan in its attacks upon Chad—sacred walls? Shall the empty words of diplomatic abstractions always drown out the cries of human suffering? How long must sovereignty triumph while men are murdered and women and children are driven bleeding, raped, and starved from their homes?

In conclusion, this Tribunal recalls the admonition of Justice Robert Jackson, who addressed the opening session of the first international tribunal at Nuremberg on November 21, 1945: "The wrongs which we seek to condemn and punish have been so calculated, so malignant, and so devastating, that civilization cannot tolerate their being ignored, because it cannot survive their being repeated." The wondrous mosaic of cultures that patterns world civilization, with some tiles shining brightly and others, as in Sudan, dangerously faded by tyranny, will be broken forever if the crimes of Omar al-Bashir and his regime go unpunished.

We, the judges of the International Citizens' Tribunal for Sudan, find the defendant, Omar Hassan Al-Bashir, GUILTY AS CHARGED.

An International Citizen's Tribunal on the Crimes Committed by the Israeli Army in Lebanon

February 22–24, 2008

The deeds committed by the Israeli army and secret services in Lebanon, as in the occupied Palestinian territories, is a violent affront to the universal human conscience. These are criminal acts, as many people feel instinctively. They are different from the acts that take place in all armed conflict committed by the aggressor as well as by the aggressed. But feeling is not enough. The facts must be established. They must then be assessed in light of existing international law. The international community is not an autonomous political and juridical body. It is but a summation of positions adopted by a certain number of governments. In many situations it has proved incapable of applying existing law by distancing itself from geopolitical or ideological contingencies. This impunity has covered up the numerous war crimes and crimes against humanity that have been committed since the end of the Second World War.

The unilateral attitude of the United States of America, like the double-speak of many European governments, make it necessary for those defending the law to take the place of failed political powers. The American administration is against any questioning of Israel's role in acts committed in Lebanon as well as in the occupied Palestinian territories. Germany, Great Britain, Finland and France refuse to support a request formulated at the UN Human Rights Council to investigate the use by the Israeli armed forces of arms that are prohibited by international law. The systematic disinformation practiced by an overwhelming majority of the media deprives Western public opinion of balanced information. All this justifies an initiative by the citizens themselves.

This initiative must aim at being of the same high quality as the tribunal initiated by Bertrand Russell during the Vietnam War. It should be carried out with the same rigor, the same credibility and the same concern to go beyond divisions which have no place when it is a question of the rights of people. It must bring together highly qualified experts and personalities who are universally recognized for their moral authority. It must not limit itself up to a restricted circle. For this reason I believe it should not follow in the footsteps of similar initiatives taken in the past, whatever the quality that such work has achieved in the past.

Such an action cannot be carried out properly in a hurry. It requires the formulation of a comprehensive project, together with a precise timetable, the mobilization of appropriate human and financial resources and an irreproachable moral framework. These requirements demand an international mobilization to support such an initiative. An international citizen's tribunal on the crimes committed by the Israeli army in Lebanon will be held in Brussels, Belgium, on February 22–24, 2008. The International Action Center has endorsed this tribunal and the work of the Committee of International Citizens that is organizing the tribunal.

http://www.iacenter.org/palestine/leb-trib-letter0208/

International Financial Institutions

Economic organizations such as the World Bank (WB) and the International Monetary Fund (IMF) represent potential constraints on criminal states through the manipulation of financial assets, trade agreements, and trade sanctions. The International Monetary Fund (IMF) is composed of 184 member countries, headquartered in Washington, D.C. Established in 1945, the IMF's goal was to promote international monetary cooperation, to foster economic growth, and to provide temporary financial assistance to needy countries. It "is the central institution of the international monetary system—the system of international payments and exchange rates among national currencies" (IMF 2006). Since the IMF was established, its purposes have remained unchanged, but its operations such as surveillance (a dialogue among its members on the national and international consequences of their economic and financial policies), financial assistance (loans), and technical assistance (structural adjustment policies) have changed. The IMF is the international system that encourages countries to adopt what it believes to be "sound economic policies," or what most commentators refer to as neoliberal economics. In part, the remedies for countries' economic hardships are ideologically placed in a global capitalistic vacuum that ignores the primacy of citizens' human rights and the overall social, political, and economic health of a nation.

The World Bank is not a "bank" in the commonly used sense of the term. Rather, it is a specialized financial agency, composed of 184 member countries. The World Bank, conceived during WWII, initially helped rebuild Europe after the war. Its first loan of $250 million was to France in 1947 for postwar reconstruction. It once had a homogeneous staff of engineers and financial analysts, based solely in Washington, D.C. More recently, the Bank became a Group, encompassing five closely associated development institutions: the International Bank for Reconstruction and Development (IBRD), the International Development Association (IDA), the International Finance Corporation (IFC), the Multilateral Investment Guarantee Agency (MIGA), and the International Centre for Settlement of Investment Disputes (ICSID) (Rothe et al. 2006). It is a closed system based upon investment. In addition to providing financing, the World Bank Group offers advice and assistance to developing countries on almost every aspect of economic development. Since the mid to late 1990s, the Bank Group utilizes the Private Sector Development (PSD) as its strategy to promote privatization in developing countries. Once its original mission of postwar European reconstruction was finished, the WB turned its lending practices to development issues. While its rhetoric was often focused on human rights, human dignity, and infrastructure development, its operational concerns strongly focused on producing returns for investors. Through the 1970s and 1980s, debtor nations were frequently unable to meet repayment demands. Therefore, during the 1980s, the Bank went through an extensive period focused on macroeconomic and debt rescheduling issues.

Due to their broad reach and economic power, these international financial institutions (IFI) do have the potential to act as a rather powerful constraint as previously noted. As an example, during the buildup to the Rwandan genocide, the IMF and WB became aware that the monies allotted to the Rwandan government for economic programs were being funneled into massive military spending and buildup of weapons in preparation for the genocide. As a result, at the beginning of 1993, the IMF and WB suspended their lending in an effort to constrain the regime from arms buildup. Nonetheless, it is most likely that these organizations would not use this coercive financial authority against some of the highly economical, political, and military empowered countries that need it (e.g., United States, France, United Kingdom, etc.). Instead, their power to act as a constraint is more likely to be used against less empowered countries and those that are subject to mandates by structural adjustment policies. Furthermore, because of their structure and voting allocations, these institutions are often mouthpieces for highly empowered countries and can be used to further a state's own political, military, or economic interest. Such was the case with the United States war on Nicaragua. Early in 1981, U.S. economic assistance to Nicaragua was terminated, and the Reagan Administration attempted to ensnarl Nicaragua into economic isolation, which included using the position of the U.S. in the World Bank and Inter American Development Bank to stop all multilateral and bilateral loans for Nicaragua. Simply, the Reagan Administration attempted to end all economic loans to Nicaragua through political pressure and its weight in the international finance institutions in an effort to delegitimize the Sandinista government during the U.S. covert war with the Contras during the 1980s. In cases such as these, the IFIs are used for illegitimate means to constrain a government from certain actions or to ensure the failing of that regime. Additionally, it should be noted that these institutions, while having the ability to act as a constraining mechanism by withholding monies or freezing trade agreements, have also been said to be criminogenic themselves (Friedrichs and Friedrichs 2002; Rothe et al., 2006, 2008).

International Reactions from States and Citizens
Social Movements

Another of the most significant constraints at the international level is negative international reaction to a state's behavior. We have seen this throughout history, where states have condemned another state's actions and attempted to use political pressures to alter a situation. Recent examples include states' denunciation of China's human rights violations, the U.S. use of Guantanamo and the invasion of Iraq, Sudan's ongoing genocide in Darfur, the political repressions by General Pervez Musharraf of Pakistan, North Korea and Iran's pursuit of nuclear weapons, and the list goes on. Having said this, it should be noted that many times, states' outrage and political pressures can be more symbolic than real. Simply, heads of states may publicly decry another regime's behaviors and even threaten them with some sort of sanction or even military intervention, while assuring the regime, behind closed doors, that such threats are for public consumption or to appease an opposing force. Nonetheless, pressures from one government or another can indeed act as a constraint. This is especially true if such pressures are put on a regime by several like-minded countries or in concert with NGOs and/or other social interest groups.

As an example, let's take a case most of us are familiar with: the U.S. desire to invade Iraq. Due to the political pressures placed on the Bush Administration by other governments, the immediate invasion of Iraq was suspended for several months. For example, in response to these pressures, the Administration made a halfhearted attempt to receive UN support for the use of military force. President Bush addressed the UN on September 12, 2002, and asked for multilateral action against Iraq. In March 2003, a U.S. sponsored war-sanctioning resolution failed to gain support in the UN Security Council. The war on Iraq faced strong political opposition from France, Germany, Russia, and China, as well as the great majority of UN member states. Mr. de Villepin of France, acting Chairman of the UN Security Council, stated, "We will not associate ourselves with military intervention that is not supported by the international community. . . . Military intervention would be the worst possible solution" (Peel, Graham, Harding, and Dempsey 2003: 1). The Administration's attempt to overcome the stiff opposition on the Security Council used "both carrot and stick, by reconsidering economic and military assistance deals as well as prospects for oil and trade in post-war" (Global Policy Forum 2005: 1). Nonetheless, the Security Council did not authorize military force against Iraq. Political reactions did indeed act as a temporary restraint. Ultimately, however, the opposition did not control the Administration's agenda to go to war with Iraq. Once the invasion of Iraq had begun, the opposition grew stronger in an attempt to have the U.S. and Britain end their occupation. For example, Russian President Vladimir Putin, in some of the harshest words by a world leader, said the war was "unjustified and must end quickly" (Reuters, 2003: 1). Meanwhile, the governments of Pakistan, Saudi Arabia, and several other Muslim countries filed formal protests with Washington. Ultimately, however, while not blocking or controlling the U.S. invasion, such efforts did temporarily alter the Administration's plans.

There were also significant public pressures in the form of an antiwar social movement that attempted to act as a constraint against the U.S. intentions to invade Iraq. Recall that, in general, what began as an overwhelming show of support for the U.S. following the September 11, 2001 attacks quickly plummeted after President George W. Bush gave his 2002 State of the Union Address in which he referred to the "axis of evil." This comment acted as a red flag that the unilateral tendencies of the Administration were resurfacing, thus estranging the vast majority of Europeans, both political leaders and the general citizenry (Heinrich Bull Foundation 2003). The general trend of lack of trust in the Bush Administration was reflected in a March 2003 Heinrich Bull Foundation opinion poll that showed that Bush was viewed as more of a security threat than terrorism was. Once the war on Iraq was being marketed, negative attitudes increased. Beginning in

September 2002, NGOs and international peace groups mobilized against the U.S./UK plan for the invasion and occupation of Iraq, forming the largest antiwar movement in history (Amnesty International 2005). A global antiwar protest involving over 10 million people took place on February 15, 2003, in an effort to constrain the Bush Administration's unilateral war on Iraq. These protests were "the single largest public demonstration in history" (Jensen 2004: xvii). Antiwar protests continued after the invasion. The Associated Press (2005) reported that "tens of thousands" of activists turned out across Europe to protest and mark the Iraq war's second anniversary, with London drawing the largest crowd of between 45,000 and 100,000.

State political pressures and international social movements have indeed resulted in regimes altering, even if temporarily or only for appeasement, acts of state criminality. While state political pressures are indeed real potentials of constraint, it must also be noted that they are highly centered on self-interests and are selective in nature. As such, political pressure by countries is only as firm as it fits with their own larger economic, political, or military interests, rather than a grander ideological or moral stance. To illustrate this point, let's take a look at a few recent examples. It is true that the U.S. has condemned China for human rights violations. They have also sanctioned Cuba for similar grounds, and referred to Iran and Syria as axes of evil for their lack of respect for human right principles. However, when it comes to U.S. allies, the government tends to condone such behaviors. For example, Saudi Arabia has a horrific human rights history and regularly suppresses freedoms. Take the most recent actions of Saudi Arabia (February 2008) where the regime arrested and are interrogating 57 men for flirting with women in front of a shopping mall in Mecca. Saudi uses religious police, The Commission for the Promotion of Virtue and the Prevention of Vice, to monitor what the state has deemed proper moral behavior, thus enforcing Saudi Arabia's strict Islamic lifestyle. It was this branch of the government that arrested the men for behavior that allegedly included dancing to pop music and wearing improper clothing. Saudi Arabia bans all other religious practices and heavily discriminates against anyone that does not fit with the Islamic lifestyle. Nonetheless, even though Saudis respect democracy, freedom, or other fundamental principles touted by the U.S., the government not only fails to condemn the Saudi policies, but supports and maintains a tight relationship among the upper echelons. This, of course, is due to state intervention, or lack thereof, when and only when it is in the interests of the government or its leader. Consequently, political pressures remain tenuous at best in many crimes of states that are occurring by governments.

Domestic Constraints

Perhaps one of the biggest challenges to presenting a section on domestic constraints is the reality of the uniqueness of each case and of various governments, cultures, and heads of state and how that makes it impossible to generalize on the potentials or means of these mechanisms. Indeed, it is the belief that, as individuals, heads of state do have agency, which makes such generalizations highly problematic. For example, while domestic media outlets may be perceived as a general constraint, a watchdog of all governments if you will, the reality is, certain heads of state can affect the ability of the media to be a constraint, while in the same country, with a different head of state, the results and expectations would be quite different; media can be censored or media blackouts be initiated by one regime but not another under similar conditions (e.g., Uganda). This is true in nearly every situation. Also, there is the issue of state-owned media outlets versus those that are run by governments, as I noted previously in the discussion of international media. States can react in various ways to suppress public outcry also. This includes imprisonments, charges of treason, outright death, or through the use of nationalism, patriotism, and a multitude of other factors. On the other hand, public protests can be acceded to by one regime but ignored or bypassed by another (e.g., Vietnam war vs. the war on Iraq). Again, type of state, agency of head of state, and actual type of crime are going to factor into whether the constraint is successful or even allowed to be enacted. Of course, in some cases, under authoritarian regimes, these domestic constraints are not even an option. We can say the same of governmental oversight agencies. These also depend upon the type of government, in some cases; they may not exist at all. Internal political pressure from within states has also been conceptualized as a constraint against a regime's criminal activities. Yet, in some conditions, such political pressure has resulted in only intensifying or creating state criminality. For example, we cannot ignore that several state crimes have resulted from a regime's attempt to maintain political power in the face of political opposition. The political opposition had been met with additional violence, coups, counter-coups, and crimes against humanity (e.g., Uganda and the multiple coups and overt violence on oppositional political pressures, or Israel and the continued camp placements within the occupied Palestinian territories).

As I pointed out in previous chapters, the importance of taking into account time/space is indeed a real consideration and should be a caution to overgeneralizations in any analysis of crimes of the state, and even more significant when promoting policies based upon successful or ineffective controls and constraints for these types of crimes. Simply, suggesting intensifications of domestic reactions, political pressures, public opinion in the form of social movements, or media exposure would be unrealistic given the realpolitik of many state circumstances at this time and may perhaps lend to additional state criminality. Recall from chapter 7, states' reactions to constraints can indeed result in additional crimes and victimization.

Summary

As this chapter has identified, the conceptualization of constraints is highly susceptible to the issue of time/space and is dependent upon the uniqueness of each case and the agentic forces at play during that specific moment. Admittedly, constraints are not omnipresent nor certain; nonetheless, given the right circumstances, the constraints discussed here have offered up great resistance to, often temporarily desisting or at best revealing, crimes of the state. Indeed, as others have rightly noted, the inability of these mechanisms to be fully capable in all circumstances to restrain has led to or further enabled the opportunity factors. On the other hand, as was pointed out in chapter 5, as defined, a constraint is not expected to fully block. Additionally, the motivating forces and opportunity for illegitimate means was already present. In view of that, the failure of these mechanisms does not empower or create additional state criminality, and the successes should be lauded, as the obstacles to these constraints' effectiveness are significant given the realpolitik of states and their power.

Chapter 11

Concluding Thoughts

There is one central theme that runs through each of the crimes discussed here: capital accumulation or capital maintenance—social, economic, or political. Whether it is a head of state, leading political players within a regime or region, militia, or paramilitary, the interest or desire to attain capital is omnipresent. As Barak (1991: 10) rightly noted, "state crimes revolve essentially around money, power, and politics"—in other words, the accumulation of some form of capital. For example, the LRA's stated reason for overthrowing the Musevini regime is to socially, economically, and politically empower the Acholi region. The stated reason for the Hutu genocide on the Tutsis was to maintain political, social, and economic capital. The reason behind the U.S. invasion of Iraq was to obtain additional political and economic capital. The systemic corruption in Zimbabwe is to obtain political, economic, and, in some cases, social capital. The Gulag was used by Stalin to maintain political capital and to acquire additional political and economic capital.

Having stated this, let there be no mistake: while capital accumulation, in some form, is behind the initial decision-making process, it by no means can explain subsequent actions or the conditions that allowed such criminal activities to occur. As was introduced in chapter 7, there is an abundance of other variables that must come into play. Nonetheless, general structural and enactment patterns emerge when we examine state crime. For example, global economics, social and/or political instability, nature and direction of power, economic collapse, and ethnic tensions are key structural conditions that undergird most of these crimes. Global economics needs little explanation. It is indeed one of the main variables to consider. Whether that be the attainment of a larger global economic market, the drive to corner a particular market (i.e., oil translating to more power), or the fluctuations or collapses in specific commodity markets that have drastic effects on national and local economies, thus affecting the state social, economic, and political instability, the need to examine economic issues at the global level is real. When state economies are overly controlled by foreign investors and/or the global market, they are reliant upon the decision making by commodity market leaders or foreign investors. When drastic fluctuations occur or when a commodity is forced to crash for economic gain of those in control of the market, weak economic states find themselves in dire conditions socially and economically. Further, transnational corporations are often directly involved in black market and/or illegal exporting and importing of state resources. The nature and direction of power and political stability is also relevant. Absolute control provides ample opportunity for the state or state actors to engage in criminal behaviors. Such states often strongly benefit only a portion of the population. State actors can quickly become corrupt, using the states' resources for their personal gain and that of their kin and allies (e.g., Amin and Obote in Uganda, or Habyarimana in Rwanda).

Common enactment procedures include the use of nationalism, religion, ethnoism or racism, propaganda, militarization, and/or fear to create or enable an environment conducive to a state's criminality. From this, regimes and/or paramilitaries utilize unique and case-specific tools to accomplish their goals, which also vary by type of crime and type of state/regime. Consider that scholars of genocides and other war crimes have long pointed toward the "otherizing" effects of ethnic polarization and dehumanization as facilitating violence in general, and widespread lethal violence in particular. This otherizing has typically been manifested through constructed ethnic or racial divisions. After all, a central element within atrocity-producing environments is a set of intense ethnic rivalries and tensions often focused on capital attainment, be it political, social, or economic. Just as colonial powers dehumanized the peoples of Africa to legitimate colonial domination, ethnic groups dehumanized each other, facilitating political and economic subordination as well as wanton violence and destruction (e.g., Rwanda Hutus). Another key factor in the creation of otherizing and/or ethnic divisiveness is the role of religious institutions. This has been especially the case in genocides. After all, "the primary driving force leading to genocide is not the pathology of individuals organizing and committing the genocide, but the pathology of the ideas guiding them" (Anzulovic 1999: 4). Ervin Staub suggested that ideologies are "almost always a part of the genocidal process" (Staub 2003: 353). Ideologies aid in the creation of the "other." Religion has offered theological, moral, and mythical groundwork for genocides (e.g., Bosnian Muslims and Croatian Serb genocides); religious institutions have knowingly and actively created ethnic, social, political, and economic divisions favoring groups of civilians over others that have led to genocides (e.g., Rwandan

Tutsis). Organizational actors and leaders (e.g., clergy) have frequently been active participants in the carrying out of mass slaughters (e.g., Hutu attacks on Tutsis and the Holocaust of the Jews). While the relationship between these social phenomena is complex and often nuanced, the interconnection is undeniable. This is not to suggest that religion in and of itself is a necessary cause of genocide, as genocidal programs have been carried out without a specifically religious framework (e.g., Stalin's purges, the Khmer Rouge, Russia's slaughter of the Circassians in the mid-nineteenth century). Further, religion is not a sufficient cause either, as even where it is a central motivating factor, other etiological factors are present (e.g., Kosovo and Serbia; the Jewish slaughters that occurred adjunct to the crusades) (Rothe and Mullins 2008).

An additional commonality is the presence and noteworthy role of bystanders in every instance of these crimes. "Third parties at the state and international level are the focal point for the prevention of gross human rights violations, because the perpetrator is unwilling and the victim is unable to prevent or stop the atrocities" (Grunfeld 2007). Grunfeld suggests that the role of the bystander "is the most decisive factor when the conflict or the human rights violations have reached a stage of repression and coercion" (2). This includes the inaction of states, international institutions of control, citizens, and others who through their complicity or "ignorance" supported or aided, directly or indirectly, the perpetrators of the crimes.

Indeed, the various types and complexities of state crime are indeed a real challenge for understanding the levels of criminality; nonetheless, it has been the goal of this book to present the tools to not only understanding, but analyzing crimes of the state. This has included the various legal standards, typologies including hybrid forms, costs and consequences of these types of illegal acts, and methodological barriers. From this, overviews of controls and constraints were presented, along with key barriers to their efficacy and dangers of overgeneralizing their applicability in all situations of state crime. Yet, the discussion would not be complete without considering future potential policies amidst the realpolitik of international relations, power, and human nature. The following section presents a general discussion of these issues along with the concepts of cosmopolitism, an international community, and universalism.

Future Directions and Policies

Cosmopolitism

The commonwealth need not to be a democracy or any form of government, but any independent community managing to protect the property of its people.
John Locke

The term *cosmopolitan* has been invoked in different ways. It is an ideology expressing that all of humanity belongs to a single moral community—an ideology for "global citizenship." As noted by Friedrichs (2007), "The notion of a cosmopolitan outlook is one that views humans as part of a world community with allegiances to all human beings, transcending particularistic attachments, and takes into account the impact of globalization on local and national issues."

Such an ideology is not new. For centuries, "philosophers and jurists have speculated on the necessary conditions for achieving enduring peace and justice between nations" (Friedrichs 2007). Consider Kant's thoughts in his 1795 essay *Perpetual Peace,* where he suggests *ius cosmopoliticum* (cosmopolitan law/right) be a guiding principle to protect people from war—grounded in the belief of universal hospitality. In more contemporary times, the idea of cosmopolitism reemerged after WWII. The post-WWII form of cosmopolitism took place in both formal and informal political realms. It is the political realm, which we will soon discuss, where the idea of cosmopolitism is reflected in the idea and terminology of an international community. Cosmopolitism is often associated with more than just an ideology for a global citizenship; it has also come to denote global governance.

The question of global governance is certain to become progressively more urgent and more widely discussed during the course of the twenty-first century, and it is quite imperative that students of international crime and law engage with the evolving transnational discussion on this question. The key terms here—including "global" and "governance"—are invoked in different ways, with popular writers tending to equate global governance with "government" whereas academics and international practitioners tend to equate it with complex public and private structures and processes. (Friedrichs 2007)

The idea of global governance, a centralized entity that in some sense governs the world,

[s]trikes many commentators as a utopian fantasy (as a positive development) and a frightening nightmare (if actually realized). A "world gov-

ernment" is profoundly problematic for those on both the conservative and the progressive ends of the ideological spectrum. For conservatives, the concession of national sovereignty is especially objectionable; for progressives, the notion of such a concentration of power is especially objectionable. But global governance in contemporary discourse transcends simplistic notions of world government. (Friedrichs 2007)

Global governance is perceived as likely to include the development of new forms of cosmopolitan citizenship and institutional heterarchy (Khagram 2006: 110). Friedrichs (2007) notes that a global civil society is one dimension of an evolving global governance and, in one view, can serve as an antidote to the activities of predatory states and unregulated markets. Nonetheless, advancing or promoting a policy rooted in achieving political and legal praxis by states, regimes, and international political players based on the ideology of cosmopolitism must take into account the realpolitiks of international relations and, more specifically, human nature. After all, ideology comes from ideas, but the ideas are expressed through the actions of humans that are rooted in basic human nature. As previously noted, a key factor involved in all the various forms of state criminality has been power. If we assume that human nature is essentially good but power corrupts, then can an ideology repress the corruptive powers of power? Or will power always tempt the weakening of the moral inhibitions we all have? If we assume human nature is both good and evil, which is an underlying assumption of this author, then we must again ask if an ideology can mask or repress a portion of our human nature. To take this one step further, let us explore the formal attempts to generate a quasi cosmopolitism at the international level: creating an international community.

International Community

> *The basic aim of the United Nations is to develop a common consciousness.*
>
> Secretary General Kurt Waldheim, 1977

> [T]he evolution of an international community. . . . We are, I believe, beginning to see the birth of such a community. But we should not take it for granted that an international community will grow by itself automatically. It must be planted, protected, nurtured, and encouraged. (United Nations Report of the Secretary General on the Work of the Organization 1977: 2)

The words *international community* invoke multiple political and moral connotations of the existing international social order. The word *international*, coupled with *community*, suggests that the international arena consists of a collective unified body that shares a common moral order. Critics have implied that the term represents nothing more than a corporate global hegemony, the superpower and its allies (Chomsky 2002), or U.S.-European relationships. Yet, there is a deeper historical, ideological, and political background that comes with the term. After all, it did not just evolve out of whole cloth. Moreover, the ideology that rests behind the words *international community* has been an ongoing promotion since WWII (Rothe and Mullins 2007b).

The end of World War II brought new alliances and new attempts to generate and legitimate an international institution designed to foster peaceful cooperation and a collective security among nations. The atrocities of WWII (i.e., the Nazi Holocaust and the Japanese treatment of civilians and prisoners of war in the Chinese theatre of operations) and the widespread destruction of life and property left in its wake created both ideological and structural responses. With the development of the United Nations, international relations and law began to take on a fundamentally different character. The expansion of public international law reflected a change in ideology, one that emphasized a universal tone previously reflected only in customary law. Attaining international social control and collective security became primary in international political agendas.

The United Nations is likely to be judged . . . by the significance of its total contribution towards building a world community in which crisis will no longer be inevitable.

Dag Hammarskjöld, 1960: 13

The mission of the UN represented the principles of a higher moral and legal authority based on social justice, control, and universalism, the legitimation of which would require creating a collective identity and consciousness—the same need seen in state formation requiring the development of nationhood: the reification of nationalism (see Brubaker 2004). As stated by Secretary General Waldheim (1987: 1), "The United Nations is the symbol of a higher and more ambitious political and social aim, the evolution of an international community with interests, aspirations and loyalties of a far more wide-ranging kind." Yet any framework of power, such as the United Nations, needs legitimacy to insulate itself from critical questions regarding its utility. When the United Nations attempted to establish itself as the guardian of peace and legal-moral authority, the generation of a truly collective morality and will to submit to universal application was needed. Hence, the ideology behind an "international community" needed to be developed, internalized, and reified to legitimate the existence of the emerging international institutions of social control (e.g., World Court of Justice, United Nations) and the incipient development of international (public) criminal law and human rights. By means of using language to identify or create a collective identity (e.g., "international community"), it was possible to promote laws that would have otherwise been considered as oppositional to existing ideology—international criminal law, universalism, human rights, collective security, and world peace. Moreover, the hope was that this collective identity would become a shared consciousness (Rothe and Mullins 2007b). Simply stated, "a community of nations with interests that encompass the welfare of all members" (United Nations Report of the Secretary General on the Work of the Organization 1973: 15).

Nonetheless, then as now, there existed a clash between idealism and realism: the realpolitik of state policies, international interests, relations, and power. For example, while having broad support for the notion of a permanent, global court, key political actors within the international arena resisted. Countries including the United States refuse to compromise their sovereignty, seeing no need to subject themselves to an international legal authority. As is true today, this position is reflective of a lack of commitment to the ideology of universalism on behalf of one of the world's most powerful citizens; realpolitik still stand in the way of the reification of a shared moral order. Simply, given the realities of international relations, the realism of a collective consciousness has and may well always falter. Usage of "international community" beckoned an end to this dichotomous relationship, yet it remains a term situated between the reality of international relations and the ideology of universalism and cosmopolitism. As noted by M. Cherif Bassiouni (2008),

> There is hardly anything to be said of an international community other than an international community of interests. . . . You don't see an international community having responsibilities deriving from commonly shared values. . . . You do not see an international community that feels a sense of social responsibility or social solidarity . . . or share resources . . . or even a community that is willing to intervene to assume the responsibilities of intervention that community knows is likely to commit genocide or crimes against humanity.

This is reflected in the lack of attention and/or response to crisis and needs of states not deemed in the political or economic interest of dominant states. For example, the lack of attention to the atrocities that occurred in Darfur and other African countries reflect the disjuncture between an "international community" or cosmopolitism and the corresponding social form or the realpolitik of international relations.

With little optimism of actuality, it is indeed a time of increased concern of international peace and security, and there is great need for an international community beyond a moral and ideological conceptualization. For the actualization of this vision to occur, while far-reaching and to date an impossible reality, global interconnection and cooperation is necessary in

---

The Contradiction: Realpolitik and Cosmopolitism

Ideology	vs.	*International Relations*
Cosmopolitism—		
International Community	vs.	*Atomistic State Interests*
Consensus		Political, Economic, Military
Shared Values		Independent Power
Common Interests		
Shared Power		
Universalism—		
Morality and Legality	vs.	*Sovereignty*
Universal Legal Jurisdiction		Self-governing States

---

the current geopolitical era. International criminal enterprises (e.g., drug and human trafficking) and security threats (e.g., terrorism) are only addressable through the development and implementation of structures of cooperation and coexistence. Further, the development of the sense of shared fate that the notion of international community embodies should also work to reduce the relational distance between global populations. Such solidarity development, in a pure Durkheimian sense, at its core can work to undermine the social, cultural, and political distances that produce alienation and are a core drive toward terrorist actions. An extant international community founded on core principles of universal human rights and justice is the best hope that disempowered and marginalized populations have to counteract the currently prevailing forces of ever-increasing domination of Western capital and of U.S. imperial ambitions on the global stage. Moreover, states must be willing to forfeit certain components of their sovereignty to allow for a true internationalism grounded in honest and complete multilateralism. For an international community to fully materialize beyond the moral concept into an existing and binding social order, states and leaders of the world would need to move toward a fully shared consciousness of identity and morals based on a global social contract that had universal application and accountability.

Universalism

The doctrine of universal jurisdiction asserts that some crimes are so heinous that their perpetrators should not escape justice by invoking doctrines of sovereign immunity or the sacrosanct nature of national frontiers. However, attempts to universally apply legal and/or moral regulations have historically been met with the same objection: state sovereignty. Consequently, sovereignty generally becomes a central wedge used to ensure international regulation is limited. To relinquish territorial domestic law to a universality of international law would have required states to accept universal jurisdiction versus international law governing only interstate issues. The result would have endangered the sovereignty that many states saw as essential for their safety, political interests, and political or national ideologies. The earliest international treaties, dating back to 1648 and the Westphalia Treaty, as well as charters, customs, and laws were based solely on interstate relations: a Hobbesian view of international order, which is very anarchical (Bassiouni 2008). The contradiction of sovereignty of states structuring an international atomistic system versus the ideology of a unified international society has resulted in decades of conflicts during attempts to create a universal system of control—an international criminal court. These conflicts and the fundamental contradiction of international society led to ad hoc international systems of justice (IMT, World Court of Justice, Court of Arbitration, and nonempowered international organizations) rather than an empowered universal criminal court. All of these international organizations are the result of attempts to address specific conflicts (Franco-Prussian War, WWI, WWII, assassination of leaders, terrorism, drug trafficking). This, coupled with a nonempowered universal system of justice, resulted in the failure of these organizations to constrain future conflicts. Historical attempts to establish an international system of justice that is empowered and universalistic have illustrated how the contradictions of an international society constrain the potential outcome for such an institution. What has resulted from the conflicts that arose as a result of these international contradictions are ad hoc entities, nonempowered systems of justice, and the establishment of new international laws without a corresponding change in ideology within international society and/or international law (during the late 1800s through the 1930s). Simply, at the core of the matter is the contradiction between the ideal type or ideology of cosmopolitism and the issue of sovereign rule.

Further, as the criminological research on state crime has shown, states with the most at risk economically, politically, and ideologically, such as the U.S., are highly unlikely to allow themselves to be regulated by outside agencies. Just as state compliance is unlikely by highly powered states, those same countries sit on, or have allies on, the Security Council, utilizing their veto power in accordance with their political, economic, and ideological interests. Indeed, the realpolitik of international relations are centered on state sovereignty. As such, the potential for a universal legal order must be pre-dated by the reification or crystallization of an international community that is truly reflective of and grounded in cosmopolitism. Yet, I am, as others are, highly skeptical that this will become a reality in the near future.

Summary

For a student or researcher of state criminality, the key question still remains—what can be done? Previous chapters have discussed in length the extremely high numbers of heads of state and/or high-ranking political players that have enjoyed impunity versus accountability. Chapters 8, 9, and 10 have explored the various controls and constraints, including their weaknesses and/or failures to fully address these types of crimes and criminals. In this chapter, I have presented a rather pessimistic view of human nature in general, but even more so concerning the potential of a "true" international community. So then, what, as scholars, as citizens, can we do to try to control, deter, and hold accountable the worst of the worst criminals? Is it an impossible task? Will there always be some form of state criminality as long as there are states and governments? Perhaps the ultimate answer to these questions lies in the assumption that we will probably never live to see the complete eradication of state criminality. However, I believe, through diligence and the growing effort to hold heads of state and other political players accountable under international laws, we can see a reduction. I also believe we can act to reduce the numbers of victims of these types of crime by taking certain courses of action:

1. Continue to expand the awareness of such crimes, whether that is through public criminology, teaching, research, or a variety of other methods. It is only through awareness that public outrage can occur. When and/or if such an outrage occurs, public demands to respond will follow, pressuring key political players to intervene even if state interests are not a key issue for involvement.

2. Work toward attaining some sense of commonality based on shared humanistic values. If each of us starts with ourselves in living out this worldview and philosophy, it can and will grow, even if it takes several generations to spread to a level wherein the majority of people share the same common outlook, goals, or vision.

3. Demand and work for both accountability for those orchestrating crimes of the state and social restoration for the areas and peoples that have been victimized by the crimes.

4. Never lose empathy for the victimized stranger that may live thousands of miles away and whose situation you believe is unrelated to your daily life. It would be and is naive to think that you are insulated from state crimes; no matter where or who you are, you have probably been a victim of such criminality, yet the degree of harm is indeed relevant to the state itself. As such, do not lose sight that you too could be a victim of state repression, crimes against humanity, genocide, slavery, torture, or a host of the most serious criminal incidents.

There is no magic answer or quick policy fix for the worst of the worst crimes. It is an ongoing problem that requires diligence, commitment, and a change in ideology, praxis, and relations.

Bibliography

Agirre, X. 2007. Personal Communication. April 14, Maastricht University.

Aglietta, M. 1990. "On a Marxist Theory of Regulation." *Monthly Review* 41(8).

———. 2000. *A Theory of Capitalist Regulation: The U.S. Experience.* London: Verso.

Akers, R. 1977. *Deviant Behavior: A Social Learning Approach.* Belmont, CA: Wadsworth.

Alexandrovna, L. 2006. *Alexander Litvinenko.* (http://www.atlargely.com/opinion/).

Almond, G. 1990. *A Discipline Divided: Schools and Sects in Political Science.* Thousand Oaks, CA: Sage.

Ambos, K. and I. Stegmiller. 2008. "German Research on International Criminal Law: With a Special Focus on the Implementation of the ICC Statute in National Jurisdiction." *Criminal Law Forum* 19(1): 181–98.

American Enterprise Institute. 2004. *American Enterprise Institute. Report and Video of Saddam's Torture at Abu Ghraib.* (http://www.aei.org/).

Amnesty International. 2002a. *Africa Report.* AFR 47/007/2002.

———. 2002b. *Human Rights Abuses Iraq.* (http://www.amnesty.org).

———. 2003. *Democratic Republic of Congo: "Our Brothers Who Help Kill Us."* New York: Amnesty International.

———. 2004. *Iraq: One Year on the Human Rights Situation.* March 18. (http://www.amnesty.org/library/Index/ENGMDE140062004).

———. 2005. *Press Release.* AFR 54/059/2005. News Service No. 150.

———. 2007. *Africa Report.* AFR 47/007:1.

———. 2008. *Amnesty International Fact Sheet.* (http://www.amnestyusa.org/women/pdf/armedconflict.pdf).

Anderson, E. 1990. Streetwise: *Race, Class, and Change in an Urban Community.* Chicago: University of Chicago Press.

———. 1999. *Code of the Street: Decency, Violence and the Moral Life of the Inner City.* New York: W. W. Norton.

Annan, K. 2004. *Address to General Assembly* [Transcript]. September 21. FDCH E-Media.

Anti-Slavery International. 2007. *Slavery Today.* (http://www.antislavery.org/).

Anzulovic, B. 1999. *Heavenly Serbia: From Myth to Genocide.* New York: New York University Press.

Asian Human Rights Commission. 2006. *Human Rights Report: The State of Human Rights in Eleven Nations.* Hong Kong: Clear-Cut Publishing.

Associated Press. 2005. *Europe Marks Anniversary of Iraq Invasion.* March 19. (http://www.globalpolicy.org/ngos/advocacy/protest/iraq/2005/0319europe marks.htm).

Aulette J. and R. Michalowski. 1993. "Fire in Hamlet: A Case Study of State-Corporate Crime." Pp. 171–206 in *Political Crime in Contemporary America, edited by* K. Tunnel. New York: Garland.

Babbie, E. 1998. *The Practice of Social Research.* 8th ed. Belmont, CA: Wadsworth.

Bachman, R., R. Paternoster, and S. Wards. 1992. "The Rationality of Sexual Offending: Testing a Deterrence/Rational Choice Conception of Sexual Assault." *Law and Society Review* 26(2):343–72.

Bales, K. 2004. *Disposable People: New Slavery in the Global Economy.* 2d ed. Berkeley: University of California Press.

Balint, J. 1996. "Conflict, Conflict Victimization, and Legal Redress: 1945–1996." *Law and Contemporary Problems* 59:231–47.

Barak, G. 1990. "Crime, Criminology and Human Rights: Towards an Understanding of State Criminality." *The Journal of Human Justice* 2:11–28.

———. 1991. *Crimes by the Capitalist State.* Albany: State University of New York Press.

———. 1993. "Crime, Criminology, and Human Rights: Toward an Understanding of State Criminality." Pp. 207–30 in *Political Crime in Contemporary America,* edited by Kenneth D. Tunnell. New York: Garland.

———, ed. 1994. *Media, Process, and the Social Construction of Crime: Studies in Newsmaking Criminology.* New York: Garland.

Barcelona Traction, Light and Power Co. Ltd. (*Belg. v. Spain*), 1970 I.C.J. 3, 32.

Barrow, C. 2005. "The Return of the State: Globalization, State Theory and the New Imperialism." *New Political Science.* (http://www.umassd.edu/cfpa/docs/annrpt05.pdf).

Basoglu, M. 2007. "Psychological and Physical Torture Have Similar Mental Effects." *General Psychiatry* 64:277–85. (http://www.eurekalert.org/pub_releases/2007-03/jaaj-pap030107.php).

Bassiouni, M. C. 1996. "Searching for Peace and Achieving Justice: The Need for Accountability." *Law and Contemporary Problems* 59(4): 9–28.

———. 1999. *International Criminal Law.* 2d ed. Vol. I. United States: Transnational Publishers.

———. 2006. *Crimes of War: The Book.* (http://www.crimesofwar.org/thebook/crimes-against-humanity.html).

———. 2008. *The Perennial Conflict between Realpolitik and the Pursuit of International Criminal Justice.* Public Speech, April 2. University of Northern Iowa.

BBC News. 1999. Front Page—World, World "Pinochet Must Go to Spain, Says Amnesty." (http://news.bbc.co.uk/1/hi/world/260124.stm).

———. 1998. Special Report. "South Africans Reconciled?" (http://news.bbc.co.uk/1/hi/world/africa/142673).

Becker, H. 1963. *Outsiders: Studies in the Sociology of Deviance.* New York: The Free Press.

Becker, T. and V. Murray. 1971. *Government Lawlessness in America.* New York: Oxford University Press.

Beitz, C. 1979. *Political Theory and International Relations*. Princeton, NJ: Princeton University Press.

Ben-Yuda, N. 2007. Personal Conversation at American Society Criminology Meeting, November.

Berg, B. 1998. *Qualitative Research Methods for the Social Sciences*. 3d ed. Boston: Allyn and Bacon.

Berger, A. A. 1991. *Media Analysis Techniques*. Rev. ed. Newbury Park, CA: Sage.

Berger, P. and T. Luckmann. 1967. *The Social Construction of Reality: A Treatise in the Sociology of Knowledge*. Norwell, MA: Anchor Press.

Berk, R., A. Campbell, R. Klap, and B. Western. 1992 "The Deterrent Effect of Arrest in Incidents of Domestic Violence: A Bayesian Analysis of Four Field Experiments." *American Sociological Review* 57:698–708.

Bertrand Russell War Crimes Tribunal on Vietnam. 1971. (http://911review.org/ Wget/www.homeusers.prestel.co.uk/littleton/v1tribun.htm).

Bijleveld, C. 2007. *So Many Missing Pieces: Some Thoughts on the Methodology of the Empirical Study of Gross Human Rights Violations*. Paper presented at the Expert Meetings, April 13–14, Maastricht University.

Blaskic Appeals Chamber Decision. 2005. Case No: IT-95-14-R. November 23, 2006. (http://www.un.org/icty/blaskic/appeal/decision-e/061123e.htm).

Boed, R. 1999. "An Evaluation of the Legality and Efficacy of Lustration as a Tool of Transitional Justice." *Columbia Journal of Transitional Law* 37:357–402.

Boyle, E. H. and J. W. Meyer. 2002. "Modern Law as a Secular and Global Model: Implications for the Sociology of Law." Pp. 65–95 in *Global Prescriptions: The Production, Exportation, and Importation of a New Legal Orthodoxy*, edited by Y. Dezalay and B. J. Garth. Ann Arbor: University of Michigan Press.

Boyle, F. 2004. *Destroying World Order: U.S. Imperialism in the Middle East Before and After September 11*. Atlanta, GA: Clarity Press.

Brahm, E. 2004. "Lustration." June. (http://www.beyondintractability.org/essay/ lustration/).

———. 2005. "The Chilean Truth and Reconciliation Commission." July. (http://www.beyondintractability.org/case_studies/Chilean_Truth_Commission .jsp?nid=5221).

Braithwaite, J. 1989a. *Crime, Shame and Reintegration*. Cambridge, England: Cambridge University Press.

———. 1989b. "Criminological Theory and Organizational Crime." *Justice Quarterly* 6:333–58.

Browning, G., A. Halcli, and F. Webster. 2000. *Understanding Contemporary Society: Theories of the Present*. Thousand Oaks, CA: Sage.

Brubaker, R. 2004. "Nationalism Reframed: Nationhood and the National Question in the New Europe." Pp. 231–44 in *The New Social Theory Reader*, edited by S. Seidman and J. Alexander. New York: Routledge.

Buncombe, A. 2003. "U.S. Admits It Used Napalm Bombs in Iraq." *The Independent* (http://www.news.independent.co.uk/world/americas/story.jsp?story= 432201).

Bunting, H. 2004. *In Testimony Given to Senate Democratic Policy Committee. Session #12: Democratic Policy Committee on Iraq Contract Abuses*. February 13. Washington, DC.

Burns, E. B. 1987. *The Reagan Doctrine and the Politics of Nostalgia*. New York: Harper and Row.

Burns, R. and M. Lynch. 2004. *Environmental Crime: A Sourcebook*. El Paso, TX: LFB Scholarly.

Bursik, R. J., Jr. and Gramsik, H. G. 1993. "Economic Deprivation and Neighborhood Crime Rates 1960–1980." *Law and Society Review* 27:263–68.

Bush, G. W. 2001. *State of the Union Address*. September 24. In "Enemies Everywhere: Terrorism, Moral Panic, and U.S. Civil Society," by Dawn Rothe and Stephen Muzzatti. *Critical Criminology: An International Journal* 12:3.

———. 2002. Pp. 47–48 in *Chain of Command: The Road From 9/11 to Abu Ghraib*, by Seymour Hersh. New York: Harper Collins.

———. 2003. *We Will Prevail*. National Review Books.

Canadian Press. 2007. "Radioactive Waste Cleanup Behind Schedule: Report." Updated Sun. Aug. 19 2007 1:43 PM ET Canadian Press. (http://www .ctv.ca/servlet/ArticleNews/story/CTVNews/20070819/Radioactive_waste _cleanup_070819/20070819).

Carty, A. 1991. "Critical International Law: Recent Trends in the Theory of International Law." *European Journal of International Law* 2(1):66–96. (http://www.ejil.org/journal/Vo2/No1/index.html).

Caruthers, T. 1991. *In the Name of Democracy: U.S. Policy Toward Latin America in the Reagan Years*. Berkeley: University of California Press.

Cassesse, A. 2002a. *The Rome Statute of the International Criminal Court: A Commentary*. Vol. I. Oxford Press.

_____. 2002b. *The Rome Statute of the International Criminal Court: A Commentary*. Vol. II. Oxford Press.

_____. 2002c. *The Rome Statute of the International Criminal Court: A Commentary*. Vol. III. Materials. Oxford Press.

Chambliss, W. 1990. "State Organized Crime." *Criminology* 27(2):183–208.

_____. 1995. "Commentary by William J. Chambliss." *Society of Social Problems Newsletter* 26(1):9.

Chambliss, W. and M. Zatz. 1993. *Making Law: the State, the Law, and Structural Contradictions*. Bloomington: Indiana University Press.

Chatterjee, P. 2004. "Controversial Commando Wins Iraq Contract." *CorpWatch*, June 9. (http://www.corpwatch.org/print_article.php?andid=11350).

Chomsky, N. 2002. *Pirates and Empires: Old and New*. Cambridge, MA: South End Press.

Christie, N. 2001. "Answers to Atrocities. Restorative Justice in Extreme Situations." In *Victim Policies and Criminal Justice on the Road to Restorative Justice. Essays in Honour of Tony Peters*, edited by Ezzat Fattah and Stephan Parmentier. Leuven, The Netherlands: Leuven University Press.

Clarke, R. 2004. *Against All Enemies: Inside America's War on Terror*. New York: Free Press.

Clifford, M. 1998. *Environmental Crime: Enforcement, Policy, and Social Responsibility*. Gaithersburg, MD: Aspen.

Clinard, M. B. 1946. "Criminological Theories of Violations of Wartime Regulations." *American Sociological Review* 2:258–70.

Cloward, R. and L. Ohlin. 1960. *Delinquency and Opportunity: A Theory of Delinquent Gangs*. New York: Free Press.

Cobban, H. 2007. *Amnesty after Atrocity? Healing Nations after Genocide and War Crimes*. Boulder, CO: Paradigm.

Cohen, A. K. 1990. "Criminal Actors: Natural Persons and Collectives." In "New Directions in the Study of Justice, Law, and Social Control." *Arizona State University School of Justice Studies*, 101–25. New York. Plenum.

Cohen, L. E. and M. Felson. 1979. "Social Change and Crime Rate Trends: A Routine Activity Approach." *American Sociological Review* 44:588–605.

Cohn, M. 2004. "Torturing Hearts and Minds." *Truthout*. October. (http://www.truthout.org/docs/04/050404A.shtml).

Collins, J. and R. Glover. 2002. *Collateral Language*. New York: NYU Press.

Colvin, M. and F. T. Cullen. 2004. "Crime and Coercion: A Test of Core Theoretical Propositions." *Journal of Research in Crime and Delinquency* 41(3): 244–68.

Commission of Inquiry for the International War Crimes Tribunal for Iraq. 1991. (http://deoxy.org/wc/warcrim2.htm).

Concerned Citizens Tribunal. 2002. *Crime Against Humanity*. Vol. II. Mumbai, India: Citizens for Justice and Peace.

Congressional Budget Office. 2008. *Long-term Implications of Current Defense Plans: Summary Update for Fiscal Year 2008*. DOC 8844. December.

Cornish, D. and R. V. Clarke, eds. 1986. *The Reasoning Criminal*. New York: Springer-Verlag.

Council of Europe Parliamentary Assembly Committee. 2005. *Need for International Condemnation of Crimes of Totalitarian Communist Regimes*. Doc. 10765. December 16. (http://assembly.coe.int/main.asp?link=/documents/workingdocs/doc05/edoc10765.htm).

Cox, R. 1996. Taken from his collection: *Approaches to World Order: Essays by Robert W. Cox*. Contributor Timothy J. Sinclair. Cambridge University Press.

Cozic, C. P. 1993. "Introduction." *Current Controversies: Nationalism and Ethnic Conflict*, edited by Charles P. Cozic. San Diego: Greenhaven Press. (http://www.enotes.com/nationalism-ethnic-article/44564).

Cressey, D. R. 1989. "The Poverty of Theory in Corporate Crime Research." Pp. 31–35 in *Advances in Criminological Theory*, edited by W. S. Laufer and F. Adler. New Brunswick, NJ: Transaction.

Creveld, M. 1999. *The Rise and Decline of the State*. Cambridge, MA: Cambridge University Press.

Dahl, R. 1998. *On Democracy*. New Haven, CT: Yale University Press.

Danner, M. 2004a. "The Logic of Torture." *New York Review*. June 24. (http://www.markdanner.com/nyreview/062404_Road_to_Torture.htm).

———. 2004b. *Torture and Truth*. New York: New York Review Books.

"Day Four of the War: Timeline." 2004. *The Guardian*, March 23. (http://www.guardian.co.uk/Iraq/Story/0,2763,920317,00.html).

Democracy Now. 2005. *Headlines*. February 18. (http://www.democracynow.org/article.pl?sid=05/02/18/156254).

Derechos News Service. 1998, October 29. (http://www.hispanianews.com/archive.htm) and (http://www.derechos.org).

Dixon, M. and S. Jonas. 1984. *Nicaragua Under Siege*. San Francisco: Synthesis.

Doctors Without Borders 2006. *International Activity Report 2006: Democratic Republic of Congo*. (http://www.doctorswithoutborders.org/publications/ar/i2006/drc.cfm).

———. 2007. *Forgotten Crises: The Top Ten Most Underreported Humanitarian Stories*. (http://www.doctorswithoutborders.org/publications/reports).

Domhoff, G. W. 1998. *Who Rules America? Power and Politics in the Year 2000.* 3d ed. Mountain View, CA: Mayfield.

Durkheim, E. 1933. *The Division of Labor in Society,* translated by G. Simpson. New York: Free Press.

Elibron Quotations Voltaire—Philosophers Dictionary. 2003. Retrieved October 7, 2003 (http://www.elibronquotations.com/author.phtml?a_id=2612).

Enloe, C. 2004. *The Curious Feminist.* Berkeley: University of California Press.

Eriksson, M. and P. Wallensteen. 2004. "Armed Conflict, 1989–2003." *Journal of Peace Research* 41:625–31.

Ermann, M. D. and R. J. Lundman. 1982. *Corporate Deviance.* New York: Holt, Rinehart and Winston.

Euro Correspondent. 2007. "EU Green Crime Proposals Seek to Improve Enforcement." April 7. (http://www.euro-correspondent.com/index.php?option=com_content&task=view&id=88&Itemid=5).

Eweld, U. 2007. *Structure of Evidence and Empirical Analysis in International Criminal Justice: A Criminological Perspective on ICTY Cases.* Presented at Experts Meetings, April 13–14, Maastricht University.

Falk, P. 1993. *Global Visions: Beyond the New World Order.* Boston: South End Press.

Falk, R. 2004. *The Declining World Order: America's Imperial Geopolitics.* New York: Routledge.

———. 2005. "The World Speaks on Iraq." *The Nation,* August 1. (http://www.thenation.com/doc/20050801/falk).

Fallows, J. 2004. "Bush's Lost Year." *The Atlantic Monthly,* October, 68–84.

Farley et al. (2003). *Prostitution, Trafficking, and Traumatic Stress.* Philadelphia: Haworth Press.

Faulks, K. 2000. *Political Sociology: A Critical Introduction.* New York: New York University Press.

Feagin, J., A. Orum, and G. Sjoberg, Eds. 1991. *A case for case study.* Chapel Hill: University of North Carolina Press.

"Fear of Terrorism Is No Excuse to Flout Laws." 2003. Ottawa Citizen, May 29, p. A17.

Felson, M. 1998. Crime and Everyday Life. 2d ed. Thousand Oaks, CA: Pine Forge Press.

Foucault, M. 1972. *The Archaeology of Knowledge and the Discourse on Language.* New York: Harper and Row.

Friedrichs, D. 1992. "State Crime or Governmental Crime: Making Sense of the Conceptual Confusion." Pp. 53–80 in *Controlling State Crime,* edited by Jeff Ross. New York: Garland.

———. 1995. *Trusted Criminals: White Collar Crime in Contemporary Society.* Belmont, CA: Wadsworth.

———. 1996a. "Governmental Crime, Hitler and White Collar Crime: A Problematic Relationship." *Caribbean Journal of Criminology and Social Psychology* 1:44–63.

———. 1996b. *Trusted Criminals: White Collar Crime in Contemporary Society.* Belmont, CA: Wadsworth.

———. 2000. "The Crime of the Century? The Case for the Holocaust." *Crime, Law, and Social Change* 34(1):21–41.

————. 2004. "White-Collar Crime in a Globalized World." Presentation at Western Michigan University.

————. 2007. *Towards a Criminology of International Crimes: Producing a Conceptual and Contextual Framework.* Presentation at Experts Meetings, April 13–14, Maastricht University.

Friedrichs, D. O. and J. Friedrichs. 2002. "The World Bank and Crimes of Globalization: A Case Study." *Social Justice* 29(1–2):1–12.

"From the Editors: The Times and Iraq." 2004. *New York Times,* May 26, p. A10.

Frulli, M. 2001. "Are Crimes Against Humanity More Serious than War Crimes?" *European Journal of International Law* 12:329–50.

Galliher, J. 1989. *Criminology, Human Rights, Criminal Law, and Crime.* Englewood Cliffs, NJ: Prentice Hall.

Gazette, The (Montreal). 2003. October: A18. Pp. 91–98, in *Missed Signals,* edited by S. Ricchiardi. American Foreign Policy Annual Edition 2006/2007.

Geis, G. 1967. "White-Collar Crime: The Heavy Electrical Equipment Antitrust Cases of 1961." Pp. 139–51 in *Criminal Behavior Systems: A Typology,* edited by Marshall Clinard and Richard Quinney. New York: Holt, Rinehart and Winston.

Giddens, A. 1987a. *The Nation State and Violence.* Berkeley, University of California Press.

————. 1987b. *Social Theory and Modern Sociology.* Stanford, CA: Stanford University Press.

Global Policy Forum. 2005. "U.S. Arm Twisting." P. 1. (http://www.globalpolicy .org/security/issues/iraq/attack/armtwistindex.htm).

Goering, H. 1947. *Testimony at the Nuremberg Trials* (Pp. 278–79). Selected and Prepared by the United Nations War Crimes Commission. London: H.M.S.O., 1947–49.

Gongloff, M. 2003. "Iraq Rebuilding Contracts Awarded Halliburton, Stevedoring Services of America Get Government Contracts for Early Relief Work." CNN, October 23.

Gramsci, A. 1971. *Selections from the Prison Notebooks.* New York: International.

————. 1995. *Further Selections from the Prison Notebooks,* edited by Derek Boothman. Trowbridge, Wilshire: Redwood Books.

Green, P. and T. Ward. 2000. "State Crime, Human Rights, and the Limits of Criminology." *Social Justice* 27(1):101.

————. 2004. *State Crime: Governments, Violence and Corruption.* London: Pluto Press.

Greenberg, K. J. and J. L. Dratel, eds. 2005. *The Torture Papers: The Road to Abu Ghraib.* New York: Cambridge University Press.

Grieder, W. 1998. *Fortress America.* New York: Public Affairs Press.

Griffen, K. 1995. "Global Perspectives for Development and Security." *Canadian Journal of Development Studies* 16(3).

Gross, E. 1978. "Organizational Crime: A Theoretical Perspective." Pp. 55–85 in *Studies in Symbolic Interaction,* edited by N. K. Denzin. Greenwich, CT: JAI Press.

————. 1980. "Organizational Structure and Organizational Crime." Pp. 211–30 in *White Collar Crime: Theories and Research,* edited by Gilbert Geis and Edward Stotland. Beverly Hills, CA: Sage.

Grunfeld, F. 2007. "The Role of Bystanders in Rwanda and Srebrencia. Paper presented at the Expert Meetings, April 13–14, Maastricht University.

Habermas, J. 1975. *Legitimation Crisis,* translated by Thomas McCarthy. Boston: Beacon Press.

Hafez, K. 2000. *Islam and the West in the Mass Media: Fragmented Images in a Globalizing World.* German Institute Middle East Studies. Cressell, NJ: Hampton Press.

Hagan, F. 1997. *Political Crime.* Boston: Allyn & Bacon.

Hall, R. 1987. "Organizational Behavior: A Sociological Perspective." Pp. 112–31 in *Handbook of Organizational Behavior*, edited by J. W. Lorsch. Englewood Cliffs, NJ: Prentice Hall.

"Halliburton." 2004. *Mother Jones Magazine.* Retrieved October 28, 2004 (http://www.motherjones.com/).

Hammarskjöld, D. 1960. "United Nations Report of the Secretary General on the Work of the Organization. General Assembly." *Official Records: First through Fifty-Ninth Session. Supplement No. I* (A/1/1–A/59/1). New York: United Nations.

Harbury, J. 2005. *Truth, Torture, and the American Way.* Boston: Beacon Press.

Harff, B. 2005. *Assessing Risks of Genocide and Politicide,* edited by Monty G. Marshall and Ted Robert Gurr, From Peace and Conflict Report.

Hartung, W. 2003. *How Much Are You Making on the War, Daddy? A Quick and Dirty Guide to War Profiteering in the Bush Administration.* New York: Nation Books.

Hathoway, O. 2004. "The Promise and Limits of the International Law of Torture." Pp. 199–212 in *Torture: A Collection,* edited by S. Levinson. New York: Oxford University Press.

Haverman, R. 2007. Oral Presentation at Expert Meetings, April 13–14, Maastricht University.

Hayner, P. B. 2001. *Unspeakable Truths. Confronting State Terror and Atrocity.* Preface of Timothy Garton Ash. New York: Routledge.

Heinrich Büll Foundation. 2003. "New Challenges Confronting CFSP After September 11." In *The Aftermath of September 11: New Challenges for a European Common Foreign and Security Policy.* January.

Helms, J. 2002. *Committee on Foreign Relations: United States Senate Press Release. Preamble.* June.

Henkin, L. 1995. *International Law: Politics and Values.* Dordrecht, The Netherlands: Martinus Nijhoff.

Henri-Levi, B. 1977. *Barbarism With a Human Face.* New York: Harper and Row.

Herman, E. S. and N. Chomsky. 1988. *Manufactured Consent: The Political Economy of the Mass Media.* New York: Pantheon Books.

Hersh, S. 2004a. *Chain of Command: The Road from 9-11 to Abu Ghraib.* New York: HarperCollins.

———. 2004b. "Torture at Abu Ghraib." *The New Yorker,* May 10, p. A1.

Hickey, N. 1998. "Money Lust: How Pressure for Profit Is Perverting Journalism." *Columbian Journalism Review* 32(3):28–36.

Hill, M. 1993. "Archival Strategies and Techniques." *Qualitative Research Methods* 31. Thousand Oaks, CA: Sage.

Hippler, J. 1993. "Foreign Policy, the Media and the Western Perceptions of the Middle East." In *Islam and the West in the Mass Media,* edited by Kai Hafez. Cresskill, NJ: Hampton Press.

Hirst, P. and G. Thompson. 1996. "No Place Like Home: A Review of Globalisation in Question." *Socialist Review* 197. Polity Press. (http://www.pubs .socialistreviewindex.org.uk/sr197/global.htm).

Hitchins, C. 2001. *Afterward and Law and Justice: Excerpts from the Book The Trial of Henry Kissinger.* Verso Press. (http://www.thirdworldtraveler.com/ Kissinger/Afterword_TOHK.html).

Hoare, M. A. 2004. "The Utasha Genocide." *South Slav Journal* 25(1–2):95–96.

Hoge, J. 1997. "Foreign News: Who Gives a Damn?" *Columbia Journalism Review* November/December.
(http://www.backissues.cjrarchives.org/year/97/6/foreign.asp).

Human Rights Watch. 1997. *The Scars of Death: Children Abducted by the Lord's Resistance Army in Uganda.* New York: Human Rights Watch.

———. 1999a. "Arms Transfers to Abusive End-Users." *World Report.* (http://www.hrw.org/worldreport99/arms/arms4.html).

———. 1999b. *Summary and Recommendations: When Tyrants Tremble.* (http://www.hrw.org/reports/1999/chile/Patrick.htm).

———. 1999c. "Uganda Historical Background Report." (hrw.org/reports/ 1999/uganda/Uganweb-06.htm).

———. 2000. *Human Rights Watch Focus on Human Rights: Civil War Sierra Leone.* March 3, p. 3. (http://www.hrw.org/campaigns/sierra/).

———. 2001. *Human Rights Watch World Report 2001 Sierra Leone.* (http://www .hrw.org/wr2k1/Africa/sierraleone.html).

———. 2003a. *Human Rights Watch World Report 2003 Middle East.* (http://www .hrw.org/wr2k3/mideast6.html).

———. 2003b. *Ituri: "Covered in Blood": Ethnically Targeted Violence in North-eastern Democratic Republic of Congo.* New York: Human Rights Watch.

———. 2003c. *Uganda: Abducted and Abused: Renewed Conflict in Northern Uganda.* New York: Human Rights Watch.

———. 2003d. *Uganda: Stolen Children: Abduction and Recruitment in Northern Uganda.* New York: Human Rights Watch.

———. 2004a. *Child Soldier Use 2003: Uganda.* New York: Human Rights Watch.

———. 2004b. *Empty Promises?* A Human Rights Briefing Paper. August 11.

———. 2004c. *Sudan-Darfur in Flames: Atrocities in Western Sudan.* April, 16(5a).

———. 2005a. *The Curse of Gold: Democratic Republic of Congo.* New York: Human Rights Watch.

———. 2005b. *Entrenching Impunity Government Responsibility for International Crimes in Darfur* 17(17A).

———. 2005c. *Seeking Justice: The Prosecution of Sexual Violence in the Congo War* 17(1A).

———. 2005d. *Sexual Violence and Its Consequences among Displaced Persons in Darfur and Chad.* A Human Rights Watch Briefing Paper, April 12. (http://www.hrw.org/backgrounder/africa/darfur0505/).

———. 2005e. *Targeting the Fur: Mass Killings in Darfur.* A Human Rights Watch Briefing Paper, January 21.

————. 2006a. *DR Congo: Army Abducts Civilians for Forced Labor*. October 13. New York: Human Rights Watch.

————. 2006b. *Report Importance of War Crimes Prosecutions in Republika Srpska*. (http://www.hrw.org/reports/2006/bosnia0306/3.htm).

————. 2006c. *What Future? Street Children in the Democratic Republic of Congo*. New York: Human Rights Watch.

————. 2007. *Women's Rights: Trafficking*. (http://www.hrw.org/women/ trafficking.html).

————. 2008a. *Enforcing the International Prohibition on the Juvenile Death Penalty*. A Human Rights Watch Submission for the Secretary-General's Report on Follow-up to General Assembly Resolution 62/149 on a Death Penalty Moratorium. May 30. (http://www.hrw.org/pub/2008/children/HRW.Juv.Death .Penalty.053008.pdf).

————. 2008b. *Human Rights Watch Child Soldiers*. (http://www.hrw.org/ campaigns/crp/index.htm).

————. 2008c. Iran: Reformist Candidates Barred From Election. March 13. (http://www.hrw.org/english/docs/2008/03/13/iran18282.htm).

————. 2008d. *World Report*. (http://www.hrw.org/wr2k8/).

"Human Rights Watch Calls on U.S. to Probe Allegations of CIA Torture." 2002. *St. John's Telegraph of Newfoundland*. December 30: A12 and D5.

Hussain, M. 2000. "Islam, Media and Minorities in Denmark." *Current Sociology* 48(4):95–116.

Huyse, L. 1996. "Justice after Transition: On the Choices Successor Elites Make in Dealing with the Past." In *Contemporary Genocides* edited by Albert Jongman. Leiden: PIOOM.

Ibrahimi, M. 2007. "The Watchdog Role of the Media—Media as the Fourth Estate." *Rrezja Journal*, January 27. (http://www.rrezja.blogspot.com/2007/01/ watchdog-role-of-media.html).

International Committee of the Red Cross. 2004. *Report*. (http://www .globalsecurity.org/military/library/report/2004/icrc_report_iraq_feb2004.htm).

————. 2007. *Annual Report. Conflicts*. (http://www.icrc.org/).

International Court of Justice. 2005. *Cases*. (http://www.icc.org).

————. 2007. (http://www.icjcij.org/icjwww/igeneralinformation.htm).

International Criminal Court. 2007. (http://www.icc-cpi.int/about.html).

International Criminal Tribunal for Yugoslavia Annual Report to the UN Security Council and General Assembly. A/62/172-S/2007/469.

International Declaration Concerning the Laws and Customs of War. Brussels, 27 August 1874.

International Monetary Fund. 2006. *Countries*. (http://www.imf.org).

International War Crimes Tribunal for Iraq. 2007. *War Crimes: A Report on United States War Crimes Against Iraq to the Commission of Inquiry for the International War Crimes Tribunal*. (http://www.deoxy.org/wc/warcrime.htm).

INTERPOL. 2007. *INTERPOL Mission Statement*. (http://www.interpol.int/ Public/Corruption/default.asp-20k).

————. 2008. Pollution Success Stories. (http://www.interpol.int/Public/ EnvironmentalCrime/Pollution/SuccessStories.asp).

"Iraq Reconstruction: How Not to Do It." 2004. *Mother Jones Magazine*. Retrieved August 10, 2004 (http://www.motherjones.com/).

"Iraqi Civilians Killed at Checkpoint." 2003. *The Guardian,* April 1. (http://www.guardian.co.uk/Iraq/Story/0,2763,927148,00.html).

IRIN. 2003. "BURUNDI: Approval of Temporary Immunity Law Sparks Heated Debate." *Humanitarian News and Analysis.* United Nations Office for the Coordination of Humanitarian Affairs, September 3, 2003. (http://www.irinnews.org/report.aspx?reportid=45911).

———. 2008. *In-Depth: Justice for a Lawless World? Rights and Reconciliation in a New Era of International Law Humanitarian News and Analysis.* UN Office for the Coordination of Humanitarian Affairs. (http://www.irinnews.org/InDepthMain.aspx?InDepthId=7&ReportId=59493).

Jackson, M. G. 2001. "Something Must Be Done? Genocidal Chaos and World Responses to Mass Murder in East Timor Between 1975 and 1999." *International Journal of Politics and Ethics* 1(1).

Jackson, R. 1946. *Case Against the Nazi War Criminals.* New York: Alfred A. Knopf. (http://www.roberthjackson.org/events/PJ092502/).

Jehl, D. and E. Schmitt. 2004a. "Afghan Deaths Linked to Unit at Iraq Prison." *New York Times,* May 24, p.1.

———. 2004b. "C.I.A. Bid to Keep Some Detainees Off Abu Ghraib Roll Worries Officials." *New York Times,* May 25. (http://www.nytimes.com/2004/05/25/politics/25ABUS.html?pagewanted=print&position=>).

———. 2004c. "Dogs and Other Harsh Tactics Linked to Military Intelligence." *New York Times,* May 22, p. A1.

Jehl, D., S. Myers, and E. Schmitt. 2004. "Abuse of Captives More Widespread, Says Army Survey." *New York Times,* May 26. (http://www.nytimes.com/2004/05/26/politics/26ABUS.html?th).

Jensen, R. 2004. *Citizens of the Empire: The Struggle to Claim Our Humanity.* San Francisco: City Lights Books.

Jorgensen, N. 2000. *The Responsibility of States for International Crimes.* Oxford: Oxford University Press.

Kant, E. 1795. *Perpetual Peace.* (http://www.mtholyoke.edu/acad/intrel/kant/kant1.htm).

Kasibante, G. 2006. *Africa's Greatest Bloodbath: The World Beyond Media Publication.* U.S. Global Peace Policy Bureau.

Kauzlarich, D. and R. C. Kramer. 1993. "State-Corporate Crime in the U.S. Nuclear Weapons Production Complex." *The Journal of Human Justice* 5(1):1–26.

———. 1998. *Crimes of the American Nuclear State: At Home and Abroad.* Boston: Northeastern University Press.

Keelman, H. C. and V. Hamilton. 1989. *Crimes of Obedience.* New Haven: Yale University Press.

Keen, David. 2001. "War and Peace: What's the Difference?" Pp. 1–22 in *Managing Armed Conflicts in the Twenty-First Century,* edited by Adebajo Adekeye and Chandra Sriram. London: Frank Cass: London.

Kekic, L. 2007. *The Economist Intelligence Unit's Index of Democracy. U.S. Economist Intelligence Unit Report to the CIA* (http://www.economist.com/media/pdf/DEMOCRACY_INDEX_2007_v3.pdf).

Kennedy, R. F. 2003. *Crimes Against Nature. Rolling Stone,* December 11. (http://www.commondreams.org/views03/1120-01.htm).

Khagram, S. (2006). "Possible Future Architectures of Global Governance: A Transnation Perspective/Prospective." *Global Governance* 12:97–117.

Klein, N. 2007. *Shock Doctrine: The Rise of Disaster Capitalism.* Metropolitan Books.

Kramer R. 1982. "Corporate Crime: An Organizational Perspective." Pp. 75–94 in *White Collar and Economic Crime,* edited by P. Wickman and Tom Daily. Lexington, KY: Lexington Books.

———. 1992. "The Space Shuttle Challenger Explosion: A Case Study of State-Corporate Crime." Pp. 212–241 in *White Collar Crime Reconsidered,* edited by K. Schlegel and D. Weisburd. Boston. Northeastern University Press.

———. 1995. "Exploring State Criminality: The Invasion of Panama." *Journal of Criminal Justice and Popular Culture* 3(2):43–52.

———. 2005. Veneestra Peace Speech. Western Michigan University. (http://www..wmich.edu/~kramer).

———. 2006. Personal Conversation. Western Michigan University, June.

Kramer, R. and R. Michalowski. 1990. *Toward an Integrated Theory of State-Corporate Crime.* Presented at the American Society of Criminology, Baltimore, MD.

———. 2005. "War, Aggression, and State Crime: A Criminological Analysis of the Invasion and Occupation of Iraq." British Journal of Criminology 45(4):446–69.

———. 2006. The Invasion of Iraq as State-Corporate Crime. In State-Corporate Crime: Wrongdoing at the Intersection of Business and Government, edited by Raymond J. Michalowski and Ronald C. Kramer. Piscataway, NJ: Rutgers University Press.

Kramer, R., R. Michalowski, and D. Kauzlarich. 2000. "The Origins and Development of the Concept and Theory of State-Corporate Crime." *Crime and Delinquency* 48(2):263–82.

Kramer, R., R. Michalowski, and D. L. Rothe. 2005. "The Supreme International Crime: How the U.S. War in Iraq Threatens the Rule of Law." *Social Justice* 32:2.

Krasner, S. 1995. "Compromising Westphalia." *International Security* 20(3):115–151.

Kristoff, N. 2005. "The Secret Genocide." *New York Times* Archive. February 23. (http://www.sudantribune.com/article.php3?id_article=8204).

Kritz, N. J., ed. 1995. *Transitional Justice. How Emerging Democracies Reckon with Former Regimes.* 3 Vols. Washington, DC: United States Institute of Peace Press.

Kupelian, D. 2004. "Saddam's Daily Horrors Make America's Abu Ghraib Abuses Seem Almost Trivial." June 21. (http://www.WorldnetDaily.com).

La Libre Belgique. 1994. P. 247 in *Introduction to Political Psychology,* edited by Martha Cottam. Mahwah: NJ: Lawrence Erlbaum Associates.

Leahy, P. 2005. *Leahy Bill Bans Outsourcing Torture to Other Countries.* (http://www.leahy.senate.gov/press/200503/031705a.html).

Lemkin, R. 1933. *Special Report Presented to the 5th Conference for the Unification of Penal Law in Madrid,* October 14–20. (http://www.preventgenocide.org/lemkin/madrid1933-english.htm).

———. 1944. *Axis Rule in Occupied Europe.* Washington, DC: Carnegie Endowment for International Peace.

Levinson, S. 2004. *Torture: A Collection.* New York: Oxford University Press.

Lie, Trygve. 1946. *United Nations Annual Review*. Words of Secretary General of the United Nations.

Lieberman, J. K. 1972. *How the Government Breaks the Law*. Briar Cliff Manor, NY: Stein and Day.

Livingston, S. and D. Stephen. 1998. "American Network Coverage of Genocide in Rwanda in the Context of General Trends in International News." Pp. 1–18 in *Early Warning and Early Response*, edited by S. Schmeidl and H. Adelman. New York: Columbia International Affairs Online.

Lynch, Frank and P. Stretsky. 2003. "The Meaning of Green." *Theoretical Criminology* 7(2):217–38.

Mandel, M. 2004. *How America Gets Away With Murder: Illegal Wars, Collateral Damage and Crimes Against Humanity*. London: Pluto Press.

Mansfield-Richardson, V. 2000. *Asian Americans and the Mass Media: A Content Analysis of Twenty United States Newspapers and a Survey of Asian American Journalists*. New York: Garland.

Martin, J. M., A. T. Romano, and J. Haran. 1988. Quoted in *Crimes by the Capitalist State: An Introduction to State Criminality*, by G. Barak, 1991. State University of New York.

Marx, K. 1906. *Capital, Vol. I: The Process of Capitalist Production*. Translated from the 3rd German edition by Samuel Moore and Edward Aveling; edited by Frederick Engels. Chicago: Charles H. Kerr.

Mathews, Susan. 2002. *Shifting Boundaries: A Conference on Moving from a Culture of Impunity to a Culture of Accountability*. Report of the Conference, November 26–28, 2001, Utrecht University.

Matthews, R. A. 2006. "State-Corporate Crime in Nazi Germany." Pp. 181–211 in *State-Corporate Crime: Wrongdoing at the Intersection of Business and Government*, edited by Raymond J. Michalowski and Ronald C. Kramer. New Brunswick, NJ: Rutgers University Press.

Matthews, R. A. and D. Kauzlarich. 2000. "The Crash of ValuJet Flight 592: A Case Study in State-Corporate Crime. *Sociological Focus* 3:281–98.

———. 2006. "The Crash of Valujet Flight 592: A Case Study in State-Corporate Crime." In *State-Corporate Crime: Wrongdoing at the Intersection of Business and Government*, edited by Raymond J. Michalowski and Ronald C. Kramer. Piscataway, NJ: Rutgers University Press.

Mayall, J., ed. 1982. *The Community of States: A Study in International Political Theory*. London: George Allen and Unwin.

Mayer, J. 2005. Outsourcing Torture: The Secret History of America's "Extraordinary Rendition" Program. *The New Yorker*, February 14. (http://www.newyorker.com/archive/2005/02/14/050214fa_fact6).

Melman, S. 1974. *The Permanent War Economy: American Capitalism in Decline*. New York: Simon and Schuster.

Merriam Webster Dictionary. (http://www.merriam-webster.com/dictionary/lustration).

Merton, R. 1938. Social Structure and Anomie. *American Sociological Review* 3(6):672–82.

Michaels, H. 2003. *Washington's Use and Abuse of the Geneva Conventions*. March 29. Retrieved from World Socialist website (http://www.wsws.org/articles/2003/mar2003/pows-m29.shtml).

Michalowski, R. 1985. *Order, Law and Crime*. New York: Random House.

————. 2008. Personal Email Conversation. February.

Michalowski, R. and K. Bitten. 2004. "Transnational Environmental Crime." In *Handbook of Transnational Crime,* edited by P. Reichel. Beverly Hills, CA: Sage.

Michalowski R. and R. Kramer. 1987. "The Space Between the Laws: The Problem of Corporate Crime in a Transnational Context." *Social Problems* 34:34–53.

————. 2006. *State-Corporate Crime: Wrongdoing at the Intersection of Business and Government,* edited by Raymond J. Michalowski and Ronald C. Kramer. Piscataway, NJ: Rutgers University Press.

Miliband, R. 1970. "The Capitalist State: Reply to Nicos Poulantzas." *New Left Review* 59:53–60.

Miller, W. 1958. "Lower Class Culture as a Generating Milieu of Gang Delinquency." *Journal of Social Issues* 14:5–20.

Mills, C. W. 1956. *The Power Elite.* New York: Oxford University Press.

————. 1968. "Some Effects of Mass Media." Pp. 32–35 in *Mass Media and Mass Man,* edited by A. Casty. New York: Holt, Rinehart and Winston.

Minow, M. 1998. *Between Vengeance and Forgiveness. Facing History after Genocide and Mass Violence.* Boston: Beacon Press.

Mitchell, T. 1991. "The Limits of the State: Beyond Statist Approaches and Their Critics." *American Political Science Review* 85(1):77–96.

Mullins, C. W. 2006. "Bridgestone-Firestone, Ford and the NHTSA." Pp. 134–48 in *State-Corporate Crime: Wrongdoing at the Intersection of Business and Government,* edited by Raymond J. Michalowski and Ronald C. Kramer. Piscataway, NJ: Rutgers University Press.

Mullins C. W., D. Kauzlarich, and D. L. Rothe. 2004. "The International Criminal Court and the Control of State Crime: Problems and Prospects." *Critical Criminology: An International Journal* 12:3.

Mullins, C. W. and D. L. Rothe. 2007. "The Forgotten Ones: The Darfuri Genocide." *Critical Criminology,* 15:2.

————. 2008. *Blood, Power, and Bedlam: Violations of International Criminal Law in Post-Colonial Africa.* New York: Peter Lang.

Nadelman, E. 2004. "International Prohibition Regimes." *Transnational Crime: International Prohibition Regimes* edited by N. Passas. (http://www.criminology.fsu.edu/transcrime/articles/GlobalProhibitionRegimes.htm).

Naqvi, Y. 2003. "Amnesty for War Crimes: Defining the Limits of International Recognition." *IRRC* 85:851.

National Law Journal. 2004. "Justices Weigh Alien Tort Act." March 29. (http://www.store.law.com/nlj_results.asp?lqry=Alien+tort+Act&x=15y=7).

National Security Council. 1982. *U.S. Policy in Central America and Cuba through Fiscal Year 1984.* April, p. 82.

Ndangiza, F. 2004. Quoted in *Rwanda Still Searching for Justice* by Robert Walker, BBC, March30. (http://www.news.bbc.co.uk/2/hi/africa/3557753.stm).

Neuman, J. 2005. *Remaking Governance: Peoples, Politics and the Public Sphere.* Bristol, UK: Policy Press.

Noyes, R. 1995. *Nuclear Waste Cleanup Technologies and Opportunities.* Norwich, NY: William Andrew.

Nuclear Decommissioning Authority (NDA). 2006. In BBC "Nuclear Clean-up to Cost £70bn." March 30. (http://www.news.bbc.co.uk/2/hi/business/4859980.stm).

————. 2007. *Report.* (http://www.nda.gov.uk/).

Nuremberg Judgment. 1947. at 41. See also Statement by the Judges of the Nuremberg Tribunal, told the Preparatory Commission for the International Criminal Court. *Secretary-General Addresses Preparatory Commission for International Criminal Court as It Concludes Ninth Session 2002.* (http://www.unis.unvienna.org/unis/pressrels/2002/l3003.html).

O'Conner, J. 1973. *The Fiscal Crisis of the State.* New York: St. Martins Press.

Ohmae, K. 1995. *The End of the Nation-State: The Rise of Regional Economics.* New York: Free Press.

ONASA News Agency. 2004. "Human Rights Watch Decries Abuses by U.S. Forces in Afghanistan." Global News Wire—Europe Intelligence Wire. March 8, p. A1.

Orentlicher, D. 2006. *Crimes of War: The Book.* (http://www.crimesofwar.org/thebook/genocide.html).

Parker, M. 1997. Cited in "Foreign News: Who Gives a Damn?" by James Hoge. *Columbia Journalism Review,* November/December. (http://www.backissues.cjrarchives.org/year/97/6/foreign.asp).

Paris, E. 1990. *Genocide in Satellite Croatia 1941–1945.* Chicago: The American Institute for Balkan Affairs.

Passas, N. 2004. *Transnational Crime: International Prohibition Regimes.* (http://www.criminology.fsu.edu/transcrime/articles/GlobalProhibitionRegimes.htm).

Paternoster, R. and A. Piquero. 1995. "Reconceptualizing Deterrence: An Empirical Test of Personal and Vicarious Experiences." *Journal of Research in Crime* 32(3): 251–286.

Paternoster, R. and S. Simpson. 1992. "A Rational Choice Theory of Corporate Crime." Pp. 194–210 in *Crimes of Privilege—Readings in White-Collar Crime* edited by Neal Shover and John Paul Wright. New York: Oxford Press.

————. 1996. "Sanction Threats and Appeal to Morality: Testing a Rational Choice Model of Corporate Crime." *Law and Society Review* 30:549–83.

Patterson, T. E. 2000. *Doing Well and Doing Good: How Soft News and Critical Journalism are Shrinking the News Audience and Weakening Democracy—and What News Outlets Can Do About It.* Joan Shorenstein Center on Press, Politics, and Public Policy, Kennedy School of Government. Cambridge, MA: Harvard University.

Pearce, F. 2003. "Foreword: Holy Wars and Spiritual Revitalization." Pp. ix–xiv in *Unmasking the Crimes of the Powerful: Scrutinizing States and Corporations* edited by S. Tombs and D. Whyte. New York: Peter Lang.

Peel, Q., R. Graham, J. Harding, and J. Dempsey. 2003. "How the U.S. Set a Course for War on Iraq." *Financial Times,* May 26, p. A1. (http://www.globalpolicy.org/security/issues/iraq/attack/2003/0526course.htm).

Perrow, C. 1986. *Complex Organizations: A Critical Essay.* Columbus, OH: McGraw-Hill.

Perrucci, R. and H. R. Potter. 1989. *Networks of Power: Organizational Actors at the National, Corporate, and Community Levels.* New York: Aldine de Gruyter.

Piquero, A. and R. Paternoster. 1998. "An Application of Stafford and Warr's Reconceptualization of Deterrence to Drinking and Driving." *Journal of Research in Crime and Delinquency* 35(1):5–41.

Politi, M. and G. Nesi. 2004. *The International Criminal Court and the Crime of Aggression.* United Kingdom: Ashgate.

Poulantzas, N. 1969. "The Problem of the Capitalist State." *New Left Review* 58:67.

———. 1976. "The Capitalist State: A Reply to Miliband and Laclau." *New Left Review* 95:63–83.

———. 1978. *Classes in Contemporary Capitalism.* London: Verso.

Proall, L. 1898. *Political Crime.* New York: D. Appleton.

Prunier, G. 1995. *The Rwandan Crisis: History of a Genocide.* New York: Columbia University Press.

———. 2005. *Darfur: The Ambiguous Genocide.* Ithaca, NY: Cornell University Press.

Quinn, J. R. 2001. Dealing with a Legacy of Mass Atrocity: Truth Commissions in Uganda and Chile. *Netherlands Quarterly on Human Rights* 19(4):20.

Rejali, D. 2008. *Torture and Democracy: Scholar Darius Rejali Details the History and Scope of Modern Torture.* Broadcast from Democracy Now, March 12. (http://www.democracynow.org/2008/3/12/torture_and_democracy_scholar _darius_rejali).

Report of the Commission of Inquiry on Human Rights Violations in Rwanda. 1992. (http://www.justiceinperspective.org.za/index.php?option=com_content&task= view&id=25&Itemid=61).

Report of the International Law Commission Covering its Second Session. 1950. June 5–July 29. Document A/1316, pp. 11–14.

Reuters Press. 2003. "Putin Turns on U.S. Over War in Iraq." March 20, p. 1. (http://www.globalpolicy.org/security/issues/iraq/attack/statement/2003/0320 putinturns.htm).

Ridha, J. 2004. "Presentation on Indiscriminate Missile Attacks as a War Crime." World Tribunal on Iraq. New York Session, May 8. (http://www.newyork .worldtribunal.org/Document/Case_2_F_Ridha.pdf).

Right to Life. 1976. Art. 6: 30.7.82, Human Rights Committee, General Comment 6, Art. 3.

Rodrigues, A. 2006. *The War Crimes Chamber of Bosnia and Herzegovina: A New Solution for the Impunity Gap.* June 23. The Hague Guest Lecture Series of the Office of the Prosecutor.

Ross, J. 1995. *Controlling State Crime: An Introduction.* New York: Garland.

———. 2000. *Varieties of State Crime and Its Control.* Mosney, NY: Criminal Justice Press.

———. 2003. *The Dynamics of Political Crime.* Thousand Oaks, CA: Sage.

Ross, J., G. Barak, J. Ferrell, D. Kauzlarich, M. Hamm, D. Friedrichs, R. Matthews, S. Pickering, M. Presdee, P. Kraska, and V. Kappeler. 1999. "The State of State Crime Research: A Commentary." *Humanity & Society* 23(3):273–81.

Rothe, D. L. 2004a. "Enemy Combatant." *Encyclopedia of Prisons and Correctional Facilities.* Vol. 1:1. Thousand Oaks, CA: Sage.

———. 2004b. "War Crimes." *Criminal Justice in the United States.* Vol. 1:2. Pasadena, CA: Salem Press.

———. 2006. "The Masquerade of Abu Ghraib: State Crime, Torture, and International Law." Ph.D. dissertation, Department of Sociology, Western Michigan University, Kalamazoo, MI.

Rothe, D. L. and D. Friedrichs. 2006. "The State of the Criminology of State Crime." *Social Justice* 33(1):147–61.

Rothe, D. L. and D. Kauzlarich. 2008. "State-Level Crime: Theory and Policy," Forthcoming in *Crime and Public Policy: Putting Theory to Work.* 2d ed., edited by Hugh D. Barlow and Scott Decker, Philadelphia: Temple University Press.

Rothe, D. L. and C. W. Mullins. 2006a. *The International Criminal Court: Symbolic Gestures and the Generation of Global Social Control.* Lanham, MD: Lexington Books.

————. 2006b. "The International Criminal Court and United States Opposition." *Crime, Law and Social Change* 45:201–26.

————. 2006c. "On the Legitimacy of International Law." *Critical Criminology Division Newsletter,* May, pp. 1–3.

————. 2007a. "Darfur and the Politicalization of International Law: Genocide or Crimes Against Humanity." *Humanity and Society* 31(1):83–107.

————. 2007b. "International Community: Legitimizing a Moral Collective Consciousness." *Humanity and Society* 30:3.

————. 2008. "Genocide, War Crimes and Crimes Against Humanity in Central Africa: A Criminological Exploration." In *Towards a Criminology of International Crimes,* edited by R. Haveman and Allette Smeulers. Antwerp, Belgium: Intersentia.

————. 2009. "Toward a Criminology for International Criminal Law: An Integrated Theory of International Criminal Violations." *International Journal of Comparative and Applied Criminal Justice* 33.

Rothe, D. L., C. W. Mullins, and K. Sandstrom. 2008. "The Rwandan Genocide: International Financial Policies and Human Rights." *Social Justice* 35:3.

Rothe, D. L., S. Muzzatti, and C. W. Mullins. 2006. Crime on the High Seas: Crimes of Globalization and the Sinking of the Senegalese Ferry Le Joola. *Critical Criminology* 14(2):159–80.

Rothe, D. L. and J. I. Ross. 2007. "Lights, Camera, State Crime." *Journal of Criminal Justice and Popular Culture* 14(4):331–43.

————. 2008. "The Marginalization of State Crime." *Journal of Critical Sociology* 34(5).

Rothe, D. L., J. I. Ross, C. W. Mullins, D. Friedrichs, G. Barak, D. Kauzlarich, and R. C. Kramer. 2009. "That Was Then, This Is Now, What About Tomorrow? Future Directions in State Crime Studies." *Critical Criminology: An International Journal* 17(2).

Roy, A. 2004. *An Ordinary Person's Guide to Empire.* Cambridge, MA: South End Press.

Rutaganda. 1999. December 6, ¶ 48–49. The Rwandan Citizens Responsible for Genocide and Other Such Violations Committed Between January 1994 and December 1994. Statutory Instrument 1996, No. 1296.

Sadat, L. N. and S. R. Carden. 2000. "The New International Criminal Court: An Uneasy Revolution." *Georgetown Law Review* 88:381–474.

Saint-Exupery, P. 1994. "Rwanda: The Assassins Remember the Massacres." Quoted in *The Rwandan Crisis: History of a Genocide* by G. Prunier, 2005, p. 255. New York: Columbia University Press.

Sampson, R. J. and S. W. Raudenbush. 1999. "Systematic Social Observation of Public Spaces: A New Look at Disorder in Urban Neighborhoods." *American Journal of Sociology* 105(3):603–51.

Sands, P. 2005. *Lawless World: America and the Making and Breaking of Global Rules.* London: Allen Lane.

Santos, D. T. 1971.*The Structure of Dependence.* Boston: Extending Horizons.

Schrager, L. and J. Short. 1978. "Toward a Sociology of Organizational Crime." *Social Problems* 25:407–19.

Schuler, D. 2007. *Citizens' Tribunal: A Symbolic Tool of Resistance.* Public Sphere Project (CPSR). (http://www.publicsphereproject.org/patterns/pattern.pl/public?pattern_id=564).

Schwendinger, H. and J. Schwendinger. 1970. "Defenders of Order or Guardians of Human Rights?" *Issues in Criminology* 5:123–57.

Scott, J. 2000. "Rational Choice." In *Understanding Contemporary Society: Theories of the Present,* edited by G. Browning, A. Halcli, and F. Webster. Thousand Oaks, CA: Sage.

Seabrooke, L. 2002. *Bringing Legitimacy Back in to Neo-Weberian State Theory and International Relations.* Department of International Relations, Research School of Pacific and Asian Studies, Australian National University, Working Paper 2002/6.

Seeley, J. 1986. *An Introduction to Political Science.* London: MacMillan.

Sells, M. 1996. *The Bridge Betrayed: Religion and Genocide in Bosnia.* Berkeley: University of California Press.

———. 2001. "Kosovo Mythology and the Bosnian Genocide." Pp. 180–204 in *In God's Name* edited by O. Bartov and P. Mack. New York: Berghahn Books.

Shalamov, V. 1980. *Kolyma Tales.* New York: Penguin Classics.

Shana, G. 2006. *The State of Corruption in Zimbabwe.* Paper presented at the Mass Public Opinion Institute, May 9. (http://www.mpoi.org/downloads/speeches/The%20State%20of%20Corruption%20in%20Zimbabwe.pdf).

Sharkansky, I. 1995. "A State Action May Be Nasty but Is Not Likely to be a Crime." Pp. 35–52 in *Controlling State Crime: An Introduction,* edited by Jeff Ross. New York: Garland.

Shaw, C. and H. D. McKay. 1942. *Juvenile Delinquency and Urban Areas.* Chicago: University of Chicago Press.

Shover, N. 1996. *Great Pretenders: Pursuits and Careers of Persistent Thieves.* Boulder, CO: Westview Press.

Shover, N. and B. Henderson. 1995. "Repressive Crime Control and Male Persistent Thieves." In *Crime and Public Policy: Putting Theory to Work,* edited by H. Barlow. Boulder, CO: Westview Press.

Shover, N. and D. Honaker. 1992. "The Socially Bounded Decision Making of Persistent Property Offenders." *Howard Journal of Criminal Justice* 31:276–93.

Sierra Leone Truth and Reconciliation Commission. 2004. *Witness to Truth: Report of the Sierra Leone Truth and Reconciliation Commission.* Database: Appendix 1:11. Accra, Ghana: Graphic Packaging Ltd.

Sierra Leone Truth Commission Charter. 2000. Reprinted in *The Final Report of the Truth & Reconciliation Commission of Sierra Leone.* (http://trcsierraleone.org/drwebsite/publish/v1c1.shtml).

Singer, P. W. 2003. *Corporate Warriors: The Rise of the Privatized Military Industry.* Ithaca, NY: Cornell University Press.

———. 2005. "Outsourcing War." Foreign Affairs. March/April. (http://www.foreignaffairs.org/20050301faessay84211/p-w-singer/outsourcing-war.html).

Skocpol, T. 1984. "Emerging Agendas and Recurrent Strategies in Historical Sociology." Pp. 356–91 in *Vision and Method in Historical Sociology*, edited by Theda Skocpol. New York: Cambridge University Press.

Smelser, N. 1964. "Towards a Theory of Modernization." Pp. 258–74 in *Social Change: Sources, Patterns, and Consequences*, edited by A. Etzioni and E. Etzioni. New York: Basic Books.

Smeulers, A. 2007. *Towards a Typology of Perpetrators of International Crimes and Other Gross Human Rights Violations.* Paper presented at the Expert Meetings, April 13–14, Maastricht University.

So, A. 1990. *Social Change and Development: Modernization, Dependency, and World System Theory.* Newbury Park, CA: Sage.

Solomon, N. 1992. *The Power of Babble: The Politicians Dictionary of Buzzwords and Doubletalk for Every Occasion.* Monroe, ME: Common Courage Press.

———. 1999. *The Habits of Highly Deceptive Media: Decoding Spin and Lies in Mainstream News.* Monroe, ME: Common Courage Press.

Solomon, N. and Lee, M. 1990. *Unreliable Sources: A Guide to Detecting Bias in News Media.* Monroe, ME: Common Courage Press.

Solzhenitsyn, A. 1973. *The Gulag Archipelago.* New York: Harper & Row.

Spiegel, S. and F. Wheeling. 2005. *Readings in World Politics: A New Era.* Belmont, CA: Wadsworth.

Stafford, M. and M. Warr. 1993. "A Reconceptualization of General and Specific Deterrence." *Journal of Research in Crime and Delinquency* 30:123–35.

Staub, E. 2003. *The Psychology of Good and Evil: Why Children, Adults, and Groups Help and Harm Others.* Cambridge: Cambridge University Press.

Stein, C. 2004. "Abu Ghraib and the Magic of Images." Pp. 102–22 in *Abu Ghraib: The Politics of Torture.* Berkeley, CA: North Atlantic Books.

Sutherland, E. 1939. "White Collar Criminality." Presidential Address to the American Society of Sociology. Reprinted 1940. *American Sociological Review* 5:1–12.

———. 1948. "Crime of Corporations." In *The Sutherland Papers*, 1956, edited by A. Cohen, Alfred Lindsmith and Karl Schuessler. Bloomington: Indiana University Press.

———. 1949. *White Collar Crime.* New York: Holt, Rinehart and Winston.

Sykes, G. and D. Matza. 1957. "Techniques of Neutralization: A Theory of Delinquency." *American Sociological Review* 22:664–70.

Tilly, C. 1985. "War Making and State Making as Organized Crime." In *Bringing the State Back In*, edited by P. Evans, D. Rueschemeyer, and T. Skocpol. Cambridge: Cambridge University Press.

Tittle, C. 1995. *Control Balance: Toward a General Theory of Deviance.* Boulder, CO: Westview Press.

Toussaint, E. 1999. Your Money or Your Life!: Tyranny of Global Finance. London: Pluto Press.

———. 2004. Rwanda 10 years On: Uncovering the Financiers of the Genocide. (http://www.redpepper.org.uk/May2004/x-May2004-Toussaint.html).

Truth and Reconciliation Commission Final Report, Section 5. March 2003. (http://www.info.gov.za/otherdocs/2003/trc/).

Truth Commission Report. 1993. Section: Recommendation F:I.

Tunnell, K. D. 1993. *Political Crime in Contemporary America.* New York: Garland.

Turk, A. 1982. *Political Criminality.* Beverly Hills, CA: Sage.

United Human Rights Council. 2006. *Genocide in Bosnia.* November 22. (http://www.srebrenicamassacregenocidemassgraves.wordpress.com/2006/11/22/united-human-rights-council-genocide-in-bosnia/).

United Nations. 2001. *Security Council Hears Reports on Making Sanctions More Effective, Lessening Harm to the Innocent.* 4,394th Meeting. November 22, 2001. Press Release. SC/7183. (http://www.un.org/News/Press/docs/2001/sc7183.doc.htm).

United Nations Environmental Program Annual Report. 2007. UNEP Online Bookstore. (http://www.unep.org/Documents.multilingual/Default.asp?DocumentID=67&ArticleID=5743&1=en).

United Nations General Assembly Twenty-ninth Session: 3314 (XXXIX). 1974. *Definition of Aggressions* A/RES/3314(XXIX) December 14.

United Nations Millennium Project. 2007. (http://www.millennium-project.org/millennium/studies.html).

United Nations Report of the Secretary General on the Work of the Organization. General Assembly. 1977. *Official Records: First through Fifty-Ninth Session. Supplement No. I* (A/1/1–A/59/1). New York: United Nations.

United Nations Resolution S/RES/1315. 2000. Adopted by the Security Council at its 4,186th meeting on August 14, 2000.

United Nations Secretary General Annual Report to the General Assembly. 1954. Supplement No. 1(A/2911).

United States Department of State. 2004. *Country Reports on Human Rights Practices.* Released by the Bureau of Democracy, Human Rights, and Labor. February 28, 2005. (http://www.state.gov/g/drl/rls/hrrpt/2004/).

United States District Court for the Southern District of New York Decision No. 86 Civ. 2500. 1986.

United States Institute of Peace. 2008. Truth Commissions Digital Collection. (http://www.usip.org/library/truth.htm).

Vann, B. 2002. *The Unquiet Death of Patrice Lumumba.* January 16. Retrieved from World Socialist website (http://www.wsws.org/articles/2002/jan2002/lumu-j16_prn.shtml).

Vanspauwen, K., S. Parmentier, and E. Weitekamp. 2007. *Restorative Justice for Victims of Mass Violence: Reconsidering the Building Blocks of Post-Conflict Justice.* Presentation at Expert Meetings, April 13–14, Maastricht University.

———. 2008. "Restorative Justice for Victims of Mass Violence: Reconsidering the Building Blocks of Post-Conflict Justice." In *Towards a Criminology of International Crimes,* edited by R. Haveman and Alette Smeulers. Antwerp: Intersentia.

Vaughan, D. 1982. "Toward Understanding Unlawful Organizational Behavior." *Michigan Law Review* 80:1377–1402.

———. 1983. *Controlling Unlawful Organizational Behavior: Social Structure and Corporate Misconduct.* Chicago: University of Chicago Press.

Vidgen, B. 1995. "A State of Terror." *Nexus Magazine* 3:2. (http://www.nexusmagazine.com/backissues/0302.conts.html).

Villa-Vicencio, C. 2000. "Why Perpetrators Should Not Always Be Prosecuted: Where the International Criminal Court and Truth Commissions Meet." *Emory Law Journal* 49:101–18.

Wagner, K. 2006. "Still Left Out? The Coverage of Critical/Conflict Criminology in Introductory Textbooks." *Academy of Criminal Justice Sciences Today* 31(4):1, 5–8.

Waldheim, K. 1977. In "United Nations Report of the Secretary General on the Work of the Organization." *General Assembly. Official Records: First through Fifty-Ninth Session. Supplement No. 1* (A/1/1–A/59/1). New York: United Nations.

Waldheim, K. 1987. In "United Nations Report of the Secretary General on the Work of the Organization." *General Assembly. Official Records: First through Fifty-Ninth Session. Supplement No. 1* (A/1/1–A/59/1). New York: United Nations.

Walker, T. 2003. *Living in the Shadow of the Eagle.* 4th ed. Boulder, CO: Westview Press.

Wallerstein, I. 1974. *The Modern World—System I. Capitalist Agriculture and the Origins of the European World-Economy in the Sixteenth Century.* New York: Academic Press.

———. 1977. *Africa: The Politics of Unity.* New York: Random House.

———. 1979. *The Capitalist World Economy.* Cambridge: Cambridge University Press.

———. 1986. *World Systems Analysis.* Stanford, CA: Stanford University Press.

Wanyeki, M. 2007. (Kenya Human Rights Commission Executive Director). Interview by Author via e-mail. October 15. (http://www.socialistunity.com/?p=1023).

Weber, M. 1946. *From Max Weber,* edited and translated by Hans Gerth and C. Wright Mills. New York: Oxford University Press.

———. 1947. *The Theory of Social and Economic Organization,* edited by T. Parsons. New York: Oxford University Press.

Weeramantry, C. G. 2003. Armageddon or Brave New World? Reflections on the Hostilities in Iraq. Ratmalana, Sri Lanka: Sarvodaya Vishva Lekha.

White, M. 1998. Military Governments. (http://www.users.erols.com/mwhite28/miltgovt.htm).

Whitney, W. T., Jr. 2008. "Tribunals Examine U.S. Role in Colombia." Peoples Weekly World Newspaper. 01/03/08. 12:12. (http://www.pww.org/article/articleview/12273/1/142/).

Whitson, S. 2004. "Introductory Presentation." World Tribunal on Iraq. New York Session. (http://www.newyork.worldtribunal.org/Document/Case_2_A_Sarah_Leah.pdf).

Whyte, D. 2003. "Lethal Regulation: State-Corporate Crime and the United Kingdom Government's New Mercenaries." *Journal of Law and Society* 30(4):575–600.

Wilkinson, T. and A. Rubin. 2004. "Pervasive Abuse Alleged by Freed Detainees." *Los Angeles Times,* May 19, p. 1.

Windsor of Ontario. 2005. February. Pp. 91–97 in *Missed Signals,* edited by S. Ricchiardi. American Foreign Policy Annual Editions 2006/2007.

Wolfreys, J. 2000. Pp. 119–48 in *Varieties of State Crime and Its Control,* edited by Jeffrey Ian Ross. Mosney, NY: Criminal Justice Press.

World Bank. 1996. *Country Report: Rwanda Country Assistance Evaluation.* (http://www.worldbank.org).

Wozniak, J. F. 2001. "Assessing Contemporary White Collar Crime Textbooks: A Review of Common Themes and Prospects for Teaching." *Journal of Criminal Justice Education* 12(2):455–75.

Wright, R. 2000. "Left Out? The Coverage of Critical Perspectives in Introductory Criminology Textbooks." *Critical Criminology* 9(1–2):100–122.

Wright, Richard and Scott Decker. 1994. *Burglars on the Job: Streetlife and Residential Break-ins.* Boston: Northeastern University Press.

———. 1997. *Armed Robbers in Action: Stick Ups and Street Culture.* Boston: Northeastern University Press.

Wright, R. A. and C. Schreck. 2000. "Red-Penciled: The Neglect of Critical Perspectives in Introductory Criminal Justice Textbooks." *Journal of Crime and Justice* 23(2): 45–67.

Yearbook of the International Law Commission. 1950. Vol. II, pp. 374–78.

Yin, R. 1984. *Case Study Research: Design and Methods,* 1st ed. Beverly Hills, CA: Sage.

Zernike, K. 2004a. "The Accused: Prison Guard Calls Abuse Routine and Sometimes Amusing." *The New York Times,* May 16, p. 3.

———. 2004b. "Only a Few Spoke Up on Abuse as Many Soldiers Stayed Silent." *New York Times,* May 22, p. 1.

Zupanov, J. 1995. "Mass Media and Collective Violence." *The Public* 2(2):77–84.

Bibliography of Documents, Legal Cases, Treaties, Charters, and Resolutions

1874 Declaration in Brussels

1899 Hague I Pacific Settlement of International Disputes

1907 Hague Convention (IV) on the Laws and Customs of War on Land

1919 Treaty of Versailles

1933 Montevideo Convention on Rights and Duties of State

1946 United Nations General Assembly Resolution 95:1

1946 United Nations Resolution 260 A (III)

1948 Declaration of Human Rights

1948 Genocide Convention

1974. Declaration of the Establishment of a New International Economic Order. Resolution 3201

1977 Additional Protocols I (Article 77:2) and II (Article 4:3c)

1979 Moon Agreement

1993 International Criminal Tribunal for Yugoslavia

1994 International Criminal Tribunal for Rwanda

1996 Draft Articles on the Law on International Responsibilities of States

2003 Norms on the Responsibilities of Transnational Corporations and Other Business Enterprises with Regard to Human Rights Agreement

African Charter on Human and People's Rights, Article 4

Agreement by the Economic and Social Council (2003)

Agreement for the Prosecution and Punishment of the Major War Criminals of the European Axis

American Convention on Human Rights, Article 4(1)

Annex Article 4 of 1907

Article 4(2)(e) of Protocol II

Arusha Accords
Barcelona Traction (1970 ICJ 3:32)
Barcelona Traction (1970 ICJ 3:32)
Basel Convention
Canadian Security Intelligence Service Act
Charter of the International Criminal Tribunal for Rwanda, 1994.
Charter of the International Criminal Tribunal for Yugoslavia, 1993
Charter of the International Military Tribunal
Child Labour Convention 182
Coalition for International Justice Reports
Common Article 3 of the Geneva Conventions
Convention (I) for the Amelioration of the Condition of the Wounded and Sick in Armed Forces in the Field. Geneva, 12 August 1949
Convention (III) Relative to the Treatment of Prisoners of War. Geneva, 12 August 1949
Convention (IV) Relative to the Protection of Civilian Persons in Time of War. Geneva, 12 August 1949
Convention (IV) Respecting the Laws and Customs of War on Land and its Annex: Regulations Concerning the Laws and Customs of War on Land. The Hague, 18 October 1907
Convention against Torture and Other Cruel, Inhuman, or Degrading Treatment or Punishment of 1984
Convention on Conservation of Antarctic Marine Living Resources
Convention on the Elimination of All Forms of Discrimination Against Women of 1981
Convention on International Trade in Endangered Species
Convention on the Prevention and Punishment of the Crime of Genocide
Convention on the Prevention and Punishment of the Crime of Genocide of 1948
Convention on the Prohibition of the Development, Production, and Stockpiling of Bacteriological (Biological) and Toxin Weapons and on their Destruction. Opened for Signature at London, Moscow, and Washington. 10 April 1972
Convention on Prohibitions or Restrictions on the Use of Certain Conventional Weapons Which May be Deemed to be Excessively Injurious or to Have Indiscriminate Effects. Geneva, 10 October 1980
Convention on the Rights of the Child
Convention on the Rights of the Child of 1989
Convention Relative to the Treatment of Prisoners of War. Geneva, 27 July 1929
Covenant of the League of Nations
Dar-es-Salaam Ceasefire
Declaration on the Elimination of Violence Against Women
Declaration Renouncing the Use, in Times of War, of Explosive Projectiles Under 400 Grammes Weight. 1868. St. Petersburg
Democratic Republic of Congo vs. Uganda. International Court of Justice, 2005
European Convention for the Protection of Human Rights and Fundamental Freedoms, Article 2(1)
Federal Registrar, Vol. 66, p. 57835
Foreign Relations Law of the U.S. (S 201)
Fourth Hague Convention
General Assembly Resolution 260 A (III), 1948

General Assembly Resolution 3314 (XXIX) of December 1974
General Assembly Resolution 3452 (XXX) of 9 December 1975
General Assembly resolution 95(1), 260 A (III)
Geneva Convention for the Amelioration of the Condition of the Wounded in Armies in the Field
Geneva Convention of 1929 (Articles 2,3,4,46, and 51)
Geneva Conventions of 1949 I, II, III, IV
Geneva Protocol of 1924 for the Pacific Settlement of International Disputes
The Hague. February 27. ICC-OTP-20070227-208-En
Hague Convention, 1907
Hague Rules of Ariel Warfare of 1923
Human Resource Exploitation Training Manual
International Commission of Inquiry Rwanda. 1959
International Covenant on Civil and Political Rights
International Covenant on Civil and Political Rights of 1966
International Covenant on Economic, Social and Cultural Rights
International Covenant on Social and Economic Rights of 1966
International Criminal Court Arrest Warrants 2005
International Criminal Court Background to Situation in Uganda 2004
International Criminal Court. First Appearance, Thomas Lubanga Dyilo. 20 March
International Criminal Court Prosecutor Opening Remarks. 2007
International Criminal Court. Warrant of Arrest: Thomas Lubanga Dyilo. 10 February
International Declaration concerning the Laws and Customs of War. 1874. Brussels
Kellogg Pact of 1928 (General Treaty for the Renunciation of War
Kubark Counterintelligence Interrogation Manual
Legal Notice No. 1 of 1986 (Transitional Government NRA)
Lomé Peace Accords of July 1999
Montreal Protocol
Nuremberg Charter, 1945
Optional Protocol to the Convention on the Rights of the Child on the Involvement of Children in Armed Conflict
Outer Space Treaty
Paquette Habana 175 US 677
Parliament of Canada Act
Principles of International Law Recognized in the Charter of the Nüremberg Tribunal and in the Judgment of the Tribunal, 1950
Prosecutor v. Akayesu. Trial Chamber (ICTR), September 2, 1998, para. 497; para. 505–506
Prosecutor v. Goran Jelisic. Appeals Chamber. Judgement (ICTY). July 5, 2001
Prosecutor v. Kayishema and Ruzindana. Trial Chamber (ICTR). May 21, 1999, para. 93, 527
Prosecutor v. Musema. Trial Chamber (ICTY). January 27, 2000, para. 157
Prosecutor v. Rutaganda. Trial Chamber (ICTR). December 6, 1999, para. 52
Protection of Civilian Populations against Bombing from the Air in Case of War
Protocol Additional to the Geneva Conventions of 12 August 1949, and relating to the Protection of Victims of International Armed Conflicts (Protocol I), 8 June 1977

Protocol Additional to the Geneva Conventions of 12 August 1949, and relating to the Protection of Victims of Non-International Armed Conflicts (Protocol II), 8 June 1977

Report of the Commission of Inquiry on Human Rights Violations in Rwanda 1992:24–25

Report of the International Law Commission Covering its Second Session, 5 June 29–July 1950, Document A/1316, pp. 11–14

Right to Life (art. 6): 30.7.82, Human Rights Committee, General comment 6, Art. 3

Rome Statute of the International Criminal Court

Royal Commission on Police Procedure and a Police Complaints Board

Rutaganda December 6, 1999, para. 48–49

Shipwrecked Members of Armed Forces at Sea. Geneva, 12 August 1949

Siderman v. Republic of Argentina, the Court of Appeals, Ninth Circuit

Stockholm and Rotterdam Convention

U.S. Appeals 2 Circuit Court in Filartiga v. Pena-Irala

U.S. Psychological Operations Manual

UN Convention Against Torture and Other Cruel Inhumane or Degrading Treatment or Punishment

UN Convention Against Torture and Other Cruel Inhumane or Degrading Treatment or Punishment

United Nations Charter Articles 1: 2, 2, 4(1), 55, 56

United Nations Convention against Corruption (UNCAC)

United Nations Convention for the Amelioration of the Condition of the Wounded and Sick in Armed Forces in the Field. 1949. San Francisco

United Nations General Assembly.

United Nations Human Rights Commission Reports

United Nations Resolution 1596, 2005

United Nations Security Council Commission Report, 2004, 2005, 2006

United Nations Security Council Report 2003

United States Federal Military Codes 18 USC Section 5; 49 USC 46501 (2)

Universal Declaration of Human Rights

Universal Declaration of Human Rights 1948

Yearbook of the International Law Commission, 1950, Vol. II, pp. 374–378

Zorea, Blatman, and Karp Commissions in Israel

Index

A

Abu Ghraib, ix, 55–57, 79, 122–23, 182, 208, 235, 238, 241–42, 245–46, 250, 253
accountability, ix, xi, 22, 57, 109, 157, 163, 177, 180, 187, 189, 193, 196-198, 201, 230, 232, 236, 247
Alien Tort Claims Act, 182
amnesty, xviii, 56, 71, 176, 179, 181, 187, 192, 197, 235, 238, 248
Argentina, 19, 36, 74, 119, 136, 141, 143, 191, 195, 259
assassination(s), xviii, 21–22, 24, 37, 57–59, 73, 84–85, 117, 119, 128, 131, 140, 183, 197, 231
authoritarian regimes, 23, 120, 143, 220
autocratic, 39, 115, 136, 144, 147

B

Bassiouni, M. Cherif, 33–34, 76, 170, 229, 231, 236
Bosnia, xvii, 39, 52–53, 80, 136, 150, 152, 157, 186, 250, 252, 254
Burma, 45, 62, 131, 136, 185, 206

C

capital accumulation, 8, 10, 14, 129–30, 144, 223

case study, 13, 86–87, 236, 240–41, 246–47, 256
Chambliss, William, 2, 5–6, 238
child soldier, 39–40, 60, 62–63, 73, 80, 83, 104, 143, 197, 243–44
Chile, xvii, 38, 117, 119, 126, 131, 137, 143, 147, 154, 185, 191, 194, 209, 250
China, 37, 116, 131, 137, 139, 143, 164–65, 172, 184–85, 206, 217–19
colonialism, 136, 146, 164
communism, xviii, 120, 126, 155, 199
corruption, xviii, 6, 22–24, 39, 54, 74, 84, 128–29, 138, 141, 143–44, 180, 223, 241, 252, 259
cosmopolitism, xix, 225–27, 229–31
Côte d'Ivoire, 52, 59–60, 143, 145, 208
crimes of aggression, xviii, 44, 64, 74, 83, 85, 121, 161, 174
criminal liability, 3, 11, 16, 37, 57, 158, 160
customary law, 3, 30, 36, 41, 45–46, 158, 175, 184, 206, 228

D

dehumanization, 147, 224
deterrence, 85, 93, 105–6, 109, 177, 194, 201, 236, 249, 253

About the Author

Dr. Dawn L. Rothe is a Professor at Old Dominion University, Department of Sociology and Criminal Justice. Her research includes corporate crime, transnational crime, state crime, and international institutions of social control. She is the author of several books, including *State Crime: Current Perspectives,* forthcoming in 2010; *Symbolic Gestures and the Generation of Global Social Control: The International Criminal Court,* coauthored with Christopher Mullins in 2006; and *Blood, Power, and Bedlam: Violations of International Criminal Law in Post Colonial Africa*, co-authored with Christopher Mullins in 2008. She has published over three dozen articles and book chapters.

Breinigsville, PA USA
20 April 2010
236480BV00002B/4/P